Massachusetts

AN EXPLORER'S GUIDE

Massachusetts

Beyond Boston and Cape Cod

AN EXPLORER'S GUIDE

CHRISTINA TREE & WILLIAM DAVIS

The Countryman Press
Woodstock, Vermont

Dedication

To Liam, Tim, and Topher
—C.T. and W.D.

Library of Congress Cataloging-in-Publication Data
Tree, Christina.
Massachusetts, an explorer's guide : beyond Boston and Cape Cod / Christina Tree & William Davis.
p.   cm.
Includes index.
ISBN 0-88150-322-3 (alk. paper)
1. Massachusetts—Guidebooks. I. Davis, William. II. Title.
F62.3.T733 1996
917.4404'43—dc 20
95-40588
CIP

Cover photograph of church on Common in North Andover, by Kindra Clineff
Cover design by Georganna Towne
Text design by Glenn Suokko
Maps by Mapping Specialists, Ltd., Madison, Wisconsin

Published by The Countryman Press, Inc.
PO Box 175
Woodstock, Vermont 05091-0175
Printed in the United States of America
10 9 8 7 6 5 4 3 2 1

Explore With Us!

Massachusetts, An Explorer's Guide was originally published in 1979 as the first in a series of travel books that now includes guides to Maine, New Hampshire, Vermont, Cape Cod, Rhode Island, Connecticut, and the Hudson Valley. This new edition has been reworked and rewritten from scratch: It's an entirely new book!

We hope you'll find its design attractive and easy to read. Although the organization is simple, the following points will help get you started on your way.

WHAT'S WHERE

In the beginning of the book you'll find an alphabetical listing of special highlights and important information that you may want to reference quickly. You'll find advice on everything from where to find the best artists and craftspeople to where to write or call for camping reservations and park information.

LODGING

Prices: Please don't hold us or the respective innkeepers responsible for the rates listed as of press time. Some changes are inevitable. The state rooms and meals tax is 5.7 percent as of this writing, but that rate varies with each town. Be sure to inquire.

RESTAURANTS

In most sections, please note a distinction between *Dining Out* and *Eating Out*. By their nature, restaurants in the *Eating Out* group are generally inexpensive.

KEY TO SYMBOLS

☞ The special value symbol appears next to lodging and restaurants that combine quality and moderate prices.

✐ The kids-alert symbol appears next to lodging, restaurants, activities, and shops of special appeal to youngsters.

We would appreciate your comments and corrections about places you visit or know well in the state. Please address your correspondence to Explorer's Guide Editor, The Countryman Press, PO Box 175, Woodstock, Vermont 05091-0175.

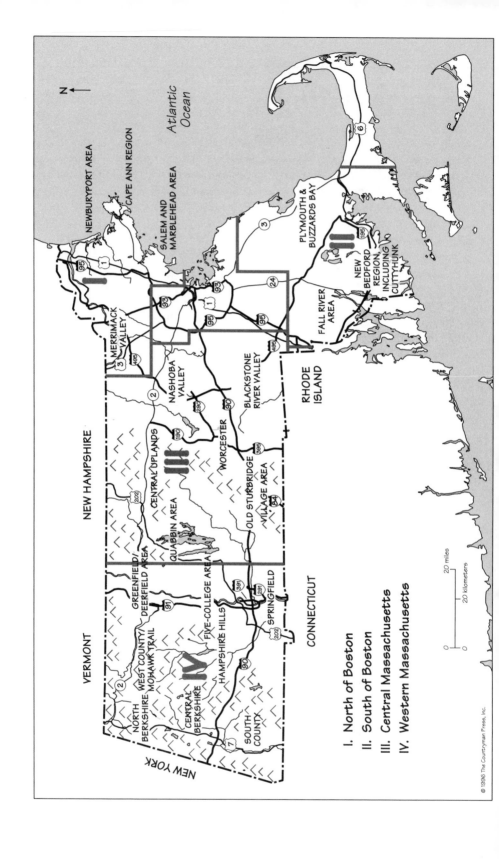

N ←

Atlantic Ocean

NEWBURYPORT AREA

CAPE ANN REGION

SALEM AND MARBLEHEAD AREA

PLYMOUTH & BUZZARDS BAY

NEW BEDFORD REGION, INCLUDING CUTTYHUNK

FALL RIVER AREA

MERRIMACK VALLEY

NASHOBA VALLEY

BLACKSTONE RIVER VALLEY

RHODE ISLAND

NEW HAMPSHIRE

CENTRAL UPLANDS

WORCESTER

OLD STURBRIDGE VILLAGE AREA

GREENFIELD/ DEERFIELD AREA

QUABBIN AREA

VERMONT

FIVE-COLLEGE AREA

SPRINGFIELD

CONNECTICUT

NORTH BERKSHIRE

WEST COUNTY/ MOHAWK TRAIL

CENTRAL BERKSHIRE

HAMPSHIRE HILLS

SOUTH COUNTY

NEW YORK

I. North of Boston
II. South of Boston
III. Central Massachusetts
IV. Western Massachusetts

20 miles

20 kilometers

© 1996 The Countryman Press, Inc.

Contents

Introduction

There's more to Massachusetts than most people see. Sure, there's Boston and its surrounding towns as well as Cape Cod and the Islands, but what about the less-populated, less-touristed three-fourths of the state—the subject of this guidebook?

Though physically just one-seventh of New England, Massachusetts accounts for almost half the region's population. Half the state's residents live within easy commuting distance of Boston, however, and often seem oblivious to the fact that most of Massachusetts lies inland. Nothing makes this point better than Massachusetts's longtime nickname: "The Bay State."

For decades we have puzzled over why many Bay Staters know so little about—and comparatively few visitors discover—the North Shore or southeastern Massachusetts, let alone inland regions such as "The Blackstone Valley," "The Five-College Area," or "The Hilltowns." One major reason why so many residents and visitors assume that there's not much worth exploring west of Concord, we think, is that most of the state beyond the crescent of I-495 is so broadly and blandly described. Labels like "western Massachusetts" and "central Massachusetts" conjure up few images likely to lure anyone.

Over the years, between us, we have written thousands of travel stories on virtually every corner of the world; yet we feel strongly that, despite its lack of a clear image, this "Other Massachusetts"—the heart and in many ways the soul of New England—constitutes one of the country's most beautiful and underrated travel destinations.

The fact that the region eludes precise definition is a tribute to its topographical and human diversity and quirky, indomitable, and unhomogenized character. To make this "Other Massachusetts" more comprehensible and easier to explore, this guide divides it into areas based on geography and the way residents define where they live— rather than on the political boundaries usually applied.

For example: "Springfield and the Pioneer Valley" is the way the 50-mile-wide, 50-mile-long swath of the state's most topographically— and in every other way—varied region is usually labeled. This name, which was coined in the 1940s, implies that the entire area is a combination of city and valley when in fact it includes the hilliest and least populated parts of the state. Within this book we divide it into several very specific and different regions.

The Massachusetts Turnpike, completed in 1952, cut the time it takes to drive across Massachusetts to less than 2½ hours. But exits are often so few and far apart, especially west of Worcester (of the Pike's 25 exits, 14 are east of I-495), that you tend to assume there's no reason to exit. The impression is that most of the state is a black hole, prudently bridged by the Turnpike Authority.

Actually, we love the Mass. Pike. It's well maintained in all weather, a quick way home after a day or two of exploring. But frequently we prefer taking Route 2 west from Boston. That way, within a half hour we are in the Nashoba Valley, following winding country roads to classic villages like Groton and Harvard, stopping at apple orchards, antiques shops, and museums.

Massachusetts is full of surprises. No other state, for instance, offers so many rural museums: world-famous art museums as well as historical museums and museum villages. There are waterfalls, ridge trails, and ocean walks, all in all an exceptional amount of the landscape preserved by Old Guard groups like the Massachusetts Audubon Society and the Trustees of Reservations (both founded in Massachusetts in the 1890s), as well as the Department of Environmental Management. The latter alone maintains more than 100 properties within the scope of this book, ranging from beaches, campsites, and bicycle paths to the 12,500-acre Mount Greylock reservation and to surprisingly elaborate "Heritage State Parks," interpreting urban or industrial history.

Just a dozen years ago many of the more beautiful parts of Massachusetts attracted few visitors because they offered almost no places to stay. When *Massachusetts, An Explorer's Guide* first appeared in 1979, it included Boston, Cape Cod, and the Islands and yet was shorter than this guide. The size of this book reflects the proliferation of inns and B&Bs throughout the state and the addition of many visitor-geared shops and new pastimes, ranging from local resident theater companies to white-water rafting. All these changes add up to myriad getaways for harried urbanities or suburbanites looking for a complete change of pace and scene.

From the island of Cuttyhunk (accessible by ferry from New Bedford) to the top of Mount Holyoke (where a restored Summit House serves as the setting for summer sunset concerts), from the dramatic granite rocks on Cape Ann's Halibut Point to the town of Mount Washington (which rises like a green island above valleys in three states), conducting the research for this book has been rewarding. The result represents far more than an update of the 1987 *Explorer's Guide* entitled *The Other Massachusetts*. Changes have been so substantial over the past decade that they have necessitated an entirely new book, reworked from scratch.

The original *Massachusetts, An Explorer's Guide* was the first in a series that now includes guides to Maine, New Hampshire, Vermont, Cape Cod, Rhode Island, Connecticut, and the Hudson Valley. Chris continues to coauthor four of these.

This, however, is the first book that Bill and Chris have coauthored together. The couple first met over a typewriter they shared in the *Boston Globe* city room. They also worked together, he as *Boston Globe* travel editor, she as assistant travel editor, for several years. Chris subsequently resigned when their first son was born (maternity leave in the early '70s was limited to 3 weeks) but has continued to contribute New England travel stories to the *Globe* ever since. Bill remains a *Boston Globe* feature writer, and articles by the couple still frequently appear together on the front page of the *Globe*'s Sunday travel section. Massachusetts is still their home.

We are grateful to all the people who took the time to contribute their expertise on particular parts of Massachusetts. For help with the North of Boston area we owe thanks to Shirley Magnanti, Linda Hodgkinson, Janice Ramsden, and David O'Neil. We couldn't have done a decent job on Bristol county without Ed Camara's help, or the Plymouth area without Kelly Spencer's good research. Thank you Mary Taft for your take on the Blackstone Valley, Marianne Gambara for your invaluable help with Springfield area dining, Sandy Ward and Terry Blunt for insights in the Five-College area, Ann Hamilton for never-failing aid throughout Franklin County, Harry and Tamsen Dodsen, Carol and Arnold Westwood and Marion Taylor for help in the Hilltowns, Mimi McDonald and the Liebert family for input in the Berkshires. More than ordinary thanks to our editors at Countryman: to Christophter Lloyd for his support and vision for this book, to Helen Whybrow for her patience when it was needed and her hard line when it wasn't, and to Laura Jorstad for her painstaking work with the manuscript.

What's Where in Massachusetts: Beyond Boston and Cape Cod

AGRICULTURAL FAIRS

A detailed list of fairs is available from the **Massachusetts Department of Food and Agriculture** (617-727-3018). The Hardwick, Topsfield, and Tri-County (Northampton) fairs all claim to be the oldest. There are a number of genuine, old-style fairs with ox pulls and livestock judging. Our favorites include those held in Middlefield and Cummington. The Eastern States Exposition, held every September in West Springfield, is in a class by itself, a six-state event with thousands of animals competing for prizes along with a midway, concessions stand, big-name entertainment, and the Avenue of States.

AIRPORTS

There are 50 public airports and seaplane bases in the state. The **Massachusetts Aeronautics Commission** (617-973-8881) in Boston is currently compiling a database that will include anything you can possibly think of asking about. Scenic rides are currently available (see descriptions within the chapters) in Newburyport, Barre, Orange, and Great Barrington.

AMUSEMENT PARKS

Unfortunately, almost all the state's amusement parks (all founded in the late 19th century by trolley companies as inducements to ride the cars out to the end of the line) have bitten the dust. The only survivors are **Riverside Park** near Springfield—the region's largest—**Whalom Park** in Lunenburg ("The Central Uplands"), and **Salem Willows** in Salem. Small but very special, there is always the boardwalk in **Salisbury Beach** (see "Newburyport Area").

ANIMALS

New England's largest collection of animals is caged at Southwick's **Wild Animal Farm,** down a back road in Mendon (see "Blackstone River Valley"). New Bedford and Springfield both have respectable small city zoos, and Worcester's **New England Science Center** features two (mother and daughter) polar bears. Also see *Farms*.

ANTIQUES

The **Brimfield Outdoor Antiques Show,** New England's largest antiques show, is held in the Sturbridge-area town of Brimfield three times per year: May, July, and September. More than 4000 dealers set up shop in the open meadows on both sides of US 20, drawing patrons from throughout the country. The best-known antiques centers in the state are in **Essex** on the

14

North Shore and in and around **Sheffield** in the Berkshires' South County.

APPALACHIAN MOUNTAIN CLUB (AMC)

Founded in 1876 and better known for its extensive presence in New Hampshire's White Mountains, the Appalachian Mountain Club (617-512-0636; 5 Joy Street, Boston) is not only based in Boston but also maintains Bascom Lodge on top of Mount Washington (see "North Berkshire"). It offers a variety of workshop, family, and outdoor programs in the Berkshires.

APPLES

Contact the **Massachusetts Department of Food and Agriculture** (617-727-3018) for a guide to local orchards that welcome visitors. Note that there are three prime orchard areas in the state: the Nashoba Valley, the Sturbridge area, and the Hampshire Hilltown/Mohawk Trail country towns.

AREA CODES

Two area codes apply to the regions described in this guide, and though generally speaking, western Massachusetts is in the 413 area and the eastern part of the state is divided between 617 and 508, it's not always clear where the dividing lines fall. On the North Shore, for instance, Salem is 508, while Marblehead is 617; south of Boston, Plymouth is 508, while Duxbury is 617. The

western fringe of the 508 area also seems rather arbitrary. Wendell and New Salem, for instance, are 508, while neighboring Shutesbury and Pelham are 413.

ART MUSEUMS

Williamstown is a pilgrimage point for art lovers from around the world. The **Sterling and Francine Clark Art Institute** has an exceptional collection of French impressionists and late-19th-century American artists, a collection that the newly expanded **Williams College Art Museum** complements with its American pieces and wealth of works by Maurice Prendergast. The **Worcester Art Museum** also has superb 19th-century American paintings, and in Springfield both the **Museum of Fine Arts** and the **George Walter Vincent Smith Art Museum** are well worth visiting. In the Five-College area, the Mount Holyoke, Amherst, and (especially) Smith museums all hold surprises. The **Berkshire Museum** in Pittsfield also has its share of American masterpieces, and the new **Norman Rockwell Museum** in West Stockbridge probably draws the biggest crowds of all. In the Nashoba Valley, **Fruitlands Museum** has among its exhibits American primitives and landscapes; the **Addison Gallery of American Art** in Andover is yet another trove of Copleys, Sargents, and Whistlers (but displays vary, so check). The **Fitchburg Art Museum** has an interesting collection of American paintings, as well as special exhibits. The recently expanded **Cape Ann Historical Association** in Gloucester showcases marine paintings by Fitz Hugh Lane and local scenes painted by Prendergast, Homer, John Sloan, and Milton Avery.

BALLOONING

The Balloon School of Massachusetts in Brimfield, **Balloon Adventures** of New Bedford, and **Paul Sena** in Worthington all offer rides. See descriptions of each within their towns' respective chapters.

BASKETBALL

The **Basketball Hall of Fame** in Springfield, where the game was invented, celebrates it in a variety of ways.

BEACHES

In this book we have listed most of those strands to which public access is clear. On the saltwater side check out **Crane's Beach** in Ipswich, **Singing Beach** in Manchester, **Duxbury Beach** (described in "Plymouth"), and both **Horseneck Beach** and **Demarest Loyd** in Bristol County. Our pick of the freshwater strands is **Wallum Lake** in Douglas (see "Blackstone River Valley").

BED & BREAKFASTS

A "B&B" used to be just a private home in which guests paid to stay and to breakfast. The definition has broadened in recent years—to include farms and fairly elaborate and formal lodging places that resemble inns in every way but do not serve dinner. Happily, B&Bs are now widely scattered throughout the state and, especially in less-touristed areas, remain reasonably priced. Many are run by longtime residents who are knowledgeable about the surrounding area and delighted to orient their guests. While researching this book we visited hundreds of B&Bs. We did not charge to include those that we found worthy of inclusion. We should also note two bed & breakfast reservation services: **Berkshire Bed & Breakfast Homes** (413-268-7244) in Williamsburg offers handy access and booking to 75 homes scattered between the Connecticut River Valley and the Berkshires; and **Folkstone Bed & Breakfast Reservation Service** (508-480-0380) lists 35 homes throughout central Massachusetts.

BICYCLING

We have noted rentals and outstanding bike routes in most sections. Mountain-bike rentals are available at Northfield Mountain and at the Swift River Inn in Cummington. The 8½-mile Norwottuck Rail Trail between Northampton and Amherst is the only formal bike path, but you might question DEM (see *Forests and Parks*) about the 22-mile Southern New England Trunkline Trail, evolving along a defunct railbed between Franklin and Uxbridge. Phone the **Bikeway Coordinator:** 617-727-3180, extension 470.

BIRDING

The **Massachusetts Audubon Society,** headquartered in Lincoln (617-259-9500) and founded in 1896 to discourage using wild bird plumage as hat decorations, is the oldest of the country's Audubon groups. Sanctuaries are found in Ipswich, Marshfield, Leominster, Wachusett, Northampton, Hampden, and Lenox; request a pamphlet guide. Perhaps the most famous birding spot in the state is **Plum Island** in Newburyport, the site of Massachusetts Audubon's biggest, newest visitors center. The prime eagle-watching spot is from **Quabbin Park** in Belchertown.

BOAT EXCURSIONS

Harbor tours are available in Newburyport, Salem, and Plymouth; ferries sail from Plymouth (to Provincetown) and New Bedford (both to Martha's Vineyard and to Cuttyhunk). You can also tour the canals and Merrimack River in Lowell and cruise a reach of the Connecticut from Northfield Mountain. (Also see *Whale-Watching* and *Fishing.*)

BOAT LAUNCHES

Sites are detailed in brochures on salt- and freshwater fishing available from the **Mas-**

sachusetts **Division of Fisheries and Wildlife** (617-727-1843), 100 Cambridge Street, Boston 02202.

BUS SERVICE

Bonanza Bus (1-800-556-3815) runs from Boston to Fall River. **Greyhound Bus Lines** (1-800-231-2222) serves Worcester and Springfield out of Boston. **Peter Pan Bus Lines** (1-800-237-8747) connects Boston with Worcester, Springfield, Holyoke, Northampton, Amherst, Lee, Lenox, and Pittsfield. **Plymouth and Brockton Bus Lines** (508-746-0378) connects Boston with Plymouth.

CAMPING

The **Department of Environmental Management** (DEM) lists state camping areas in its "Massachusetts Forests and Parks Recreational Activities" brochure available from DEM (617-727-3180), 100 Cambridge Street, Boston 02202. You can now reserve campsites at eight of the public campgrounds described in this book. They are: the **DAR State Forest** in Goshen (413-268-7098); **Mohawk Trail State Park** in Charlemont (413-339-5504); **Savoy Mountain State Park** in Savoy (413-663-8469); **Tolland State Forest** in East Otis (413-269-6002); **Lake Dennison State Recreation Area** in Baldwinville (508-939-5960); **Wells State Park** in Sturbridge (508-347-9257); **Salisbury Beach State Reservation** in Salisbury (508-462-4481); and **Harold Parker State Forest** in North Andover (508-686-3391). Campsite reservations can be made as much as 6 months prior to arrival for stays of 7 consecutive days or longer; for fewer than 7 days they can be made as much as 3 months in advance. The cost of the reservation is a deposit equal to 2 nights.

A "Massachusetts Campground Directory" to commercial campgrounds is available from the Massachusetts Association of Campground Owners (617-544-3475).

CANALS

The country's first canal was supposedly built in South Hadley in 1794 (scant trace remains). The country's first major canal was the **Middlesex,** built to connect Boston and Lowell and opened in 1808. The **Blackstone Canal,** which once connected Worcester and Providence, Rhode Island, is now evolving into a linear park (see "Blackstone River Valley"). The **Farmington Canal,** which ran from Northampton through Westfield and Southwick on its way to New Haven, is also visible in parts. In Holyoke and Lowell, power canals have become important parts of Heritage State Parks, as they will in Turners Falls.

CANOEING

The canoe is making a comeback. Early in this century it was a common sight on Massachusetts rivers, and within the last decade canoe lessons and rentals have proliferated. We detail specific canoe routes and rentals for the Ipswich, the Blackstone, and the Housatonic Rivers; they're also noted in "The Nashoba Valley."

CHILDREN, ESPECIALLY FOR

Children's museums are found in Dartmouth and in Holyoke. The **Toy Cupboard Theater and Museum** in Lancaster is a delight for children of all ages. Within this book we describe attractions such as amusement areas, waterslides, and minigolf under the heading *For Families.*

CHRISTMAS TREES

The **Massachusetts Department of Food and Agriculture** (617-727-3018), 100 Cambridge Street, Boston 02202, supplies a current list of Christmas tree farms at which you can cut your own.

COVERED BRIDGES

See Charlemont, Colrain, Conway, Greenfield, Pepperell (Groton Street, over the Nashua River), Sheffield, and Old Sturbridge Village for examples.

CRAFTS

The country's largest concentration of craftspeople is reportedly in the Five-College area and the hills just to the west. **Northampton's Main Street** showcases much of this work, as does **Salmon Falls Artisans** in Shelburne Falls. The region's outstanding crafts fairs are the **A.C.C. Craftfair** held each June at the Eastern States Exposition Grounds in West Springfield, and the far smaller but quality **Deerfield Crafts Fairs** (June and September) in Old Deerfield.

CRANBERRIES

The Pilgrims called these berries, introduced to them by the Native Americans, "crane berries," since the pink blossoms reminded them of the heads of cranes. Harvesting in Plymouth County gets under way in late September and is especially colorful if the bog is flooded, making billions of berries bob to the surface. The **Cranberry World Visitors Center** in Plymouth presents the history of the industry and serves as an information source about annual harvest events (early October).

FACTORY OUTLETS

Fall River and nearby New Bedford in southeastern Massachusetts pride themselves on their factory outlets, but the **Worcester Common Fashion Outlet Mall** in downtown Worcester is also worth noting, as are the genuine factory stores in downtown Lawrence.

FALL FOLIAGE FESTIVALS

The most colorful fall festivals in the state (and they rank right up there with the most colorful in all of New England) are the **Conway Festival of the Hills** and the **Fall Foliage Festival** in Ashfield on Columbus Day weekend (see "West Franklin County/ Mohawk Trail").

FARMERS' MARKETS AND FARM STANDS

Lists for both are available from the **Department of Food and Agriculture** (617-727-3018).

FARMS

"Agri-tourism" is big in Massachusetts. A number of farms scattered from the Nashoba Valley through central Massachusetts, and concentrated most densely in the Hilltowns, offer bed & breakfast. A few more offer cottage rentals on their property. Many more farms offer pick-your-own (apples, strawberries, blueberries, etc.), depending on the season; still others invite you in to watch them milk. A couple sell their own goat cheese, and one (see "Cape Ann Region") makes its own wine as well as offering just about everything else you can think of. Farms in South Hadley, Sterling, and North Andover feature petting zoos. A visit to a farm invariably gets you off the main drag and into beautiful countryside you might otherwise not find. Request a "Massachusetts Agri-tourism Directory" from the **Department of Food and Agriculture** (617-727-3018).

FISHING

Freshwater fishing options range from mountain streams in the Berkshires and Hilltowns to the wide Connecticut and Merrimack Rivers. In all there are more than 28,000 stocked lakes, ponds, and reservoirs in the state. For a listing of stocked fishing sites, best bets, and areas with handicapped access, call 1-800-ASK-FISH (275-3474). For pond listings and maps send a self-addressed, stamped envelope to the Information and Education Section, Division of Fisheries and Wildlife, Field HQ, Westboro 01581, or call 508-792-7270. For deep-sea fishing charters and party boats check *Boating* and *Fishing* in the "North Shore" chapter and "South of Boston" section.

GOLF

More than 200 golf courses in Massachusetts welcome visitors. We have listed golf courses under *To Do* in each chapter. A list of "Bay State Fairways" for the entire state is available from the **Massachusetts Division of Tourism** (617-727-3201).

GUIDANCE

Phone the Boston-based **Massachusetts Division of Tourism** (617-727-3201) to access a recorded events line ("Great Dates in the Bay State") and to request information about other free publications; for a copy of the free "Massachusetts Getaway Guide" phone 1-800-447-6277.

HERITAGE STATE PARKS

Conceived and beautifully executed by the Department of Environmental Management (DEM) as a way of revitalizing old industrial areas, each "park" revolves around a handsome visitors center in which multivisual exhibits dramatize what makes the community special. Though they have served as prototypes for similar parks

throughout the country, the six Heritage State Parks within the scope of this book have all suffered severe financial cutbacks under recent administrations. Only the **Holyoke** and **Lawrence** parks seems to have rallied enough local volunteer support to continue operating as envisioned. The film in the **Fall River** park remains the most compelling. But be sure to visit the exhibits at the **Western Gateway Heritage State Park** in North Adams, the **Gardner Heritage State Park,** and the brand-new **Riverbend Farm Visitors Center** at the Blackstone River and **Canal Heritage State Park** in Uxbridge. All are detailed within their respective chapters.

HIKING AND WALKING

The Department of Environmental Management (DEM) maintains thousands of miles of hiking trails in more than 100 state parks and preserves within the scope of this book. Trails worth special note include the **Midstate Trail,** traversing ridges that run much of the way from Ashby on the New Hampshire line, over Mount Wachusett, and on down to the Connecticut line; and the section of the **Appalachian Trail** that winds 90 miles through Berkshire County. The **Taconic Skyline Trail,** originally blazed by the CCC in the 1930s, offers many spectacular views along its 21-mile route, also in the Berkshires. Another dramatic, but not easy, hike follows the ridgeline of the east/west Holyoke Range (accessible from the state-run Notch Visitors Center in Granby). Elsewhere in the Five-College area, the Amherst Conservation Commission maintains some 45 miles of walking and hiking trails. It's also worth noting that many miles of trails are maintained by the Essex County Greenbelt Association on the North Shore and throughout the state by the Trustees of Reservations. Within this book dozens of walks are suggested in each chapter (see *Hiking* and *Green Space*). The "bible" for hiking throughout the state is the *Appalachian Mountain Club's Massachusetts and Rhode Island Trail Guide,* which appeared in its seventh edition in 1995. *Fifty Hikes in Massachusetts,* by John Brady and Brian White (Backcountry Publications), is also a nicely written guide to trails throughout the state.

HORSEBACK RIDING

Over the past decade a number of Massachusetts livery stables have closed or limited their scope to lessons and clinics. See "Nashoba Valley," "Old Sturbridge Village Area," "Quabbin Area," "Central Berkshire," and "North Berkshire" for operating stables. Note that two farms in the Hilltowns also offer horseback riding when combined with bed & breakfast.

HOSTELING

The American hosteling movement began in Northfield, where there is still a summer hostel, in 1934. Although geared to bicyclists, hostels are not limited to serving them. For a mapped guide to New England hostels send a stamped, self-addressed envelope to the Greater Boston Council, AYH, 1020 Commonwealth Avenue, Boston (617-731-5430 or 617-731-6692 weekdays). Also see "The Nashoba Valley."

HUNTING

The source for information about licenses, rules, and wildlife management areas is the **Massachusetts Division of Fisheries and Wildlife** (617-727-3151), 100 Cambridge Street, Boston 02202. Request the current "Abstracts" and a list of the division's wildlife management areas.

LAKES

The state's largest lake is the human-made

Quabbin Reservoir, offering fine fishing; **Wachusett Reservoir,** the next largest, is also artificially constructed and also good for fishing. The largest lake with public swimming is Lake Chargoggagomanchauggagogchaubunagungamaug in Webster; unfortunately it is not in this book because it falls between the Blackstone Valley and the Old Sturbridge Village area, but it is very much there, complete with bathhouse. Other lakes with public access have been described in each chapter.

MAPLE SUGARING

Native Americans reportedly taught this industry to early settlers in Tyringham (South Berkshire) in the early 18th century. Sugaring is thriving today, primarily in the Hilltowns, an area with more sugarhouses than the rest of the state put together. During sugaring season in March, visitors are welcome to watch producers "boil off" the sap, reducing it to the sweet liquid that is traditionally sampled on ice or snow. A "Massachusetts Maple Producers Directory," listing dozens of sugarhouses that welcome visitors when they are "boiling" in March and that cater to customers year-round, is available from the **Massachusetts Maple Producers Association** (413-628-3912), Watson-Spruce Corner Road, Ashfield 01330.

MASSACHUSETTS TURNPIKE

It's impossible to explore much of Massachusetts without encountering the "Mass. Pike" (I-90). Completed in 1952, this super-highway cuts as straight as an arrow 135 miles across the state from Boston to the New York line, with just 25 exits, 14 of them east of I-495. Unlike other Massachusetts roadways, the turnpike receives no state or federal money and charges accordingly (the toll from Boston to the Berkshires is $5.60). It was the first road in Massachusetts on which you can officially drive 65 miles per hour (between Auburn and Ludlow and again between Westfield and the New York line). Eleven service centers (most with fast-food restaurants) are scattered along the route, and four of these include information desks. They are located near the intersection with I-84 in Charlton (eastbound 248-4581; westbound 248-3853); in Lee (243-4929); and in Natick (650-3698).

MOUNTAINS
Mount Greylock is the state's highest, and you can get to the top (3491 feet) by car. You can also drive up Mount Everett ("The Berkshires—South County"), Mount Wachusett ("Central Uplands"), Mount Sugarloaf ("Pioneer Valley—Greenfield/Deerfield Area"), Mount Tom and Mount Holyoke ("Pioneer Valley—Five College Area"). All these offer hiking trails, as do Mount Toby ("Pioneer Valley—Greenfield/Deerfield Area") and Mount Grace ("Quabbin Area"). For some dramatic ridge trails see *Hiking.* Note that you can stay on top of Mount Greylock (see "North Berkshire"—*Lodging*).

MUSEUM VILLAGES
Old Sturbridge Village in Sturbridge recreates New England rural life in the 1790s–1830s. It is one of New England's biggest tourist attractions and has spawned thousands of adjacent "beds," dozens of shops, restaurants, and some smaller museums in town. Plimoth Plantation in Plymouth is a smaller but equally painstaking reconstruction of the Pilgrim village. Hancock Shaker Village is a restored Shaker complex in Central Berkshire, and Historic Deerfield near Greenfield preserves more than a dozen 18th- and 19th-century homes. In West Springfield, Storrowton is small but

represents one of the country's earliest re-created villages.

MUSIC
Music festivals are a growing phenomenon. The oldest (since 1858) is the Worcester County Music Association Festival in October. The best known is the Tanglewood Music Festival, during July and August in Lenox. Other summer series of note include the Aston Magna Festival in Great Barrington, the Berkshire Choral Festival in Sheffield, the Sevenars in South Worthington, the Mohawk Trail Concerts in Charlemont, the Castle Island Festival in Ipswich, and the popular series of organ concerts at Hammond Castle, in Gloucester, and in the Methuen Memorial Music Hall.

PICK-YOUR-OWN
Listings of places where you can pick your own apples, blueberries, and strawberries are available from the Massachusetts Department of Food and Agriculture (617-727-3018), 100 Cambridge Street, Boston 02202.

RAIL SERVICE AND EXCURSIONS
The Massachusetts Bay Transportation Authority (MBTA; 617-722-3200) offers daily commuter service north to Salem, Gloucester, Rockport, and Ipswich, and west to Fitchburg and Worcester. AMTRAK's (1-800-USA-RAIL) Lake Shore Limited from Boston to Chicago stops in Springfield and in Pittsfield every evening (departing Boston at 4:20, arriving in Springfield at 6:35); reservations are required. The Mystic Valley Railway Society (617-361-4445) runs a variety of excursions throughout New England every year. Holyoke Heritage State Park (413-534-1723) stages 1-hour round-trip rides on weekends. The Providence and Wor-

cester Railroad (508-799-4000) runs occasional excursions over the line on which it hauls freight on weekdays, and the **Berkshire Scenic Railway** (413-637-2210) offers short, narrated train rides on the grounds of its Lenox railroading museum.

ROOM TAX

In contrast to most states, which impose one state tax throughout, Massachusetts has given local communities the option of adding an extra 4 percent—theoretically for local promotion—to the basic 5.7 percent room tax. Although resort towns tend to add the extra 4 percent, there is no hard-and-fast rule: Salem does, while neighboring Rockport doesn't; Great Barrington does, and neighboring Egremont doesn't. It's worth asking. It's also worth noting that B&Bs with only two or three rooms are exempt from room tax.

SAILING

Sailing lessons and rentals are offered by the **Coastal Sailing School;** see "Salem and Marblehead Area."

SEA KAYAKING

Several outfitters are described in "Cape Ann Region."

SKIING, CROSS-COUNTRY

A couple dozen years ago the Finns of Fitchburg were about the only Bay Staters skiing through the Massachusetts woods. There are currently more than a dozen commercial touring centers and hundreds of miles of marked cross-country trails in Massachusetts. Trails are noted throughout the book under *Cross-Country Skiing* and *Green Space.* The state's most dependable snow conditions are found in the western Massachusetts snowbelt, which runs north-south through Stump Sprouts (a lodge and touring center) in East Hawley; the Windsor Notch Reservation in Windsor; and Hickory Hill Ski Touring Center in Worthington. The Swift River Inn in Cummington offers the most elaborate lodge and limited snowmaking on cross-country trails.

SKIING, DOWNHILL

A "Ski Massachusetts" brochure is available from the **Massachusetts Division of Tourism** (617-727-3201), 100 Cambridge Street, Boston 02202. Within this book we have described each area. In the Berkshires there are Jiminy Peak, Brodie, Bousquet, Catamount, Butternut Basin, and Otis Ridge. There's also Berkshire East in Charlemont, Mount Tom in Holyoke, and Mount Wachusett in Princeton.

THE SOCIETY FOR THE PROTECTION OF NEW ENGLAND ANTIQUITIES (SPNEA)

Founded in 1910 to protect New England's cultural and architectural heritage, SPNEA maintains four properties described in this book, two of which—Beauport in Gloucester and the Spencer-Pierce-Little Farm in

Newbury—are as spectacular as historic houses can be. For a "Visitors Guide" to all 33 house museums in five states and a list of current events, phone 617-227-3956.

STATE FORESTS AND PARKS

Would you believe that Massachusetts has the eighth-largest state park system in the country? The Department of Environmental Management (DEM) is responsible for more than a quarter million acres of public forests and parks. It's the largest single landholder in the state. The system began in 1898 with the gift of 8000 acres of land around Mount Greylock; in 1915 the DEM acquired the Otter River State Forest in Winchendon. Initially its mandate was to purchase logged-over, virtually abandoned land for $5 per acre, and during the Depression the Civilian Conservation Corps (CCC) greatly expanded the facilities (building roads, trails, lakes, and other recreation areas). The DEM continues to expand and diversify its holdings. This book describes roughly 100 forests, parks, and reservations under *Green Space,* suggesting opportunities for camping, canoeing, swimming, skiing downhill (at Mount Wachusett and Butternut) and cross-country, rock climbing, and hang gliding—not to mention hiking. "The Massachusetts Forest and Park Map/Guide" is a cryptic but indispensable key to this vast system, available, along with an excellent pamphlet guide to "Massachusetts Historic State Parks," from the DEM (617-727-3180, extension 482), 100 Cambridge Street, Boston 02202. For specific information it's best to contact the regional offices: in the Berkshires, 413-442-8928; for the Connecticut River Valley, 413-545-5993; for the central region, 508-368-0126; for the northeast, 617-369-3350; and for the southeast, 508-866-2580.

THEATER

Summer theaters are described in Beverly ("The North Shore"), Stockbridge ("Central Berkshire"), Williamstown ("North Berkshire"), South Hadley ("Five-College Area"), Gardner and Fitchburg ("Central Uplands"), and Greenfield. **StageWest** in West Springfield is a year-round theater company, and the **Little Theater** of Chester offers small but superb off-Broadway drama.

TRUSTEES OF RESERVATIONS

A nonprofit organization founded in 1891 to preserve the public use and enjoyment of historic places and beautiful tracts of land (much as a person enjoys outstanding paintings in museums), the Trustees of Reservations now owns and manages more than 40 properties described in this book. Several of these are beautifully maintained historic houses (in Stockbridge, New Ashford, and Cummington), but most are exceptional pieces of land, several of which include waterfalls. Check under *Green Space* throughout the book; details about properties and special events are available from the Trustees of Reservations (508-921-1944), 572 Essex Street, Beverly 01915.

VINEYARDS

The number and quality of Massachusetts wineries have increased substantially in the past decade; we have described them in Ashburnham, Bolton, Colrain, Ipswich, Raynham, Westport, and West Dudley.

WATERFALLS

Waterfalls can be found in Ashfield, Barre, Becket, Blandford, Cheshire, Chesterfield, Dalton, Middlefield, Mount Washington, New Marlboro, North Adams, Royalston, Sheffield, Shelburne Falls, Williamsburg, and Worthington.

WHALE-WATCHING

More than a dozen major whalewatching operators now offer thousands of trips spring through fall to watch the whales that congregate to feed on Stellwagen Bank, a dozen miles off Cape Ann. Check the listings for Newburyport, Cape Ann, and Plymouth. If you are inclined to be seasick, Dramamine is very helpful; you might also opt for a larger, newer boat. Be sure to bring a sweater and windbreaker on even a hot day. For many landlubbers these excursions are their first encounter with a small boat on the open sea.

I. NORTH OF BOSTON

The North Shore
The Merrimack Valley

Wintertime along Hawthorne Boulevard in Salem

JIM McALLISTER

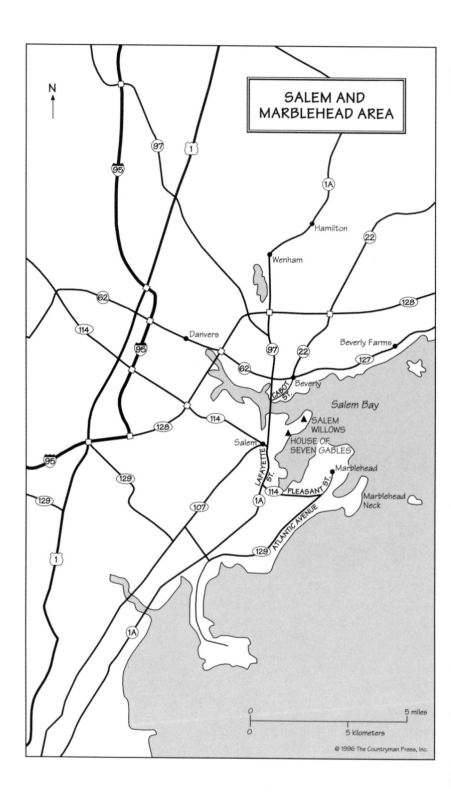

N

SALEM AND
MARBLEHEAD AREA

95

97

1

1A

Hamilton

22

Wenham

128

62

114

Danvers

95

97

22

Beverly Farms

62

127

CABOT ST.

Beverly

Salem Bay

114

SALEM
WILLOWS

128

HOUSE OF
SEVEN GABLES

Salem

95

Marblehead

129

LAFAYETTE ST.

114

PLEASANT ST.

Marblehead
Neck

129

1A

107

ATLANTIC AVENUE

1

129

1A

0   5 miles

0   5 kilometers

© 1996 The Countryman Press, Inc.

The North Shore

For touring purposes, Boston's North Shore begins in Marblehead and runs 30 miles or so, tacking and jibing around Cape Ann and along the ragged edge of Ipswich Bay to Newburyport at the mouth of the Merrimack River. Here old families, old money, and the purest of Massachusetts accents prevail.

What strikes visitors is the way old seaports remain much the way they did in their heyday—a time that varied from place to place. Ipswich, with its sheltered harbor and vast salt marshes, prospered in the 17th century and boasts the greatest number of houses from that era of any town its size in this country. In Marblehead many buildings along narrow streets were built just prior to the Revolution on profits from the Triangle Trade. Both Salem and Newburyport are distinguished by their unusual number of graceful Federal mansions built by the sea captains and merchants who pioneered trade with the Far East after the Revolution, while Gloucester's look dates from the late 19th century, an era when it ranked as one of the world's foremost fishing ports.

In the late 19th century all of these old ports emerged as summer havens. Trains, ferries, and trolleys linked the shore to Boston. Beaching and yachting came into vogue. Blue-collar workers flocked to the boardwalks at Salisbury Beach and Salem Willows, and millionaires built summer mansions on Marblehead Neck and Gloucester's Eastern Point. Summer cottages mushroomed on Plum Island, and on Little Neck in Ipswich. Hotels appeared along the length of the North Shore—from Swampscott to Salisbury. The 750-room Oceanside in Magnolia billed itself as the largest resort hotel in New England.

By the middle of this century most of the hotels had vanished, summerhouses were winterized, and the North Shore communities, many of them connected by commuter trains and buses with Boston, were suburbanized. Cape Cod—a bit farther from home and offering more sand, warmer water—supplanted the North Shore as Boston's preferred summer spot.

Quietly, however, the North Shore has been evolving again as a tourist destination, one of the most interesting in the Northeast. Many miles of oceanside walks and inland beauty spots have been opened to the public, water excursions have multiplied, the area's outstanding museums—notably the Peabody Essex Museum in Salem and the Cape Ann Historical Society in Gloucester—have substantially expanded, and lodging options have proliferated with the spread of small inns and B&Bs. Rockport remains the area's only real resort town, but, as their traditional industries fade, Salem, Gloucester, and Newburyport are also turning to tourism. Bostonians haven't yet caught on. They still think of the North Shore as a place to day-trip.

GUIDANCE

In 1993 the National Parks Service opened this state's most elaborate visitors center in Salem. It includes an excellent film dramatizing the history of Essex County and makes Salem the logical gateway to this area (see "Salem and Marblehead Area").

The North of Boston Convention & Visitors Council (508-921-4990; 1-800-742-5396) also publishes a useful guide to the entire region.

SALEM AND MARBLEHEAD AREA

Although Salem and Marblehead abut, the old town centers are several miles apart, positioned on opposite sides of Salem Harbor. Both are bordered on three sides by water and pervaded by a sense of the sea.

Salem is a city of 40,000 people with fine Federal-era mansions, a very walkable downtown, and an immense, superb museum. The Peabody Essex is New England's ultimate treasure chest of exotica, all of it brought from the farthest points of the globe by Salem sea captains and "supercargoes." The Salem Maritime National Historic Site on the waterfront also recalls the era between the Revolution and the War of 1812 when Salem's merchant fleet numbered 185 proud vessels.

Oh, yes, Salem also has witches: wax witches, multimedia witches, candy witches, witch houses, and real witches. Back in 1692, Salem was the site of the infamous "Witch Trials" during which hundreds of men, women, and children were accused by their neighbors of practicing witchcraft. Today Salem's busiest season (it's been extended to three weeks of "Haunted Happenings") is Halloween.

Half the size of Salem, Marblehead has a delightfully walkable historic district that's a tangle of crooked streets, with old houses perched like so many seabirds above the harbor. Most of the older homes are modest, clustering around the Old Town House (1727), their token gardens recalling that only fishermen, not farmers, were permitted to live downtown. Today Marblehead is still synonymous with sailing vessels, but fishermen have been upstaged by yachtsmen for more than a century—ever since the Bay State's most prestigious yacht clubs located here. Once known for its summer hotels as well as mansions, Marble-

JIM McALLISTER

The homes of old sea captains line Chestnut Street in Salem.

head Neck is still a great spot from which to watch the thousands of boats competing each July during Marblehead Race Week or just to sit a spell any day and smell the sea.

Beverly claims to have seen the birth of the American navy (a claim disputed by Marblehead and Whitehall, New York). It also claims America's oldest house (disputed by Dedham) and says it put a stop to Salem's witch hysteria. The town itself was transformed in the 19th century by the shoe industry, but Prides Crossing and Beverly Farms still harbor a number of estates, many of them now parts of private schools.

The summertime North Shore Music Theater and the year-round magic of Le Grand David, whose troupe has restored two vintage Cabot Street theaters, draw large audiences.

It was actually in Danvers that the slave Tituba fired the imagination of two young girls by telling them ghost stories back in 1692. The girls then accused village women of witchcraft, sparking the "Salem Witch Hunt." Danvers was part of Salem at the time.

AREA CODE
508 for Salem; 617 for Marblehead.

GUIDANCE
National Park Visitor's Center (508-740-1650), 12 Liberty Street, Salem. Open daily 9–6. Opened in late 1994, this major center features a film dramatizing the history of Essex County and information for the entire region.

Salem Office of Tourism; 1-800-777-6848 is the number to call to order the area's map/guide.

Salem Chamber of Commerce (508-744-0004), Old Town Hall, 32 Derby Square; a friendly walk-in information center open weekdays 9–5.

Marblehead Chamber of Commerce (617-631-2868), PO Box 76, Marblehead 01945. This unusually friendly office at 62 Pleasant Street is open weekdays 9–3; request copies of its guides to lodging, dining, and shopping, and the downtown walking tour. A seasonal information booth at the corner of Pleasant and Essex Streets is open from Memorial Day on weekends, and daily July through Columbus Day, 10–6.

GETTING THERE
By train: MBTA (1-800-392-6100; 617-722-3200) commuter trains connect Salem with Boston's North Station.

By bus: MBTA (see numbers above) buses from Boston's Haymarket Square (daily, at least once every half hour).

Airport shuttle: **North Shore Shuttle** (617-631-8660) connects the Salem/ Marblehead area with Logan Airport.

By car: Marblehead is 17 miles north of Boston via MA 1A to Lynn, then MA 129 North. But the simplest and quickest way from Boston to Salem is MA 128 to Exit 25A (MA 114 East). Within Salem signs lead you to the Salem Visitors Center and downtown parking.

GETTING AROUND
The Salem Heritage Trail. A 1.7-mile red line down the center of Salem sidewalks links most of the obvious sights to see here. Begin in East India Square with the visitors center and Peabody Essex Museum and walk the short way down Hawthorne Boulevard to Derby Street and the Maritime National Historic Site. The House of Seven Gables is a few blocks beyond. Inquire about a printed guide to the Samuel McIntire Trail.

The Salem Trolley (508-744-5469) operates July through October, stopping at all the obvious tourist sites, including Salem Willows Park and the House of Seven Gables, every half hour. $8 adult, $7 seniors, $3 children and students. Good for one entire day. You might want to take an initial hour-long tour and then use it for transportation the rest of the day.

PARKING

In Salem: The good news is that the "P" signs lead to the municipal parking garage ($4 all day and free on weekends) adjoining the National Park Visitor's Center and Peabody Essex Museum. The bad news is that this parking garage is the one from hell (you'll understand why). We recommend the Church Street lot instead (free on weekends). Beware the town's zealous meter maids.

In Marblehead: Aside from summer weekends you can usually find curbside parking, and there are limited lots on Rockaway Street, Harris Street, Fort Sewall, and, if it's your lucky day, the Town Landing. Pick up a walking map from the chamber of commerce or information booth; shops, museums, restaurants, and parks are all within walking distance, and during the summer it's better to take a bike than a car onto Marblehead Neck; to find it, head south on MA 114 and turn left onto Ocean Avenue.

MEDICAL EMERGENCY

North Shore Medical Center (508-741-1200), 81 Highland Avenue, Salem; for ambulance: 508-744-4414.

TO SEE

In Salem

MUSEUMS

Peabody Essex Museum (508-745-9500), East India Square. Open Monday through Saturday 10–5, Sunday noon–5, Thursday evenings until 8. Closed major holidays. Admission to museum buildings or historic houses: $6 senior, $5 student, $3.50 children aged 6–18, $15 per family. Admission to the entire complex, including historic houses: $10 adult, $8.50 senior/student, $6 children, $25 per family. In 1992 the Peabody and Essex Museums merged, but it's still impossible to lump them into one description. They still physically stand across the street from each other and retain identities formed over more than 150 years.

The Peabody is one of New England's leading maritime museums with its ultimate treasure chest of exotica. It was founded in 1799 by 22 of the city's overseas traders as the East Indian Marine Society. The idea was to share navigational information, to support the widows of those lost at sea, and "to form a museum of natural and artificial curiosities such as are to be found beyond the Cape of Good Hope and Cape Horn." Almost 200 years later the museum's collection totals more than 300,000 objects. Thousands of visitors come each year from Japan and China to see priceless porcelain, silver, ivory, and the lacquered screens and exquisite furniture made in their countries during the 16th through

19th centuries (an entire Asian Export Art wing was added in 1988 when the Peabody absorbed the former Museum of the American China Trade in Milton). We are always particularly struck by the 18th- and early-19th-century paintings of the "Hongs," or trading houses in Hong Kong and Canton, and of the traders themselves. The maritime art and history department is also impressive, ranging from a horn fashioned from the penis of a sperm whale to works by artists like Fitz Hugh Lane and Gilbert Stuart. The natural history regional collection, with rare examples of the flora and fauna of Essex County, includes a 750-pound turtle found in Ipswich 200 years ago and still exuding oil. The Arts of Asia and the Pacific gallery continues to delight kids with its huge, fierce (and authentic) sculptures of South Pacific gods, and the heart of the museum remains the grand, 1820s East Indian Hall, lined with ships' figureheads and the kind of old-fashioned "cabinets of curiosities" that the museum's founders envisioned.

The former Essex Institute was founded in 1848 and houses a collection of portraits, period rooms, local silver, and county archives—including the actual records of the 1692 witch trials in Salem. This era is dramatized through exhibits within the museum and, in summer months, through role playing outside the 17th-century John Ward House, one of several historic houses on the museum grounds. The neighboring Gardner-Pingree House (1804) is a 14-room mansion generally believed to represent Samuel McIntire's work at its best. (McIntire is known for the airy, four-square mansions garnished throughout with delicately carved detailing, arches, and stairways. The lineup of these homes makes Chestnut one of the handsomest streets in America.) The heart of this museum remains its two-story, balconied hall, containing period rooms and a wide assortment of local memorabilia. Inquire about the museum's elaborate changing exhibits and about daily guided tours. See the museum's café under *Dining Out*. The Ropes Mansion and Garden (508-744-0718) is open on a reduced schedule at this writing but well worth inquiring about.

Salem Maritime National Historic Site (508-744-4323), 178 Derby Street. Open daily 9–6, 10–5 in winter. The site includes the brick Custom House (1819) in which Nathaniel Hawthorne worked, a Bonded Warehouse and West India Goods Store, and the brick mansion built by Elias Hasket Derby, better known as "King Derby," who pioneered a new sailing route around the Cape of Good Hope and is said to have been America's first millionaire. A maritime film is shown in the visitors center at the head of Derby Wharf, which dates from 1752 and is the last of some 50 wharves that were once lined with warehouses.

HISTORIC HOUSES

House of Seven Gables (508-744-0091), 54 Turner Street. Open daily year-round except major holidays and the last two weeks in January for 45-minute guided tours, 10–4:30, and July through Labor Day, 9–6. No one

Fort Pickering Lighthouse on Winter Island

should leave Salem without a visit to this very special place, a waterside complex that includes the dark clapboard, vintage-1668 house (complete with hidden staircase and penny-candy shop) that inspired Nathaniel Hawthorne's gloomy novel. The complex also contains the house in which Hawthorne himself was born and two more 17th-century homes. A new visitors center with interactive videos and a continuous audiovisual representation, also a snack bar and garden café, eases you into the site and the story of how it was restored as a tourist attraction back in 1910 as a way of supporting the settlement house across the street, a cause the site still benefits. $7 adults, $4 ages 13–17, $3 ages 6–12.

Stephen Phillips Memorial Trust House (508-744-0440), 34 Chestnut Street. Open Memorial Day to mid-October, Monday through Saturday 10–4:30. $2 adults, $1 children. The only house open to the public on Chestnut Street displays paintings, Chinese porcelain, and Oriental rugs. There is also a carriage house with antique cars and carriages. $1.50 adults, $1 seniors, $.75 children.

Pickering House (508-744-1647), 18 Broad Street, Salem. Open Monday, year-round, 10–3, and by appointment. Built in 1651, it is the oldest house in America to be continually occupied by the same family. $4 adults.

Salem 1630 Pioneer Village (508-744-0991), off MA 114 and West Avenue in Forest River Park. Open Memorial Day through October, Monday through Saturday 10–5, Sunday noon–5. The town's initial settlement was reconstructed for the city's 300th anniversary and is now staffed by costumed interpreters. Visitors are invited to churn butter, spin wool, and play the era's games, and there are barnyard animals, also ducks in the

Halloween in Salem

adjacent reeds. $4.50 adults, $3.50 seniors and children aged 13–17, $2.50 children aged 6–12.

WITCHES

Salem Witch Museum (508-744-1692), 19½ Washington Square North. Open year-round, daily 10–5, until 7 PM in July, August. With "computerized sound and light," this so-called museum tells the whole lurid tale of how 14 women and 5 men were executed in 1692, of the 4 who died in jail, and of the 55 more who saved their necks by accusing others. $4 adults, $3.50 seniors, $2.50 aged 6–14 (under 6 should not be admitted).

The Witch House (508-744-0180), corner of Essex and North Streets.

Open mid-March through June and September to December 1, 10–4:30; July through Labor Day 10–6. Restored and furnished by the City of Salem in the 1930s, this 1642 building was the home of Magistrate Jonathan Corwin, a judge in the 1692 witch trials. Pretrial examinations of many of the accused were held here. $5 adults, $1.50 children aged 5–16.

The **Witch Dungeon Museum** (508-741-3570), 16 Lynde Street. Open May through October, 10–5. Yet another dramatization of the witch trials, this one with mannequins. $4 adults, $3.50 seniors, $1.50 children aged 5–12.

Salem Wax Museum of Witches and Seafarers (508-740-2929), 288 Derby Street. Open daily 10–7, $4 adults, $3.50 seniors, $2.50 children. The story is told with wax figurines.

In Marblehead

HISTORIC HOUSES AND SITES

Jeremiah Lee Mansion (617-631-1069), 161 Washington Street. Open mid-May to mid-October, Monday through Friday 10–4; Saturday and Sunday 1–4. Nominal fee. Lee was a shipowner who could import his own building materials: mahogany from Santo Domingo for the grand staircase, and wallpaper from England. Today the striking building is headquarters for the Marblehead Historical Society, whose third-floor exhibits include bright early-20th-century primitives of Marblehead scenes by J.O.J. Frost and early-19th-century portraits by William Bartoll.

King Hooper Mansion (617-631-2608), 8 Hooper Street; daily 10–4, Sunday 1–5. The rare, five-story section of this remarkable house dates from 1728; the three-story, block-front facade and front rooms were added in 1745. The building now serves as headquarters for the Marblehead Arts Association. Changing exhibits are in the former third-floor ballroom. Donations welcome.

Abbot Hall, Washington Square. Open year-round, Monday, Tuesday, Thursday, and Friday 8–5; Wednesday 7:30 AM–7:30 PM; Saturday 9–6; and Sunday 11–6. A brick Victorian town hall that stands on the highest point of land and towers over the town. The famous (and not disappointing) *Spirit of '76* painting commissioned for the 1876 centennial is in the Selectmen's Room. It depicts Washington being rowed across the Delaware by General Glover's hardy company of "Headers." In the lobby is the 17th-century deed to the town, complete with totem signatures of the sachems.

Old Town House, Market Square. No longer open to the public, this bright yellow building was built in 1727, designed like Boston's Faneuil Hall to house butcher and produce stalls on its ground floor, with a meeting hall on its second floor (it was here that General Glover organized his Essex Regiment). It is an unusually graceful building but compromised by the heavy granite first floor added in 1830.

The Lafayette House (privately owned) at the corner of Hooper and Union Streets is a local landmark because its lower corner was obviously cut out to make passage for carriages and wagons. According to legend it was altered to allow the Marquis de Lafayette to pass in 1824.

In Beverly

The Beverly Historical Society (508-922-1186), 117 Cabot Street, maintains three outstanding houses, all open mid-May through mid-October, Wednesday through Saturday 10–4, Sunday 1–4; $2 adults, $.50 children; $4 adult admission to all three, $1 children. **The Balch House,** 448 Cabot Street, is a Tudor-style clapboard house built in 1636, now within sight of the mammoth United Shoe factory. It is reportedly the home of the first male born in the Massachusetts Bay Colony, and it has its own witchcraft story. **Cabot House,** 110 Cabot Street, is a handsome brick Federal home built for John Cabot, shipowner and co-founder of America's first cotton mill. There are relics here from the city's privateering and Far Eastern trade, and antique toys. The **John Hale House,** 39 Hale Street (off MA 22), was built partially in 1694 by a minister who was involved in the Salem witch trials, until his own wife was accused of being a witch; he quickly helped end the trials.

In Danvers

Rebecca Nurse Homestead (508-774-8799), 149 Pine Street. Open mid-June to September, Tuesday through Sunday 1–4; weekends through October. $3.50 adults, $1.50 children under 16. The vintage 1678 house is starkly silhouetted against its old pastureland, and Rebecca's body lies buried on the grounds, only because her family risked their own necks to retrieve it by night from Gallows Hill in Salem. The 72-year-old mother of eight stoutly refused to say that she was a witch.

TO DO

BICYCLING
Salem Cycles (508-741-2222), 316 Derby Street in Salem, rents cycles.
BOATING
East India Cruise Company (508-741-0434), 123 Bay View Avenue, Salem, offers seasonal harbor cruises from Pickering Wharf; also shuttle service to Marblehead and back, and 10 AM daily whalewatching cruises to Stellwagen Bank.
Note: For whalewatching options see "Cape Ann Region" and "Newburyport Area."
The Rockmore Company (617-639-0600), 208 Beacon Street, Marblehead. Narrated harbor tours aboard the *Hannah Glover.* Thursday night music cruises are actually based at The Rockmore in the middle of the harbor (see *Eating Out*).
Coastal Sailing School (617-639-0553), 81 Front Street, Marblehead. The 20-hour course, conducted entirely on a 26- or 30-foot sailboat, can be

spread over 5 weeks or compressed into 5 days. A 5-day, live-aboard cruise is $695 plus food. Bareboat Sailboat rentals are also offered: two Rainbow 24s ($85 a half day, $115 a full day); a Pearson 26 ($115 a half day, $155 a full day). Sailboat charter: The 30-footer is available for daysails.

Westwind Sailing Charters of Salem (508-740-9890), at Hawthorne Cove Marina, 10 White Street (next to the House of Seven Gables). May through October, the 43-foot ketch *Alexandra Rose* offers 2-hour cruises: lunch, dinner, and sunset.

Black Cat Fishing & Cruise Private Charters (508-622-2108), Congress Street Bridge at Pickering Wharf. May through October, a 25-foot Hydrapost takes two to six passengers with expert fishing guide.

SWIMMING

Devereux Beach, Ocean Avenue, at the causeway to Marblehead Neck; rest rooms, covered seating, barbecue grills. $3 weekdays, $5 weekends.

Forest River Park, off MA 114 at West Avenue, Salem. Two small beaches and "the largest outdoor swimming pool in the state." City owned, nominal fee.

Lynch Park, Beverly, Ober Street off MA 127. Once part of a grand estate, this park includes two beaches as well as a grassy expanse for sunning; also a sunken rose garden, rest rooms, concession stands, picnic tables, and there's a great sledding hill. Band concerts in the shell Sunday evenings 6–8. Parking is $5 per car on weekends, $10 weekdays.

GREEN SPACE

PARKS

Salem Willows (508-745-0251), Salem. Follow signs out along Derby Street to Fort Avenue. This is one of New England's few surviving old-fashioned amusement areas, and it's set in a landscaped park overlooking the Beverly waterfront on one side, Salem Sound and the coast from Marblehead to Cape Ann on the other. The willows were planted in 1801 to form a shaded walk for patients at the smallpox hospital. Note the round-roofed Hobbs Pavilion, still a source of burgers, popcorn, hot peanuts, taffy, and ice cream cones. (Everett Hobbs is said to have introduced the ice cream cone to New England in 1905.) The carousel in neighboring Kiddieland dates from the same era; the arcade and Cappy's Fried Clams are also local institutions.

Derby Wharf, Derby Street in front of the Customs House. The wharf itself extends some 2000 feet into Salem Harbor and, now grassed over, forms a great picnic and relaxing spot. It is now part of the Salem Maritime National Historic Park.

Winter Island Maritime Park (508-745-9430), 50 Winter Island Road, off Derby Street just before you get to Salem Willows. A former Coast Guard station with some fairly ugly buildings left from that chapter in its history, RV campsites, a boat launch, and beach; $2 for nonresidents, but the snack bar validates 2 hours' parking.

Crocker Park, Front Street, Marblehead. This park includes a grassy rise with a harbor view and old-fashioned stone seats, all found up beyond a house designed to look like a Viking castle. Bring a sketch pad.

PICNICKING

Old Burial Hill and Fountain Park, Pond Street, Marblehead. Gravestones surround the site of the town's 1638 meetinghouse and mark the resting places of some 600 Revolutionary War soldiers. There is a great view of the town and harbor, and you can picnic just up the way (turn right) at Fountain Park, site of a Revolutionary-era fort. Below Fountain Park (access off Orne Street) is a small, sandy beach, and at low tide you can walk out to a little island. Redd's Pond, nearby on Norman Street, is also a place to picnic in summer and to watch skaters in winter.

WALKS

Massachusetts Wildlife Sanctuary, Marblehead Neck, Risley Road. Massachusetts Audubon maintains 15¼ acres here; the pond is used for winter skating.

Chandler Hovey Park and Lighthouse Point, tip of Marblehead Neck; a great spot to picnic, get your bearings, and watch summer boat races.

Fort Sewall, Marblehead; at the eastern end of Front Street. Begun as an earthenworks during the 17th century and improved as the Revolutionary-era fortification that still stands, it is now a pleasant park.

Long Hill (508-921-1944), 572 Essex Street (MA 22), is a brick mansion built as a summer home for Ellery Sedgwick, author, editor, and publisher of *The Atlantic Monthly* from 1909 to 1938. The mansion itself now houses the offices of the Trustees of Reservations, and the 114-acre grounds are open to the public. The big draw here is Sedgwick Gardens, a remarkable collection of trees, shrubs, and flowers, including Japanese maple, weeping cherry, rhododendron, and azaleas. Walking trails thread through fields, forest, and wetland.

Hospital Point, Beverly. Driving north from the city on Hale Street (toward MA 127), turn right on East Corning Street for a short detour to an 1871 lighthouse overlooking Salem and Marblehead. This was also the site of a Revolutionary fort, and later of a smallpox hospital.

Misery Islands Reservation, Salem Bay. Accessible only by boat, this second-largest island between Boston Harbor and Cape Porpoise, Maine, was once the site of summer cottages, a clubhouse, and a golf course; now the rolling fields are a favorite destination for weekend sailors.

SPECIAL SPACES

Salem Common (Washington Square). Set aside for public use early in the 1700s, this once swampy, hilly space was leveled in the early 19th century into the classic Common that survives today, complete with benches and bandstand.

Derby Square and Essex Street, Salem. From Washington Square you can now walk down Essex Street, a pedestrian way lined with museums and shops, to Derby Square, the original market area around the Old Town Hall. At East India Square stone benches surround a large fountain.

State Street Landing, Marblehead. A landing since 1662, this is a place to watch people and boats (some 3000 sailing craft summer in the sheltered inner harbor).

LODGING

Note: Local tax on lodging varies: In Marblehead it's 5.7 percent, and in Salem, 9.4 percent.

HOTEL

Hawthorne Hotel (744-4080; 1-800-729-7829), 18 Washington Square West, Salem 01970. A fine six-story, three-sided, 89-room hotel that was built by public subscription in the 1920s and has managed to keep its standards high in an era during which few small city hotels have survived. By far the tallest building around, it has the best views in town. The lobby, with its fluted columns and potted palms, is quite elegant, and rooms are furnished in reproduction antiques; all have private baths. Facilities include the Tavern on the Green (an oak-paneled bar) and Nathaniel's Restaurant. $92–137 per room, $195–295 per suite.

BED & BREAKFAST INNS

Two remarkably similar facilities, one in Salem and the other in Marblehead, offer the feel and facilities of a full-service inn but serve only breakfast.

The Salem Inn (508-741-0680; 1-800-446-2995), 7 Summer Street, Salem. A four-story, brick double townhouse built in 1834 with 21 rooms, private baths. Dick and Diane Pabich have created an appealing place in keeping with its surroundings. There's a comfortable living room with fireplace and suitable ancestor hanging above it. Rooms vary widely, from spacious, bright doubles with working hearths (Duraflame logs), to top-floor family suites with cooking facilities, to smaller rooms (some with fireplaces) with baths down the hall. Around the corner at 331 Essex Street, **The Curwen House,** a vintage 1854 Italianate-style house, has recently been added to the inn. It has its own living room and a meeting room plus the guest rooms, six with working fireplaces and three of these with two-person whirlpools and canopy beds. All rooms have cable TV and phone, and half have in-room coffeemakers. Breakfast, served in the inn's restaurant and on the patio, is included in the rates: $89–149, higher during Haunted Happenings. Add tax.

The Harbor Light Inn (617-631-2186), 58 Washington Street, Marblehead. Two Federal-era mansions have been joined to create this elegant 21-room inn. It's flush to the sidewalk of a narrow, busy street near the heart of old Marblehead, with parking and a small, landscaped pool in the rear. Owner Peter Conway has a sure touch. There's ample common space between the formal living rooms and the dining room (a continental breakfast is served 7:30–9:30). A dozen of the guest rooms have working fireplaces and five, Jacuzzis; all have phone, TV, and private bath, and many have canopy beds. From $85 for rooms to $185 for suites.

BED & BREAKFASTS
Note: Tax is only levied on B&Bs with five or more rooms.
In Salem 01970

Amelia Payson House (508-744-8304), 16 Winter Street. The feel inside this striking, vintage-1845 Greek Revival house is bright, crisp, and friendly. Ada and Don Roberts have been welcoming guests for more than a decade and obviously enjoy what they do. Guests are invited to gather in the living room with its baby grand and around the dining room table for breakfast (an expanded continental, served 8:30–10). The four rooms consist of two doubles and two with an extra bed, one of them a studio with microwave and fridge. $75–85 double, less off-season.

The Inn at Seven Winter Street (508-745-9520), 7 Winter Street. A very Victorian, mansard-roofed townhouse conveniently positioned just up from Salem's Common. Sally Flint lived here for more than 20 years before deciding to turn her home into a B&B; the 10 units range from rather gloomy first-floor rooms to third-floor efficiency units. We found the second-floor rooms with working fireplace to be the most attractive; the "honeymoon suite" comes with a Jacuzzi and complimentary champagne. All have direct-dial phones, private baths, cable TV, and air-conditioning. A continental breakfast is served in the combination living/dining room. Rates: from $85 off-season to $145 plus tax. No smoking.

The Suzannah Flint House (508-744-5281; 1-800-752-5281), 98 Essex Street. A classic Federal house with large, square, attractive guest rooms. It's tucked unceremoniously behind the Hawthorne Hotel parking lot but manages to retain its grace. At this writing the only common space is a second-floor breakfast room. $59–119.

The Stephen Daniels House (508-744-5709), 1 Daniels Street. This is a real find for people who appreciate a vintage-1667 house with a 1745 wing that's furnished with period antiques. Owned until 1931 by the family who built it in 1731, the house stood vacant until restored and reopened as a tea room in 1945. Kay Gill has owned the house for 30 years, taking in guests long before "B&B" was a concept in Salem. Several of the five guest rooms have working hearths, and the hearths in the common room and original kitchen are huge. Period paneling and ceilings apply throughout. Common space includes the old kitchen and a parlor, as well as the dining room and the pleasant garden with flowering shrubbery and wisteria. Children under 10 are not appropriate but are welcome, and so (amazingly enough) are pets. Baths can be private or shared. $65–95 per room, $135–175 per suite (two rooms with a connecting bath). *Note:* If no one answers when you call, call back. There's no answering machine or call-waiting, but persevere. It's worth it.

In Danvers 01923

The Cordwainer Bed & Breakfast (508-774-1860), 78 Centre Street. Open May through September. Located in the Old Salem Village part of Danvers (formerly part of Salem). An 1850s Greek Revival house with canopy beds. Rooms from $55.

In Marblehead 01945

The Golden Cod B&B (617-631-1846), 26 Pond Street. This house isn't on the water, but it consistently gets rave reviews for the two guest rooms with private bath. $75 includes breakfast.

The Seagull Inn B&B (617-631-1893), 106 Harbor Avenue. This is a real find—the remaining segment of a waterside hotel on Marblehead Neck that functioned from 1893 to 1940. It has been owned by Skip and Ruth Sigler for more than 20 years and modernized to create some great spaces, including the kitchen and the living room. Choose from three suites, all with TV, phone, and bath. The largest sleeps five and has a real kitchen and two baths. Our favorite is the third-floor aerie. Guests have free access to a health club and the fax machine. Rates, which include an expanded continental breakfast, are $85–200.

The Guest House at Lavender Gate (617-631-3242; 639-0400), One Summer Street. This bibliophile's delight is subtitled "Literary Lodging." It is an 18th-century house in the middle of the historic district, with just two suites, both furnished with flair. The Kelmscott Suite features William Morris wallpaper, a brass bed, and a claw-foot tub, and the Hogart Suite has an antique, hand-painted bed. Instead of a TV there's good bedside lighting and an ample supply of books, all for sale. Hosts Olson and Nash Robbins own the nearby Much Ado, an antiquarian bookstore. A breakfast of homemade breads, cheese, and fruit is served in the low-beamed dining room, which is decorated with literary memorabilia, including a pair of Eugene O'Neill's boxer shorts. $90–100.

Spray Cliff (617-637-6789; 1-800-626-1530), 25 Spray Avenue. It would be hard to beat the location of this rather grand mansion right on the rocks, overlooking open ocean. Most of the seven rooms have water views and are unusually large, with ample bathrooms, and three have working fireplaces. Although you have to drive into town (bring a bike), you can walk to Preston Beach. Our only problems with this beautiful place are that the common space consists of a sunroom—albeit a large sunroom—and that guests must use a side entrance when they are paying $169–189 B&B (less off-season).

Brimblecomb Hill B&B (617-631-3172; days: 632-6366), 33 Mechanic Street. Nicely located in the center of the Old Town, this vintage-1721 house has three comfortable first-floor guest rooms. The one with a private bath, a tall four-poster, and its own library is a beauty. The remaining two are smaller and share a bath but are pleasant and have private entrances. The living room features its original hearth and a blue piano (guests are invited to play). Continental breakfast is served here or, weather permitting, in the garden. Gene Arnould, who owns a nearby frame shop/gallery, has been hosting visitors for some years and makes you comfortable. $60–75 double, $55–70 single.

Harborside House (617-631-1032), 23 Gregory Street. Susan Livingston's talents as a professional dressmaker are evident in the bright and neat guest rooms; the look is tailored rather than frilly, and the feel is very comfortable. The front room with twin beds has a water view, and the back room is a double. The living and dining rooms are gracious, and there's a third-story sun deck. Livingston, a Marblehead resident for more than three decades, tunes guests into what the area offers and lends out a couple of bikes. Tea as well as breakfast is included in $60–75, cheaper off-season.

Compass Rose (617-631-7599), 36 Gregory Street. Carol Swift's waterside house offers just one room, but it's a beauty: a snug studio apartment with a great view of the harbor. Facilities include a kitchenette and use of the garden just outside the door. $85.

Stillpoint B&B (617-631-1667; 1-800-882-2891), 27 Gregory Street. An 1830s house with a handsome living room and formal dining room, three attractive guest rooms, and two full baths (a private bath can be requested). Weather permitting, breakfast is served on the deck overlooking the garden and Marblehead Harbor. Sarah Lincoln-Harrison strives to keep her breakfasts as healthy and the house as ecological as possible; she recently replaced her lawn with an organically maintained mix of grass, herbs, flowers, and vegetables. **Lindsey's Garret B&B,** her other property, is an attractive studio apartment with a water view, available only by the week. Rooms: $70–80.

The Nesting Place B&B (617-631-6655), 16 Village Street. Louise Hirshberg caters to frazzled women looking for a soothing getaway, but really everyone (families included) is welcome in this airy house, which offers two rooms with shared bath and outside hot tub (great for star gazing). Hirshberg is a massage therapist and offers spa getaways as well as B&B rates of $55–65.

In Beverly Farms 01915

The Jon Larcom House Bed & Breakfast (508-922-6074), 28 Hart Street. Nicely situated to take advantage of both the Cape Ann area and Marblehead/Salem sites, yet off the beaten track, within walking distance of the train and a beach. Two of the three bedrooms have fireplaces, and all feature feather beds and handmade quilts. Breakfast and afternoon tea are included in $65 (shared), $85 (private) bath, more in October.

WHERE TO EAT

DINING OUT

Lyceum Restaurant (508-745-7665), 43 Church Street, Salem. Open daily for lunch and dinner. Housed in the city's 19th-century Lyceum, the forum for a number of celebrities including Alexander Graham Bell, who gave his first public demonstration of the telephone here. There are now a number of different dining rooms, ranging in atmosphere from the brick-walled barroom to the back glass-walled area overlooking Salem Green. This is a great place to lunch on a grilled portabella mushroom sandwich or Caesar and grilled shrimp salad ($5.50–7.50). The à la carte dinner menu features entrées like grilled Maine salmon steak with warm watercress and sesame-soy vinaigrette ($14.95) and the "Grill of My Dreams" ($17.95).

Rosalie's Restaurant (617-631-5353), 18 Sewall Street, Marblehead. Open for dinner nightly at 5:30, Sunday at 5. Closed Monday. Housed in a skillfully decorated (upscale Victorian) factory space. The northern Italian menu includes creative pastas (like angel hair with a cream sauce, peas, and prosciutto) and nightly specials like grilled swordfish with a wine and butter sauce. Entrées: $9–17.

Hawkes Street Cafe (617-631-4440), 26 Hawkes Street, Marblehead. Open for lunch Tuesday through Friday and dinner Tuesday through Sunday. Nonsmoking on Friday and Saturday evenings. Reservations suggested. Just off the beaten track, an attractive café, good for either lunch or dinner. The menu changes seasonally. On an autumn day we lunched well on grilled eggplant and goat cheese pizza with tomato sauce and parsley pasta ($5.95). Dinner might have been scallion ravioli stuffed with pumpkin in a ginger vegetable broth sauce ($12.95) or black-and-white ravioli stuffed with lobster and crabmeat, with a champagne, basil, and garlic cream sauce ($15.95). The wine list is extensive, and regional microbrewery beers are on tap.

Pellino's (617-631-3344), 261 Washington Street, Marblehead. Open daily 4:30–10:30. Early dining specials, Sunday through Thursday 4:30–5:30. Free parking. This is a small place specializing in fine Italian dining. Try the slow-roasted lamb with fresh mozzarella ($11.95) or the roasted duck breast with apple and herb honey ($15.95).

The Red Raven (508-745-8558), 75 Congress Street, Salem. Salem's "bistro," featuring an eclectic menu and atmosphere that locals rate highly.

Peabody & Essex Museum Cafe (508-745-1876), East India Square, Salem. Open Tuesday through Friday 11–4, also for a "Tea Buffet" 3–4:30 and for Sunday brunch noon–3. We don't have an "elegant lunching out" or "brunch" category, but if we did this place would be in it, because the relatively small café with its rare china within built-in cabinets has a distinctly elegant feel and the service is formal. You can lunch on chicken salad ($5.50), a grilled ham and Swiss sandwich ($6.75), an omelet, quiche, or one of the daily specials like penne marinara ($5.50). You might brunch on strawberry pinenut pancakes ($7.25), on a shrimp, scallop, and wild mushroom quesadilla served with fresh fruit salsa ($8.25), or on sautéed chicken with artichokes, capers, and olives tossed in a tomato pesto over linguine ($8.25). Our only complaint is that, in this palace built largely on the tea trade, tea comes in packets. Obviously you don't have to pay a museum admission to eat in the café.

Michael's House (617-631-5255), 26 Atlantic Avenue, Marblehead. Open for lunch and dinner daily, Sunday brunch. A local landmark, this 17th-century house has low-beamed ceilings and fireplaces. Sandwiches run $3–9, and the Italian/Continental dinner menu, $9–16. Live entertainment Thursday through Sunday.

EATING OUT
Between Salem and Marblehead

The Rockmore (617-639-0600), Salem Harbor. A seasonal, floating eatery with seafood and local specialties, regional beers. It's smack in the middle of the harbor, accessible from both Salem and Marblehead by launch service from Village Street Landing in Marblehead and from Pickering Wharf in Salem. Entrées are $5–12.

In Salem

Red's Sandwich Shop (508-745-3527), 15 Central Street. Open Monday through Saturday, 5 AM–3 PM, Sunday 6 AM–1 PM. Just off Essex Street and around the corner from the Old Town Hall, this shop is housed in an ancient-looking building with a plaque stating it was once the London Coffee House, established 1691. This is the kind of place every town should be lucky enough to have. The curvy counters are pink, and an old-style coffee mug is filled the moment you sit down. Breakfast possibilities range from one egg any style to a corned-beef omelet, and beverages range from frappes to Miller's. We recommend the BLT on whole wheat ($2.20) and the custard pie ($1).

Victoria Station (508-745-3400), Pickering Wharf. Open daily for lunch and dinner, Sunday brunch. It's difficult to beat the tip-of-the-wharf location.

Stromberg's Restaurant (508-744-1863), 2 Bridge Street. Open daily 11–8:30 except Monday (open Monday holidays). Claiming to be the oldest restaurant on the North Shore, Stromberg's proudly displays its 1935 menu. There is a water view, and although fresh fish is featured, the nightly special can be lamb, boiled dinner, or prime rib.

Dodge Street Bar & Grill (508-745-0139), 7 Dodge Street. Open noon–1 AM. Billing itself as "Salem's friendliest neighborhood pub," the grill is good for ribs, burgers, and seafood; live music nightly.

The Grand Turk Tavern Restaurant (508-745-7727), 110 Derby Street. Open daily for lunch, Sunday brunch. Housed in an 18th-century house, it is touristy but good for moderately priced seafood dishes and pasta.

In Marblehead

Flynnie's at the Beach. Open daily May through November for all three meals (from 6 AM on weekends). You can park (no small matter on weekends) and enjoy the view from the deck or beach; fried seafood is the specialty, and it's good; so are the steak tips. Ice cream and sandwiches are also served.

The Barnacle (617-631-4236), 141 Front Street. Open daily for lunch and dinner, right on the water. Closed Tuesday in winter. No reservations, checks, or credit cards. Seafood, of course, broiled scallops and jumbo shrimp scampi (sautéed in butter, herbs, and white wine), or maybe try the steamers served with drawn butter and natural broth or freshwater smelts. This place is so popular that it's wise to come early in the lunch and dinner hours.

Maddie's Sail Loft (617-631-9824), 15 State Street. Open for lunch Monday through Saturday; full menu 5–10 PM, but not on Monday. No credit cards. A neighborhood bar with good chowder and blackboard specials; really hops on yachting weekends. Fish-and-chips are $8.95, and the Marblehead Seafood Pie is $14.95.

The King's Rook (617-631-9838), 12 State Street. Open Monday through Saturday for lunch and dinner; closed Monday evening. This is a café and wine bar in a vintage 1747 building, the place for a curried egg sandwich or gourmet pizza with a glass of wine, or a lemon tart and espresso. Cocktails too.

ENTERTAINMENT

North Shore Music Theatre (508-922-8500), 62 Dunham Road, Beverly. Off MA 128, Exit 19, April through December: professional performances, popular plays, musicals, concerts, and children's theater.

Cabot Street Cinema Theater (508-927-3677), 268 Cabot Street, Beverly. A jewel of a 750-seat theater restored and owned by Le Grand David and his own Spectacular Magic Company, which has been performing every Sunday (3 PM) year-round since 1976. The company has also restored the 500-seat **Larcom Theatre** up the street, scene of another 2-hour program on selected Saturdays (2 PM) since 1985. Adults bring their children and grandchildren to see these shows, and then come back again. Art films are shown on weeknights at the Cabot Street Cinema Theater.

Marblehead Summer Music Festival (617-631-3421), a series of Saturday performances by the Cambridge Chamber Players in the Old North Church.

Marblehead Summer Stage (617-631-4238), a series of performances by a resident repertory company in varied locales.

Summer Jazz (617-631-6366), a series of summer concerts in the Unitarian Universalist Church.

SELECTIVE SHOPPING

Salem's Pickering Wharf and Marblehead's historic district both harbor a number of specialty shops, galleries, antiques shops, and bookstores, but two categories of store in this area stand out.

BOOKSTORES

The Spirit of '76 Bookstore (617-631-7199), Pleasant and School Streets, Marblehead. A superb bookstore guided with the personal touch of the owner, Bob Hugo.

Derby Square Bookstore (508-745-8804), 215 Essex Street, Salem. General and regional books in abundance.

Book Shop of Beverly Farms (508-927-2122), 40 West Street, Beverly Farms. Frequented by North Shore readers and authors.

CANDY

Ye Olde Pepper Companie (508-745-2744), 122 Derby Street, near the House of Seven Gables, Salem. Open daily. Established in 1806, billed as America's oldest candy company, specializing in blackjacks, Gibraltar, and other 19th-century treats.

Harbor Sweets (508-745-7648), 85 Leavitt Street, Salem. Handmade chocolates like Sweet Sloops (chocolate, almond, butter crunch sailboats) are made here and distributed throughout the country.

Stowaway Sweets (617-631-0303), 154 Atlantic Avenue, Marblehead. Open daily 9:30–5:30, noon–5 on Sunday. A name known to candy connoisseurs: 87 varieties of candy, much of it hand-dipped chocolate. In business since 1929, shipping throughout the country.

OCCULT AND PSYCHIC

Crow Haven Corner (508-745-8763), 125 Essex Street, Salem. Laurie Cabot, "official witch of Salem," offers tarot card readings, psychic consultations, and love readings; the shop is appropriately stocked.

Pyramid Books: The New-Age Store (508-745-7171), 214 Derby Street (across from Pickering Wharf), Salem. Open daily and five nights. Metaphysical books, music, audios, gifts, jewelry, quartz, healing stones, crystal balls, incense, oils, herbs, and tarot decks.

Angelica and the Angels (508-745-9355), 7 Central Street, Salem. Psychic and medium readings, tarot cards and tea leaves, healing through angels, angelic collectibles.

SPECIAL EVENTS

July: **Independence Day celebrations** in Marblehead (fireworks and harbor illumination), also **Marblehead Festival of the Arts.**

Late July: **Marblehead Race Week** draws thousands of boats to compete.

August: **Beverly Homecoming Week** (first week); **Heritage Week** in Salem—a citywide festival that includes concerts, exhibits, sidewalk sales, fireworks, parade.

October: **Haunted Happenings** in Salem—2 weeks of dances, parties, tours, concerts, and spooky events climaxing with Halloween.
December: **Marblehead Christmas Walk.**

CAPE ANN REGION

Cape Ann is a rocky fist of land thrusting from the North Shore up and out into the Atlantic. It's virtually an island circled by a 15-mile road that we challenge anyone to drive in less than a day—ignoring the beaches, shops, seafood restaurants, and smooth oceanside rocks obviously made for sunning.

Cape Ann has a split personality. It's divided between the very different towns of Gloucester and Rockport.

Founded by fishermen back in 1632, Gloucester prides itself on being the "oldest continuous working harbor in America." Around the turn of this century Gloucester was the country's leading fishing port, and in the 1930s it still boasted 400 proud, graceful, two-masted fishing schooners. A typical crew included the Yankees, Italians, and Portuguese fishermen portrayed in Rudyard Kipling's *Captains Courageous.*

Gloucester remains home for 200 draggers and trawlers. Current federal regulations, however, threaten to reduce the fleet drastically, and there's understandable malaise over the idea that tourism rather than fishing and fish processing may soon be the city's mainstay.

Tourism has been part of the Gloucester mix for well over a century. In 1880 artist Winslow Homer spent the summer on Ten Pound Island in the middle of the inner harbor, recording and popularizing what he saw. Other artists, including Childe Hassam and John Sloan, summered on Rocky Neck, converting fishermen's shacks into studios. A large hotel and summer theater soon followed, and by the turn of the century a half-dozen hotels lined the shore in East Gloucester. In Magnolia, just south of Gloucester, the 750-room Oceanside billed itself as the largest resort hotel in New England. Elaborate summer mansions, which continued to be built into the '30s, included 40-room Beauport on Eastern Point and John Hays Hammond's fantasy castle across the harbor.

Rockport, one-third the size of Gloucester and on the opposite (ocean) side of Cape Ann, also began as a fishing village. Early in the 19th century it grew as a granite quarrying center, and as early as the 1840s it, too, began attracting summer people and artists. Rockport remains primarily a resort—but on its own terms. Since 1856 the town has been "dry," and guests at the North Shore's largest concentration of inns and B&Bs are advised that local dining rooms are BYOB. In contrast to Gloucester, beaches are free, but parking is extremely limited; summer day-trippers are encouraged to come by train and trolley or to stay at one of the many inns and B&Bs within walking distance of the shops, restaurants, and beaches.

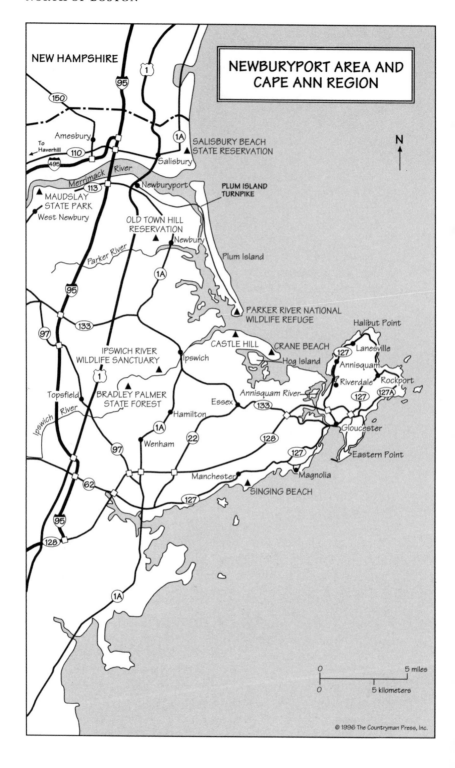

Essex, just a few miles west of Gloucester, is another appealing anomaly. Having produced more vessels per capita over the past three centuries than any other community in America, it has also been catering to day-trippers since the 1870s—when Sunday excursion trains began running to the town's "Centennial Grove." Today the causeway that once supported 15 shipyards is top-heavy with restaurants (including two claiming to have invented the fried clam) and the North Shore's largest concentration of antiques shops. The Essex Shipbuilding Museum preserves the town's amazing history.

Neighboring Ipswich boasts more 17th-century homes than any other American town its size. It still prides itself on the fact that in 1686 its residents refused to pay taxes without representation, a gesture hailed locally as the "birth of American Independence." Most visitors, however, pass quickly through the village on their way to Crane Beach. Richard T. Crane was a Chicago plumbing magnate who acquired the North Shore's most beautiful beach and built a 59-room "Great House." Luckily the mansion (site of summer concerts and theatrical productions) and some 1400 surrounding acres of beach, garden, woodland, and salt marsh are preserved by the Trustees of Reservations.

This may be the best known, but it's just one among dozens of spectacular preserves in Essex County. Despite the fact that this area has been settled since the early 1600s and lies within 40 miles of Boston, dozens of waterfront preserves are open to the public, thanks to a half-dozen groups ranging from "The Trustees" (founded in 1891) to the Essex County Greenbelt Association (founded in 1961).

Still, the Cape Ann region is known primarily as a place to set out on a whalewatching or fishing expedition or to go to the beach. To date, it seems few visitors explore the areas described here under *Green Space* or take advantage of the relatively new ways out into the salt marshes via excursion boats and sea kayaks. The ocean- and riverside inns and B&Bs in this area remain little known and reasonably priced. This beautiful heart of the North Shore is, in fact, far less of a destination than it was a century ago, but is still just as beautiful and hospitable.

AREA CODE
508

GUIDANCE
Cape Ann Chamber of Commerce (283-1601), 33 Commercial Street, Gloucester. Open May through October weekdays 8–6, Saturday 10–6, Sunday 10–4; otherwise weekdays 8–5; this is a walk-in information center with rest rooms on the waterfront across from St. Peter's Park. Another major information center (rest rooms) at Stage Fort Park on the western fringe of town is open June to mid-October 9–5 daily. Pick up a map/guide to the Gloucester Maritime Trail.

The Rockport Chamber of Commerce (546-6575) maintains a seasonal information center (with rest rooms) on MA 127 just south of town. It's

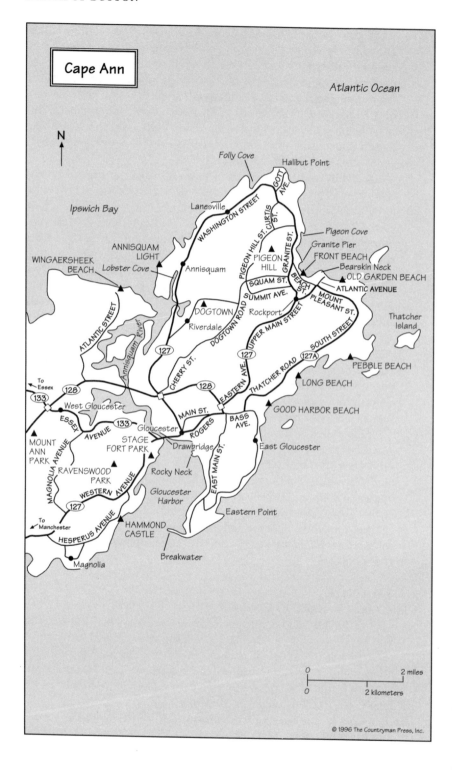

Cape Ann

Atlantic Ocean

N

Folly Cove

Halibut Point

GOTT AVE.

Ipswich Bay

Lanesville

WASHINGTON STREET

Pigeon Cove

Granite Pier

ANNISQUAM LIGHT

CURTIS ST.

PIGEON HILL ST.

GRANITE ST.

PIGEON HILL

FRONT BEACH

WINGAERSHEEK BEACH

Lobster Cove

Annisquam

Bearskin Neck

SQUAM ST.

BEACH ST.

OLD GARDEN BEACH

ATLANTIC AVENUE

ATLANTIC STREET

SUMMIT AVE.

MOUNT PLEASANT ST.

DOGTOWN

Rockport

Thatcher Island

DOGTOWN ROAD

Annisquam River

Riverdale

127

CHERRY ST.

UPPER MAIN STREET

SOUTH STREET

127

127A

PEBBLE BEACH

To Essex

128

133

128

EASTERN AVE.

THATCHER ROAD

LONG BEACH

West Gloucester

ESSEX AVENUE

MAIN ST.

ROGERS

BASS AVE.

GOOD HARBOR BEACH

133

Gloucester

MOUNT ANN PARK

STAGE FORT PARK

Drawbridge

EAST MAIN ST.

East Gloucester

MAGNOLIA AVENUE

RAVENSWOOD PARK

Rocky Neck

WESTERN AVENUE

Gloucester Harbor

127

Eastern Point

To Manchester

HESPERUS AVENUE

HAMMOND CASTLE

Breakwater

Magnolia

0   2 miles

0   2 kilometers

© 1996 The Countryman Press, Inc.

open daily mid-May to mid-October, 11–5, Sunday 1–5; the chamber office at 3 Main Street (just off Dock Square) is open weekdays 10–5. **Ipswich Chamber of Commerce** (356-3231) publishes a pamphlet guide and maintains a seasonal information center on South Green (MA 1A), May 30 through Labor Day, 9–5 daily.

GETTING THERE
By train: The T commuter trains serve both Gloucester and Rockport from North Station (617-227-5070; 1-800-392-6099), and CATA (283-7916) buses meet some weekday trains. There are also Gloucester-based taxis: **Cape Ann Yellow Cab** (283-9393) and **Charlie's Cabs Inc.** (281-4747).

By car: From Boston, MA 128 runs to Gloucester, and there are two ways into town. Exit 14 (MA 133) shadows the Annisquam River, bringing you in along the waterfront from the west to the Stage Fort Park information center (running the risk of getting stuck at the Blynman Canal drawbridge on Western Avenue); or you can go all the way to the rotary and follow signs for downtown and the chamber of commerce.

For Rockport, you continue on through to MA 127 and follow signs. For Essex take Exit 14 and MA 133 West, and for Ipswich take MA 128, Exit 20 (MA 1A North).

GETTING AROUND
The Cape Ann Transit Authority (283-7916) offers frequent daytime service around Cape Ann itself and June through mid-September, weekends, and holidays runs **Salt Water Trolleys,** circulating all day (10–10, until 11 on Saturday) within Rockport, and between Rockport, Gloucester, and Essex.

PARKING
In Gloucester: Try Stage Fort Park, the chamber of commerce, St. Peter's Park, two more lots off waterfront Rogers Street, and another lot on Pleasant Street.

In Rockport: Weekend and holiday parking is found behind the information center on MA 127, with shuttles connecting with downtown; parking on Broadway and along streets and on wharves in the village is adequate except on summer weekends. Several lots are "residents only"; beware. At peak tourist times it can make more sense to come by train or stay in a B&B within walking distance of a beach.

MEDICAL EMERGENCY
911 except in Gloucester, where ambulance numbers are 283-2424 and 283-8670.

TO SEE

MUSEUMS
In Gloucester
Cape Ann Historical Association (283-0455) 27 Pleasant Street. Open

Tuesday through Saturday 10–5; $3.50 adults, $3 retirees, $2 students, free aged 6 and under. This is one of New England's outstanding small museums, founded in 1873, now filling an 1804 house, an attached formal museum, and another attached (via an atrium) three-floor brick building added in 1993. The pride of the collection continues to be the 35 paintings plus sketches and lithographs by Gloucester-born marine artist Fitz Hugh Lane (1804–56), but there are also paintings of mostly local scenes by Maurice Prendergast, Winslow Homer, John Sloan, Milton Avery, and Augustus Buhler. In addition, fine china from China, silver by Paul Revere, and early-19th-century furniture and furnishings contrast with the Fisheries and Maritime collections, which tell the story of the city's Sicilian population. The collection includes antique photos and tools of the fishing industry and several historic boats: the dory *Centennial,* in which a young Gloucester fisherman sailed solo to England in 1876, and the 25-foot Gloucester sloop *The Great Republic,* in which the city's Howard Blackburn, a fisherman whose hands had been reduced to stumps in a previous, seemingly superhuman adventure at sea, sailed solo from Gloucester to Portugal in 1901 (in 1899 he had sailed to England). With its mix of paintings and a sense of the city's very human history, this place is one in which you tend to linger longer than you had intended.

Beauport (283-0800), Eastern Point in East Gloucester, off MA 127A. Open for guided tours on the hour from mid-May to mid-September, weekdays 10–4, weekends in spring and fall 1–4. $5 adults, $2 children. Even historic-house haters shouldn't pass up this one: a mansion of some 45 rooms, most of them representing a phase in American history. "Beauport," incidentally, is the name that Samuel de Champlain gave Gloucester Harbor when he charted it in 1604. This Beauport evolved between 1907 and 1934 and is the work of one of America's leading interior decorators of the 1920s, Henry Davis Sleeper. His arrangement of his carefully collected treasures (which include Lord Byron's bed) is said to have inspired Delaware's Winterthur Museum. It is maintained by the Society for the Preservation of New England Antiquities. To get there, you must ignore the "Private" signs at the entrance to Eastern Point. Summer programs include evening concerts and a sunset tour.

Hammond Castle Museum (283-2080; events line: 283-7673), 80 Hesperus Avenue, Magnolia (5 miles south of Gloucester off MA 127, or take MA 128, Exit 14, east on MA 133). Open Memorial Day weekend through September, daily 10–4, otherwise weekends 9–4; $6 adults, $5 for seniors, $4 children 4–12. This castlelike mansion was built in the 1920s by John Hays Hammond Jr., an eccentric inventor who held more than 800 patents including breakthroughs in radio, radar, and remote control. More of a stage set than a home, its props include artificial rain and a Roman bath; its centerpiece is a cathedral-like, 60-foot-high grand hall housing a 10,000-pipe organ that Hammond designed himself (he is not, however, the Hammond of Hammond organs). Organ concerts ($15) are scheduled regularly throughout the year and usually sell out well in advance (so if you are interested, call ahead), and it's worth inquiring about other scheduled concerts and functions. From the grounds you can see the pile of off-shore rocks known as Norman's Woe, immortalized by Longfellow in his poem "The Wreck of the Hesperus."

Essex Shipbuilding Museum (768-7541), housed in an 1830s schoolhouse at 28 Main Street (MA 133) in the center of the village. Open year-round, Thursday through Monday 11–4, Sunday 1–4. Over three centuries some 4000 vessels are said to have been built within a few miles of each other along the tidal Essex River in this town with a population that never topped 1500. In the 1700s it launched Chebacco boats, then dogbodies, pinkies, and finally schooners. From 1850 until 1900, a period during which Gloucester ranked as one of the world's top fishing ports, Essex built its fishing schooners, and the town's fame spread as the place to get a vessel built reasonably and well. In 1852 the tiny town had 15 different shipyards, and by the 1870s the ships were so big that it frequently took a number of tides to make it down the river. Steamers and yachts as well as schooners were sent to sea by the hundreds. The Causeway, former site of most of the boatbuilding yards, is now top-heavy with restaurants and antiques shops, but the museum tells the town's story well through photographs, ship models, tools, dioramas, and hands-on exhibits. At the museum's Story Shipyard (66 Main Street), the *Evelina M. Goulart,* one of five currently surviving Essex-built fishing schooners, is being restored.

HISTORIC HOMES AND SITES

In Gloucester

The Sargent House Museum (281-2432), 49 Middle Street. Open June through October from Saturday through Monday 1–4, and by appointment other times of the year. $3 adults, $1 seniors, free 12 and under. Built in 1783, this late-Georgian house tells a fascinating story about Judith Sargent, the first American to have a play produced in this country (it ran two nights in Boston in 1793). The house is preserved, however, because Judith's second marriage was to John Murray, the founder of Universalism in this country. Superb paneling and staircase, paintings by John Singer Sargent, locally crafted highboys and lowboys, and a wealth of period furnishings grace this historic site.

Gloucester Fishermen's Statue, on Western Avenue or Stacy Boulevard (as MA 127 is known at this point) near Blynman Bridge. This stalwart seaman at the wheel honors the more than 10,000 Gloucester fishermen who have died at sea and all "that go down to the sea in ships." The nearby drawbridge spans an 18th-century canal between Gloucester Harbor and the Annisquam River.

Stage Fort Park, Western Avenue. This is where the fish stages were set up by the Dorchester Company in 1623. It's the site of the city's major seasonal information center and of summer Sunday band concerts. Pathways climb the smooth rocks overlooking the harbor.

Gloucester Waterfront. Park and stroll by the boats tied up here; there's a Hidden Park behind the Gloucester House Restaurant from which you can take in the scene.

Schooner *Adventure* (281-8079), built in Essex in 1926, represents the famous fishing schooners for which Gloucester was once known. Her docking space shifts from time to time, but she can usually be found when not on a summer sail and is generally open Tuesday through Sunday 10–4 ($3 adults, $1.50 children); Sunday mornings breakfast is served aboard 9–noon ($5).

Independent Christian Church (283-2410), Middle and Church Streets. Now Unitarian-Universalist, this is the mother church of Universalism in this country. Built in 1804, it is a graceful building with a Wren-style steeple, a Paul Revere bell, a Willard clock, and a Sandwich-glass chandelier.

Our Lady of Good Voyage Church (283-1490). A church of unusual warmth and grace, modeled on the cathedral of San Miguel in the Azores, the origin of much of its congregation. Models of fishing vessels are mounted on the walls.

Eastern Point Light and Dog Bar Breakwater. See directions for Beauport (ignore the "Private" signs at the entrance to Eastern Point). Marking the entrance to Gloucester Harbor, the lighthouse is owned by the US Coast Guard and open for tours 9:30–3:30 daily. It dates from 1890, and the breakwater marks the presence of a treacherous sandbar beneath. This is a great spot to clear your lungs and head. The view is of Gloucester's rocky shoreline and of Boston's skyscrapers hovering improbably above the horizon.

Thacher Island and **Cape Ann Lighthouse,** off MA 127A heading north from Eastern Point, south from Good Harbor. The small island marked by twin lights is named for a couple who survived the 1625 shipwreck in which they lost four children. The island, with its two vintage-1851 towers, is now maintained by the volunteer Thacher Island Association as a wildlife refuge, with eight hiking trails. Visitors are welcome May through October, and it's possible to spend the night in the lighthouse keepers' house (but not on a bed & breakfast basis); for details about lodging, camping, hiking, and a seasonal launch service from Rockport, phone the association secretary: 546-2326.

In Rockport

Sandy Bay Historical Society and Museum (546-9533), 40 King Street (corner of Granite, near the train station). July through Labor Day, open daily 2–5, weekends through September. Free. The museum is located in the Sewall-Scripture House, an unusual Federal-style granite home built in 1832. It holds an extensive collection of town memorabilia. The

GEORGE M. CUSHING PHOTOGRAPHY

News from the Fleet (1918), by Augustus W. Buhler, is in the Cape Ann Historical
Association's collection.

historical society also offers tours, by appointment, of the Old Castle
(set back from MA 127 north of Rockport in Pigeon Cove), a 1715 gar-
rison-style saltbox.

Paper House (546-2629), Pigeon Hill Street. Open July and August 10–5;
ages 15 and over, $1, ages 6–14, $.50. North of Rockport on MA 127,
turn up Curtis Street. At first you might think this house is just a modest
summer cottage set in a rock garden. On closer inspection you find that
even the exterior walls are made of newspaper: 215 layers of paper,
pressed under two tons of pressure. Inside, a fireplace, a piano (the
casing), a grandfather clock, chairs, tables, a desk, and more are all made
of "newspaper mâché." The creator was Elis F. Stedman, a Swedish
immigrant who read a half-dozen newspapers a day.

James Babson Cooperage Shop, MA 127 midway between Gloucester
and Rockport. Open July and August, Tuesday through Sunday 2–5.
This small, shedlike building is a restored barrel-repair shop, displaying
early tools; also good for local information.

Bearskin Neck. This rocky, natural neck extends off Dock Square and has
always formed the heart of Rockport, first as a fishing center, then an
artists' enclave, and now a tourist magnet.

Motif #1, a much-painted red fish shed at the end of Tuna Wharf off Bearskin Neck, has become the symbol of Cape Ann.

Granite Pier, MA 127 north of Rockport. Across from the quarry, accessible by car, is this great spot to enjoy the view.

Pigeon Cove, farther along MA 127, is hidden behind Cape Ann Tool Company. It's a quiet inlet where fishing boats tie up. The New England Lobster Company at the end of the pier has a reasonably priced selection of fish and lobster.

Folly Cove, MA 127. A good spot to pull off MA 127 and walk the rocks.

In Ipswich

The John Whipple House (356-2811), 53 South Main Street, on South Village Green. Open April to mid-October, Tuesday through Saturday 10–5, Sunday 1–5. $2 adults, $3 for two houses (see John Heard House). The major part of this weathered, double-gabled house, one of the oldest buildings in New England, was built in 1640 by "clothiers of good estate." It remained in the family for two centuries and in 1898 became one of the country's first houses to be restored. It is well furnished, and the herb garden contains 60 varieties of medicinal plants.

John Heard House (356-2541), 40 South Main Street. Built in 1795, this stately Federal mansion is crowned with four corner chimneys. Maintained, like the Whipple House, by the Ipswich Historical Society, it is filled with China-trade treasures; there is also a collection of carriages, from a doctor's surrey to a funeral rig. For hours and admission, see Whipple House.

Castle Hill (356-4351), Argilla Road. The Great House, a majestic, 59-room brick mansion built by Chicago plumbing magnate Richard Crane, is open for tours every Tuesday, May through October, 1–4 ($5 adults, $3 children under 12, and free under 6). The house is maintained by the Trustees of Reservations and is the scene of summer concerts, plays, Circus Smirkus, an antique-auto show, and other happenings in July and August, as well as spring and Christmas house tours. The setting is on 200 acres that include a Grand Allée and the North Shore's most spectacular beach.

Also in Ipswich, the Feoffees, a group of town property trustees who have been perpetuating themselves since 1642, manage lucrative **Little Neck,** thickly covered with summer cottages. Most of the town's late-17th- and 18th-century houses are grouped around **Meeting House Green** (the Meeting House itself burned and has been replaced by a modernistic church). The **Old Burying Ground** on High Street contains stones dating from 1634, and the carvings on many gravestones are outstanding. Also note the **Choate Bridge,** in the middle of the village, said to be the oldest stone-arched bridge (1764) in English-speaking America.

In Manchester

The Trask House (526-7230), 10 Union Street. Open July and August, Wednesday through Saturday 2–5. This curbside, Federal-style home houses the Manchester Historical Society collection. It was owned origi-

nally by Abigail Trask, wife of a sea captain who traded with Russian Czar Nicholas I (Abigail was happily married, but insisted that the house remain officially hers).
Along Union Street note the **Orthodox Congregational Church,** a graceful 1809 classic. The **Manchester Memorial Library** next door was designed by Charles McKim. **Masconomo Park** on Beach Street is the site of periodic concerts and a good picnicking spot, with a view of Manchester's largely hidden harbor and two yacht clubs. This seaside town separated from Salem in 1645, traded with Europe and the West Indies in the 18th century, and became the first North Shore summer resort in the 1840s. Splendid **Singing Beach** remains open to anyone willing to walk a mile-plus from the train or public parking. Also note the **Old Burial Ground** on Summer Street (MA 127), a beautiful plot with 17th- and 18th-century headstones.

In Annisquam
This village within the town of Gloucester is known for its narrow streets and crooked old homes dating from its improbable 18th- and early-19th-century status as a thriving port. The **Annisquam Village Church** was built in 1830, and the **Village Hall,** as a Baptist meetinghouse, in 1828. On the Green is the Old Leonard School, now the **Annisquam Exchange and Art Gallery** (open mid-June to mid-September except Sunday). Also note the **Lobster Cove Bridge,** built in 1847.

ART CENTERS
Since the mid-19th century artists have gathered on Cape Ann to paint its fishing boats and beaches. The cape's special, luminous light, as well as its land- and seascape, continues to draw them.
Rocky Neck, off MA 127A. There is a parking lot at the entrance to this picturesque peninsula, traversed by a narrow, one-way (no parking anywhere in summer) road. Home of one of the country's oldest art colonies, it is also the place where Rudyard Kipling wrote *Captains Courageous* in the company of seamen at the marine railway that's still there. Fairly quiet these days, it sports a colorful jumble of art galleries and restaurants. It's accessible directly from Boston via excursion boat *Virginia C.* (see *To Do*).
The North Shore Art Association (283-1857), 197 East Main Street near the entrance to Rocky Neck. Open June through late September, daily 10–5, Sunday 1–5. Housed since 1922 in a large wharf building, the association features an unusual number and variety of juried work in changing exhibits.
Rockport Art Association (546-6604), 12 Main Street, Rockport. Open daily 9:30–5, Sunday 1–5. This former tavern has galleries meandering off into the skylit barn out back. The works of art on display are by association members. Art classes and concerts are also held here, and the small gift shop sells cards and prints.

FOR FAMILIES

New England Alive (256-7013), 163 High Street (MA 1A/MA 133 north of the village), Ipswich. Open April through November, weather permitting, daily. $5 adults, $3 children aged 12 and under, $2 seniors. This petting farm features barnyard animals as well as woodland animals ranging from pheasants and skunks to coyotes and bears, with some exotic snakes like the Burmese python and boa constrictors.

Wolf Hollow (356-0216), MA 133 near the Essex line. Open weekends at 1; presentations at 1:30 and 3:30. Pure wolves on view, gift shop.

SCENIC DRIVE

From Gloucester take MA 133 West to Essex (see *Museums, Green Space, Antiques Shops,* and *Eating Out*), and turn south on MA 22 through Essex Falls. Bear right when Essex Street splits and follow it through farms as it turns into Larch Row. Turn left on MA 1A into Wenham, site of the **Wenham Museum** (468-2377) at 132 Main Street; it's open year-round daily (just 1–4 Saturday, 2–5 Sunday), a 17th-century house with a famous doll collection and a gallery with changing art and antiques exhibits. The **Wenham Tea House** (468-1398) at the corner of Monument and Main Streets is a North Shore tradition. It's open Monday through Saturday 9–5, specializing in homemade soups and desserts and "teatime favorites" like hot cinnamon sticks and scones with real whipped cream. There's also a classic "gift shop." Turn back north on MA 1A through Hamilton, an aristocratic town known for its polo matches (Memorial Day weekend through Columbus Day every Sunday at 3; phone the Myopia Hunt Club at 468-1402). Note **Appleton Farms** on your left as you head north into Ipswich; a portion of this 123-acre estate, which has been in the Appleton family since 1638, is open. The Trustees of Reservations maintains 5 miles of mowed paths—"Grass Rides" for hiking and ski touring. Continue on MA 1A to its junction with MA 133 and return to Essex.

TO DO

BICYCLING

Although the roads are heavily trafficked, they border the water in many places. You can park your bike (in places you cannot park a car) and clamber onto the rocks or browse in shops, where you will pay far less than at the beaches. Bikes can be rented from **Giles of Gloucester** (283-3603) and **Seaside Cycle** (526-1200) in Manchester.

BOAT EXCURSIONS

The Dixie Belle (283-5110), Rose's Wharf, 415 Main Street, Gloucester. Leaves hourly on summer days; offers a 1-hour tour around the harbor. It makes a pickup stop at Rocky Neck.

Sandpiper Boat Tours (283-1776), from Seven Seas Wharf, Gloucester. Harbor and Annisquam River tours.

The Virginia C. (617-261-6633), 290 Northern Avenue, Boston, from Sunday through Wednesday, runs from Boston to Rocky Neck. Bikes permitted.

Gloucester Ocean Adventures (283-1979; 283-5110), Rose's Wharf, 415 Main Street, Gloucester. June through September, narrated circuit cruises of Cape Ann; also lobstering trips and harbor tours.

Lady Diane (546-2889), T Wharf, Rockport. Captain Ted offers 1-hour cruises.

Lobstering "cruises" are offered by **Lobster Hauling Cruise** (283-1979) from Rose's Wharf, 415 Main Street, Gloucester, and by **"Dove" Lobstering Trips** (546-3642) from Town Wharf in Rockport.

Gloucester to Provincetown Boat Express (283-5110), late June through September 1 from Rose's Wharf, Gloucester. A 2½-hour cruise to the tip of Cape Cod and back, with 4 hours in Provincetown.

Tiny Tug Tours and Charters (281-1572), Lighthouse Marina, Parker Street, Gloucester. *Time Being,* a 23-foot, six-passenger miniature tugboat designed with a shallow draft to cruise the salt marshes, tours the Annisquam River and harbor several times daily in summer.

Essex River Cruises (768-6981), 35 Dodge Street, Essex Marina. April through October; scheduled cruises aboard the 34-foot pontoon boat *Essex River Queen* to Crane Beach and Hog Island. Clambakes available on charters. Cliff Amero narrates the 90-minute tours, pointing out osprey nests, egrets, and local landmarks.

Good Harbor Beach in Gloucester

Moby Duck Tours (281-DUCK), Rogers Street, Gloucester. Fifty-minute harbor/land tours on amphibious vessels.

BOAT RENTALS

Old Harbor Yacht Club (596-9411), Wharf Road, Rockport. Powerboats and a variety of sailboats are rented.

CANOEING

The Ipswich River is navigable for 30 miles. Rental canoes and put-in advice are available from **Foote Brothers Canoes** (356-9771), 230 Topsfield Road, Ipswich; reservations for rentals are recommended.

FISHING PARTY BOATS

The Yankee Fleet (283-0313), Cape Ann Marina, 75 Essex Street, Gloucester, offers all-day, half-day, and overnight deep-sea fishing trips. All-day trips leave at 6 and 7 AM, return at 3 and 4 PM. Bait is supplied, and tackle can be rented. Inquire about cruises to Nantucket.

Lady Diane (546-2889), T Wharf, Rockport. Tuesday through Sunday, 5-hour, deep-sea fishing trips, from late June through Labor Day.

GOLF

Rockport Golf Club (546-3340), South Rockport; nine-hole course. **Candlewood Golf Club** (356-5377), MA 133, Ipswich; nine-hole public course. **Cape Ann Golf Course** (768-7544), MA 133, Essex; public nine-hole course.

SAILING

Salt Marsh Charters (768-7035), Rocky Neck, Gloucester. Day-sailing aboard the Friendship sloop *Kim* is offered by her owner-captain Arnold Burnham. $10 per person per hour.

Rockport Schooner Co. (546-9876). The 56-foot schooner *Appledore III* sails from Tuna Wharf in Rockport five times daily in summer.

SCUBA DIVING

Cape Ann Divers (281-8082), 17 Eastern Avenue, Gloucester. Rentals, boat charters, dive trips, instruction, snorkeling equipment.

SEA KAYAKING

Essex River Basin Adventures (768-ERBA), based at the Essex Shipbuilding Museum boatyard, MA 133, Essex, offers a variety of guided tours.

Cape Ann Sea Kayak Company (356-5264), Ipswich. Day trips, clinics.

Davensport Kayak (777-5228), 123 Liberty Street, Danvers, offers lessons, guided tours, and clinics in the Danvers River, Salem Sound, and Beverly Harbor.

SWIMMING

In Gloucester: Beaches all forbid the use of inflated tubes and the like. Lifeguards are on duty 9–5, and the nonresident fee (charged 8–4) is $15 per car. All have bathhouses and snack bars. On weekends it's best to be there before 10 to ensure a spot. **Good Harbor Beach,** Thatcher Road, is the most popular, and **Wingaersheek Beach** on Atlantic Street (Exit

14 off MA 128) is favored by families with small children (great climbing rocks and relatively small surf). **Half Moon** and **Cressy Beaches** at Stage Fort Park are city beaches.

In Rockport: Beaches include **Long Beach** (lined with cottages) and **Cape Hedge Beach** (one parking area serves both); also **Old Garden Beach,** accessible by foot from many Rockport inns; **Front** and **Back Beaches** on the other side of the village; and well-named **Pebble Beach** on Penzance Road. There are rest rooms at Front Beach, which, along with Back Beach, is accessible to anyone who can find a legal parking space. Most people come by trolley or on foot from local inns and B&Bs.

In Ipswich: **Crane Beach** (356-4354) is part of the Richard T. Crane Jr. Memorial Reservation, Argilla Road. Open daily 8 AM–sunset, the summer services include lifeguards, bathhouses, and refreshment facilities. Admission in 1995: January to mid-May, $5 per car; Memorial Day through Labor Day, $14 per car; weekends, $8 per day; midweek, shoulder prices in shoulder seasons. This property, maintained by the Trustees of Reservations, includes more than 4 miles of sand on Ipswich Bay. The superb, dune-backed beach never quite fills, but the parking lot frequently does, despite the stiff fee. Overflow parking is at Steep Hill Beach (a section of the main strand), entailing a fair walk down a steep hill; not ideal if you are trying to manage both gear and small children. Both sides of the beach are also plagued by greenhead flies in late July and early August. (See *Historic Homes and Sites* and *Entertainment* for more on Castle Hill.)

In Manchester: **Singing Beach** is a wide, smooth beach now backed by mansions. There is an elegant little beach house with a weather vane and fanlight. Anyone can use the snack bar and rest rooms, but changing rooms are for Manchester residents only. Parking is by sticker only, but you can leave your car in town or come by train from Boston and walk the mile or so to the beach.

WHALE-WATCHING
Whales fast all winter and feast during the months that conveniently coincide with tourist season. They feed on sand eel—a tiny, wormlike creature that thrives on Stellwagen Bank, a dozen miles off Cape Ann. Some 200 whales—humpbacks, minkes, finbacks, and right whales—feed here from April through October. They add up to the world's greatest concentration of whales, not only in numbers but also in species. The massive mammals seem to respond to whale-watchers by breaching (flinging their entire bodies—up to 50 feet and 40 tons' worth—out of the water). They also "spy-ho" (shove their massive snouts out of the water) and "lob-tail" (wave their huge tails in the air). All the Cape Ann boats offer half-day trips with naturalists aboard to narrate the whale story.

Cape Ann Whale Watch (283-5110; 1-800-877-5110), Rose's Wharf at the

Halibut Point State Park and Reservation in Rockport

eastern end of the Gloucester waterfront. Captain Fred Douglas was the first (in 1979) to take whale-watchers out from Gloucester.

Yankee Whale Watch (283-0313; 1-800-WHALING), at Cape Ann Marina, 79 Essex Avenue, Gloucester. Two trips daily, three on summer weekends.

Seven Seas Whale Watch (283-1776; 1-800-238-1776) departs from the wharf behind the Gloucester House Restaurant. A 90-foot Privateer.

Capt. Bill's Whale Watch (283-6995; 1-800-33-WHALE), 9 Traverse Street (Harbor Loop), Gloucester.

GREEN SPACE

We recommend securing a copy of the ***Passport to Essex County*** ($15), published by the Essex County Greenbelt Association (768-7241); you can find it in local bookstores or pick it up at the association's headquarters, the farm at the Cox Reservation on MA 133 in Essex. Since its 1961 founding, Greenbelt has preserved some 5000 acres of land in the county. Inquire about monthly guided walks.

Walking Cape Ann by Helen Naismith ($11.95) is also a handy tool, containing 22 maps and written descriptions of dozens of widely varied trails running the length and breadth of the cape. These descriptions are based on walks with Ted Tarr, a direct descendant of a Rockport founding father. Tarr meets with anyone wishing to take a long walk (the trail varies each week, but many of the following destinations are included) at the Whistlestop Mall, Sunday (year-round) at 10 AM.

WALKS

Ravenswood Park, off Western Avenue (MA 127), southwest of Gloucester; the parking lot is some 2 miles west of the junction with MA 133. The 300-acre park was laid out in 1889 and contains miles of wide, wooded paths, good for jogging and cross-country skiing. This spot is reportedly the northernmost point that the wild magnolia grows in.

Dogtown. Best accessed from Cherry Street in the Riverdale section of Gloucester. A 3000-acre tract that's best explored on a guided Sunday morning walk (see above). No houses survive, but there are a few dozen cellar holes, the traces of the 80 families who lived here between the early 1700s and the 1830s. The Essex County Greenbelt Association has been instrumental in acquiring land, removing trash, and improving signs to this area. It's a superb place for birding in spring and fall and for blueberrying in July, but it can be confusing. Detailed trail descriptions can be found in both guidebooks listed above.

Eastern Point Sanctuary at the tip of Eastern Point. A 26-acre Massachusetts Audubon Sanctuary with a pebbly beach, rocky shore, salt marsh, and woods, with a spectacular view of Boston. Persevere past all the "Private" and "For Eastern Point Residents Only" signs. Access available to a long breakwater.

Halibut Point, Gott Avenue off MA 127. North of Rockport a narrow path leads down to one of the most dramatic sites on the Eastern Seaboard. First there is the 12-acre Halibut Point property maintained by the Trustees of Reservations; a path leads through low scrub to flat rocks and a fine view across Ipswich Bay. The adjoining 54-acre Halibut Point State Park (546-2997) section commands the same view (on a clear day Mount Agamenticus in York, Maine, looms at the end of the sweep of coastline) and includes deep granite quarries (a sign says no swimming; admission is $3 per car). This rocky headland forms the northern tip of the cape, off which sailing vessels have always had to tack ("Haul-About"). This spot is great for picnics, and there are tidal pools to explore; also a self-guided trail detailing the granite industry.

Mt. Ann Park, New Way Lane off MA 133 east of MA 128. The 87 acres are maintained by the Trustees of Reservations. It's forested land, containing the highest elevation on Cape Ann and commanding views as far as Blue Hill to the south and Mount Agamenticus to the north.

The Cox Reservation, MA 133, Essex (first driveway west of Farnum's Restaurant). The headquarters for the Essex County Greenbelt Association is in an old farmhouse, former home of Allyn Cox (his murals grace Grant's tomb). A path leads down past the gardens and orchard, through marsh to a landing on the Essex River with a fine view of Hog Island and Crane Beach in the distance. Bring paper and paints.

Crane Wildlife Refuge (356-4351), Argilla Road, Ipswich. Open year-round 9 AM–4 PM, maintained by the Trustees of Reservations. Day-use fee: $2 adults, $1 children 6–12. Almost 1400 acres include Castle Hill (see *To See*), Castle Neck, and islands, as well as a 4-mile beach (see *Swimming*). A mile-long interpretive trail explores the barrier-beach system, leading to a woodland where sand dunes are slowly engulfing pine trees.

Ipswich River Wildlife Sanctuary (887-9264), 87 Perkins Row, Topsfield. From US 1 turn east on MA 97 at the lights, left at the first intersection. This is the largest sanctuary maintained by Massachusetts Audubon: 2800 acres of marsh, pond, and upland along the Ipswich River. There are 10 miles of paths, marked for skiing in winter. Year-round admission: $3 adults, $2 children.

Stony Cove and Presson Reservation, Exit 13 off MA 128, Gloucester, near the confluence of the Annisquam and Little Rivers. This 45-acre property includes a granite pier, tidal inlet, salt marsh, and upland white pine, oak, and sweet birch. Detailed directions and descriptions are in the *Greenbelt Passport*.

Back Shore, Atlantic Avenue, Gloucester. From MA 128 turn left at the second light after the second rotary. Follow Bass Avenue to the ocean for a wonderful dune walk to view the rocky shoreline and large summer homes. Great surf watching after storms.

BEACHES

Whittemore Marsh. Open only October through May, this 75 acres of salt marsh and barrier beach is owned by Greenbelt. Access is from Wingaersheek Road in West Gloucester.

Coolidge Point Reservation, Manchester, off MA 127 just past its junction with Hesperus Avenue. Small parking lot. Easy trail leads through woods, past salt marshes, and by a salt marsh pond to Magnolia Beach. Great birding.

(Also see *Swimming.*)

PICNICKING

Pigeon Hill, Landmark Lane off MA 127 near Pigeon Cove, Rockport. A great picnic spot above Sandy Bay if you don't mind sharing it with a water tank.

The Headlands, Atlantic Avenue, Rockport. A rocky point at the entrance to Rockport Harbor with benches great for boat watching.

James N. and Mary F. Stavros Reservation, Island Road off MA 133 (just west of Cape Ann Golf Course). A short foot trail leads to the top of White's Hill, just 116 feet high but with a view that takes in Castle Hill, Hog Island, and the meanderings of the Castle Neck River. The 53-acre refuge includes a salt marsh, and pine, cedar, and cherry trees. A great spot to sketch or picnic.

Rafe's Chasm, Magnolia; off Hesperus Avenue, about ¼ mile after Hammond Castle heading toward Magnolia. There's a small parking area and a short, easy path leading to spectacular rock perches for swimming and views of Norman's Woe.

Agassiz Rock in Manchester, east side of School Street, Essex; ½ mile north of MA 128, Exit 15. This 106-acre property is wooded upland with two glacial boulders said to have been discovered by Harvard naturalist Louis Agassiz. A great spot for a picnic.

STATE FORESTS

Bradley Palmer State Forest (887-5931) in Topsfield (from US 1 turn right at second light north of the Topsfield Fairgrounds, then onto Hamilton Road) offers picnic areas, fishing, and canoeing on the Ipswich River; 35 miles of hiking and ski trails.

Willowdale State Forest (887-5931), Linebrook Road in Ipswich, is 2400 acres with 40 miles of trails, canoeing, and fishing.

LODGING

INNS AND BED & BREAKFASTS

In Gloucester 01930

Harborview Inn (283-2277; 1-800-299-6696), 71 Western Avenue (Stacy Boulevard). Open year-round. The five guest rooms have all been wall-papered and painted by *Better Homes & Gardens* magazine and are bright, crisp, and flowery to the max. Rooms vary from the small Rockport Room with shared bath to the Boulevard Penthouse, which fills the entire third floor and has two baths and a living room, as well as a bedroom. The Gloucester suite features a working fireplace, and most rooms have ocean views. Note the painting of the fishing boat above the mantel; it belonged to innkeeper John Orlando's father. A continental breakfast is included in $79–169, cheaper off-season.

Gray Manor (283-5409), 14 Atlantic Road. Open May to October 18. This is a comfortable, unpretentious old home within walking distance of Good Harbor Beach. Mrs. Madelaine Gray has three guest rooms and six efficiencies. All rooms have private baths, air-conditioning, cable TV, refrigerators, some decks. No breakfast, but Charlie's Place (see *Eating*

Out) is a short walk; $40–50 a night, $425 per week for efficiencies; cheaper off-season.

Riverview Bed & Breakfast (281-1826). Sequestered down a side street near the hospital, this pleasant home is right on the Annisquam River. The Swinsons offer four rooms, two with riverview decks; all share two baths. Guests share a library and TV.

In Rockport 01966

Addison Choate Inn (546-7543), 49 Broadway. Although the 1860s house is right downtown on Broadway, it offers peace: a deep garden with a nicely landscaped swimming pool, six rooms and three suites artfully decorated with a mix of antiques and modern furniture and original art. The coach house has the feel of a country cottage and sleeps four, and the Celebration Suite is fit for honeymoons and anniversaries. The buffet breakfast features homemade granola; it's served either in the dining room or on the long, flower-filled porch. $81–118 per couple for rooms, more for suites, breakfast included.

Beach Knoll Inn (546-6939), 30 Beach Street. The core clapboard house was one of the first on Sandy Bay, and it has a wide old hearth with a hidden passage. Rooms all have private bath, some have fireplace and refrigerator. Back Beach is just across the street. $63–87 for a room, more for two-room and three-room apartments, also weekly rates, cheaper off-season.

The Captain's House (546-3825), 109 Marmion Way. This large, white stucco, vintage-1913 house is sited right on the ocean, 1½ miles from the center of town. Open March through mid-December. The five bedrooms with private baths are all pleasant. A continental breakfast is laid out in the seaside sun room. $90–105.

Cove Hill Inn (546-2701), 37 Mount Pleasant Street. Built in 1791, this classic Federal-style house has a curving staircase with 13 steps, representing the 13 colonies. Legend has it that it was built with pirate gold found at nearby Gully Point. There are 11 guest rooms, most of them doubles, 2 with an extra bed. There's also a bright little single on the third floor. The wide-planked floors gleam, and moldings and doors have been preserved. Rooms are papered in designer prints and furnished with family antiques, comforters, and canopies made by forebears. $47–98 including continental breakfast.

Eden Pines Inn (546-2505), Eden Road. A turn-of-the-century mansion set right on the water, 2 miles south of the village. The six upstairs bedrooms have luxurious baths and ocean views (several are large enough to accommodate four people). There is a paneled living room with a stone hearth and a bright breakfast room overlooking the ocean. Best of all are the porch and patio overlooking Thacher Island and the ocean; the smooth rocks below are great for sunning. $80–135 includes an ample breakfast.

Linden Tree Inn (546-2494), 26 King Street. This friendly Victorian home on a quiet street is within easy walking distance of both railroad station and beaches. There are 18 nicely decorated rooms, some ideal for families, and a spacious living room; also a sun porch. Inquire about efficiency units. Continental breakfast is included in the $63–98 per room, less off-season.

Old Farm Inn (546-3237; 1-800-233-6828), Pigeon Cove. This 1799 saltwater farm offers low-beamed common rooms and three pleasant guest rooms in the inn itself, four in the Barn Guesthouse (one with a kitchenette, the others with fridge and hotpot). All have private bath and TV. There is a comfortable sitting room for guests in the inn, and continental breakfast is provided in the sun room. It's a bit far from the village but is set in 5 acres of lawn and meadow and adjacent to Halibut Point (see *Green Space*). $73–120 (for a two-room suite) in summer, $50–90 off-season.

Peg Leg Inn (546-2352; 1-800-546-2352), 2 King Street. Rooms are in several adjoining 19th-century houses, all very clean and handy to the beach and shops. $65–120.

Pleasant Street Inn (546-3915; 1-800-541-3915), 17 Pleasant Street.. The view from the expansive porch is across town to the bay, unquestionably one of the most pleasant places in town to sit on a summer day. The eight rooms are also comfortable, all with private baths and all different, from spacious tower rooms and a snug double under the eaves to a private basement-level room with its own entrance and a Jacuzzi. Inquire about the Carriage House apartment. Roger and Lynn Norris have nicely renovated and landscaped this large Victorian house that sits high above town, within walking distance of shops and restaurants. $78–98 includes a buffet breakfast.

Ralph Waldo Emerson House (546-6321), Green Street. Open mid-April through November. Off by itself beyond Pigeon Cove, this is one of the few 1850s summer hotels left on the New England coast, the kind with a formal check-in desk, large common rooms, and a sub-lobby recreation area (table tennis, large-screen TV, whirlpool, and sauna); there's also an outdoor pool. Rooms are old-fashioned, all with private ('50s) baths; $96–130 EP. Breakfast and dinner are served. This is a good place for weddings.

Rocky Shores (546-2823; 1-800-348-4003), 65 Eden Road. Open mid-April through October. This is one of those unusual places that are equally good for families, singles, and couples. A brown-shingled 1905 mansion forms the hospitable centerpiece for 11 two- and three-bedroom housekeeping cottages. Renate and Gunter Kostka encourage guests to mingle in the living room and on the porch, which commands a splendid view of the ocean and twin lighthouses on Thacher Island. Guests in the main house also meet over breakfast. Beaches are within walking distance. $76–110 per couple for rooms; cottages run $640–825 per week.

Seacrest Manor (546-2211), 131 Marmion Way. A large old mansion with eight big guest rooms, all with private bath, some with deck space and ocean views. There's a friendly clutter to the public rooms, and the guest rooms, although not furnished in antiques, are pleasant. The house is set on 2 acres of grounds. $90–124 in summer, less in winter, full breakfast included.

Seafarer Inn (546-6248), 86 Marmion Way. Open April through November. A homey, gambrel-roofed inn with a great water view. There are 10 airy guest rooms hung with paintings by local artists. The best views are from the two third-floor rooms with breakfast nooks and efficiency kitchenettes (rented on a weekly basis). Most rooms have their own bath. A continental breakfast is included in $65–90 in summer.

Seaward Inn and Cottages (546-3471; 1-800-648-7733), Marmion Way. Open April through September 22. After 50 years of welcoming guests, Roger and Anne Cameron sold this very special place to Rockport residents Fred and Jane Fiumara in 1995, but they continue to summer on the property—which hasn't changed noticeably as yet. The 31 rooms (all with private bath) are scattered among the main house, The Breakers (directly on the water), and assorted small cottages, some with fireplaces and/or kitchens. A path winds along the shore of a sheltered, spring-fed pond (with a small sandy beach) and into a small wood. Old Garden Beach is a 5-minute walk, and the village is a mile away. The main house itself offers a spacious, comfortable sun porch, a fairly formal living room with a grand piano, and an old-fashioned dining room that is now open to the public as the Sea Garden (see *Dining Out*). $98–138.

Seven South Street (546-6708). This 18th-century house offers six attractive rooms, as well as a cottage and a one-bedroom suite. There is a small pool out back, and Old Garden Beach is a short walk. The rest of the village is just up South Street (MA 127A). In summer, rooms are $60–80 double; less off-season.

Tuck Inn B&B (546-7260), 17 High Street. Open year-round. An early-19th-century home on a quiet corner with nine nicely furnished rooms, including one suite that can accommodate four. In winter, fireplaces warm the common rooms, and in summer there's a pool; beaches and shops are all within walking distance. Continental breakfast is served. $77–107 double, less off-season.

Yankee Clipper (546-3407), PO Box 2399, MA 127 north of the village. The main inn is hedged off below the road, facing Sandy Bay and, across the bay, the village. The living room is carpeted in Orientals, richly paneled, and decorated with ginger jars, ships models, and the portrait of Mehitable Lamon, great-grandmother of innkeeper Barbara Wemyss Ellis. Barbara's parents opened the Yankee Clipper in 1946. There is a sense of tradition here and of everything in its place. A total of 29 rooms are scattered among the inn, its annex, "The Captain's Quarters," and the Bulfinch House across the road (named for its architect), which caters to more transient guests. Grounds are terraced in flowers, and rocky promontories overlook the water. There is an outdoor pool. $95–219 with breakfast; MAP rate also available, less in off-season; midweek packages available.

In Magnolia 01930

The White House (525-3642), 18 Norman Avenue. This gracious Victorian house has 8 rooms, also 10 in a motel-style wing (open all year). It is within walking distance of Magnolia shops and restaurants and offers access to a private beach. Continental breakfast featuring home baking is included in $75–90 per couple.

In Essex 01929

George Fuller House (768-7766), 148 Main Street (MA 133). Tucked between the seafood restaurants and antiques shops, between the main drag and the salt marshes, this cheerful old house is unusually welcoming. The snug, square parlor with paneling and Indian shutters is in the Federal (1830) part of the house, but rooms ramble off into Victorian-era spaces and porches. All six guest rooms have private baths, phones, air-conditioning, and color TVs, but each is different. Some have canopied beds. Three have working fireplaces. Generally speaking, we prefer the second- and third-floor rooms in back because the view is off across the salt marshes, but the downstairs rooms are also attractive. The penthouse, with its efficiency sink and stove, is a real find. Breakfast might include French toast drizzled with brandied lemon butter or piña colada pancakes. Bob and Cindy Cameron are genial hosts with plenty of suggestions about local options. From $70 for the Story Room off-season to $125 for the penthouse in summer. The Andrews suite, two rooms with a working fireplace, is $100–115.

In Hamilton 01936

The Miles River Country Inn (468-7206), 823 Bay Road (MA 1A). This is a genuine North Shore estate, and one on which you are made to feel like an invited (not just paying) guest. Gretel and Peter Clark's home is a 24-room mansion dating from a number of periods between 1774 and the 1920s, set in lawns and outstanding flower gardens stretching back to the river. Four of the eight guest rooms are named for the Clarks' children, and each has a different feel. They come with and without private baths and working fireplaces. The common rooms are luxurious, most with working fireplaces. A study is paneled with 19th-century wooden bedsteads from Brittany. The full breakfast features eggs laid by the resident hens and honey from the apiary. Gretel delights in sharing her garden with guests and in directing them to other little-known show gardens in the area. Needless to say, this is a great place for a wedding. $80–105.

MOTELS

In Rockport 01966

Captain's Bounty (546-9557). This multistory facility has 25 basic units, some of them with kitchenettes. Its appeal is its location, right on Front

Beach on the edge of the village. $95–105 (for the efficiency suite) in summer, $10 for each additional person over two.

Sandy Bay Motor Inn (546-7155), 173 Main Street. The rooms are basic: two double beds, a phone, and TV, but facilities include an attractive indoor pool and whirlpool and outside tennis courts; also a pleasant coffee shop where breakfast and lunch are served daily. $88–94 per room, $132–158 for suites.

In Gloucester 01930

Cape Ann Marina Motor Inn (283-2116), 75 Essex Avenue. Right at the marina, a 53-room facility is geared to those who are setting out on 7 AM fishing expeditions or morning whale-watches, but it still maintains a nice seaside atmosphere. Facilities include a swimming pool, hot tub, and seasonal restaurant. $69–90 per room, $150 for the penthouse in summer; less off-season.

Cape Ann Motor Inn (281-2900), 33 Rockport Road. This three-story motel stands right on Long Beach. Open year-round. $95 double in summer, $6 for each extra person (under age 10, free), $105 with kitchenette, less off-season.

Good Harbor Beach Inn (283-1489), Salt Island Road. Open spring through fall. This place has charm. The check-in desk is a pine-paneled living room with Oriental rugs and a fireplace. The 17 rooms are pine-walled too, furnished in traditional beach cottage style, and each has two double beds and full baths. There are also efficiency apartments. Good Harbor Beach is just over a hedge. Breakfast and lunch are served in an oceanfront dining room; $89–95 in summer, less in shoulder seasons.

WHERE TO EAT

DINING OUT

In Gloucester

The White Rainbow (281-0017), 65 Main Street. Open for dinner only, closed Monday. The dining room is candlelit and low beamed in a vintage-1800 commercial building. Long established and generally regarded as the best restaurant in town with prices to match ($18–25 for entrées) for dishes like lobster Monte Carlo or seafood Capellini. The Cafe Wine Bar offers lighter fare and slower prices (lobster stew $6.50) and an outdoor garden.

Square Cafe (281-3951), 197 East Main Street. Open Monday through Saturday for lunch and dinner, Sunday for dinner only. An elegant, storefront dining room with stippled walls. The luncheon menu features reasonably priced but unusual sandwiches (fried catfish with jalapeño/lime mayonnaise, salsa, and jack cheese) and pasta dishes. The à la carte dinner menu also includes a couple of sandwiches but features appetizers like pan-fried salmon cakes ($5.50) and fried calamari, and entrées like "Fusian pork chops" (grilled and marinated, stuffed with oriental pesto, and served over a sweet-and-sour plum sauce: $10.50).

Au Beaujolais Cafe and Wine Bar (283-5200), 287 Main Street. The walls are ocher, and the atmosphere is reminiscent of a French brasserie; the à la carte menu is in French but still reasonably priced. You might begin, for instance, with "crêpes au fromage chevre et champignons" (goat cheese and spinach stuffed crêpes with mushroom sauce, $5.75) and a cassoulet of duck, pork, and lamb baked with white beans and herbed crumbs ($11.75).

Le Bistro (281-8055), 2 Main Street. Housed in a striking, four-square brick building at the head of Main Street, the restaurant is open Tuesday through Sunday from 5:30 for dinner. The brick-walled dining area is pleasant. The menu changes frequently but is constantly creative; on a winter evening you could dine on acorn squash bisque ($5.50), followed by tea-smoked duck with mango chili chutney and a vermicelli spring roll ($17.50).

The Rudder (283-7967), 73 Rocky Neck Avenue. April through October, lunch weekdays, dinner until 12:30. A waterfront restaurant on Smith Cove to which Bostonians drive for dinner and to see the Parsons—mother (Evie) and daughters Susan and Paula—perform. Built in the 1880s as a fish-packing and -processing plant, it subsequently served as studio space and has been under present ownership for more than 30 years. Specialties include roast leg of lamb, and shrimp scampi, clam, and scallop farci. Piano music and after-dinner sing-alongs. From $12.95 for steamers as an entrée to $17.95 for lamb farci; children's menu items are $7.95.

The Studio (283-4123), 51 Rocky Neck Avenue. Seasonal. Open daily for lunch and dinner. Built in the 1880s as a fish house, then an isinglass factory, and then a summer art school, the building now houses a large, airy dining space with an open hearth, windows, a piano bar in the evening, and a deck on Smith Cove. The *Virginia C.* excursion boat from Boston docks here. Entrées range from spinach fettucine and fish-and-chips ($9.95) to baked lobster casserole ($17.95), and the "Little Sailors" menu includes a grilled frankfurter ($2.95).

Passports (281-3680), Main Street. Fewer than a dozen tables and so new at this writing we haven't had a chance to check it out—but local reviews are good.

Gloucester House Restaurant (283-1812), Seven Seas Wharf on Rogers Street. A large, waterfront fish restaurant with views of the boats out the windows and from the open-air Cafe Seven Seas on the back deck, as near to the water as you can get. Geared to groups and tourists but locally respected. Open daily for lunch and dinner; entrées $5.95–27.

In Rockport
Note: Rockport is dry; all restaurants are BYOB.

Peg Leg Restaurant (546-3038), 18 Beach Street. Open April through October, daily for three meals, but only from noon on Sunday. A long-established place with views over Front Beach through large windows and a converted greenhouse. The traditional menu features broiled scrod, baked stuffed shrimp, and lamb chops. Dinner entrées $7.95 and up.

Glass Verandah at the Yankee Clipper (546-7795), MA 127, north of Rockport village. Open daily for breakfast and dinner. Oceanfront dining, creative New England cuisine. Dinner entrées $13.95–21.95.

My Place By-the-Sea (546-9667), tip of Bearskin Neck. Open most of the year Thursday through Sunday for lunch and dinner. Sited at the very end of Bearskin Neck, with an outdoor deck and a view from the inside. Sandwiches, salads, and omelets at lunch; dinner is the time to come here, to dine on marinated shrimp kabob ($17.50) or tuna Mediterranean, baked with fresh tomato, onion, Shiitaki mushrooms, garlic, wine, and herbs ($16.50), as the sun sinks over the water.

Sea Garden (546-3471), Seaward Inn, Marmion Way. The dining room at this low-key inn opened to the public for the first time in 1995 and quickly gained a reputation for serving some of the most interesting food in town. You might begin with sautéed mussels in a leek and tarragon broth ($5), and dine on squid-ink linguine with shrimp, lobster, grilled eggplant, fresh corn, and herbs ($17) or grilled tenderloin of beef, apple-smoked bacon, goat cheese casserole, and cabernet reduction ($19).

Brackett's Ocean View Restaurant (546-2797), 27 Main Street. Open most of the year for lunch and dinner; picture windows overlook Sandy Bay. This is a white-tablecloth but family-geared place with a traditional Yankee menu and seafood specialties.

The Hannah Jumper (546-3600), Tuna Wharf off Bearskin Neck. Open daily for lunch and dinner. Great view of Rockport Harbor from the dining room and deck above. A big, moderately priced, tourist-oriented place, named for the 75-year-old Rockport seamstress credited with inciting a citizens' assault on the town's saloons in 1856. Entrées $5–15.

In Manchester

Seven Central Publick House (526-4533), 7 Central Street, opposite Manchester Town Hall. Open daily for lunch and dinner, patio dining in-season. Housed in a former farmers' market dating from 1753, with a patio overlooking Mill Brook. The menu is large; specialties include seafood and prime rib. Entrées $6.95–18.95.

In Magnolia

The Patio (525-3230; 525-3110), 12 Lexington Avenue. Open year-round weekdays for lunch, daily for dinner. A family-owned, locally favored place priced for local residents; fish-and-chips at lunch is $4.95; dinner entrées from $9.95 for lemon-pepper chicken to $16.95 for filet mignon. Try the haddock Portuguese style ($11.95). Entrées come in junior and regular sizes.

In Essex

Tom Shea's Restaurant (768-6931), on the causeway. Open for dinner from 4 PM daily, brunch on weekends. The atmosphere is casual, with antique decor; a view of the marshes. Generally rated as the best of the more expensive seafood places on the causeway. Scallop-stuffed shrimp ($17.95) and Cajun blackened salmon ($18.95) are particular favorites. Pasta dishes begin at $14.95, and steak entrées average $20.

Jerry Plonzi's Hearthside (768-6002; 768-6003), MA 133. Open 11:30–5:45 Monday through Friday, until 5:15 Saturday. You dine in the loft of a converted barn or in the fireplaced dining areas of a 250-year-old farmhouse overlooking the marshes. Leisurely lunches are the specialty of the house; seafood dishes include deep-fried smelts ($12.95) and baked finnan haddie with egg sauce ($14.95); filet mignon Hearthside is $18.95.

In Ipswich

Chippers River Cafe (356-7956) at the Choate Bridge, open daily for breakfast (from 6 AM on weekdays), lunch, and dinner; a seasonal deck. Omelets, Belgian waffles, interesting sandwiches, salads, dinner entrées like mustard-lemon chicken and Chippers Cioppino (seafood simmered in marinara sauce); entrées from $9.95.

Steep Hill Grill (356-0774), behind Bruni's Market on MA 133 near the Essex line. Open daily (closed Tuesday off-season), brunch on Sunday; no lunch on Saturday, nor on Sunday in summer. Brunch is particularly popular, and the daily choice of soups and salads (like lentil salad topped with grilled shrimp on a bed of red-leaf lettuce) and sandwiches is extensive; try the jalapeño-barbecued pork with spicy coleslaw on an onion-dill roll. For dinner this is one of the best values around. The menu is large and varied, and there are always intriguing specials like pan-roasted game hen. Entrées $10–16. The wine list is also unusually good and reasonably priced.

EATING OUT

In Gloucester

Halibut Point (281-1900), 289 Main Street. Open daily 11:30–11:30. Occupying the original tavern built by Howard Blackburn in 1900 after his amazing voyage (see the Cape Ann Historical Society under *To See*), the place has a pub atmosphere and is a favorite with residents. Specialties include a spicy Italian fish chowder, burgers, deli-style sandwiches, and reasonably priced entrées like "spicy shrimp" (cooked on the grill, seasoned with garlic, dill, and shallots).

Japaleños (283-8228), 86 Main Street. Open for lunch and dinner daily. Atmosphere is minimal, but the *pollo mole* (chicken in a spicy chocolate sauce), chile relleno (stuffed polblano chiles), and Tampiquena (marinated steak) draw patrons from near and far.

La Lanterna (283-6334), 118 Main Street. Open Tuesday through Saturday 11–9. Rosa and Joe make a good pizza and reasonably priced pastas.

El Caliente Cafe (283-4113), 17 Rogers Street. Open daily for breakfast, lunch, and dinner. The food is fine, and the harbor view is great.

Charlie's Place (283-0303), 83 Bass Avenue near Good Harbor Beach. Open daily year-round, 7 AM–8 PM. A bright, Formica place with a counter and tables, Styrofoam cups, paper plates, a huge fried shrimp roll, luscious crabmeat, a haddock plate. Breakfasts are a specialty (fresh-squeezed orange juice).

Gull Restaurant (283-6060), 75 Essex Avenue at the Cape Ann Marina. Open seasonally 5:30 AM–9:30 PM; geared to the owners of the motor yachts tied up here and passengers on the Yankee fleet's fishing and whale-watching expeditions. A great old standby on the Annisquam River. Cocktails served.

Gleason's (283-4414), 42 Eastern Avenue. Open daily year-round 8–8. Lobster-in-the-rough is the specialty: reasonably priced crab and lobster rolls and boiled lobster.

In Manchester

The Coffee Cup (526-4558), 25 Union Street. Open daily 6 AM to 9 PM. Greek specialties, homemade soups, grinders, and pizza. $3.25–4.95.

The Edgewater Cafe (526-4668), 69 Raymond Street. Open daily 5–10 PM. Specializing in Mexican food; casual atmosphere. BYOB.

In Rockport

Ellen's Harborside (546-2512), T Wharf. *The* place for budget dining in Rockport, right on the harbor, open daily from 6:30 AM for breakfast, lunch, and dinner. Counter and tables, authentic atmosphere, seafood specialties, but hamburgers too; dinner specials.

Portside Chowder House (546-7045), Bearskin Neck. Open 11–8 in summer, year-round for lunch. A pleasant place with a hearth that's lit in winter, water view, good chowder, lobster stew, daily specials.

The Greenery (546-9593), 15 Dock Square. Closed November through March; open daily in-season for lunch and dinner, also Sunday breakfast. A bright, casual place with a great harbor view, salad bar, gourmet sandwiches, fresh fruits, lobster.

In Essex

Woodman's (768-6451), MA 133. The most famous clam house on the North Shore. Open daily for lunch and dinner. The claim is that "Chubby" Woodman invented the fried clam over 75 years ago, and the house specialty remains fried seafood by the plate and bucket. Patrons eat at picnic tables, in the rough. As with most legendary places, you hear it's too crowded, not as good as it used to be, but judge for yourself; everyone has to try it at least once. Beer on tap. This is also one of the few places that cater old-fashioned clambakes.

Farnham's (768-6643), MA 133. Open seasonally, daily from 5 AM until 10 PM. Wooden booths and windows that overlook the Essex marshes; chowder, fried clams.

Village Restaurant (768-6400), MA 33. Closed Monday, otherwise open for lunch and dinner. The Riccis began with five booths and seven counter stools 30 years ago, and they now seat 225. They specialize in local seafood; an Essex River Sampler includes sautéed haddock, shrimp, and clams.

Fortune Palace II (768-3839), 99 Main Street, Essex. Open for lunch and dinner. Enthusiastically recommended by locals. No MSG, a wide choice, including salads and pan-fired dishes; try the plum-flavored crispy duck. White tablecloths, bright, cheerful atmosphere.

In Ipswich

The Clam Box, High Street on MA 1A just north of the village. Open March through Memorial Day daily except Monday, then daily until Labor Day; closed Monday again until Columbus Day, then open Wednesday through Sunday until December 15. This landmark dates back to the '30s and derives its name from its original shape: a 15- by 15- by 30-foot clam box. There is now space for eating in as well as taking out.

Stone Soup (356-4222), Mitchell Road (turn off MA 1A/MA 133 on the road across from the Dairy Queen). Open Tuesday through Friday 7–2, Saturday and Sunday 7–midnight. Thursday through Saturday night reservations are a must for one of the two dinner sittings (6 and 8). Very small, very reasonably priced for breakfast and lunch, dinner entrées from $7.50, Italian specialties.

Choate Bridge Pub (356-2931), middle of village at the bridge. Open daily 11–10. A comfortable village pub like too few villages have. There's a smoky bar side and a dining room with booths and blackboard specials. The burgers are outstanding, and in the evening you can also feast on a kielbasa pizza.

TAKEOUT

Virgilio's Grocery (283-5295), 29 Main Street in the West End, Gloucester, features sandwiches made to order with "fisherman's bread" fresh from the oven (request the St. Joseph's); also pizza by the slice.

Destino's Submarine Sandwiches (283-3100), 129 Prospect Street, Gloucester opposite Our Lady of Good Voyage Church, may just offer the best lunch deal in town; every sub comes with a free side order of slaw, macaroni salad, or three-bean salad, plus (weekdays only) soup. (Also see *Selective Shopping—Seafood.*)

SNACKS

Caffe Sicilia (283-7345), 40 Main Street, Gloucester. Outstanding espresso and Sicilian pastry.

Donut Jim's (283-3383), 24 Washington Street, Gloucester. Very good doughnuts, pastries. Locally loved.

The Glass Sailboat (283-7818), 3 Duncan Street (just off Main), Gloucester. Open 8–5:30, and Thursday evenings. A café/deli in the back of a natural-foods store: croissants, homemade soups, pocket-bread sandwiches.

Helmut's Struedel (546-2824), 49 Bearskin Neck, Rockport. Memorable pastries, also coffee and sandwiches, with seating on an outside deck.

BREAKFAST

Eating breakfast out is a popular local custom around Gloucester and a good way of tuning in.

Sailor Stan, off MA 127A at the entrance to Rocky Neck, is open for breakfast and lunch; counter and tables, good chowder, local gossip center, bargain priced.

Lee's, corner of East Main Street and Eastern Avenue, **The Gull Restaurant** and **Charlie's** (noted above), as well as **Captain's Lodge** at 237 Eastern Avenue in Gloucester, **Flav's Red Skiff** in Rockport, and **The Firehouse** in Lanesville are all popular morning spots.

ENTERTAINMENT

MUSIC

Rockport Chamber Music Festival (546-7391), the Rockport Art Association, Rockport. Throughout the month of June distinguished chamber musicians perform at the art association and other local places. Performances are Thursday, Friday, and Saturday at 8, Sunday at 5.

Hammond Castle Organ Concerts (283-2080), Hesperus Avenue, Gloucester. Performances on the 10,000-pipe organ, housed in the 100-foot-long Great Hall with its 85-foot tower, are scheduled throughout the year.

Castle Hill Festival (356-7774), Argilla Road, Ipswich. A July and August series of concerts and other special events at the Concert Barn; all events are at 5 PM with picnicking permitted beforehand on the Grand Allée of the Great House.

Band concerts in July and August, Sunday at 7:30, at the bandstands in Rockport (near Back Beach) and Gloucester (at Stage Fort Park).

THEATER

Gloucester Stage Co. (281-4099), 267 East Main Street, Gloucester, mid-May through December, Wednesday through Sunday. Staged in a 150-seat theater in a former Gorton's Fish Company warehouse near Rocky Neck. Affordably priced.

FILM

Little Arts Cinema (546-2973), 18 Broadway, Rockport, shows a variety of classic and popular films.

The Strand (356-0184), MA 1A in Ipswich, shows the latest.

Cape Ann Twin Cinema (281-1990), Essex Avenue (MA 133), Gloucester, shows current hits.

SELECTIVE SHOPPING

ANTIQUES

Essex styles itself the "Antiques Center of New England." In 1966, the first year the town required licenses to sell used goods, six permits were issued. Today there are some 60 dealers. **The White Elephant** (768-6901), 32 Main Street, bears special mention because it was the village's first antiques shop (when it opened in 1952, the legend is that someone found a Winslow Homer painting here for $10 and an original Rembrandt sketch for $1). It's still one of the best, a clutter of everything from sleds and vases to license plates, beds, radios, quilts, and almost anything else you can think of; the outlet is up MA 133 near Essex. **Main Street Antiques** (768-7619) in Essex is four floors, and **Robert C. Coviello Antiques** (768-7039) is three floors. Needless to say, antiques dealers are also scattered around Cape Ann itself.

Rockport also offers a half-dozen antiques shops within a few blocks. Pick up an "Antiques in Rockport" flyer. **The Rockport Trading Company** (546-8066), 67 Broadway, features a wide variety of fun stuff and is open year-round.

ART GALLERIES
Rockport is home to more than two dozen art galleries, all within a mile or so of each other. Pick up a copy of "The Rockport Fine Arts Gallery Guide" from the Rockport Chamber (see *Guidance*). (Also see *To See— Art Centers.*)

BOOKSTORES
Toad Hall Bookstore (546-7323), 51 Main Street, Rockport. Open daily, evenings in summer. Housed in an old granite bank building and walled with inviting titles, this exceptional store donates net profits to cultural and ecological projects.

The Bookstore (281-1548), 61 Main Street, Gloucester. A pleasant store with a rear view of the harbor.

Bookends (281-2053), 132 Main Street, Gloucester. Good selection of paperbacks. Best magazine rack in town.

Olde English Book Shop, Rocky Neck, Gloucester. Owned by a British transplant married to a local fisherman; features British publishers and titles.

FARMS
Goodale Orchards (356-5366), Argilla Road, Ipswich. Open June through December 24, a 179-acre farm on the verge of the marshes with an orchard store in an 18th-century barn. The Russell family specializes in fruits, vegetables, and flowers all grown on the farm, pick-your-own strawberries in June, raspberries in July, blueberries in August, apples and tomatoes in September, also fruit and dandelion wines, cider (hard as well as regular), and a daily barn menu of soups and sandwiches. In October there's a haunted barn.

The Boundary Turkey Farm (768-7718), Chebacco Road, Essex. Home-grown, all-natural turkey, turkey pies.

SEAFOOD
J.A.H. Seafood, 10 Railroad Avenue, Gloucester, sells the catch of the day, Essex clams, lobster meat.

Northeast Seafood, 2 East Main Street, Gloucester, features a "clambake special": two lobsters, steamers. Also fresh fish, scallops, shrimp.

Roy Moore Lobster Co., Bearskin Neck in Rockport, sells lobster cooked to order that you can eat "in the rough" outside at round wooden tables (the kind formerly used for spooling cable).

New England Lobster Co., in Pigeon Cove (north of Rockport, hidden behind Cape Ann Forge), offers flapping fresh fish, shrimp, and lobster. The boats dock a few feet away.

SPECIAL SHOPS

Bearskin Neck, Rockport. A finger of land dividing Sandy Bay from Rockport Harbor, this is one of the pleasanter places along the Eastern Seaboard to stroll, nosh, and browse. As in Ogunquit, Maine, the several dozen seasonal shops and restaurants are housed in former fish shacks. The **Sun Basket** specializes in North American Indian carts. **Serendipity** features some local craftspeople, and **Half Moon Harry's** hand-painted clocks are truly special.

John Tarr Store, Main Street, Rockport. An old-fashioned haberdasher with a bargain corner and women's wear.

Pierce & Company (356-3755), 30 Brownville Avenue, Ipswich. Open Monday through Saturday 9–5. Designer oak furniture made on the premises.

Glass Sail Boat Wearhouse, 199 Main Street, Gloucester. Women's clothing: natural-fiber, nicely styled skirts, dresses, jumpers, sweaters, and things woven; cosmetics.

Hibiscus (283-3848), 114 Main Street, Gloucester. Sandy and Michael Koolkin have created an unusual shop filled with furnishings, women's clothing, and gifts.

Local Colors (283-3996), 108 Main Street, Gloucester. Features locally crafted products.

SPECIAL EVENTS

May: **Prince of Whales Ball** to celebrate the return of the whales. five-mile road race. **Motif No. 1 Day Celebration** in Rockport.

June: **Rockport Chamber Music Festival** (546-2825), series of concerts by prominent performers at the Hibbard Gallery in the Rockport Art Association. **Rocky Neck (studios) Open House. St. Peter's Fiesta**— biggest event of the year in Gloucester. A week of music, sporting events, parades, a blessing of the fishing fleet. **Swedish Midsummer Festival** of Swedish dances, foods in Rockport.

July: **Independence Day parades** in Gloucester, Rockport, and Manchester. **Renaissance Fair** at Hammond Castle.

August: **Olde Ipswich Days** includes a block dance, marathon, public dinners. **Gloucester Waterfront Festival**—art and crafts show, weekend fish fry. **Manchester Sidewalk Bazaar**—races, parade of sail. **Annual Crane Beach Sand Castle Contest.**

September: **Gloucester Schooner Festival.**

Labor Day: 15-mile **Cape Ann Road Race** around the cape. **Essex Clamfest**—chowder festival, clam-shucking contest, clambake.

October: **North Shore Antiques Show**—major display by area dealers at Woodman's Function Hall in Essex. **Amateur Art Festival,** Rockport. **Haunted Halloween Nights** at Hammond Castle.

December: **Christmas in Rockport**—ice sculpture, tree lighting, strolling carolers and minstrels, climaxing with Christmas pageant. Also **Annual Santa Claus Parade** in Gloucester, **Victorian Christmas Festival** at Hammond Castle.

NEWBURYPORT AREA

The Bay State's smallest city contains the country's largest collection of Federal-era buildings.

Sited at the mouth of the Merrimack River, Newburyport was an early shipbuilding center, and by the outbreak of the Revolution was the fourth largest town in America. Thanks to its privateers, fortunes were made *during* the War for Independence, and the ensuing decades, judging from its present look, were unusually prosperous. Architecturally Newburyport is frozen in the 1790s to 1830s.

Driving into town along High Street you can't help but notice the 2-mile lineup of white, wooden, "Federal-style" homes with their distinctive three stories, spare, symmetrical lines, and shallow-hipped roofs. The commercial buildings down along State Street and around waterfront Market Square are also older and more graceful than those of most other American downtowns. They were built of brick after a fire in 1811.

The Federal era also bred an unusually deep split between High Street residents and the craftsmen and mariners who lived above their shops down by the river. Each party supported its own fire company, bank, Masonic lodge, and militia company. A century later in 1930, when a five-volume study focused on Newburyport as "Yankee City," the "upper-uppers" were still living on High Street, and social status sloped downward through five distinct strata to the "lower-lowers" along the waterfront. Hometown novelist John P. Marquand satirized the study and its subject in *Point of No Return,* a story about a city in which "everyone instinctively knew where he belonged."

This picture altered, however, in the 1960s when urban renewal razed the old distilleries and post–Civil War factories along 20 acres of the city's waterfront and turned menacingly to the city's early brick commercial rows. Newburyporters of every ilk rallied in protest, attracting many preservation-minded newcomers in the process.

Today more than a hundred shops—a mix of basics, boutiques, and antiques—are housed in waterfront complexes like the Inn Street Mall, the Tannery, and Merrimac Landing, and mellow brick buildings run the length of State Street. On the river itself the granite Custom House, a Greek Revival temple designed in 1835 by the architect of the Washington Monument, is now a museum, and the vintage-1823 firehouse is a combined theater and gallery. The waterfront itself is a landscaped place to walk and watch river traffic, as well as to board whalewatching, fishing, and excursion boats.

Plum Island, an 8½-mile, stringbean-shaped barrier island minutes from downtown, offers miles of beach and wildlife refuge trails known to birders from around the world. Although the Massachusetts Audubon chapter owns some 23,000 other acres in the state, it has chosen to buy 3 acres on the Plum Island Turnpike as a site for its most elaborate visitors center, and guided bird walks are offered by an increasing number of groups, both commercial and private, year-round. Maudslay State Park, on the other arm of town, beckons with hiking and biking trails on the Merrimack River.

As noted in the introduction to this section, Newburyport is a hinge between the Merrimack River Valley and the North Shore, a logical hub from which to explore both.

AREA CODE
508

GUIDANCE
Greater Newburyport Chamber of Commerce (462-6680), 29 State Street, Newburyport 01950. Open weekdays 9–5, Saturday 10–4, Sunday noon–4. A seasonal information booth in Market Square, with rest rooms, welcomes visitors on summer weekends.

GETTING THERE
By bus: **Commuter Coach** (1-800-874-3377) offers frequent service to Boston during commuter hours. **C&J Trailways** (465-2277; in Boston, 617-426-6030) also offers frequent service to Boston and Logan Airport.
By boat: Dockage downtown.
By car: I-495 is the most common approach; MA 113 exit.

PARKING
Ample free parking in downtown Newburyport can be found in lots off Green and Merrimack Streets.

MEDICAL EMERGENCY
Anna Jacques Hospital (462-6601), Highland Avenue, Newburyport.

TO SEE

MUSEUMS
Cushing House (462-2681), 98 High Street. Open May through November, Tuesday through Saturday 10–4. $3 adults, $1.50 students. This brick mansion, housing the town's historical collection, was built in

1808 and served as home to Caleb Cushing, our first ambassador to China. Twenty-one rooms are filled with elegant furnishings, silver, paintings, and vintage clothing. The 1700s French-style garden is under restoration.

Custom House Maritime Museum (462-8681), 25 Water Street. Open April to late December, Monday through Saturday 10–4, Sunday 1–4. $3 adults, $2 seniors, $1.50 children, $6 per family. Built in 1835 of Rockport granite, designed by Robert Mills, architect of the Washington Monument and US Treasury Building, sold in 1913 and used for hay storage and, eventually, as a junk shop, this handsome building is now a fine museum with a small, permanent historical exhibit and the Marquand Library, furnished and filled with the novelist's treasures. Major exhibits dramatizing some aspect of the city's history change each year.

HISTORIC HOUSES

Spencer-Pierce-Little Farm (462-2634), 5 Little's Lane, Newbury; MA 1A just south of the light at Rolfe's Lane, a way to the Plum Island Turnpike. Open June to October 15, Thursday through Sunday noon–5. $4 adults, $3.50 seniors, $2 children, free to SPNEA members. Hauntingly beautiful and set in 240 acres of meadow and salt marsh, this house is one of New England's oldest and the only grand Jacobean-style manor built of stone and brick. Built in the late 1600s, it has recently been stabilized at a cost of $1 million by the Society for the Protection of New England Antiquities (SPNEA). Although still unfurnished, the mansion is skillfully interpreted on tours that begin by introducing you to the family who lived here in the 20th century. You then move back through the rooms and generations, into the wooden Federal-era wing and back again to the second-floor, 17th-century kitchen. Don't miss the attic, with its early-19th-century graffiti. The fields, presently leased to local farmers, stretch to the Plum Island Turnpike.

Coffin House (617-227-3956), 14–16 High Street, MA 1A, Newbury. Open June through mid-October, Thursday through Sunday noon–5; $4. This weathered house was begun circa 1654 and grew considerably over the next two centuries. Its old kitchens and early wallpaper, as well as its furnishings, are interesting. Owned by the Society for the Protection of New England Antiquities.

HISTORIC SITES

Bartlett Mall, High Street, Newburyport. The high-splashing fountain here is known as Frog Pond; the mall as a whole was the gift of a merchant in 1800. The adjacent brick courthouse was designed by Charles Bulfinch. The old **Hill Burying Ground** across the way contains many of Newburyport's most memorable residents.

The Old Jail (north end of the mall), built of Rockport granite, dates from 1823.

Newburyport Public Library (465-4428), 94 State Street. Patrick Tracy's

1771 brick mansion has hosted George Washington, the Marquis de Lafayette, Aaron Burr, and Benedict Arnold. During the Revolution, Patrick's son Nathaniel made a fortune from his privateers (selling cargoes from the captured ships for more than $4 million), but eventually he lost it all and was forced to sell both this house and his country property (now the Spencer-Pierce-Little Farm; see *Historic Houses*). This mansion has been a library since 1865 and contains marine paintings and a model of the clipper ship *Dreadnought*, built in Newburyport.

Unitarian Church (465-0602), 26 Pleasant Street, Newburyport. This 1801 structure is thought to have been designed by Samuel McIntire and has an unusually graceful facade and spire with a Paul Revere bell. The interior is also graceful and airy. Services are held every Sunday.

Old South Presbyterian Church (465-9666), 29 Federal Street, Newburyport. Built in 1756 with a bell cast by Paul Revere, this dignified church has a whispering gallery; at one time it boasted a sea captain "at the head of every pew on the broad side."

FOR FAMILIES

Amusement Area (465-3581), Salisbury Beach. An old-time carnival boardwalk atmosphere prevails adjacent to 5 miles of beach: arcades, family entertainment center, midway. In the course of researching a *Boston Globe* story on this area in the '60s, Chris was told by a fortune teller here that she would write books, marry a stubborn man, and have three sons; all have come to pass.

SCENIC DRIVES

Amesbury. From Newburyport drive out Merrimac Street to the Chain Bridge. After the bridge bear left onto Main Street and look for **Lowell's Boat Shop** (388-0162), open year-round weekdays 9–5, at 459 Main Street; it's brown shingled and wedged between the road and river. Founded by Simeon Lowell in 1793, it is the country's oldest boat-building shop and has produced some 150,000 boats over the years. Dories and small wooden sailing skiffs are the specialty of the house. It's a sweet-smelling place, filled with boats and men working on them; inquire about workshops and special programs. The shop is administered by the Custom House Museum, and visitors are welcome. Beyond the shop lies the picturesque, small village of Point Shore. Continue along Main Street into the middle of town. The **Bartlett Museum** (388-4528), 270 Main Street, open Memorial Day to Labor Day, Friday through Sunday 1–4, houses an interesting town historical collection, including Native American artifacts. You learn that Amesbury was known as the "Carriage Center of the World" in the late 19th century. The former carriage-mill buildings are under restoration as a shopping and restaurant complex adjoining the **Amesbury Chamber of Commerce** (388-3178) at 5 Market Square (open weekdays 9–3). Also worth searching out, the **Whittier Museum** (388-1337), 86 Friend Street, (open May through October, Tuesday through Saturday 10–4), the home of John

Greenleaf Whittier for 46 years, conveys a genuine sense of the poet and his poems.

West Newbury and Haverhill. From Newburyport drive west on MA 113 to the village of West Newbury. This was a bustling spot until the 19th-century construction of the Chain Bridge prevented larger vessels from sailing this far upriver. Take either Bridge or Church Street to the Rocks Village Bridge (it still has to be opened manually with a capstan for boats to pass) and follow Country Bridge Road (note the old houses in Rocks Village) to MA 110. West on 110 you come to the birthplace of John Greenleaf Whittier (373-3979) at 305 Whittier Road (open May through October, Tuesday through Saturday 10–5; Sunday 1–5; November through April open Saturday 10–5, also Tuesday through Friday and Sunday 1–5; $2 adults, $1 seniors and children), and then to the entrance to **Winnekenni Park,** a former 214-acre estate with Winnekenni Castle (open for special exhibits, concerts, and other events: 521-1681). At the junction with 113 continue west to the **Buttonwoods Museum** (374-4626) at 240 Water Street; this complex includes a shoe shop, an 1814 home furnished to period, and Tenney Hall, housing Native American relics and town exhibits. Continue along the river past 19th-century brick mills and shops all compressed into a relatively small area; this **Washington Street Shoe District** is billed as the finest Queen Anne–style industrial street in America. Try contacting the Greater Haverhill Chamber of Commerce (373-5663).

TO DO

AIR RIDES
Air Plum Island (462-2114), Plum Island Turnpike, offers sightseeing rides. Inquire about helicopter rides, flight instruction, charters, plane rentals; private planes accommodated and serviced.

BICYCLING
The bike paths in Maudslay State Forest and the 7-mile road (6 miles are now hardtopped) through the Parker River reservation on Plum Island are particularly popular.
Aries Sports and Bikery (465-8099; 1-800-501-BIKE), US 1, one mile south of the Newburyport traffic circle. Sales, service, and rentals.

BIRDING
Plum Island has long been recognized as one of the world's better places to view a wide variety of shorebirds and migrating waterfowl.
Newburyport's place on the global birding map dates from the 1985 sighting of the Ross' gull, a rare species associated with Siberia. Dan Rather and the front page of *The New York Times* featured the story, and birders, as well as birds, have been flocking to Newburyport ever since (see Plum Island under *Green Space*). As we go to press, Massachusetts Audubon is completing a major interpretive facility on the Plum Island

Turnpike, due to open in 1996. Two shops cater to birders: **The Bird-watcher of Newburyport** (463-2473) at 50 Water Street (the Tannery) sponsors both guided walks and birding boat tours on the Parker River; and **Birdwalker's Supply** (462-0775) at the US 1 traffic circle also offers guided walks.

BOAT EXCURSIONS

Capt. Bill Taplin (948-2375) runs Yankee Clipper Harbor Tours all summer, departing every hour, 11 AM–6:30 PM from the Boardwalk (wharf next to Hilton's) in Newburyport. $7 adults, $3 children. Special sunset tours and charters.

Merrimack Queen Riverboat (372-3420), a 150-passenger paddle-wheeler, sails Sunday (Memorial Day weekend to mid-October) from the MA 197 bridge in Haverhill. The 4-hour cruise to Newburyport and back costs $12 adults, $6 children.

FISHING

Hilton's Fishing Dock (465-9885; 462-8381), 54 Merrimac Street, Newburyport. There is ample free parking on the wharf and a shop from which you can set out for a full day of fishing. (Also see *Whale-Watching.*)

Capt. Lew (465-9885; 1-800-848-1111) is a 65-foot charter and party boat; tackle and rod rental, heated cabin, passenger limit, sailing April 1 through fall.

Captain's Fishing Parties (462-3141), April through October, Plum Island. Fishing and whale-watching, also weekly dinner cruises.

The *Barracuda* (465-3022), Merrimac Marina, Newburyport. A 28-foot sport-fishing vessel is also available for deep-sea fishing, whale-watching, and cruising; it takes up to six.

GOLF

Evergreen Golf Course (465-3609), 14 Boyd Drive, Newburyport. Nine holes, open to the public daily. **Ould Newbury Golf Club** (462-3737), US 1, Newburyport. Nine holes, open to the public weekday afternoons.

SEA KAYAKING

Adventure Learning (346-9728; 1-800-649-9728), 67 Bear Hill, Merrimac. One-day clinics, weekend tours.

SWIMMING

Salisbury Beach State Reservation (462-4481), off US 1, Salisbury, is a 3.8-mile-long expanse of sand, frequently crowded in summer. Facilities include bathhouses, picnic facilities, boat launch, and interpretive programs (ranging from guided walks to live entertainment). (Also see Plum Island under *Green Space.*)

WHALE-WATCHING

Hilton's Newburyport Whale Watch (465-7165; 1-800-848-1111), Hilton's Fishing Dock, 54 Merrimac Street. April through October. One of the oldest and best known of the region's whalewatch excursions, founded by Scott Mercer, who does much of the narrating. Naturalist-narrated runs depart twice daily July through mid-September, weekends in spring and fall; the vessel is 100 feet.

GREEN SPACE

BEACHES
Plum Island. This stringbean-shaped, 8½-mile-long barrier island is accessible via Water Street, which turns into the Plum Island Turnpike. Beginning in the 1890s when a horsecar line reached Plum Island from downtown Newburyport, this area has been a summer cottage colony. Since the 1940s the southern two-thirds of the island has been maintained as the **Parker River National Wildlife Refuge** (465-5753), a natural landscape of dunes, bog, tidal marsh, and beach. The refuge is open dawn to dusk, year-round; $5 per car, $2 per bicycle or walk-in during warm-weather months. A 7-mile road bisects the refuge, with parking areas strung along its length and access both to the beach and to Parker River at scattered intervals. The beach is closed April through June (tern nesting season), and when it opens parking spaces tend to fill by 10 AM, even in green-fly season (mid-July to mid-August). The beach is famous for surf fishing but is not a good place to bring small children: It's a hike over the dunes, and the surf and undertow are unusually strong. In spring (through early June) and fall (beginning in August and especially in September and October) the refuge makes a good place to watch migrating wildfowl: 300 species of birds have been sighted (see *To Do—Birding*). In winter there is still a surprising number of birds, also deer and rabbits. A self-guiding wildlife trail at Hellcat Swamp (Parkinson #4) is rewarding any time of year. *Warning:* Parking throughout the refuge is limited to 300 cars and it tends to fill up early on many weekends.
Sandy Point State Reservation (462-4881), at the end of the 7-mile gravel access road on Plum Island (see above), is a 72-acre area with a sandy beach backed by rolling dunes and a small hill called Bar Head. Parking is limited to 50 cars (attendants at the gate to the national wildlife refuge keep tabs on availability).
Town of Plum Island Beaches. The 3½ miles of sand north of the wildlife refuge on Plum Island is public, accessible from parking lots scattered among the cottages and a larger one at North Beach at the mouth of the Merrimack River. This is a popular area for fishing and wading out onto the sandbar; beware of currents near the jetty.
WALKS
Maudslay State Park (465-7223), West Newbury. Marked from MA 113: Take Story Lane 1⅔ miles to its junction with Geoffrey Hoyt's Lane; turn right and follow signs. Open year-round, 8–sunset. This 480-acre property includes 19th-century estate gardens, rolling agricultural land, and mountain laurel. It also includes 2 miles of frontage on the Merri-

mack River in one of its loveliest segments. The mansions (one had 72 rooms) are gone, but the formal gardens, designed by Charles Sprague Sargent (who also designed Harvard's Arnold Arboretum in Boston), remain, along with the glorious mountain laurel that inspired John Greenleaf Whittier to write a number of poems, among them "The Laurels" and "June on the Merrimack." Over 16 miles of carriage roads and trails provide hiking, biking, cross-country skiing, and horseback riding. Guided walks are offered spring through fall, and performances by a resident group called Theater in the Open, along with children's theater and concerts, are also staged.

Old Town Hill Reservation. In Newbury turn left off MA 1A at Newman Street—at the far end of the Green, the first left after crossing the Parker River. The Trustees of Reservations own these 230 acres. The steep path takes less than a half hour round-trip, and it is one of the most delightful walks in the state: You climb gradually, following old stone walls and wild rose bushes. Benches are scattered along the way, and the view is not only of Newbury and Plum Island but also as far north as Mount Agamenticus in Maine and south to Cape Ann.

Mosely Pines (465-7336), Merrimac Street near the Chain Bridge; tennis courts, fireplaces for cookouts, swings, play equipment.

Waterfront Park. Two acres and boardwalk at Market Square, landscaped and fitted with benches and gas-style street lights, a favorite spot from which to watch boat traffic.

Newbury Perennial Gardens (462-1144), 18 Liberty Street, Newburyport. Open mid-April through June 8–6 daily, Friday until 8; July through September 10–5 daily. Nominal fee. Begun in 1974, 20 theme gardens are scattered throughout the grounds of a private estate; the Garden Store sells seeds, bulbs, and garden accessories.

LODGING

INNS AND BED & BREAKFASTS
Note: All listings are in Newburyport 01950.

Morrill Place (462-2808), 209 High Street. A three-story, Federal-style mansion built in 1806, Morrill Place offers nine guest rooms (most with private baths). The decor is a mix of formality and fun. Some rooms have sleigh beds, others, four-posters and canopies; a few have fireplaces, and a number have a third bed tucked discreetly in a corner. Guests gather for breakfast and tea around the formal, lace-covered table in the rose-colored dining room but otherwise spread throughout the house. There's a formal parlor, a wicker-filled upstairs TV room, a luxurious library with hearth, a glass-sided winter porch, and a wraparound veranda. Innkeeper Rose Ann Hunter is a warm host who also conducts workshops on innkeeping and brokers inns. Continental breakfast and afternoon tea are included in $82–90 per couple, $55 single.

Clark Currier Inn (465-8363), 45 Green Street. Another classic, three-story Federal mansion, built in 1803, near the heart of Newburyport. The parlor features graceful window arches and a Samuel McIntire mantel and is furnished with wing chairs and appropriate antiques. Guests can also relax in the upstairs library or in a comfortable skylight sitting room off the garden—itself another inviting space with a gazebo and fish pond. A light breakfast of muffins, bread, and fresh fruit is served by the hearth in the dining room. The eight guest rooms all have private baths but vary in shape, decor, and size. The Merrimac Room is fitted for families, the Hale Room features a Franklin stove, and several rooms have canopied beds. Your hosts are Mary and Bob Nolan and their daughter Malissa. $85–125.

The Windsor House (462-3778), 38 Federal Street. Guests gather for full English-style breakfasts around the table in the kitchen of this 18th-century brick house. Afternoon tea is served in the formal common room beneath the portrait of Queen Elizabeth II. Innkeeper Judith Harris is an enthusiastic Anglophile, and John hails from Cornwall. The six guest rooms are all large and four have private baths. The Merchant Suite, originally a chandlery and now a pleasant ground-level room with its own entrance, is usually reserved for guests with pets or children, and upstairs the candy-pink nursery is equipped with a crib and toys as well as a single and a double bed. $85 per couple with shared bath, $99 with private, $180 for a two-room suite sharing a hall bath. Add 15 percent tax and 15 percent service. Additional persons in a room are $25 but under 3 years, free.

Garrison Inn (465-4017), 11 Brown Square. The atmosphere is that of a small, formal hotel (with an elevator and a handicapped-accessible room); built as a residence in 1803, it has been an inn of one sort or another since the turn of the century. The 24 guest rooms (private baths, color TV) are furnished with reproduction antiques; six suites have lofts with spiral or Colonial-style staircases, and a number of rooms have fireplaces. Although the downstairs level is devoted to dining areas (see *Dining Out*), staff are helpful in orienting and otherwise serving guests. $85 per room, from $135 per suite.

Essex Street Inn (465-3148), 7 Essex Street. Feels like an apartment house rather than an inn (no public space), but all 17 rooms are air-conditioned, with private baths, antiques. One-room suites have a fireplace and whirlpool; two-room suites have fireplaces, kitchen, and deck. $55–155.

Market Street Inn (465-5816), 22 Market Street. Apartment-sized suites with kitchens; includes maid service, backyard, cable TV. Rent by the week or month, also by the night if available. No smoking. No pets. $1050–1200 a month; $350–440 per week; $75–95 per night.

CAMPGROUNDS

Salisbury Beach State Reservation (462-4481), MA 1A, Salisbury, offers more than 500 campsites for trailers on a first-come, first-served basis.

WHERE TO EAT

DINING OUT

Scandia Restaurant (462-6271), 25 State Street, Newburyport. Open Monday through Friday, lunch and dinner; Saturday, dinner only; Sunday, brunch and dinner. This storefront dining room is quite elegant with white tablecloths and fresh flowers, blue walls, and antique mirrors. It's a popular spot for soups, salads, and sandwiches at lunch, and the weekday buffet (not offered every day) is one of the best values in town. Dinner entrées range from $9.95 for black pepper pasta Putennesca (seasoned with garlic, anchovies, onion, tomato, and black olives) to $16.95 for veal and lobster sauté or steak Diane (flamed with brandy and topped with scallions, mushrooms, Dijon, and parsley).

David's Restaurant (462-8077), 11 Brown Square, Newburyport. Downstairs, in the brick-walled basement, the mood and menu are informal; upstairs it's quite elegant. Here is a place you can bring the kids anytime because there's a nursery with a big-screen TV, games, and kid food (children must be 18 months; the charge is $5). You might dine on oysters baked with sun-dried tomatoes and spinach cream, followed by crisp boneless breast of duck carved over apple sage stuffing and dressed with cranberry port wine sauce; entrées are $15.95–21.00.

Joseph's Winter Street Cafe (462-1188), 22 Winter Street, Newburyport. Open Monday through Saturday from 5:30, Sunday from noon. The food and atmosphere are Italian. A locally favored dining place with standout veal dishes, choices like grilled shrimp and prosciutto, calamari, and penne pasta. Live jazz on Sunday afternoons.

Ten Center Street (462-6652), 10 Center Street, Newburyport. Open for lunch and dinner daily. An 18th-century mansion with informal Molly's Pub downstairs and a more formal white-tablecloth dining room upstairs with specialties like veal Firenza ($19.95); entrées range from pastas ($14.50) to twin filet mignon béarnaise ($21.95).

Glenn's Galley (465-3811), 44 Merrimac Street, Newburyport. "World class cuisine in a funky casual atmosphere," clean and modern with exquisite food and plating; specializes in dishes cooked on a wood-fired grill like bourbon pecan chicken.

Amesbury House (388-5249), 62 Haverhill Road (MA 110), Amesbury. Open for lunch and dinner weekdays, dinner on weekends. fine dining and an extensive wine list; specialties include fresh seafood, beef, and poultry. $11.95–16.95 for dinner.

EATING OUT

Captain's Quarters Restaurant (462-3397), 54R Merrimac Street, Market Square, Newburyport. Open 5 AM–9 PM, Sunday through Thursday; until 10 PM Friday and Saturday. Our favorite place on the waterfront: deep booths, decks, right on the water; burgers and sandwiches around

$5.50, seafood dinners from $13.95. Seafood marinara with fresh mussels, shrimp, scallops, and haddock over linguine is $14.95.

The Grog Shop (465-8008), 13 Middle Street, Newburyport. Open for lunch and dinner daily. Usually crowded in the less formal pub space downstairs; slower-paced but the same menu upstairs in a living room setting with a hearth. You can lunch on pasta or burgers, dine on a selection of seafood, pasta, and Mexican dishes; try the Key lime pie. Nightclub entertainment downstairs after 8 PM.

Michael's Harborside (462-7785), Tournament Wharf (under the Salisbury bridge), Newburyport. Open for lunch and dinner. An informal place right on the water; fried and broiled seafood, chowder. Mixed reviews.

Fowle's Restaurant (465-0141), 17 State Street, Newburyport. Open 6 AM–6 PM Monday through Friday; from 7 AM on weekends until 6 PM Saturday, 1 PM Sunday. Sit at the marble counter or in a small booth. This is a 1930s combination of a magazine and tobacco store with soda fountain; its art deco fountain (complete with an intricate wooden scene behind the counter) has been spiffed up, and the menu has tipped to sprouts, veggies, and whole-grain muffins. The soups are all hearty, fresh-made, and the sodas come in ice cream parlor glasses.

The Mall (465-5506), corner of High and Green Streets, Newburyport. Open for lunch and dinner. Pronounced "Mal," this local dining landmark caters to families, with tablecloths that kids can draw on; reasonably priced, varied menu ranging from West Indian to Mexican.

Ciro's Restaurant (463-3335), 1 Market Square, Newburyport. Open for lunch and dinner. One in a chain of local Italian restaurants: slick, good food, reasonable prices, great location in the firehouse with outside dining on the waterfront park in season. Pizza, calzones, and pasta dishes.

Jacob Marley's Restaurant (465-5598), 22 Pleasant Street Newburyport. Open for lunch and dinner. A large, family-geared place with a large menu ranging from Mexican through pizza and pastas to burgers, sandwiches, lots of greens, children's menu. Sunday buffet brunch 11–2.

The Agawam Diner (948-7780), US 1, near the junction with MA 133 in Rowley. Open daily 5 AM–12:30 AM. A chrome classic. Breakfast is served all day, and there are blue-plate specials, homemade cream and fruit pies, reasonably priced fried clams and shrimp.

Abraham's Bagels (465-8148), 11 Liberty Street, Newburyport. Open 6 AM to early afternoon. A distribution bakery—great bagels and other bakery basics.

Szechuan Taste & Thai Cafe (463-0686), 19 Pleasant Street, Newburyport. Open daily for lunch and dinner until midnight, except Friday and Saturday, when it closes at 1 AM. This attractive restaurant does not use MSG and offers an unusually wide choice of Chinese dishes, especially seafood. Try the fresh scallops with ginger sauce.

Taffy's (465-9039), corner of State Street and Prince Place, Newburyport.

Open Monday through Saturday 4 AM–2:30 PM, in winter, 4 AM–2 PM. Little changed since it opened 45 years ago, this old-fashioned luncheonette with a counter and booths is clean, friendly, and cheap. Try the soups of the day or luncheon special.

SNACKS

Middle Street Foods (465-8333), 25 Middle Street, Newburyport. Open daily 7 AM–8 PM. A great little white-and-blue bakery and café with pressed-tin walls. The menu features soups and vegetarian dishes like spinach pie and roasted eggplant.

Gretta's Great Grains (465-1709), 24 Pleasant Street, Newburyport. Open 7:30–5. A bakery featuring fragrant, good-for-you breads and muffins; some tables and coffee.

ENTERTAINMENT

The Firehouse Center for the Performing Arts (462-7336) is a vintage 1823 firehouse in Market Square, Newburyport, that now includes a 195-seat theater, two art galleries, and a restaurant (Ciro's). Year-round productions (Wednesday through Sunday) include a wide variety of concerts and plays, also children's theater. Contact the box office (open daily, varying hours) for a current calendar; tickets are rarely more than $12.

The Playhouse Dinner Theater (388-9444), 109 Main Street, Amesbury (town parking lot off MA 150); near the junction of I-95 and I-495 (Exit 54). Performances by a resident troupe of 60 actors; classics like *Arsenic and Old Lace* and *Can-Can*.

The Screening Room (462-3456), 82 State Street, Newburyport. A small, unusually comfortable cinema specializing in classic flicks.

SELECTIVE SHOPPING

ANTIQUES

No fewer than 15 antiques stores can be found within a half-dozen downtown blocks: Federal, Water, State, and Merrimac Streets. Pick up a list at any store.

ART GALLERIES

The Newburyport Art Association (465-8769), 65 Water Street, Newburyport. Open daily 1–5 except Monday. The gallery shows and sells works by members.

Piel Craftsmen Company (462-7012), 307 High Street, Newburyport. Open weekdays 8:30–noon, 1–4:30. Visitors are welcome to watch shop models of 1800s ships made by hand.

BIRDING

Birdwatcher's Supply (462-0775), US 1 traffic circle, Newburyport. Open daily 9–6, until 8 Thursday. Books, feeders, etc.; guided walks offered.

The Birdwatcher of Newburyport (462-2473), 50 Water Street in the

Tannery. Birding supplies, bird feeders; guided walks and boat tours on the Parker River.

BOOKSTORES

Jabberwocky (465-9359), the Tannery, 12 Federal Street, Newburyport. Open Monday through Saturday until 9 PM, Sunday noon–6. A large, full-service bookstore with an adjoining café.

Middle Street Bookstore (463-2000), 3 Middle Street, Newburyport. A small store with a large selection of titles.

The Book Rack (462-8615), 52 State Street, Newburyport. A full-service bookstore.

Old Port Book Shop (462-0100), 18 State Street, Newburyport. Open daily. In addition to 18,000 of its own antiquarian titles, 15 dealers from around New England are also represented.

FARM STANDS

Long Hill Orchard (363-5545), Main Street (MA 113), West Newbury. Open daily, year-round. Own vegetables in-season, apples, cider, peaches, pears, blueberries, jams, honey.

Tender Crop Farm (462-6972), High Road (MA 1A), Newbury. Open spring through Christmas. Home of "Buffy the Buffalo" as well as home-grown fruits, seasonal vegetables, dried flowers, nursery plants.

SHOPPING COMPLEXES

State Street and the **Inn Street Mall.** The lower State Street shops back on delightful pedestrian courts and more shops. The buildings themselves, all built of sturdy brick after an 1811 fire destroyed this area, are wonderful places to browse.

The Tannery (465-7047), 12 Federal Street; a pleasant indoor mall with some 30 specialty shops: antiques, flowers, books, and clothing.

SEAFOOD

David's Fish Market (462-2504), Bridge Road (MA 1 a mile or so beyond the bridge), Salisbury. Open daily 8–6. This white cinderblock building should be the last stop on every day-tripper's list; the fish is flapping fresh, and you can get fish stock and chowder fish as well as lobsters from the tank and native shellfish at good prices.

SPECIAL EVENTS

May: **Spring Wildlife Plover Festival** at Parker River National Wildlife Refuge, Maudslay State Park, and throughout the city. **Custom House Antique Show** at Plum Island Airport. **Salmagundi Fair**—craft fair; Sunday, Monday of Memorial Day weekend, includes food, dancing.

June: **Garden Tour,** sponsored by Cushing House.

July through August: **Yankee Homecoming**—last week in July, climaxing first weekend in August. Races, contests, sidewalk sales, concerts, buggy rides, fireworks.

September: **Annual Country Auction** at Upper Green, Newbury. High-quality antiques, collectibles, and books attract bidders from throughout New England.

October: **Fall Harvest Festival,** Sunday and Monday of Columbus Day weekend—craftsmen, performances, food, farm exhibits.

November: Santa parade, tree lighting.

December: Choral concerts and candlelight services, caroling, and open houses at shops.

The Merrimack Valley

LOWELL

In the 1980s this brick mill city enjoyed a rebirth as sudden as its 1820s birth. Because Lowell was the country's first major industrial city, its more than 5 miles of canals and several of its mammoth brick mills were restored to form a National Historical Park. Trolleys now shuttle visitors from exhibit to multimedia exhibit, and in summer tour boats ply the canals.

An introductory film dramatizes the way Boston merchant Francis Cabot Lowell memorized the mechanics of the power looms he viewed on a visit to Britain in 1810. At the time only cotton yarn—not cloth—was being manufactured in the US, and upon his return Lowell was able to produce cloth—from bale to bolt—in a factory in Waltham on the Charles River. His Boston Manufacturing Company quickly outgrew its power source, and in 1821 some 400 acres surrounding a major drop in the Merrimack River was selected as a site for an entire company-planned town of mills.

By 1836 Lowell boasted eight major textile mills, employing 7500 workers. By 1855, after completion of the world's largest waterpower canal system, 9000 women and 4000 men were producing more than 2 million yards of cloth a week. The women were Yankee girls who had come from upcountry farms to live together in tidy boardinghouses; they were well paid and spent their limited free time attending lectures, reading, and writing. This was the Lowell that drew sightseers from Davy Crockett to Charles Dickens, but it was short-lived.

By the 1850s other mill towns had emerged, many established by the same "Boston Associates" who had developed Lowell. Competition soon forced longer hours, lower wages. Yankee mill girls were replaced at the looms by immigrant families willing to accept work at any pay and to live in the flimsy wooden tenements that mushroomed around town. Irish families arrived in the 1850s, French Canadians in the 1860s and 1870s, and Greek, Polish, and East European families in the 1890s and early 1900s. By the turn of the century mill hands were working a

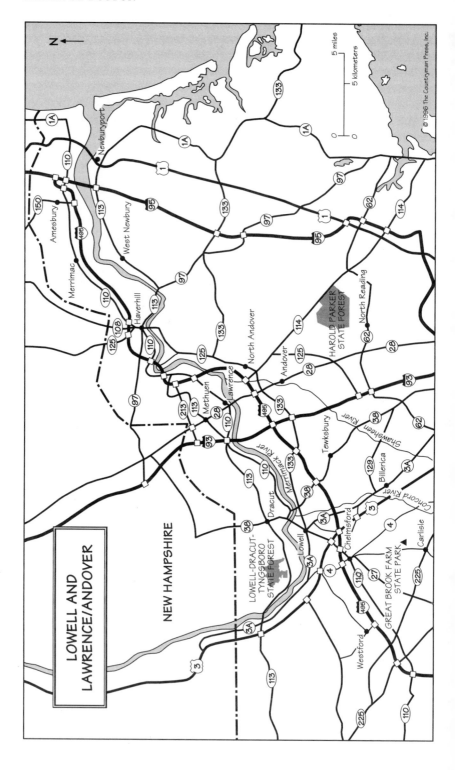

Trolley car in Lowell

72-hour week for $5 or less. A major strike in 1912 brought some con-cessions. The city's population, with its 40 nationalities, peaked during World War I at 126,000.

Textile companies, however, soon began transferring their opera-tions to the South to take advantage of cheaper labor. Then came the Depression, and one mammoth mill after another closed. The World War II demand for cloth and munitions brought a short reprieve, but by the 1950s Lowell itself looked like a war zone, filled with crumbling brick buildings—obvious targets for urban renewal.

It was school principal Patrick J. Mogan who first fired residents with the idea that Lowell had a history so special that it deserved a national park. Business leaders and local politicians rallied to the cause, and the Lowell National Historical Park was established in 1978. In the 1980s more than 100 downtown buildings were rehabilitated, attract-ing a variety of tenants. The University of Massachusetts at Lowell (formed in 1975 when Lowell State College and Lowell Technological Institute merged) also expanded, becoming a palpable downtown presence.

In the 1990s, however, Lowell has been among the communities hardest hit by the recession. Beyond its restored core it remains a city of recent immigrants. The latest arrivals are from Cambodia, Laos, Latin America, and the Caribbean.

Visitors are surprised by the present quality and quantity of the national park exhibits. In Building #6 in the Boott Mills, the center-piece of the national park, visitors are greeted with the deafening clat-ter of 88 belt-driven power looms and must pass through this "weave room" to reach the elaborate displays upstairs. Exhibits in the neighboring Boarding House are devoted to Lowell's workers from the 1830s through today.

Park rangers offer a variety of narrated tours year-round. Seasonal tours combine boat and trolley rides. You might request self-guiding walks to the canals and the river (be sure to at least drive by mighty Pawtucket Falls) and to sites in town connected with Lowell-born and -bred author Jack Kerouac. Note the annual Lowell Celebrates Kerouac festivities in autumn.

AREA CODE
508

GUIDANCE
The National Park Visitors Center (970-5000), 246 Market Street, open daily 8:30–5. The place to phone before you come and to check into as soon as you arrive for an idea of the day's tour and events schedule.

GETTING THERE
By train and bus: MBTA Commuter Service offers frequent daily service from Boston's North Station (227-5070) to the Charles A. Gallagher Transportation Terminal (459-7101) on Thorndike Street, also the local depot for Trailways and Vermont Transit. Shuttle service to downtown Lowell runs every 15 minutes Monday through Saturday.

By car from Boston: Either MA 128 to US 3 or I-93 to I-495; either way, exit onto the Lowell Connector and follow signs for the park visitors center at Market Mills; free parking in back.

GETTING AROUND
From March through November, classy replica 1901 trolleys, powered by an electric overhead line, shuttle between the visitors center and other points of interest like the Boott and Suffolk Mills and Lower Locks; open-sided cars are used in warmer months. The distance between the visitors center and Boott Mill is actually just a short and interesting walk.

MEDICAL EMERGENCY
Saints Memorial Medical Center (453-1761), 220 Pawtucket Street (west end of Merrimack Street), 24-hour emergency service.

TO SEE

Note: All places are in Lowell unless otherwise indicated.

National Park Visitors Center and Tours (470-5000), 246 Market Street, in the former Lowell Manufacturing Company Mill Complex, now called "Market Mills." A multi-image slide show, "Lowell: The Industrial Revelation" (presented twice each hour), describes the dramatic rise of Lowell as well as its factory system, its turn-of-the-century excesses and rich ethnic life, as well as its subsequent decline. Here you also sign up for one of the day's tours (it's best to call ahead to reserve a spot).

An operating gatehouse on the canal within Lowell National Historical Park

Boott Cotton Mills Museum. Open daily 9:30–4, admission $3 adults, $2 seniors, $1 youths, children 5 and under free. Visitors are startled by the noise and vibration of the 88 looms (earplugs are available); walk the length of the room reading quotations by workers; just 6 looms here now actually produce cloth, reproduction Boott Mills towels that are sold in the museum store. These particular looms were first used in Fall River and later in Tennessee. You learn that when the Boott Mills first opened in the 1830s each weaver tended 2 looms, but a century later it was common to assign 20 looms to each weaver. At the far end of the Weave Room, stairs lead to the second floor (there's also an elevator) with its elaborate displays describing the transition from pre-industrial to industrial society; "Wheels of Change," a 24-minute, nine-projector slide program, also tells the story, and another exhibit, "Lowell Heyday: Bale to Bolt," details the production process. Another room depicts an empty mill room and videos present workers' memories of the city in decline. A final room theoretically presents Lowell as it is today.

Elsewhere in the Boott Mills: Check to see whether the **New England Folklife Center** (970-5190), located on the fifth floor, is open. Note that the **Tsongas Industrial History Center** (970-5080) offers a variety of hands-on, experiential exhibits.

Working People Exhibit at the Patrick J. Mogan Cultural Center, 40 French Street. Open same hours as Boott Mills. Free. Housed in the vintage-1836 boardinghouse adjacent to the Boott Mills, this is one of 70 boardinghouses built and operated by Lowell's original textile corporations. The tables are set for a meal, and you hear invisible girls discussing their lives. Extensive exhibits upstairs draw you on into another part of the center, all depicting actual workers, from mill girls through a variety of immigrants; part of the gallery is devoted to changing exhibits.

The New England Quilt Museum (452-4207), 18 Shattuck Street, Lowell. Open Monday through Saturday 10–4 and Sunday noon–4. Closes earlier November to May. $3 adults, $2 seniors and students. Changing exhibits, crafts gift store.

Whistler House (452-7641), 243 Worthen Street, one block from the National Park Visitors Center. Open June through August, Tuesday through Saturday 11–4, Sunday 1–4; September through May, Wednesday through Saturday 11–4, Sunday 1–4; closed major holidays. Built in 1823, this house served as home for three years to Major George Washington Whistler, the engineer charged with supervising construction of the locomotives for a rail line between Lowell and Boston. His son James Abbott was born here in 1834, but never returned when he left at age 3.

Here you learn that James's artistic training began in St. Petersburg (his father supervised construction of the railroad from there to Moscow beginning in 1843) and that he later attended West Point (like his father) but was discharged for failing chemistry and getting too many demerits. He went on to become a celebrated artist, living in Paris and London. Since 1908 this building has housed the Lowell Art Association; rooms display late-19th-century landscapes and portraits from the collection, and the adjacent Parker Gallery stages changing exhibits.

Jack Kerouac's Lowell. From the National Park Visitors Center pick up a descriptive map/guide to sites associated with Jack Kerouac, born March 12, 1922, in the Centraville section of Lowell. The writer's Underwood typewriter and backpack are exhibited, with copies of his most famous works (*On the Road* and *Mexico City Blues*) in the Working People Exhibit at the Patrick J. Mogan Cultural Center. He frequented the City Library, the Worthen (still on Dutton Street), and Nicky's Bar (now La Boniche) on Gorham Street. Kerouac's grave is in the Sampas family plot at the Edson Cemetery (corner of Gorham Street and the Lowell Connector). Kerouac, who died in 1969, draws an increasing number of fans from around the world to Lowell; for details about the series of exhibits, poetry readings, and musical performances honoring him in autumn, phone 441-3800.

Pawtucket Falls. This 30-foot drop is impressive, best viewed from the Pawtucket Canal Gatehouse, School Street.

The Acre. Bounded by Merrimack and Dummer Streets. The city's oldest and most densely settled immigrant neighborhood is constantly changing. Begin with the Whistler House and walk a couple of blocks, checking out the ethnic restaurants and markets.

The Butterfly Place (392-0955), 120 Tyngsboro Road, Westford. Exit 34 on US 3 North from Lowell. Also accessible from I-495, Exit 32. Call for directions. Open mid-April to Columbus Day. $6 adults, $5 seniors and children over age 3. A 3100-square-foot atrium with 122-foot-high walls that then taper to make a 27-foot-high peak is filled with flowering plants and some 500 butterflies said to represent 40 species.

CHURCHES

St. Anne's Episcopal Church, corner of Merrimack and Kirk Streets and built in 1825, is supposedly haunted by the first minister, who sided with the rebellious mill girls (who refused to pay tithes to the church as they were ordered). It's also said to be built from stone excavated during the construction of the Merrimack Canal. Note the stained-glass windows by Tiffany.

St. Joseph The Workers Shrine in the Lee Street Church (between Kirk and John Streets, one block north of Merrimack). Built in 1850 of the same stone as St. Anne's, the shrine was originally a Universalist church but later was bought by the Boston archdiocese to be the state's first French-Canadian church. More than anywhere else in downtown Lowell, you get the sense of the people who still live here.

St. Patrick's Church (459-0561), 282 Suffolk Street. The city's oldest church and the center for the Irish community; inquire at the National Park Visitors Center about periodic tours.

TO DO

Lowell National Historical Park Tours (970-5000). Programs are offered year-round, departing from the visitors center (see *To See*). Reservations are strongly advised. Walking tours follow portions of the canalway trails, explore ethnic neighborhoods and churches, and include boat rides on portions of the canal system. $3 for adults, $2 for seniors, $1 for youths (6–16) for narrated boat and trolley tours offered several times daily June through Columbus Day.

SWIMMING

Privately operated **Wyman's Beach** (692-6287) in Westford offers swimming, camping, and picnicking. A public beach on the Merrimac at the Bellegrade Boathouse is due to open.

CROSS-COUNTRY SKIING

Great Brook Farm Ski Touring Center (369-6312), Lowell Street, Carlisle. Open in ski season daily 9 AM–4:40 PM, until 9 PM Tuesday and Thursday; 12 groomed miles of trails, instruction, rental equipment, night skiing on a 1.5-kilometer loop. Located on a working dairy farm.

GREEN SPACE

Vandenberg Esplanade River Front Park, Pawtucket Boulevard, Lowell, is a 2.5-mile paved walkway with benches and landscaped lawns along the north bank of the Merrimack River, maintained by the Department of Environmental Management (DEM). The Sampas Pavilion stage is the site of live performances, and the boathouse offers community sailing and rowing programs.

Lowell Waterpower Trail. A system of trails, called canalways, has been laid out to guide you around the canal system. This 3-mile walk links the visitors center and the Boott Cotton Mills via two spurs along the canals and travels past the mills to Pawtucket Dam and the Vandenberg Esplanade. Request the printed guide from the visitors center.

Lowell-Dracut-Tyngsboro State Forest (452-7191), Trotting Park Road off Varnum Avenue, Lowell. This 997-acre park sports a 30-acre lake for skating and fishing, picnicking and scenic trails for hiking, cross-country skiing, and bicycling. A spring and the springhouse were used by a former bottling works. Granite from the forest's quarries was a resource for mill foundations and canal embankments.

Great Brook Farm State Park (369-6312), Lowell Road, Carlisle. Open meadows, wooded trails, and a scenic pond, 15 miles of hiking trails, a working dairy that sells ice cream, and a ski-touring center in winter. From Lowell take MA 110 South to MA 4 through Chelmsford. South of the village the road splits; bear right where MA 4 bears left (Lowell Road). The 950-acre park is on the left just over the Carlisle line.

Carlisle State Forest (369-6312), Forest Road, Carlisle. A 22-acre area, this former estate is webbed with hiking and touring trails.

Warren Manning State Park (369-6312), Chelmsford Road, Billerica, MA 129. A 380-acre wooded spread with picnic tables, a children's spray pool, bridle paths, hiking trails.

LODGING

HOTEL

Sheraton Inn, Lowell (452-1200), 50 Warren Street, Lowell 01852, at the Lower Locks. A 251-room hotel overlooking the Pawtucket Canal, within walking distance of all the park sites and downtown shops. Facilities include a swim and fitness club, two restaurants, and two lounges. Packages begin at $49 per couple.

BED & BREAKFASTS

Note: The following B&Bs are located in Lowell's two posh Victorian neighborhoods, Belvedere and the Highlands, both set high above the downtown.

Sherman-Berry House (459-4760), 163 Dartmouth Street, Lowell 01851. David Stromeyer and Susan Scott have furnished their spacious house with Victoriana, but it is not the least bit stuffy. Three comfortable rooms. $50 double, $40 single, $10 surcharge for a 1-night stay.

The Barnes House (453-9763), 30 Huntington Street, Lowell 01852. Judy Hayden's stately old house in the Belvedere section offers three rooms.

Coddington Hall (454-1763), 353 Wilder Street, Lowell 01851. Linda

Coddington offers one or two rooms, one with double bed and private bath; the second room is good for an accompanying child. Breakfast served, kitchen privileges.

WHERE TO EAT

DINING OUT
Note: All restaurants are in Lowell. Be forewarned that the names of places change frequently in Lowell but the quality and value of the ethnic restaurants—which actually serve the communities they represent—remain outstanding.

La Boniche (458-9473), 110 Gorham Street. Open for lunch Tuesday through Friday and dinner Tuesday through Saturday. Jack Kerouac frequented this place when it was a bar called Nicky's. In its present incarnation this is exactly the kind of culinary find you don't expect in Lowell: a sophisticated and informal French restaurant. You can lunch handsomely on the soup and pasta or pizza of the day and dine on pan-fried shrimp or grilled chicken and penne, saving room for memorable desserts. The wine list is exclusively French. Entrées $13.50–18.50.

The Speare House (452-7191), 525 Pawtucket Boulevard, is one of the city's leading Greek restaurants. Closed Monday, otherwise open for lunch and dinner. The decor is plush medieval and the large menu, Greek/American. This was *the* place to eat in Lowell for a long time and continues to be the place where business deals are made and special occasions celebrated. Dinner will run you $21–30 per person.

Athenian Corner (458-7052), 207 Market Street. Open daily for lunch and dinner, boasting the "largest variety of fine Greek food in New England." Handy to the park's visitors center, daily luncheon specials ($4.50–5.95), dinner entrées from $7.50. The menu is classic Greek, and the specialty is shish kabob. The music on weekends can be lively.

Cobblestones (970-2282), 91 Dutton Street, near the Merrimack Gatehouse and St. Anne's Church. A former agent's mansion is now a large, fairly formal restaurant that's surprisingly reasonable in price for dinner; smoked chicken and wild mushrooms tossed with fettucine and cashews in cream is $11.95, and roast pork loin is $9.95. The bar side is pleasant.

EATING OUT
Diners

Arthur's (452-8647), 112 Bridge Street. Also known as the Paradise Grill. A shabby but friendly and clean diner, source of one of the best pastrami sandwiches we've ever had; the Boott Mill sandwich will set you up for the day.

Club Diner (452-1679), 145 Dutton Street, across from the visitors center. Open Monday through Friday 11 AM–3 PM, closing Sunday at 12 PM. The yellow-bodied classic, here since 1933, was owned by Mlle le

Vasseur from 1928 until 1962 and is still in the family. Red Jell-O, baked stuffed haddock, stuffed peppers, coffee in heavy mugs, clean and friendly.

Four Sisters Owl Diner (453-8321), 244 Appletown Street. Open 6 AM–2 PM. Diner buffs will recognize this place as a "Semi-streamer," and in Lowell it's an institution. Note the artwork in the dining room. Reliable food and atmosphere.

Other

Southeast Asian Restaurant (452-3182), 351 Market Street. Open daily 8 AM–7:30 PM. Thai, Laotian, Cambodian, and Vietnamese specialties, all made from scratch. Descriptions of the exotic dishes are detailed on the menu, but you might also take advantage of the luncheon buffet ($5.95) and dinner buffets (Monday, Tuesday, Wednesday: $9.95).

Cong Ly, 124 Merrimack Street. Reasonably priced buffet, specializing in Vietnamese noodle soups. A very popular place with the local Vietnamese community.

Bombay Mahal (441-2222), 45 Middle Street. Authentic Indian menu. Monday through Saturday, northern Indian traditional dishes are the specialty, but Sunday brunches feature southern Indian food. Beer and wine.

Dubliner (459-9831), 197 Market Street. Open daily except Sunday for lunch and dinner, around the corner from the park's visitors center. An Irish pub atmosphere featuring sandwiches, steaks, and seafood—all day.

The Brewery Exchange (937-1200), 199/201 Cabot Street. Open weekdays for lunch, Tuesday through Saturday for dinner, noon–8 on Sunday. Home of the Lowell Brewing Company, a pleasant pub with good food and brew.

The Melting Pot, 246 Market Street in the Market Mills complex, adjacent to the visitors center. Mall-type counters selling Greek, American, Italian, and Mexican foods, which you consume at tables or in the courtyard.

The Old Worthen Tavern (458-3132), open Monday through Saturday for lunch. The city's oldest tavern and bar; a genuine neighborhood bar but obviously conscious of its status as a former Jack Kerouac haunt. The window proclaims, "Historic Tours Welcome"; inquire about Kerouac nights.

Mill-Town Deli (937-3876), corner of Middle and Palmer Streets. Open 6:30 AM–4:30 PM Monday through Saturday. Daily specials, homey, busy.

ENTERTAINMENT

Note: The **Lowell Office of Cultural Affairs** (441-3800) publishes a bimonthly calendar of events and serves as a constant source of information about ongoing entertainment.

Merrimack Repertory Theatre (454-3926), Liberty Hall, 50 East

Merrimack Street, Lowell. A professional equity theater presenting a full program of plays; also special summer events.

University of Massachusetts/Lowell Center for the Arts (934-4444), Durgin Hall, South Campus, Pawtucket and Wilder Streets. A performance series that includes top-flight Broadway productions, children's entertainment, and musical groups.

Boarding House Park Summer Performance Series (441-3800), French Street at Boott Mills. The outdoor stage here serves as a lively performance center on summer weekends.

Lowell Memorial Auditorium (454-2854), East Merrimack Street, Lowell. The theater seats 1200 and is the frequent stage for nationally known groups and Broadway shows, as well as for world-class wrestling matches.

SELECTIVE SHOPPING

Note: Unless otherwise noted, all shops are in Lowell.

A Brush with History (459-7819), 246 Market Street, across the courtyard from the park's visitors center, includes 12 studios and a gallery. Open Tuesday through Sunday 11–5, Thursday until 9 PM.

Wells Emporium (454-4401), 169 Merrimack Street. Hand-crafted gifts.

Hub Mills Factory Outlet (937-0320), 12 Perkins Street (off Cabot Street). Closed Sunday and Monday. Wool, mohair, cotton, and silk yarns; wool sweaters, blankets, and lingerie.

Parrot Hat Shop (453-4622), 73 Middlesex Street. Billing themselves as New England's largest hatters, this great shop has been in business since 1923.

George's Textile Company (452-0878), 360 Merrimack Street. A find for anyone looking for fabrics; great selection and prices. Note the wall of old Lowell photographs.

Cote's Market (458-4635), Salem Street. A French-Canadian market with prepackaged specialties like bread pudding and baked beans.

BOOKSTORE

Paperback Booksmith (256-3514) Chelmsford Mall, 265 Chelmsford Street, Chelmsford. General selection of hard cover and paperback books.

SPECIAL EVENTS

April: **Thoreau's Portage Whitewater Invitational Slalom**—the New England championships, with members of the US Whitewater Racing Team and other kayak and canoeists running the rapids on the Concord in Lowell; a great spectator event.

Mid-April: **Cambodian New Year** is April 13, celebrated with a 3-day festival of rituals, music, and games.

July: **July 4th Celebration. Lowell Folk Festival** (last weekend), the city's biggest weekend of the year, draws thousands of visitors for traditional folk music, dance, parades, crafts, ethnic food; performances are on five outdoor stages and along the canals, on downtown streets.

September: **Banjo and fiddle contests** at Market Mills (Saturday after Labor Day).

October: **Lowell Celebrates Kerouac!** Exhibits, poetry readings, musical performance.

November: **Lowell's City Lights Celebration** begins the weekend after Thanksgiving.

December 31: **Family First Night.**

LAWRENCE/ANDOVER

In 1845 the Essex Company selected a rural stretch of land along the Merrimack River, known as Deer Jump Falls, as a site on which to build a planned mill town. By 1847 Lawrence (named for Abbot Lawrence, a partner in the company) was incorporated, and its population zoomed to 3550. By 1848 the company had already built the Great Dam, which still stands, as well as two canals, a machine shop to build locomotives, the Prospect Hill reservoir, 50 brick buildings, a large boardinghouse, and the Atlantic Cotton, Pemberton, Upper Pacific, and Duck Mills. The Essex Company also conscientiously planted elms, laid out a Common and parks, and built its mills and workers' boardinghouses solidly. By 1850 the 6-square-mile town boasted 11 schools and a lecture series that drew Emerson and Melville.

This town was the Lawrence that attracted trainloads of Bostonians to breathe its clean air and stroll its handsome streets—and it vanished quickly. In 1860 the five-story Pemberton Mill collapsed, killing 88 and seriously injuring 116 more, an ominous sign of things to come as the town doubled and redoubled its size. Cramped wooden "four-deckers" housed immigrants from Italy, Germany, Britain, Russia, Austria, Poland, and Syria, among other places. Those born in the city rarely lived beyond 40, if they survived infancy. The whole sorry scene became one of national concern with the "Bread and Roses Strike" of 1912.

At the time of the strike, the city was the "worsted center of the world," a city of 86,000 in which 74,000 were foreign born or of foreign parentage. In the wake of the strike, wages increased slightly, and immigration dropped off, largely because an investigation of conditions in Lawrence led to the passage of a federal quota law.

The city's population today is 73,000, and it continues to attract new arrivals from Southeast Asia and Latin America. Hispanics now account for more than 40 percent of the total population. It remains one of the country's most vividly ethnic cities.

Many visitors come to Lawrence to shop in its factory stores—not the kind of slick "outlets" you find by the dozen these days, but shops selling quality products that haven't yet left the building in which they were made. The factories are in the mills lining the river and power canals, most on or near Canal Street, which is well marked from the highway and nicely landscaped—thanks on both counts to the Lawrence Heritage State Park.

This park is one of the most successful among the nine Heritage State Parks founded in Massachusetts since the late 1970s. Housed in a canalside, 1840s mill boardinghouse, it tells the city's story and also serves as a visitors information center for the area and a community center for Lawrence.

From the Heritage State Park, request directions to the museums and historic houses across the river in Andover and North Andover. Within a few miles of the city's colossal brick mills, you can pick peaches on a centuries-old farm or view Americana at a prestigious prep school museum or in a colonial-era house set in a rural Yankee village.

AREA CODE
508
GUIDANCE
Lawrence Heritage State Park Visitors Center (794-1655), One Jackson Street, corner of Canal. Open daily 9–4.
Merrimack Valley Chamber of Commerce (686-9900) in Lawrence furnishes publications and information by phone.
GETTING THERE
By train: The T Commuter Service (617-722-3200; 1-800-392-6100) terminal is a reasonable walk across the Casey Bridge from the canal area sites.
By car: I-495, Exit 45, follow "Downtown" and Heritage State Park signs.
PARKING
The Heritage State Park has a parking lot. Follow signs.
MEDICAL EMERGENCY
Lawrence General Hospital (685-2151), 1 General Street.

TO SEE

In Lawrence
Lawrence Heritage State Park (794-1655), One Jackson Street. Open daily 9–4. The 1847 brick boardinghouse contains two full floors of exhibits depicting life from the point of view of the various immigrant groups (totaling more than 50) that have worked in the mills. A video depicts the 1912 Bread and Roses strike, and displays include a tenement kitchen; the third floor doubles as a gallery, with changing exhibits and a theater running regularly scheduled performances.
Phillips Academy Museums, Main Street (MA 28), Andover. Founded in

1778, this academy is one of the country's leading prep schools, with a college-sized (450 acres) campus. **Addison Gallery of American Art** (457-7515), closed August, otherwise open daily except Monday 10–5, Sunday 2:30–5. Note that the collection includes only American art, and you might want to call ahead to ask what's on display; shows change frequently. Don't miss the collection of exquisite ships models in the basement. **Robert S. Peabody Foundation of Archeology** (749-4990), Phillips and Main Streets. Open Tuesday through Friday 10–5, closed most holidays. Collections of shards and Native American implements unearthed in digs around the region and in the Southwest. This is a teaching museum and only 1 percent of the collection is on view at any one time.

HISTORIC HOUSES

Andover Historical Society (475-2236), 97 Main Street, Andover. Open Monday through Saturday 9–5 and by appointment. An unusually lively town historical society featuring the early 19th century in the Blanchard House and Barn Museum. Five period rooms illustrate the decorative arts of that period; there are also an extensive archives, a tool collection, and an early pumper. Ask about changing exhibits and walking tours.

North Andover Historical Society (686-4035), 153 Academy Road, North Andover. The Johnson Cottage (open year-round Tuesday through Friday 10–noon and 2–4) is a vintage-1789 artisan's cottage. The Parson Barnard House (1715), open June through September, Tuesday through Thursday and by appointment, is a mustard-colored saltbox with some unusual features, like a Federal-era mantel that folds away to reveal the original hearth, and panels displaying successive wall coverings.

Stevens-Coolidge Place (682-3580), Andover Street, North Andover. Open April through October, Sunday 1–5; adults $3, children free. An exceptional summer mansion, actually two older buildings transformed around the turn of the century by noted Colonial-revival architect Joseph Chandler. Furnishings include Chinese porcelains, early American pieces, Oriental rugs, and cut glass. Many personal mementos convey a sense of its owners, Helen Stevens Coolidge (a North Andover native who inherited this farm) and John Gardner Coolidge (a Boston Brahman who, after graduating from Harvard, spent almost 20 years traveling with long stints in Japan and Brazil and in 1902 served as a diplomat in Peking). In 1909 the couple married (he was 44, she, 36), and although this was just their summer home (North Andover was a fashionable summer address at the time), the couple devoted immense energy to the estate. They even acquired the old center Common in the 1920s when the state planned to widen adjoining streets, granting a right-of-way through their property instead. The 90-acre grounds include elaborately landscaped gardens, including a sunken-walled rose (36 varieties) garden. Inquire about the spring plant sale.

HISTORIC SITES

Great Stone Dam. The largest in the world when completed in 1848: 35 feet high. Descend below the John W. Casey Bridge to Pemberton Park; drive or walk beyond the parking lot to the viewing platform.

Ayer Mill Clock Tower. The pride of Lawrence, the world's largest mill clock. The dial, just 6 inches smaller than that of Big Ben, recently was restored through donations by former mill workers and their children.

Immigrant City Archives (686-9230), 6 Essex Street, Lawrence. Open Monday through Thursday 9–4:30 and by appointment. Former offices for the Essex Company, which built and managed the city for much of a century. It's the place to research genealogies of the city's social history or simply to see the big old safes and collection of record books.

First Church Congregational at Methuen (687-1240), 26 Pleasant Street. Open September through May, weekdays 9–3, also Sunday services and by appointment. The opaque glass window depicting the resurrection by Robert LeFarge is memorable, and it's set above an altarpiece designed by Augutus Saint Gaudens. Below the church note the Civil War monument with lions smiling toward the North, scowling toward the South.

Shawsheen Village, junction of MA 28 and MA 133 in Andover. A classic, early-20th-century mill village built by the American Woolen Company with shops and suburban-style housing as well as mills.

TO DO

BOATING

The Greater Lawrence Community Boating Program (681-8675), Eaton Street, off Andover Street, Lawrence. There's a seasonal fee, and a swimming test is required to take out a sailboat or canoe; inquire about the Sunday excursion boat cruises in July and August.

Merrimack River Watershed Council (681-5777), 56 Island Street, Lawrence 01840. This nonprofit group, dedicated to promoting the entire length of the river, has published a detailed map ($3.95) showing launch areas. It is also the source of a pamphlet guide to canoeing, fishing, and bicycling along the river, and of guided canoe trips and special events. "A Guide to Trails from Canada to the Atlantic Ocean" includes details about the New Hampshire Heritage Trail as well as a section on hiking the Merrimack River Trail.

CANOE RENTALS

Moore & Mountain (475-3665), Park Street, Andover. $25 for first day plus $300 security deposit (credit card acceptable).

FISHING

The **Shawsheen River** is stocked with trout. For details about the Merrimack see the Merrimack River Watershed Council's guide (under *Boating*).

GOLF

Rolling Green (475-4066); nine holes in Andover. **Hickory Hill** (686-0822); 18 holes in Methuen.

GREEN SPACE

PARKS

Campagnone Common, Lawrence. An unusually large Common, just off Essex Street, contains the Leonard Bernstein Stage and Robert Frost Fountain (both named for former Lawrence residents).

Pemberton Park, on the Casey Bridge end of the island between North Canal and the Merrimack, accessible from the bridge near the dam.

Merrimack Riverfront State Park (795-1655), adjoining the boathouse on Everett Street, off Shattuck. Still under constuction at this writing, the 47-acre park will include a boat-launch ramp and walking trails.

Den Rock Park on the Shawsheen River, known as a practice ground for technical rock climbers.

STATE FOREST

Harold Parker State Forest (686-3391), Middleton Road, North Reading. A 3000-acre preserve with a total of 135 campsites, 11 ponds (9 artificially created), picnic grills, 35 miles of trails and woods roads.

WALKS

Charles W. Ward Reservation, Prospect Road, east of MA 125, North Andover. A self-guided interpretive trail explores a typical northern bog; hiking and cross-country ski trails traverse woodland. The 640-acre reservation includes Holt Hill, highest hilltop (just 420 feet) in Essex County, with views from Boston to Maine.

Deer Jump Reservation, River Road west of I-93. A 130-acre area on the river with trails leading west (follow the blue blazes) along the river to the Tewksbury line. This land belongs to the Andover Village Improvement Society and accesses 5.1 riverfront miles. See *Boating* for details about the Merrimack River Watershed Council's guidebook that describes the Merrimack River Trail.

Dogwood Park (from I-495 North take the Marston Street Exit to the end of Training School Road; park behind the white fence). There are no dogwoods, but dogs are allowed on the 2.2-mile riverside trail. Turn right to Flamingo Beach and pass under I-495 to the confluence of the Merrimack and Spicket Rivers.

LODGING

Andover Inn (475-5903; 1-800-242-5903), Chapel Avenue, Andover 01810. This columned brick inn is an integral part of the Phillips Academy campus, but it sits on the edge, almost like a gatehouse. It dates from 1930, the gift of an alumnus. The lobby is formal, and the dining room, elegant and popular (see *Dining Out*). There are 33 rooms, 23 with private bath. Although it caters to Phillips Academy parents, other travelers are welcomed warmly. From $70 double, $130 for a suite; all rooms have phones, color TV, radio, and air-conditioning.

WHERE TO EAT

DINING OUT

Bishop's (683-7143), 99 Hampshire at Lowell Street, Lawrence. Open weekdays for lunch and dinner, Saturday from 4 PM, Sunday from 2 (from 4 in summer). The atmosphere and menu are Middle Eastern, but lobster and roast beef are also specialties. Friday evenings offer music and dancing, bar until 1 AM. Average $8 for lunch, $15–20 for dinner.

The Andover Inn (475-5903), Phillips Academy, Chapel Avenue, Andover. The dining room is formal: white tablecloths, chandeliers, courteous service. You might lunch on chicken pot pie ($9.50) or chicken salad on a croissant ($6.50) and dine on veal scallops with cognac shallot butter ($22) or shrimp stir-fry on pasta ($19.55). The specialty of the house on Sunday (only on Sunday, 5–8:45) is an authentic Indonesian rijsttafel ($21.50): dry steamed rice with an indefinite number of side dishes like roast chicken on sticks, marinated cucumbers, and pork in soya sauce and ginger (reservations a must).

Top of the Scales (681-8848), 4 Johnson Street, North Andover, center of the village. Open for all three meals, Sunday brunch. A downstairs crafts center, with upstairs dining inside and on the sun porch: fresh-baked croissants, quiches, soups, salads for lunch, and specializing in seafood and chicken at dinner. Entrées ($8.95–13.95) include starch, salad, and rolls; full liquor license. This was the first smoke-free restaurant in Massachusetts.

Vincenzo's (475-4411; 475-7337), 12 Main Street, Andover. Open for lunch and dinner weekdays, dinner only on weekends. This is a pleasant upstairs restaurant in the middle of Andover's brick shopping street. It's Italian as opposed to Italo-American (no spaghetti and meatballs). Sauces are carefully prepared with fresh herbs from natural stocks. You might lunch on *zuppa di cozze rosso o Bianco* (fresh mussels poached in your choice of white broth or spicy marinara sauce over angelhair pasta, $6.95) and dine on *pollo al Limone* (chicken medallions sautéed with Shiitake mushrooms and finished with lemon and fresh rosemary, $15.50).

EATING OUT

Lawton's Hot Dog Stand, corner of Broadway and Canal Streets, Lawrence, features unique hot dogs fried in oil, highly rated. This stand evolved from a pushcart and was asked to move when first a street, then a walking path ran right through it. Popular support kept it where it is; note the original sidewalk and fire hydrant inside the stand.

Ellie's Restaurant (688-7587), 76 South Broadway, South Lawrence. Lunch and dinner, lounge. A cheerful little Lebanese restaurant with great combo platters and specialties like *kafta* (lean ground beef mixed with onions, parsley, and spices), stuffed grape leaves, lamb skewers, and eggplant dishes. You can also have chicken soup or a turkey dinner.

Ye Loft and Ladle (687-3933), 337 Essex Street, Lawrence. Open Monday through Wednesday 7:30–5, Friday until 9, Saturday until 2 PM. This is a great downtown lunch spot with good, reasonably priced sandwiches, soups, and salads; also dinner specials. The anadama bread and muffins are baked fresh daily, and the beer list is extensive.

Cafe Azteca (689-7393), 180 Common Street, Lawrence. Open for breakfast, lunch, and until 5 Monday through Saturday. Friends tell us this is the real thing, not just Tex-Mex. You can start the day with *sincronizada* (a cheese, ham, and flour tortilla melt), lunch on tacos or flautitas, and finish off the day with *chilis rellenos de puebla* (cheese-covered green peppers filled with egg batter and topped with red salsa) or steak fajitas. Nothing is more than $6.95.

Larry's Cedar Crest Restaurant (685-5722), 187 Broadway (MA 28), Lawrence. Open for breakfast, lunch, dinner. Family restaurant, reasonable prices, daily specials.

Al's Diner (682-9678), 297 South Broadway, Lawrence. A classic diner, great meat pies.

Sam's Steak Out, MA 28 at the Stone Dam, South Lawrence. Open early and late; better than it looks.

Jude's Takeout (681-0896), 37 Hampshire Street. Open 6–5, closing Wednesday and Saturday at 3. Rolled pita bread sandwiches, Italians, grape leaves.

Lobster Den (686-7494), 255 Merrimack Street, Methuen. Open 9–8, Sunday noon–8. A great Cajun chicken sandwich and good fried seafood (clean batter).

ENTERTAINMENT

Methuen Memorial Music Hall concerts (683-6108; 683-2323), 192 Broadway (MA 28), Methuen. You have to see this organ—and the cathedral-shaped hall built to house it—to believe it. Built in 1863 in Germany for the Boston Music Hall, it is huge and baroque. After 21 years it was sold to make room on the stage for the Boston Symphony Orchestra, so it was acquired by Methuen native and millionaire Edward Searles in 1897. The music hall, which Searles commissioned, has a 65-foot vaulted ceiling, marble floors, and rich paneling. Concerts here are events, especially the "Mai Fest," a pops-style concert with Bavarian dancing that's always held the third week in May. Starting in

June, recitals are held on 18 consecutive Wednesdays, 8 PM; all tickets are sold at the door.

SELECTIVE SHOPPING

BOOKSTORE
Andover Bookstore (475-0143), 89 R Main Street, Andover. Exceptionally well stocked, and offers a crackling fire and coffee in winter.

FACTORY STORES
Note: All listings are in Lawrence.

KGR (659-1221), 300 Canal Street. Classic women's suits and separates. Faye and Chet Sidell have created a thriving business employing upward of 1000 men and women who cut, stitch, and otherwise help produce the clothing sold only in this handsome mill store—which is only open one Saturday a month, and not at all in February or July. The trick is to get on their mailing list and to be in line early the day of the sale; savings are at least 50 percent below retail. Missy, petite, and women's sizes.

Blotner Woodworks (682-9412), 399 Canal Street. Open Monday through Friday 9–5. A long-established pilgrimage point for parents and nursery school teachers: piles of wooden balls, beads, tubes, rings, cubes, and pegs for creating.

Malden Mills (1-800-252-6688), 600 Broadway. Open Monday and Wednesday 10–3, Tuesday, Thursday, and Friday 10–6. Full line of Polartec and polarfleece as well as cotton fleece and upholstery fabrics.

Cardinal Shoes (686-9706), 468 Canal Street. Monday through Friday 10–5, Saturday 10–3. Great savings on women's shoes: sizes 6–10, medium width only, made here.

New Balance (682-8960), 5 South Union Street. Open daily, Thursday until 7. Sneakers and jogging clothes for men, women, and children.

Southwick (794-2474), 50 Island Street. Open Wednesday through Saturday 9–5. Men's fine suits, sportscoats, trousers, shirts, ties, outerwear.

Hy-Sil Gift Wrap (689-3900), 250 Canal Street. Open Monday through Saturday 8:30–4:30. Quality gift wrap, bows, ribbons, bags, and tissue.

Hampshire Printed Fabrics (683-5433), 300 Merrimack Street. Open Monday through Thursday 8:30–5, Friday until 4, Saturday until 5, Sunday noon–4. Designer fabrics and accessories.

SHOPPING STREET
Main Street, Andover. A number of small specialty stores add up to interesting shopping.

FARM
Smolak Farm (682-6332), 315 South Bradford Street, North Andover. Open 7–6 daily. A 160-acre farm with 35 acres of apple trees (including 20 antique varieties), a total of 2700 fruit trees, cut-your-own Christmas trees, walking trails, barnyard petting animals, a greenhouse, hayrides, haunted barn at Halloween. The farm stand is known for its baked goods

as well as produce. Pick-your-own apricots, cherries, peaches, nectarines, and pumpkins, as well as apples and flowers.

SPECIAL EVENTS

Note: All events are in Lawrence.

June: **Hispanic Week.** Eight-day celebration of 25 Central and South American countries.

June through September: **Organ Recital Series** at Methuen Memorial Music Hall.

September: Labor Day weekend—**Bread and Roses Celebration.** This event is big, with multi-stages in major parks. The **Common Street City Block Festival** and **Feast of the Three Saints** are the same weekend.

October: **Octoberfest.**

II. SOUTH OF BOSTON

Plymouth County
Bristol County

The Mayflower II *in Plymouth Harbor*

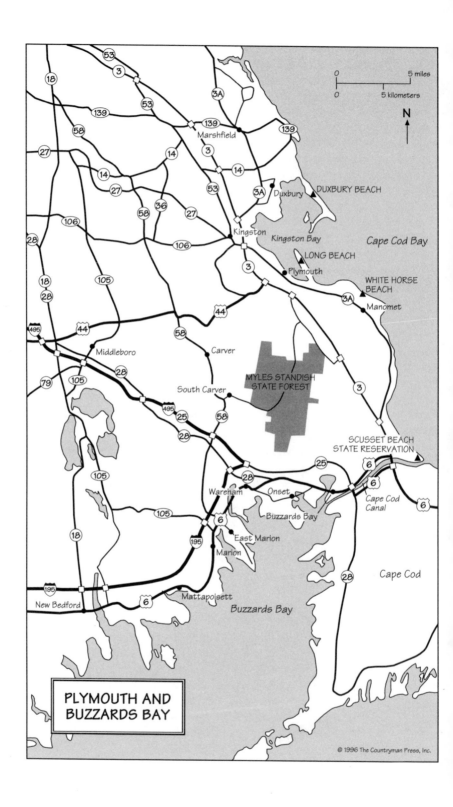

PLYMOUTH AND
BUZZARDS BAY

© 1996 The Countryman Press, Inc.

Plymouth County

PLYMOUTH

As you might suspect, "America's Home Town" is a mix of tourist-geared attractions and landmarks. During the summer months the medley can be cacophonous, but if you look past the tour buses and T-shirt shops, you'll see a genuinely interesting community with some well-preserved colonial-era homes and one of America's more successful museum villages.

The thatched homes and Fort-Meetinghouse of the museum village, within their diamond-shaped stockade, are a modern pioneering effort in their own right. The idea of dramatizing the Pilgrims' daily life was conceived by Harry Hornblower. In 1945 Harry's father, Ralph (a partner in the brokerage firm of Hornblower and Weeks), offered a founding gift, and his grandmother Hattie eventually donated her 100-acre estate for a reconstructed village. Decades ago the Plimoth Plantation rid itself of any authentic Pilgrim pieces (these can be found in the Pilgrim Hall Museum) and encouraged visitors to sit on carefully re-created chairs and bedsteads and to thumb through Bibles. The staff dress in bright colors rather than the blacks and browns in which Victorian artists picture the settlers, and each has adopted a particular Pilgrim to portray as authentically as possible.

Plymouth is actually the state's biggest town in the area, and it is an old summer resort. Both its bay and its lakeshores are lined with summer cottages and offer public beaches, and a fleet of fishing boats are based at Town Wharf.

Duxbury, a short drive up the coast, has its own Pilgrim sites, stately historic homes, and outstanding beach, and the tiny inland hamlets of Carver and Middleboro represent the state's largest concentration of cranberry bogs. They also harbor enormous state forests.

AREA CODE
508
GUIDANCE
Massachusetts Tourist Information Center (746-1150; 746-1152), Exit

5 (Long Pond Road) on US 3 South. Open year-round, 8:45 AM–5 PM. An information clearinghouse with a large selection of maps, brochures from local hotels, motels, restaurants, museums, and other attractions. The staff are ready to answer questions from visitors in person as well as over the phone. The large facility has lots of parking, rest rooms, and picnic tables.

Plymouth Visitors Information Center/Discover Plymouth (747-7525; 1-800-872-1620), Water Street. Open daily April through December, 9–5, and June through August, 9–9. Right on the waterfront, this visitors information center has a broad selection of tourist-oriented literature. There are public rest rooms, too, and baby-changing stations in each bathroom.

GETTING THERE

By car: To reach Plymouth from Boston, drive south on US 3 (approximately 45 minutes) and follow signs from the highway. The fastest approach is from Exit 6 on MA 44 East. If you're not in a rush, take MA 3A South from Duxbury. The scenic road winds along the coastline through affluent commuter villages, beside lovely coves and harbors, and in view of lighthouses, fishing boats, and graceful old homes.

By bus: **Plymouth and Brockton Street Railway Company** (746-0378) isn't a train line; it's a bus company that runs frequent trips between Plymouth and the rest of the South Shore to Boston, including Logan Airport. One-way fare is $7.75.

By boat: Private boats can dock at **Brewers Plymouth Marina** (746-4500).

GETTING AROUND

Since it's an old seaside community, Plymouth is eminently walkable. Other than Plimoth Plantation, most of the sites you'll want to see are within 10 minutes' walking distance from one another. If you get tired of walking, or if you'd rather see everything quickly, the **Plymouth Rock Trolley** (747-3419), 22 Main Street, is an excellent resource. In 45 minutes, the trolley stops at all the major sites, including the Rock and the *Mayflower II*. During the summer months it goes all the way to Plimoth Plantation and Long Beach. It operates from the first weekend in May through Thanksgiving weekend, 9 AM to 5 PM, and until 8 PM during the summer. Per-day tickets are $6 for adults and $3 for children; you may get off and on the trolley as often as you'd like for the day.

MEDICAL EMERGENCY

Jordan Hospital (746-2000), 275 Sandwich Street (Exit 5 off US 3), Plymouth.

TO SEE

Note: The following listings are in Plymouth unless otherwise indicated.

MUSEUMS

Plimoth Plantation (746-1622), MA 3A, Warren Avenue. $15 adults, $9

TED CURTIN ©PLIMOTH PLANTATION

The Plimoth Plantation in Plymouth

children 5–12, under 5 free. A one-day ticket for both the Plantation and the *Mayflower II* is $18.50 adults, $11 children. Open April through November, 9–5. Three miles south of Plymouth proper, this living museum is populated by men and women in period costumes who live the lives and play the parts of the residents of a 1627 Pilgrim village (see chapter introduction). The small wooden houses with thickly thatched roofs straggle along a dirt road. The "settlers" speak in Old English; they are as much a part of the museum as the tools they use and the lives they lead, and they're eager to answer your questions about their daily activities. A Wampanoag tribe site on the premises exhibits a typical Native American encampment of approximately the same period as the Plantation.

Pilgrim Hall Museum (746-1620), 75 Court Street. Open daily 9:30–4:30. Continuously operating since 1824, the Greek Revival building houses the largest collection of Pilgrim possessions, including richly styled Jacobean furniture and the relic of the *Sparrow-Hawk*, one of the many ships that brought the early colonists to Plymouth. The ship's hull is especially fascinating for modern viewers: It was hewn from naturally curved tree trunks and branches. The museum also owns the only known painting of a *Mayflower* passenger, Edward Winslow.

Cranberry harvest in Plymouth

WINERY
Plymouth Colony Winery (747-3334), MA 44 West. Open year-round. Free wine tastings and tours of a working cranberry bog. Since this is cranberry country, cranberry wine is one of the 14 wines they make.

HISTORIC HOMES
Mayflower Society Museum (746-2590), 4 Winslow Street (mailing address: PO Box 3184, Plymouth 02361). Admission. This striking white building, built in 1754, boasts a fabulous double staircase and a wealth of stories. Here are three tidbits from the house's history: The original owner was Edward Winslow, a Tory leader who was forced to flee to Canada during the Revolution; Ralph Waldo Emerson got married in the front parlor in 1835; and ether was discovered here in 1842. If you think you may be a descendant of one of the *Mayflower* passengers, you may research your own genealogical history in the library, which is run by the General Society of Mayflower Descendants.

Spooner House (746-0012), 27 North Street. Admission. The 1749 Spooner House is humbler than many historic houses, but its vast collection of five generations of Spooner family possessions is truly impressive.

Richard Sparrow House (747-1240), 42 Summer Street. Donations requested. The Sparrow House was built in 1640 by Richard Sparrow and his family. It's now Plymouth's oldest surviving wooden-frame house. Inside, the spartan furnishings and primitive construction give visitors an honest glimpse back into life in the 17th century.

Hedge House (746-9697), 126 Water Street. Open daily, late June to Labor Day, 10–5 Monday through Saturday, noon–5 Sunday; weekends in June and September to mid-October; closed mid-October through May. Admission. Next to the visitors information center on Water Street is this stately 1809 Federal building, originally the home of a shipping family. The building is filled with period pieces, including a fine selection of quilts and Chinese porcelain.

Jabez Howland House (746-9490), 33 Sandwich Street. Open late May to mid-October and Thanksgiving weekend, 10–4:30. In a town full of "oldests," the Howland House is the only surviving house to have been inhabited by *Mayflower* passengers. John Howland and Elizabeth Tilley arrived in Plymouth in 1620, married soon after, and produced 10 children. Their youngest son, Jabez, purchased the house in the late 1660s; his parents lived here during the winters in order to be close to their church, and Elizabeth continued living with Jabez and his family after John died in 1673 (at the age of 80). The John Howland Society, formed by Howland descendants, did extensive restorative work on the building during the 1940s. They finished their work by furnishing the house with many fine examples of period chairs, tables, and beds.

HISTORIC SITES

Most first-time visitors to Plymouth head straight for **Plymouth Rock** on Water Street, on a hill overlooking the harbor. Purported to be the landing place of Plymouth's first white settlers, the smallish boulder is now housed inside a neo-Grecian portico. The green area that surrounds the portico is Massachusetts's smallest state park.

Mayflower II (746-1622), State Pier. $5.75 adults, $3.75 children 5–12, under 5 free (see Plimoth Plantation for special boat-and-Plantation rates). Down the hill from the Rock is the *Mayflower II,* a reproduction of the original. By modern standards, the boat seems ridiculously small for 102 passengers, its load during the boat's first crossing from England to the New World. During the summer, guides in period costume conduct fact-filled tours that are worth the wait in line. The *Mayflower II* is usually open, although it makes several trips each summer to destinations along the Massachusetts coastline (including Provincetown, its predecessor's first "real" stop in the New World).

1749 Court House and Museum (830-4075), Town Square. Open year-round. Free. The courthouse was the site of several cases tried by none other than John Adams, before he became the second president of the United States. Today, the building is the oldest wooden courthouse in the country. The first floor is a museum, and the second floor is a re-creation of the courtroom as it looked during the mid-18th century. Other than the building itself, which is remarkably interesting, there are several items on view in the museum that will draw visitors' attention: a hand-drawn suction pumper from 1828 used by Plymouth's early firefighters, and an intricately carved oak bench from 1740.

FOR FAMILIES

Cranberry World Visitors Center (746-2350), 225 Water Street. Open May through November. Free. Sponsored by Ocean Spray, the center displays a scaled-down "bog," several exhibits on the history of cranberry cultivation around the world, and lots of free samples.

The Children's Museum of Plymouth (747-1234), 46–48 Main Street. Open daily mid-April to Labor Day; Labor Day to mid-April, open weekends, holidays, and during school vacations. Admission. The Children's Museum is a kid-sized version of everyday places in and around America's Home Town. Kids may take part in a variety of activities, such as operating the weather station at Gurnet Lighthouse, climbing onto a fire engine, DJ-ing at a radio station, and even working behind the counter at Dunkin' Donuts.

Plymouth National Wax Museum (746-6468), 16 Carver Street. Open March to December. $5.50 adults, $2 children 5–12. The depictions of Pilgrim life at this museum are fanciful and, at times, even awkward; they're geared more toward kids than adults. Bring your sense of humor, and you'll probably have a good time, too.

TO DO

BICYCLING

Bike Line (830-0100), 127 Samoset Street, Plymouth, has standard, mountain, racing, and hybrid bicycles for rent, as well as helmets, carriers, locks, and other equipment.

Biking trails: **Myles Standish State Forest** (866-2526), Cranberry Road, South Carver. Open mid-April through Columbus Day weekend. Miles of bike trails wind through the 15,000-acre reservation area. To get there, take US 3 to Exit 5, turn south on Long Pond Road, and look for the sign to the forest, approximately 2.5 miles south. **Scusset Beach State Reservation**—take US 3 to the rotary before the Sagamore Bridge, then follow the signs. The park has 7 miles of paved bike trails.

BOAT EXCURSIONS

Plymouth-to-Provincetown Ferry (1-800-242-2469), State Pier, Plymouth. Late May through late September. Adults $22, seniors $18, children under 12 $14, bikes $2. The 90-minute ferry ride across Cape Cod Bay to Provincetown on the *Cape Cod Clipper* saves you the drive, and it's twice as fast. Reservations recommended.

Plymouth-Bristol Charters (746-3688), Plymouth Town Pier. $22–34 per person. Enjoy a morning, afternoon, or sunset cruise around Cape Cod Bay from Plymouth Harbor on Captain John Lifrieri's 41-foot sloop *Jehovah Jireh.*

Also see *Fishing* and *Whale-Watching.*

CANOEING

Palmer River Canoe (252-4246; 336-2274), Myles Standish State Park.

This outfitter has a wide range of canoes, kayaks, clothing, and other equipment on hand; they also offer guided trips and group discounts.

FISHING

Massachusetts's waters support a world-class striped bass fishery, and the South Shore is one of the country's most overlooked striper hot spots. Migratory striped bass enter area waters at the beginning of May and stay well into November. The area also sees good fishing for such game species as bluefish and blue shark.

Henry Weston Outfitters (617-826-7411), 15 Columbia Road (MA 53 at Pembroke Crossing), Pembroke, can supply you with tackle, information, and guides. Shop owner Jim McKay retains the services of five Coast Guard–licensed guides who specialize in fly-fishing and light spin-fishing for striped bass and bluefish. Two also book charters for blue shark using both conventional and fly tackle.

Andy Lynn Boats (746-7776; 1-800-540-3474), Town Wharf, Plymouth. A full-service fleet of boats that offer sport fishing, off-shore fishing, and year-round deep-sea fishing. Trips of various lengths are available, from 4 hours to overnight. Reservations recommended.

GOLF

Plymouth Country Club (746-0476), 18 holes. **Squirrel Run** (746-5001), MA 44 (5 miles west of US 3); 18-hole course, rentals, pro shop, carts, and sandwich shop.

PARASAILING

Plymouth Parasail and Water Sports (746-1415), 14 Union Street, Plymouth. No experience or special equipment necessary.

SWIMMING

Duxbury Beach, in Marshfield, is one of the finest barrier beaches in Massachusetts (see *Green Space*).

Nelson Street Beach, off Water Street just north of Cranberry World, is a pleasant beach with good swimming. Parking is free, though limited. Since the beach is part of a park with a playground, there are lots of kids.

Long Beach is a straight, 3-mile-long beach popular with both locals and day-trippers (see *Green Space*).

Stephens Field Beach, Park, and Playground is at the end of a dead-end lane called Stephens Field, just off MA 3A, 1 mile south of Plymouth; take the first left after the fire station. Playground, picnic tables, a small duck pond, a short beach, tennis courts, and free parking (limited number of spaces).

Myles Standish State Forest, South Carver, has freshwater swimming at College and Fearing Ponds (see *Green Space*).

White Horse Beach, Mahomet, is the favorite of many locals (see *Green Space*).

TENNIS

Stephens Field (see *Swimming*) has three public courts available on a first-come, first-served basis.

WHALE-WATCHING
Captain Tim Brady and Sons (746-4809), Town Wharf, Plymouth. **Captain John Boats** (746-2643; 1-800-242-2469), Town Wharf, Plymouth.
CROSS-COUNTRY SKIING
Myles Standish State Forest has miles of touring paths through its meadows and forests (see *State Forests*).

GREEN SPACE

BEACHES
Duxbury Beach (617-837-3112 for information), accessed via MA 139 through Marshfield's Green Harbor area, is a 5-mile-long stretch of clean white sand that juts out into the ocean. Be cautious: The surf on the Cape Cod Bay side of the beach can be rough at times. A few areas of the beach are accessible by four-wheel-drive vehicles only. Lifeguards, rest rooms, showers, changing rooms, and snack bar at the beach; restaurants and groceries available nearby. From late May through early September, parking is $8 on weekends, $7 weekdays.
Long Beach, also known as Plymouth Beach, on MA 3A, 3 miles south of Plymouth center. Located in a half-rural, half-residential area, this popular beach has lifeguards (June through Labor Day), rest rooms, showers, a snack bar, excellent fishing, and good swimming. Part of the beach is roped off; this area serves as a nesting ground for migratory shorebirds such as terns and sandpipers. Parking is $10 per car on weekends, $7 weekdays.
White Horse Beach, Manomet. South of Plymouth center, take MA 3A South, then follow signs when you get to Manomet. The locals keep it quiet, but they love this beach. It's just as popular with the folks who rent the beachside cottages summer after summer. Parking is hard to find: It's off-street only, usually in a resident's driveway for approximately $7–10 per car. Spend some time at this pretty beach; it's well worth your effort.
STATE FORESTS
Myles Standish State Forest (866-2526), Cranberry Road, South Carver. To get here, take US 3 to Exit 5, turn south on Long Pond Road, and look for the sign to the state forest, approximately 2.5 miles south. The roads, walking trails, and bike paths that wind through this 14,635-acre park's forest and meadows seem to go on forever. Even during the busiest summer weekends, visitors can easily find some space to be alone. The park, Massachusetts's first state forest when it was created in 1916, has 15 ponds and two freshwater beaches (at Fearing and College Ponds). Motorcycle, bicycle, bridle, and hiking paths, fishing, picnic areas, rest rooms, camping, bathhouses, swimming, and interpretive programs. Picnic tables, fireplaces, and parking ($5) are available. Open mid-April through Columbus Day weekend.

LODGING

Probably because it's a popular holiday destination for families, Plymouth has plenty of motels that are as unremarkable in decor as they are budget oriented. For travelers who are looking for pleasanter, more unusual lodgings in and around Plymouth, there are several nice bed & breakfasts available.

INNS AND BED & BREAKFASTS

Windsor House Inn (617-934-0991), 390 Washington Street, Duxbury 02332. Some 15 minutes north of Plymouth, in the town of Duxbury, is this inn/restaurant, a black-shuttered white building in a neighborhood that's filled with houses that are on the National Register of Historic Places. The inn's two bedrooms and one suite are gracefully decorated with light blue paneling and pretty, blue-and-white stenciling; furnishings are a mix of Shaker and Federal reproductions. Breakfast is served in the restaurant. $85–115.

The Jackson-Russell-Whitfield House (746-5289), 26 North Street, Plymouth 02360. This red-painted brick building's unusual name is actually a listing of its provenance: Samuel Jackson built the house in 1782. His daughter Mary married into the Russell family, and after she died, her descendants occupied the house until Brian Whitfield purchased it in the late 1980s. Whitfield has restored the house's original woodwork—the hand-carved newel post and banisters of the front staircase are especially striking—and filled the house with antique furniture and art. There are two large rooms, one with a queen-sized bed and one with two twins, both with fireplaces; the arrangement is easily converted into a suite. $80–140.

The Mabbett House (1-800-572-7829; fax 508-830-1911), 7 Cushman Street, Plymouth 02360. Three large, sun-filled bedrooms, all with private bath, in a home that's surrounded by gardens. Breakfast is served in the screened-in porch. $95–165.

On Cranberry Pond (946-0768), 43 Fuller Street, Middleboro 02346. If you're looking to escape busy Plymouth, this peaceful bed & breakfast is a 25-minute drive away. Located in the heart of cranberry country, the house is surrounded by horse pastures and cranberry bogs. The three rooms are furnished with contemporary furniture. Reservations required. $75–105.

MOTELS

The John Carver Inn (746-7100; 1-800-274-1620; fax 746-8299), 25 Summer Street, Plymouth 02360. A large, imposing motel on the south side of Burial Hill that attracts lots of tour groups during the busy summer months. The 79 rooms are decorated in tans and beiges and are furnished with Colonial-style reproductions. The hotel has a restaurant, lounge, gift shop, and pool. $69–105.

Cold Spring Motel (phone/fax 746-2222), 188 Court Street, Plymouth 02360. Among Plymouth's many motels, this one is probably the most attractive with its cheerful yellow awnings and carefully landscaped grounds. The rooms are exceptionally clean, if not inspiringly furnished or decorated, but the very reasonable rates make up for lack of atmosphere: $43–76.

Pilgrim Sands (747-0900; 1-800-729-7263), 150 Warren Avenue/MA 3A, Plymouth 02360. The prime attraction of this oceanside motel is its private beach, which is an extension of Long Beach. It's also very close to Plimoth Plantation. Various sizes of rooms (some with kitchenette) are available to accommodate families, couples traveling together, and groups, and most rooms have balconies. Amenities include indoor and outdoor pools and a whirlpool. $85–115.

CAMPGROUNDS

Myles Standish State Forest (866-2526), Cranberry Road, South Carver 02566. Open mid-April through Columbus Day weekend. The state forest has 470 tent/RV sites (no hookups) with rest rooms, hot showers, and a fireplace and picnic table at each site. Rates are $6 per night with showers, $5 per night without showers. To get there, take US 3 to Exit 5, turn south on Long Pond Road, and look for the sign to Myles Standish State Forest, approximately 2.5 miles south.

WHERE TO EAT

DINING OUT

The Inn for All Seasons (746-8823), 97 Warren Avenue/MA 3A, Plymouth. Open year-round, Tuesday through Saturday for dinner only, Sunday brunch and dinner. Set on a wooded hilltop with four carpeted dining rooms in contemporary decor. Entrées include veal Oscar, fruits de mer, and oysters Rockefeller. Chocolate lovers shouldn't skip the chocolate mousse cake. $8.95–15.95.

Crane Brook Restaurant (866-3235), 229 Tremont Street, South Carver. Open year-round except for one week in January and the last week in June; lunch Wednesday through Friday, dinner Wednesday through Sunday. Located in a retired iron foundry that's surrounded by a mix of forests, pastures, and cranberry bogs, this restaurant is a terrific spot for lunch or dinner. The dining room looks out over a pond. Lunch entrées include grilled duck breast sandwich; dinner might be rack of lamb or spicy pork-loin roast. Reservations required. $8.95–27.

Windsor House Inn (617-934-0991), 390 Washington Street, Duxbury. Open year-round for dinner. Established in 1803, this black-shuttered white inn is a favorite celebration-dinner destination for South Shore residents. Dining available in the elegant main dining room (weekends only) or in the carriage house (daily). Typical entrées include marinated tomato and eggplant pizza, balsamic tatsoi-grilled quail salad, agnolotti lobster with grilled scallions, pan-seared talapia with stir-fried noodles and curry, and herb-crusted lamb. $3.50–22.

EATING OUT

1620 Restaurant (746-9565), 158 Water Street, Plymouth. Open year-round for lunch and dinner. Perched on one of the busiest street corners in Plymouth, this second-floor restaurant is a good place to have a meal and watch the traffic in the harbor. The dining room has vaulted ceilings and glass walls on three sides; try to get a table with a view of the harbor. Appetizers include lobster tartlet; entrées include traditional turkey dinner and baked tortellini with scallops. $5–13.

Iguana's (747-4000), 170 Water Street, Plymouth. Open for lunch and dinner. A Mexican/southwestern restaurant in the Village Landing complex, with good quesadillas, taco salads, and fajitas with your choice of fixings. Try to sit in the glassed-in addition on the north side; you'll have a view of the harbor. $5–10.

✐ **Persy's Place** (617-585-5464), 117 Main Street, MA 3A, Kingston. Open daily for breakfast and lunch. You may be distracted by the old-time country store decor and feel of the place, but take a few minutes to read the lengthy list of offerings; this family-oriented eatery asserts that it has "New England's largest breakfast menu." There's something for everyone here, from fish cakes to chipped beef on toast, from catfish and eggs (no-cholesterol eggs are available) to thick pancakes. $3–12.

All-American Diner (747-4763), 60 Court Street, Plymouth. Open daily 5:30 AM–2 PM for breakfast and lunch; takeout also available. This cheerfully decorated new restaurant already feels like it's an institution, serving traditional as well as unusual egg dishes, crunchy French toast (their invention), and sandwiches with a choice of home fries or rice pilaf. $1.55–5.90.

Wood's Seafood and Fish Market (746-0261), end of Town Wharf, Plymouth. Open year-round for lunch and dinner, weekdays 11 AM–8 PM, weekends until 9 PM; closed in January. Sit indoors or at an outdoor picnic table on Town Wharf and feast on a clam roll, fresh fish sandwich, or a cup of fish or clam chowder. Fresh fish and lobster sold at the adjacent market. $4–15.

The Lobster Hut (746-2270), Town Wharf, Plymouth. It's slightly more crowded with bus traffic than Wood's, but the atmosphere is still authentic New England seaside, as is the cuisine: clam rolls, lobster salad, and lots of fries. $4.95–15.95.

Star of Siam (224-3771), MA 3A, Manomet. High-quality, take-out Thai food may not be what you expect to find in staid old Plymouth/Manomet, which makes this place such a pleasant surprise. Do what the locals do—pick up a spicy pad Thai lunch or dinner and bring it to the beach. $4.95–12.95.

SNACKS

✐ **Farfar's Danish Ice Cream Shop**, Millbrook Station, St. George's Road,

Duxbury. In a converted train depot, the proprietors make all their ice cream daily on the premises. There are wooden benches and tables inside and a big porch out back.

Corner Bakery and Deli (747-2700), Court Street (corner of Brewster Street), Plymouth, offers several flavors of gourmet coffee and fresh-baked scones, croissants, and enormous cookies.

ENTERTAINMENT

MUSIC

Village Landing Marketplace (746-3493), Water Street, Plymouth. During the summer months, free concerts here range from swing music to Irish ballads, with special performances for kids.

THEATER

Priscilla Beach Theatre (224-4888), Rocky Hill Road, Manomet. June through mid-September. The country's oldest summer-stock barn playhouse presents children's shows Friday and Saturday at 10:30 AM, performing-arts day camps throughout the summer (1-week and 2-week programs only), and adult shows Monday through Saturday at 8:30 PM. Call for specific show schedule.

NIGHTLIFE

The Pub at the Sheraton Plymouth (747-4900), 180 Water Street, Plymouth, offers live music on weekends.

The Full Sail (224-4478) is beside White Horse Beach in an innocuous building that looks like a ranch house. Its clientele are locals and summer folks who love this beach, which is bordered by tiny beach houses. No food is served here, just beverages.

SELECTIVE SHOPPING

ANTIQUES SHOP

Simon Hill Antiques (617-934-2228), 453 Washington Street, Duxbury. Located in the scenic Snug Harbor area of Duxbury, this shop carries a fine selection of antique furniture and decorative pieces, as well as antique jewelry.

BOOKSTORES

Westwinds Bookshop (617-934-2128), 45 Depot Street, Duxbury. Charming atmosphere and location. Splendid children's books section.

Yankee Books and Antique Shop (747-2691), 10 North Street, Plymouth. Open year-round, Monday through Saturday 11–5, Sunday noon–4. Specializes in hard-to-find books and Pilgrim history.

FACTORY OUTLETS

Cordage Park Marketplace (746-7707), MA 3A, North Plymouth, is a former cordage rope factory that's surrounded by ponds, fountains, gazebos, lawns, and flower gardens. Manufacturers with discounted merchandise include American Tourister, Van Heusen, and Maidenform.

FARM STANDS

On MA 3A in Manomet, just south of the Purity Supreme grocery store, you'll see a farm stand that some locals swear by as their primary source of fresh vegetables and fruits. The only sign next to this weathered white building said "Roses $6.99."

Carvelli's Farm Stand: On MA 44, approximately 5 miles west of MA 3A, a large farm tops a hill. Set back from the road, a small, red, wooden building serves as the farm stand for a brisk business in corn and other fresh produce, all sold in a setting that looks like a bit of Iowa here in Plymouth.

SPECIAL SHOPS

Little Shoes (747-2226), 359 Court Street, Plymouth, has—you guessed it—shoes for kids. A great selection and some bargains, too.

Plimoth Plantation has an extensive gift shop and bookstore.

Scarecrow (747-6776), 8 Main Street Extension, Plymouth, is a specialty shop indeed—it features snowboards and skateboards as well as the requisite baggy padded clothing.

The Stencil Shoppe (830-1163), 16 Court Street, Plymouth, has a selection of ready-made stencils and other materials you'll need if you decide to try your hand at stenciling; there's plenty here to inspire you.

Village Landing Marketplace, Water Street, Plymouth. Housed in a group of clapboarded buildings, this seaside mall contains T-shirt shops, crafts stores, ice cream shops, a deli, and restaurants.

SPECIAL EVENTS

June: **John Carver Day,** Carver.

July: **Waterfront Festival,** Plymouth.

October: **Cranberry Harvest Festival.** Second week in October. The Cranberry World Visitors Center, Plymouth and Edaville Bog, South Carver.

November: **Thanksgiving observances,** Plymouth. Reasonably priced turkey and fixings served continuously in Memorial Hall 11 AM–5 PM. Square dancing and other entertainment.

December: **Christmas on North Street,** Plymouth.

BUZZARDS BAY: ONSET TO MATTAPOISETT

South of the Cape Cod Canal and north of New Bedford lies a ragged strip of coast jokingly known as "the armpit of Cape Cod." Quite beautiful in parts, it receives few tourists because the most spectacular areas are all private. Onset, the one summer resort village, is now a bit worn and funky but is still fun. It began life in 1876 as a camp-meeting site for church groups from Boston and Rhode Island, and it retains its Victorian look and feel. The nearby towns of Marion and Mattapoisett are really New Bedford bedroom towns with more than the usual number of shops and restaurants, because they also cater to the yachting crowd in summer. Many Bostonians keep their boats in Marion (from which it's an easy sail to the islands), which is best known for its whaling history and for prestigious Tabor Academy. Mattapoisett's Shipyard Park, with its tall flagpole and gazebo, occupies the site of the town's six defunct shipyards (the *Acushnet*, in which Herman Melville went whaling, was built here), and the flagpole incorporates the mizzenmast from the town's last whaleship.

AREA CODE
508

GUIDANCE
Onset Bay Association (295-7072; fax 295-7070), 215 Onset Avenue (mailing address: PO Box 799, Onset 02558). Open year-round, but hours vary. When a staff member is present, this small office can be very helpful to visitors; you'll be provided with brochures, information about activities in the area, and suggestions for lodgings. Staff also answer questions over the phone. If you plan to spend a few days in the area, call ahead to get a copy of the latest edition of the *Onset Village Voice*, the association's informative quarterly publication.

Cape Cod Canal Region Chamber of Commerce (759-6000), 70 Main Street, Buzzards Bay. Located in a retired train depot by the railroad bridge, this small office stocks current brochures, maps, and lists of lodging options in the Onset and nearby Canal area.

New Bedford's Waterfront Visitors Center (979-1745), Pier 3, New Bedford, offers information about Mattapoisett and Marion.

GETTING THERE
To reach Onset from Boston, drive south on US 3 until you reach the rotary before the on-ramp to the Sagamore Bridge. Take the exit marked "US 6/MA 28." At the rotary beside the Bourne Bridge, take the US 6/MA 28 exit, heading toward New Bedford. Stay on US 6. After approximately 3 miles, watch for the sign marked "Onset/Onset Beach." Mattapoisett and Marion are south on US 6, accessible from I-195.

GETTING AROUND
Onset is a small place; one of its charms is in the fact that you can—and, if you're staying in the village, should—park your car and walk everywhere. Alternatively, you can get around quite easily by remembering that most streets lead you back to Main Street/Onset Avenue, which has signs for US 6.

MEDICAL EMERGENCY
Falmouth Hospital (548-5300), Ter Heun Drive, Falmouth. **St. Luke's Hospital** (997-1515), 101 Page Street, New Bedford.

TO SEE

MUSEUMS
Sippican Historical Society Museum (748-1116), Front Street, Marion. Open year-round, Wednesday 2–5, Saturday 11–5, Sunday 2–4 (with teas and tours), and whenever the flag's flying (which means the caretaker is in). This small museum features exhibits on Marion's whaling days, along with the mystery of the *Mary Celeste*, which was found in 1872 at sea under full sail—and bereft of passengers.

Mattapoisett Historical Society (758-2844), Main Street, Mattapoisett. Open July and August, Tuesday through Saturday 1–4:30 ($2 admission). The old meetinghouse of the Mattapoisett Christian Church is filled with local memorabilia and whaling exhibits.

TO DO

BOAT EXCURSIONS
Cape Cod Canal Cruises (295-3883), Town Pier, Onset (mailing address: Box 3, Onset 02558). Many of the people who come to Onset are here for the *Viking's* cruises up and down the calm waters of Cape Cod Canal. Cruises are available from May through October. Trip times vary from 2 to 4 hours; special excursions include sunset cruises and live music sessions.

BOAT RENTALS
Maco's Bait and Tackle Shop (759-9836), US 6, Wareham. This bait and tackle shop has powerboats for rent: 15-foot skiff with 10 HP, $55 per day; 17-foot Boston Whaler, $180 per day, not including gas.

FISHING
Shell Point (291-2028), Town Pier, Onset (mailing address: 37 Buzzards Bay Drive South, Plymouth 02360). Try your hand at deep-sea fishing out of the Onset Town Pier for $10 per person, plus $5 for rod and bait.

GOLF
Bay Pointe Country Club (759-8802), Bay Pointe Drive, off Onset Avenue. Eighteen-hole course on pretty grounds. Greens fee is $25 Monday through Friday, $27 on weekends, $12.50 per cart. The club also offers a pool and tennis courts ($5 for both for a day). **Marion Golf Club** (748-0199), 10 South Drive, Marion. A nine-hole course.

SWIMMING
Onset Town Beach, off Onset Avenue, is the only sizable public beach in the area; most of the others are either private or else too rocky or inaccessible for swimming. Parking is found on the Town Pier and at meters along Onset Avenue.

Island Park and Beach, Front Street, Marion, is a nice, though small, beach with some public parking.

TENNIS

Bay Pointe Country Club (759-8802), Onset, offers two courts, available to the public when club members aren't playing. $3 per hour; $5 per day includes swimming in the club pool.

GREEN SPACE

Onset Town Park is a small, grassy, hilltop park overlooking the Town Pier. The bandshell is a nice place to stop for a view of the coastline.

Shipyard Park, Mattapoisett, is a waterside park in the center of town. The bandstand is used during the summer for evening concerts; the flagpole is the mizzen from the town's last whaling ship, *The Wanderer*, which was launched in 1878.

Great Hill Farm (748-1052), Delano Road in East Marion, is open weekdays only. The 700-acre estate on Buzzards Bay has woodland paths.

Ned's Point Light in Veterans Park, Mattapoisett, is a prime spot for sunset watching.

(Also see *Swimming*.)

LODGING

INNS AND BED & BREAKFASTS

☞ **Mattapoisett Bed & Breakfast** (758-9347), 16 Shipyard Lane, Mattapoisett 02739. Bill and Janet Muldoon share their amazing, early-19th-century house with guests lucky enough to find it. The Mattapoisett Suite is a large bedroom and sitting room furnished with antiques, and the Tower Suite occupies the entire third floor (a tower)—it's a large bedroom and sitting room with a view of the harbor. Rollaways can be fitted into either suite. $60.

The Mattapoisett Inn (758-4922), 13 Water Street, Mattapoisett 02739. Open April through November. This classic old summer hotel offers three rooms, each with private bath, which were all filled when we stopped by to see them. All have harbor views, but you may want to inquire about dining room noise. $63.

Onset Pointe Inn (295-8442), 9 Eagle Way, Onset (mailing address: PO Box 1450, Onset 02558). The mansion is open year-round, the Cottage and Guest House are open May to October. The pale yellow inn claims the best spot in town: flanked by Onset Beach, the three buildings perch on a point that juts into Buzzards Bay. Fourteen rooms total, three with kitchens. Long-term renters requested in Cottage and Guest House during winter months. $75–150.

Reynolds House B&B (291-4036), 11 South Boulevard, Onset 02558. Open year-round. Built in 1890, this comfortable house has three rooms, all doubles, with a shared bath. An expanded continental breakfast is served either in the dining room or on the front porch overlooking the harbor and the canal. $65–75.

COTTAGES

Mary Crowley Associates (759-4430; mailing address: PO Box 261, Buzzards Bay 02532). A local real estate agent who helps visitors find houses or cottages to rent.

HOTELS/MOTELS

Onset Harbor Inn (295-4600; 1-800-475-4606), Onset Avenue, Onset 02558. Almost directly across the street from Onset Harbor, this hotel has 12 small rooms, all with water view and private bath. Amenities include a restaurant, a pool, a poolside bar, and a tavern-type cocktail lounge. In-season $40–95.

Bay View Motel (295-5937), 181 Onset Avenue, Onset 02558. Open year-round. The turreted, slate-blue motel has 17 rooms furnished with rather standard-issue furniture and bathrooms, but its location—overlooking Onset's town pier—and reasonable prices ($40–60) are attractive.

WHERE TO EAT

DINING OUT

The Mattapoisett Inn (758-4922), 13 Water Street, Mattapoisett. Open April through November for lunch and dinner, Sunday brunch. Entertainment on Friday and Saturday. An old summer hotel with low-beamed dining rooms, atmosphere, early-bird specials. The menu includes Cajun dishes, frogs' legs, and roast duckling.

EATING OUT

Oxford Creamery (758-3847), US 6, Mattapoisett. Open 11–7 Tuesday through Sunday, Friday 11–8, closed Monday. A family-run grill/creamery, with tables inside and under a tree outside. Ice cream and yogurt as well as sandwiches, fried seafood, and healthy low-fat meals. Take-out meals also available. $1.80–11.

Ansel's Pantry, in the Ansel S. Gurney House (748-1111), 403 Country Road, Marion. Open for lunch year-round. This Federal-period tavern is now a large gift/crafts shop with a small luncheon room. The menu features homemade soups and desserts. $4.95–10.95.

The Boat Club at the Onset Harbor Inn (295-4600), Onset Avenue, Onset. Open year-round. A small hotel restaurant with a varied menu that may include mussels in lobster marinara, barbecued chicken, build-your-own burger, or linguine with marinara and homemade meatballs. $2.95–11.95. During warm weather, have a drink out on the deck at the hotel's **Lower Deck Pub and Tavern** before your meal.

Joseph's (758-3400), US 6, Mattapoisett, just over the line from Fairhaven. Open for lunch and dinner. The owners of Antonio's in New Bedford have created a popular place with a variety of dishes. Dinner prices from $7.95 for a chicken special to $17.95 for a seafood bucket for two. Reservations and credit cards accepted.

Pier View Restaurant (295-5968), 201 Onset Avenue, Onset. Open year-round for breakfast, lunch, and dinner. On Onset's two-block-long commercial district, this old-style, small-town restaurant has plenty of room between tables; if you'd prefer, you can twirl on a stool at the counter. Omelets, burgers, sandwiches, and various fried seafoods. $1.95–8.95.

Mattapoisett Chowder House (758-2333), US 6, Mattapoisett. Open year-round for lunch and dinner. A family-style restaurant, known locally for its homemade chowder, stuffed quahogs, and pies. $4.95–9.95.

SNACKS

Nana's Ice Cream Parlour, 190 Onset Avenue, Onset. Ice cream, frozen yogurt, and beverages served either inside or from a window along the Onset Avenue sidewalk.

COFFEE SHOPS

Dunkin' Donuts (291-2214), Onset Avenue, Onset. This must be the nicest Dunkin' Donuts in New England—it's harborside, on the ground floor of a shingled, hexagon-shaped building.

ENTERTAINMENT

The **Lower Deck Pub and Tavern** at the Onset Harbor Inn (295-4600) has DJs on weekends.

Onset Town Park Bandshell has concerts on Wednesday nights and some weekends during the summer. Music runs the gamut from blues, to marches, to swing-band tunes.

Square Dancing at the Mattapoisett Town Wharf, Saturday evenings in late June through August.

Band concerts at the gazebo in Shipyard Park, Mattapoisett, Wednesdays in summer.

SELECTIVE SHOPPING

Grainger Pottery (748-1238), US 6, Marion. Open year-round. Handmade pottery with a nautical theme.

Marion General Store (748-0340), 140 Front Street, Marion. Open Monday through Saturday 8:30–5:30. A genuine, small-town general store with something for everyone, from jelly beans to refrigerator magnets.

Tremont Nail Company (295-0038), Elm Street, Wareham. This old-fashioned country store is owned and operated by the world's oldest nail-manufacturing company; wares include antique nails and other hardware.

BOOKSTORE

The Bookstall (748-1041), 151 Front Street, Marion. Nautical books a specialty.

SPECIAL EVENTS

August: **Onset Blues Festival.** An all-day festival in the Onset Town Park Bandshell that features five or six blues bands. **Onset Intertribal**

Homecoming Pow Wow, Lopes Field, Wareham. A Wampanoag tribal powwow sponsored by the Wareham Historical Commission, with a grand parade of tribal flags, circle dancing, crafts fair, and storytelling.
September: **Harvest Moon Festival,** Onset. Music, parades, fireworks, and crafts fair.

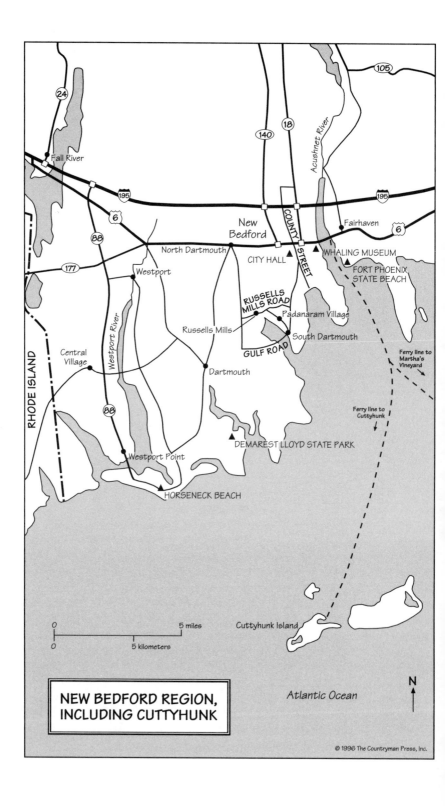

24

Fall River

195

105

140

18

Acushnet River

6

88

177

New
Bedford

North Dartmouth

CITY HALL

COUNTY STREET

195

Fairhaven

6

WHALING MUSEUM

FORT PHOENIX
STATE BEACH

Westport

RUSSELLS
MILLS ROAD

Padanaram Village

Russells Mills

South Dartmouth

Ferry line to
Martha's
Vineyard

Central
Village

Westport River

GULF ROAD

Dartmouth

RHODE ISLAND

88

Ferry line to
Cuttyhunk

DEMAREST LLOYD STATE PARK

Westport Point

HORSENECK BEACH

0   5 miles

0   5 kilometers

Cuttyhunk Island

N

**NEW BEDFORD REGION,
INCLUDING CUTTYHUNK**

Atlantic Ocean

© 1996 The Countryman Press, Inc.

Bristol County

NEW BEDFORD REGION, INCLUDING CUTTYHUNK

The physical size and shape of Manhattan Island, New Bedford has a population that's less than that of Cambridge, a heady mix of Portuguese, old-line Yankee, and a couple of dozen ethnic groups. In the 19th century, New Bedford—first as the world's leading whaling port and subsequently as a major textile center—drew workers from all the world's corners.

"I'm an Irishwoman, who married a Greek, and I run a Jewish delicatessen," is the way our tour guide introduced herself. "That's the way it is in New Bedford. Everyone's very ethnic, but we're all mixed up together, very friendly." The summer walking tours are led by local volunteers.

Generally perceived as a pass-through place, New Bedford is actually well situated to serve as a hub from which to day-trip to Newport, the islands of Martha's Vineyard and Cuttyhunk (both accessible by ferry), and Cape Cod.

In Dartmouth, southwest of the city, quiet, shady roads wind through farms and salt marshes to public beaches and conservation land, and the yachting village of Padanaram offers some unexpected dining and shopping. In nearby Westport, the state's number-one dairy town, fields sweep to tidal rivers, and one farm is now an outstanding winery. On the island of Cuttyhunk you can walk for an hour and meet only birds, and maybe a rabbit.

Across the Acushnet River from New Bedford, Fairhaven is a genuinely salty town with large boatyards and splendid public buildings funded by Henry Huttleston Rogers, a local boy who made his fortune in Pennsylvania petroleum rather than in whale oil.

AREA CODE
508

GUIDANCE

New Bedford maintains two visitors information centers. The **Waterfront Visitors Center** (979-1745), Pier 3, occupies the former Wharfinger Building, for many decades the scene of daily fish auctions; it offers free parking and rest rooms. **The Historic District Visitors Center** (991-6200), North Second Street, is handy to the Elm Street Garage. Both are open Monday through Saturday 9–5, Sunday 10–4; both are departure points for walking tours. See *Getting There* for directions.

Bristol County Convention and Visitors Bureau (997-1250), 70 North Second Street, New Bedford; in the Historic District, handy to the Elm Street Garage. Good for information on the entire county.

GETTING THERE

By car: From the west and New York, take I-95 to I-195 East, Exit 15 to MA 18, downtown exit. From points north and Boston, take MA 24 to 140 to I-195 East to Exit 15 (MA 18) to the downtown exit. For the North Second Street visitors center and the Whaling Museum, park in the Elm Street Garage, a right just off the exit. For the Pier 3 Visitors Center take the downtown exit but continue straight ahead to Union Street, then turn left on Union Street and cross MA 18; turn left onto Frontage Road and onto Fisherman's Wharf (Pier 3).

By bus: **Bonanza** (1-800-556-3815) offers service to Providence and New York. **American Eagle Coach Company** (1-800-453-5040) offers frequent service to Boston.

By air: New Bedford Regional Airport is served by **Cape Air** (flying to Nantucket and Martha's Vineyard). **Island Shuttle** (997-4098) also offers seaplane service to Cuttyhunk and the other islands.

By ferry: See *To Do—Ferries and Excursions.*

GETTING AROUND

Although the "Downtown Connector" (MA 18) disconnects the waterfront from the water, there are pedestrian crossways to the wharves where scallopers and draggers are docked. Guided tours of the area depart from both visitors centers, mid-June to mid-September.

PARKING

The **Elm Street Garage** (on your right just off the downtown exit) costs less than a meter, max of $5 per day.

MEDICAL EMERGENCY

St. Luke's Hospital (997-1515), 101 Page Street, New Bedford.

ISLANDS

Cuttyhunk Island. Accessible by the M/V *Alert II* (see *To Do—Ferries and Excursions*) from Pier 3 in New Bedford, and by air with Island Shuttle (see *Getting There*). Cuttyhunk is the westernmost of the 16 Elizabeth Islands that together form the town of Gosnold. The islands trail off in a line from Woods Hole, dividing Buzzards Bay from Vineyard Sound, and Cuttyhunk is one of only two not owned by Boston Brahman families. It is little more than 2 miles long and an irregular ¾ miles wide, home for fewer than 60 people in winter, maybe 400 in summer. It's best known for bass fishing.

From the dock you walk past the old life-saving station and, skirting the village, find the footpath through the cemetery and up the bluff. The panoramic view is off across the neighboring, very private islands to the dramatic cliffs at Gay Head on Martha's Vineyard. It's difficult to imagine a more perfect picnic spot, unless it's the observation platform on the island's height-of-land, overlooking the village, the harbor, and the sandy public beach on Copicut Neck.

In Cuttyhunk's one-room schoolhouse, the pupils (who seldom number more than three) learn that their island was the site of the Bay State's first English settlement. Bartholomew Gosnold built a stockade here in 1602 and set about planting a garden and gathering sassafras (valued for medicinal uses); but Native Americans, lurking in the brush, made the settlers jumpy. After a 22-day stay, the would-be colonists sailed away. A singularly ugly stone tower, erected in 1902, now marks the fort's site on a mini-island in the middle of a salt pond (in which oysters are presently being cultivated) at the western tip of the island.

From town it is a pleasant hour or day's walk to the monument, depending on how frequently and long you pause on the smooth boulders to watch the surf breaking or the sun glinting on beach grass. (It's advisable to wear socks and long pants against wood ticks.)

Although there are no longer inns or B&Bs, rooms and cottages can be rented by the day, weekend, week, or month; contact **Cuttyhunk Boat Lines** (992-1432). You might also inquire about bass boats, "with tackle, boat, and the guidance of their owners," which can be rented by the day or the tide. There's a small general store, and in summer the Cuttyhunk Breakfast and Lunch Shoppe serves meals.

If you can't spend the night, Cuttyhunk is still worth a day trip. The hour's ride down Buzzards Bay is a pleasant interlude, but, still, the absolute peace of the island comes as a jolt.

Martha's Vineyard. This isn't the place to describe New England's largest island and one of its most popular tourist destinations. (Contact the Martha's Vineyard Chamber of Commerce: 693-0085). The Vineyard is generally accessed by car ferry from Woods Hole on Cape Cod, but getting a reservation for your car is frequently difficult, not to mention expensive, and traffic to Woods Hole can be impossible. The 450-passenger ferry *Schamonchi* (see *To Do—Ferries and Excursions*) from New Bedford docks (as do ferries from Cape Cod) in Vineyard Haven. Day-trippers can bring bikes and spend up to 8 hours on the island, taking the bike path along the shore and into Oak Bluffs and Edgartown, then back the short way to Vineyard Haven. Rental bikes and cars are also available, and you can step right from the boat onto a tour bus or

The Whaling Museum's fully rigged, 89-foot half-scale model of the whaleship Lagoda

OLD DARTMOUTH HISTORICAL SOCIETY WHALING MUSEUM

take advantage of the island's (seasonal) visitor-geared bus system. Parking at the ferry dock in New Bedford is $7 a day.

TO SEE

MUSEUM
The New Bedford Whaling Museum (997-0046), 18 Johnny Cake Hill, New Bedford. Open Monday through Saturday 9–5, Sunday 1–5 (11–5 in July and August). Internationally known for its scrimshaw collection (more than 2000 pieces), the museum displays vivid paintings of life aboard whaling vessels from Tahiti to the Arctic Circle. Whaling voyages are illustrated on a quarter-mile-long panorama (produced in 1848 to show in traveling tents), etched on whale teeth, and dramatized in movies (shown regularly in summer months). You can clamber aboard the world's largest ship model—a half-scale model of the New Bedford bark *Lagoda*, fully equipped. The museum showcases more than the whaling chapter in the area's history. There is a room full of the ornate art glass for which New Bedford was known beginning in the 1880s, and there are always major changing exhibits. Admission: $4.50 adults, $3.50 seniors, $3 children aged 6–14.

WINERY
Westport River Vineyard and Winery (636-3412), 417 Hixbridge Road, New Bedford. Open daily April through December noon–5; tours Saturday and Sunday. Winter tours by appointment. "We made a climatic study and discovered that this area between Newport and Cape Cod offered the longest, sunniest growing season in New England," explains Carol Russell about why she and her husband, Robert, chose Westport as a vineyard site. More than 40 of the 110 acres (making this the physically largest vineyard in New England) on this former farm are now planted in Vinifera grapes, a third of which are annually turned into table wines, notably a Chardonnay of unusual quality. Another third has been reserved for champagne, the first 12,000 bottles of which were released in 1994. Inquire about frequent special events at the winery.

HISTORIC SITES
In the Waterfront Historic District of New Bedford
Seamen's Bethel (992-3295), 15 Johnny Cake Hill. Open May through October, weekday afternoons and weekends. The pulpit, shaped like a "ship's bluff bow," such as Melville described, was actually installed after the publication of *Moby Dick*. The remainder of the 1830s chapel conveys a sense of the men who have prayed here (and continue to) before setting out to sea. The walls are covered with memorial tablets to men who have died in every watery corner of the earth, cenotaphs from the 1840s side by side with those from the 1970s and '80s. It is a Quaker-plain, moving place. It's also a popular place for weddings because of the myth that marriages made here last. The **Mariner's Home** next door, like the Bethel, is run by the Port Society, founded in 1830 "for the moral and religious improvement of seamen." The building itself dates from 1787, and there is a nominal charge to fishermen for a night's lodging (not open to the public).
Coast Guard Lightship *New Bedford*, State Pier. This retired lightship saw long service in Atlantic waters until 1971 and is a waterfront landmark awaiting restoration.
Double Bank Building, 56-60 North Water Street. One of the city's most distinctive buildings, built in 1831–35 as a classic Greek Revival temple of finance, originally for two different banks (notice the two kinds of pillars); it now houses the Fisherman's Union and related firms.
Custom House (994-5158), corner of William and Second Streets, built in 1834–36, is impressive both inside and out. It is still operating as the oldest custom house in the country.
Third District Court of Bristol County, corner of William and Second Streets (kitty-cornered to the Custom House). Built in 1852 as a bank, it housed the Third District Court of Bristol County from 1899 to 1914 and was subsequently auctioned to the Nonquiet Tribe of Red Men. It served a number of unlikely purposes until it was eventually reclaimed and restored as a bank in 1979. Closed once more in 1994, it will per-

haps serve as headquarters for New Bedford's proposed National Historic Park.

City Hall, Pleasant, William, and Sixth Streets. Dating from the city's whaling era (it was built in 1856), the building contains an ornate open-cage elevator, said to be the oldest functioning elevator in the US, that dates from 1906.

New Bedford Free Public Library, Pleasant Street next to City Hall. The building dates from 1837, constructed of native granite with Egyptian Revival detailing (boasting the world's only Egyptian Revival elevator). A Melville Whaling Room includes a superb collection of log books and other whaling-era material. Note the handsome rotunda added in 1905 and, outside, the Whaler's Memorial.

Along County Street, New Bedford
"Nowhere in America will you find more patrician-like houses," Herman Melville wrote about County Street; "brave houses and flower gardens, . . . harpooned and dragged hither from the bottom of the sea." One of the oldest streets in the city, County Street runs along the crest of the hill from which the city slopes down to the harbor. It was the obvious place to build for the wealthiest whaling merchants, followed by textile-mill owners.

Rotch-Jones-Duff House and Garden Museum (997-1401), 396 County Street. Open Tuesday through Saturday 10–4, Sunday 1–4. One of New Bedford's finest mansions, built in 1834 by Nantucket whaling merchant William Rotch Jr. at age 72 for his second wife. The 28 rooms are filled with furnishings illustrating the lifestyles of the three different families who lived here and their respective eras. We found the locally made Pairpoint glass chandeliers, the extensive costume collection, and Captain Jones's study particularly interesting. The formal gardens, which occupy an entire city block, are an oasis filled with boxwood hedges, a dogwood allée, wildflowers, and roses. In July and August there are Friday evening concerts; guests are invited to spread blankets and to picnic in the garden beforehand. Admission $3 adults, $2 seniors; free aged 12 and under. Concerts $6; half price for children over 6.

In Fairhaven
Just across the Acushnet River (take the US 6 bridge) from New Bedford, Fairhaven is a proud old shipbuilding and whaling town, distinguished today by its elaborate public buildings—virtually all the gifts of Henry Huttleston Rodgers. A multimillionaire who made his fortune in Pennsylvania petroleum rather than in whale oil, H.H. Rodgers donated the huge, castlelike high school (US 6 and Main Street), the Masonic Hall, the splendid Unitarian church (102 Green Street), and, most notably, the library.

The Millicent Library, 45 Centre Street, dedicated to the memory of Rodgers's daughter, who died at age 17, is worth a stop simply to see its ornate, Victorian interior. Many Japanese visitors come to see its collection of memorabilia relating to Manjiro Nakahama, a shipwrecked Japanese boy who was rescued by a Captain William Whitfield in 1841. The Fairhaven captain brought the boy home and sent him to private school. Nakahama later returned to Japan, serving as interpreter for Admiral Perry in negotiating the 1853 treaty that opened Japanese ports. The late emperor of Japan stopped at the library in 1987, and Japanese tourists continue to come to sign their names in the same book that he used.

The library also displays memorabilia of Joshua Slocum, who set sail from Fairhaven in his small boat, *The Spray,* to circumnavigate the world. Samuel Clemens (Mark Twain), who dedicated the library in 1894, pronounced it "the ideal library, I think. Books are the liberated spirits of men, and should be bestowed in a heaven of light and grace and harmonious color and sumptuous comfort, like this." H.H. Rodgers is said to have saved Clemens from bankruptcy.

Fort Phoenix, on the bay, is the other Fairhaven site to see: Pre-Revolutionary in origin, it claims the first naval engagement of the Revolution (May 14, 1775). The fort maintains its original shape. One cannon (still here) had been captured by John Paul Jones in the Bahamas. The fort was overcome in 1778 but fended off a British invasion party in 1814, and again saw service in the Civil War. The smooth rocks and small beach below the fort at the base of the Acushnet River breakwater are free and locally favored for sunbathing. (Also see *Swimming.*)

Also in Fairhaven: For a sense of the town's active waterfront, stop by the Public Boat Landing across from **Cushman's Park** (Middle Street), and check out the scallopers at **Kelley Boat Yards** and in the **Fairhaven Ship Yard.** Note that most boats here and in New Bedford bear the letters "F.V." ("Fishing Vessel").

FOR FAMILIES

Children's Museum (993-3361), 276 Gulf Road, South Dartmouth. Open year-round, Tuesday through Saturday 10–5, Sunday 1–5. Housed in a huge old dairy barn, it is now filled with a kaleidoscopic range of hands-on exhibits: a fishing boat; a fantastical revolving pillar of trucks, cranes, and mechanical contrivances; a plethora of blocks and Legos; and, outside, a "windfarm" and 60 acres of conservation land. Inquire about frequent special events. Admission $3.75 per person.

New Bedford Fire Museum (992-2162), corner of Bedford and South Sixth Streets, New Bedford. Not far from the center of town, but a fire engine shuttles visitors up from the visitors centers. Open July and August only, daily 9–5. Housed in a former stable next to 19th-century Fire Station #4, this museum maintains a collection of antique equipment: shiny pumpers, buckets, horns, and more. There is a corner for children to dress up in firemen's uniforms and a pole for them to slide down (grown-ups are permitted to slide, too). It is staffed by veteran firefighters. $1 adults, free for children 12 and under.

Westport Waterslide (636-6750), Westport, on US 6 near Lincoln Park.

Open mid-May through September, weekends until mid-June, then daily 11–6.

(Also see Demarast Lloyd State Park under *To Do—Swimming* and the Lloyd Center under *Green Space.*)

SCENIC DRIVE

Just southwest of New Bedford lies some of the most beautiful seaside farmland in the state. We suggest that you explore it from west to east, but obviously this route can work in either direction. Take MA 88 South from I-195 to **Westport Point,** one of the oldest settlements between Newport and Plymouth and a major shipbuilding village in the 1850s. It's now a quiet, gray-shingled village with a main street that ends at the fishing pier and Lees Wharf Fish Market. Most of the town's shops cluster in Central Village, several miles up Main Road, from which you should detour on Hixbridge Road east across the river to find the **Westport River Winery** (see *Winery*). Westport ranks as the state's number-one dairy town, and the scenery along its back roads—with farms reaching to the river—is memorable, beloved by bicyclists. Note the range of Westport listings under *Where to Eat.*

From Westport Point continue on to West Beach Road past **Horseneck Beach** (see *Swimming*). This area was an upscale resort (FDR convalesced here from polio) with a large hotel until the 1938 hurricane savaged the area. It's possible to walk out onto Gooseberry Neck or into the Audubon Sanctuary at Allens Pond; both come before **The Bayside** (see *Eating Out*). Continue on Old Horseneck Road (note the turnoff for **Demarest Lloyd State Park**; see *Swimming*), up along the Slocum River and into **Russell Mills Village** in which houses are scattered, each on its own rise of land, around an old mill pond (note Davoll's General Store and Salt Marsh Pottery under *Selective Shopping*). Ask directions to the **Apponagansett Friends Meeting House,** a weathered building built in 1790 (closed except for a Sunday meeting in summer months). The graveyard is a quiet, moving place with the same names on the plain tombstones that appear on local mailboxes: Allen, Slocum, Gifford, Russell. Take Rock O'Dundee Road to Potomska Road and the **Lloyd Center** (see *Green Space*) and continue south along the salt marsh on Little River Road to Smith Neck Road, one of the area's more prestigious summer addresses. The most famous mansion (on the shore side) on this gold coast is **Round Hill,** an estate built by the son of Hetty Green, known as "The Witch of Wall Street" and supposedly the richest and most miserly woman in the world around the turn of the century. Hetty's son and daughter built Round Hill, now converted into condominiums and part of a private development. The huge satellite dish resembling a fountain is a legacy from the decades in which the mansion was owned by MIT. Note **Salt Marsh Farm B&B** just up the road, and turn left on Gulf Road into **Padanaram Village.** This marks the spot of a 17th-century settlement.

In the 19th century there were saltworks and shipyards; now it is a fashionable yachting resort with some fine little restaurants. The view of the yacht-filled harbor from the bridge and causeway is exceptional, as is the ride along Smith Neck Road.

TO DO

BALLOONING
Balloon Adventures of New Bedford (636-4846), 564 Rock O'Dundee Road, South Dartmouth. One-hour champagne flights available year-round, specializing in coastal flights, 17 years' experience; $200 per person, $225 on weekends.

BICYCLING
The route described under *Scenic Drives* is eminently suited to bicycling. Salt Marsh Farm B&B offers use of bikes to its guests and specializes in mapping routes of varying distances.

FERRIES AND EXCURSIONS
Cape Island Express Lines, Inc. (997-1688), Billy Wood's Wharf, New Bedford. The 450-passenger *Schamonchi* departs mid-May to mid-October, making one to four runs (depending on the day and month) to Vineyard Haven on Martha's Vineyard. Parking is $6 per day at Billy Wood's Wharf (next to Davey's Locker) at the southern end of the city. Round-trip fare to the Vineyard is $15 adults, $7.50 children; $8.50 and $4.50 one-way; $2.50 for bicycles. (Also see *Islands.*)

Cuttyhunk Boat Lines, Inc. (992-1432; 992-6076), Fisherman's Wharf/Pier 3, New Bedford. Mid-June to mid-September daily; Tuesday, Friday, and weekends in spring and fall; Tuesday and Friday only in winter. Obviously designed as much for freight as for passengers, this 60-passenger, aluminum-hulled ferry serves as the life and information line to Cuttyhunk. On summer weekends prepaid reservations are suggested. $15.50 adults round trip, $10.50 one-way, and $8.50 for children round trip. Inquire about harbor tours and other excursions at the Waterfront Visitors Center next door.

FISHING
Captain Leroy (992-8907) departs from the Fairhaven Bridge (US 6) April through November daily at 7:30 AM, returning at 4 PM. His 50-foot and 65-foot party boats are equipped with fish and depth finders; rods and reels available for $7. (Also see Cuttyhunk Island under *Islands.*)

GOLF
Emerald Park Golf Club (992-8387), North Dartmouth, 18 holes. **Whaling City Country Club** (996-9393), New Bedford, 18 holes. **Hawthorn Country Club** (996-1766), North Dartmouth. **Marion Golf Club** (748-0199), nine holes.

SWIMMING
Demarest Lloyd State Park (636-8816), Barney's Joy Road, South

Dartmouth. This is one of my favorite state beaches, crowded on Sunday but otherwise relatively deserted, ideal for small children since there is no surf. There are roughly 2 miles of beach with a view of Cuttyhunk; picnic tables, grills, and fireplaces. A large sandspit jutting into the mouth of the Slocum River is a pleasant place to walk. In-season there is a $2 parking fee.

Horseneck Beach (636-8816), Westport Point, accessible from I-195 by MA 88. The highway stretches almost to the blacktopped parking lot and camping area and nearly to the futuristic concrete shower/restroom/snack-bar complex. There is even a blacktop strip between the dunes and the beach. The vast expanse of beach is spectacular, and the surf is just challenging enough. $3 admission.

Apponagansett Point Beach (parking fee for nonresidents) is a small, pleasant beach on Gulf Road, South Dartmouth, near the Children's Museum.

New Bedford Beaches. Follow MA 18 South to Rodney French Boulevard. Hazelwood Park and East Beach both have changing rooms and snack bars; open late June until Labor Day, 9–6; free.

Fort Phoenix State Beach (992-4524), Fairhaven. Take Green Street from US 6. This beach can be windy, but it is otherwise pleasant and uncrowded on weekdays; an urban beach, bathhouse, lifeguards, $2 parking fee.

GREEN SPACE

Buttonwood Park (993-5686), US 6, New Bedford. Designed by the prestigious firm of Olmsted/Elliot in 1894, this 97-acre park includes tennis courts, picnicking space, and paddleboats.

Brooklawn Park (995-6644), Acushnet Avenue, New Bedford; a kiddie pool, tennis courts, and picnicking facilities.

Lloyd Center for Environmental Studies (990-0505), 430 Potomska Road, South Dartmouth. A former home that's been fitted with touch tanks, aquariums, an environmental library, and a third-floor observatory overlooking a 55-acre preserve on the Slocum River. The nature trails are varied, snaking through wooded hills, sloping through large holly stands to Osprey Point, and winding around a swamp filled with salamanders and spotted turtles. Inquire about canoe trips and frequent guided walks.

Fort Phoenix, Fairhaven. See *To See*.

Fort Tabor, Rodney French Boulevard (the end), New Bedford. At the far southern end of the city, this massive granite complex was designed by Captain Robert E. Lee in 1846, long before his command in the Confederate Army.

LODGING

BED & BREAKFASTS

☞ **Edgewater Bed & Breakfast** (994-1574), 2 Oxford Street, Fairhaven 02719. Parts of this unusual house, on Fairhaven's Poverty Point, were built as a store in the 1760s. It is now a rambling 1880s home with some of the best views of New Bedford across the Acushnet River, which seemingly surrounds the house and moves so quickly by its many windows that you actually feel afloat. There are five rooms, each with a TV and private bath. The Captain's Suite has a private sitting room with a working fireplace and water views on three sides. The Clara Anthony Room has water views and a clawfoot tub. The Joshua Slocum Suite (good for families) in the 1760 part of the house has a private entrance and deck, a sitting room, and kitchenette. The Eldridge Room and East Indies Room in the old part of the house lack views but are nicely furnished. A muffins-and-juice breakfast is served in the formal dining room, and guests have full access to the handsome, sunken living room. Cathy Reed, a college professor, is a warm host and is knowledgeable about local restaurants and sights. $70–85 double.

Salt Marsh Farm (992-0980), 322 Smith Neck Road, South Dartmouth 02748. The hip-roofed farmhouse dates from 1727, and it's set in its own 90 acres, with access to a nearby beach. The homestead has been in Sally Brownell's family since World War II, and she shares with guests her special sense of the area. There are two guest rooms with private baths, antique and handmade quilts, each room with its own hall and stairway besides. The living rooms and dining room are slant-floored, furnished in comfortable antiques. Larry Brownell nurtures an extensive garden and Sally prides herself on fairly spectacular breakfasts: Dutch Babies (puffy shells and waffles topped with fresh strawberries and syrup), omelets from fresh-hatched eggs laced with Brie, blueberry muffins made with yogurt and scented with lemon. Guests are welcome to use the house bikes (or bring their own) and follow a variety of routes through the countryside (see *Scenic Drive*). $75 per couple, including tax and breakfast. No smoking.

Cynthia and Steven's Bed and Breakfast (997-6433), 36 Seventh Street, New Bedford 02742. Just off County Street, within New Bedford's historic district, is a long-established B&B in a Victorian home with private baths. Contact Cynthia Poyant.

The Little Red House (996-4554), 631 Elm Street, Padanaram Village 02748. Two rooms in a gambrel-roofed house; $55 and $65.

MOTEL

Days Inn (997-1231), 500 Hathaway Road, intersection of MA 140 (Exit 3) and I-195, New Bedford 02719. This is a 133-room, recently refurbished

motel with a locally respected restaurant, indoor pool. $55–60 double.
CAMPGROUND
Horseneck Beach (636-8816) offers 100 campsites.

WHERE TO EAT

DINING OUT
Bridge Street Cafe (994-7200), 10-A Bridge, South Dartmouth. June to Labor Day, open Tuesday through Saturday for lunch and dinner (brunch on Sunday). A garage turned restaurant, specializing in fresh, local ingredients and in "bridging the gap between the mundane and the much too fancy"; Greg and Sally Morton feature ginger chicken, barbecued baby-back ribs, soft-shell crabs, grilled lamb, a variety of homemade pasta and seafood dishes, and Sally's outrageous desserts. Dinner entrées $13.95–19.50.
Le Rivage (999-4505), 7 Water Street, Padanaram Village. Jean-Claude Galan offers locally acclaimed fine dining in the yacht haven.
Huttleston House (999-1791), 111 Huttleston Avenue, Fairhaven. Open daily for lunch and dinner. Traditional American fare, friendly service. Complete dinners average $20, and daily specials are $7.95.
The Candleworks (992-1635), 72 North Water Street, New Bedford. Open for lunch and dinner Monday through Saturday, 4–9 on Sunday. Regional fish, Italian dishes. Housed in a granite building built by Samuel Rodman in 1810 to produce spermaceti candles. Patio dining. Dinner entrées $15–22.
Moby-Dick (636-6500), Westport Point (the last right off MA 88 before Horseneck Beach). Open for lunch and dinner. An old dining landmark, expanded and upscaled when it was rebuilt (after a fire) several years ago. Accessible by boat as well as car. The menu goes with the Oriental rugs: chilled littlenecks, bouillabaisse, grilled salmon with black truffle butter. Still offers the classic New England clambake (steamers, potatoes, onion, sausage, hot dog, linguica, and scrod) for $10.95; $19.95 if you add lobster.
Kate Cory's Restaurant at Bittersweet Farm (636-5559), 438 Main Road, Westport (between Westport Point and Central Village). Open for lunch and dinner except Monday. A nicely converted, open-beamed barn with an airy feel and views of manicured grounds; a locally favored dining place. Try the billi bi soup and poached mussels in cream with herb butter.
EATING OUT
In New Bedford
Freestone's (993-7477), 41 William Street. Open daily 11 AM–11 PM, Sunday brunch. This is both a casual and serious dining spot, depending on the time of day and what you order. In 1979 Debbie Sequin and Kerry Mitchell dislodged a raunchy bar and restored this early-19th-century

bank building, preserving the original mahogany paneling and working fireplace. Specialties include prize-winning fish chowder, grilled Louisiana scallop and crab cakes, and a wide choice of salads, sandwiches, and seafood.

Antonio's Restaurant (990-3636), 267 Coggeshall Street. Open Sunday through Thursday 11:30–9:30; Friday and Saturday until 10. One of the best places for Portuguese food in the state; an informal, friendly place with a bilingual menu. You smell the spices the moment you walk in. Of course you start with kale soup and make a satisfying, reasonably priced meal of the Cacoila Platter; the specialty of the house is "Mariscada a Antonio's," a seafood casserole usually split between two. From I-195 West take Exit 17 (Coggeshall Street) and turn left. Go through the traffic light, and the restaurant is on your right. Free parking is in the lot across the street. No credit cards or reservations. Try the Sagres (Portuguese) beer in the stand-up lounge while waiting for a table. The "Seafood Antonio" serves two starving adults at $17.95. Entrées begin at $5.50.

Davey's Locker (992-7359), 1480 East Rodney French Boulevard. Open daily 11 AM–10 PM. A large dining landmark at the south end of the city, overlooking the water, this is generally agreed to be the best reasonably priced place to eat fish in New Bedford. The clam chowder is outstanding. Note the nightly dinner specials. Steaks and other meat staples are part of the large menu.

Phoebe's Restaurant (999-5486), 7 South Sixth Street. Open for breakfast and lunch, Sunday brunch, dinner Thursday and Friday. Housed in the former storefront of a 19th-century building that's been a Turkish bathhouse and an undertaker's parlor, this attractive, brick-walled space with mismatched antique oak tables and chairs offers imaginative egg dishes, salads, and sandwiches.

Maxie's Deli, Purchase Street across from City Hall. Open 4 AM–2:30 PM. A bright, friendly eating and gossip spot with exposed brick walls and hanging plants; the day's paper is stacked for guests. Jurassic-sized two eggs and toast, $1.05. NYC-style deli sandwiches.

Shawmut Diner (993-3073), Shawmut Avenue. Open 5:30 AM–7 PM daily, until 8 Thursday through Saturday. A chrome classic, but roast leg of lamb is the specialty. $5.95 buys dinner; $2.99 for fish-and-chips.

In Fairhaven

Mike's (996-9810), 714 Washington Street (US 6). No reservations. Cash only. Usually a wait in the lounge until your name is called. The attraction here is steak and seafood—lots of both at bargain prices: clam chowder, a full, boiled lobster, and side order of potato (or spaghetti) for $6.99. Twin lobster dinners for $11. A slab of the best prime rib for $12. Also good for thin-crust pizza, and where else can you get an Italian Pu Pu platter?

Margaret's, corner of Main and Water Streets, breakfast and lunch, dinner on Friday. A hangout for locals and boatyard workers. Coffee-shop atmosphere, but café-style food: Norwegian fish cakes, Portuguese-style codfish salad, sautéed chicken with tomato, garlic, spinach, and feta, and, if you must, peanut butter with jelly and fluff. Desserts the day we stopped by included almond torte and apricot meringue cream cake.

Pumpernickel's (990-2026), 23 Centre Street. The menu is printed on a paper bag. Good for chowder or kale soup, linguica, or a seafood medley; fabulous desserts.

The Pasta House, Bridge Street. Homemade pasta, dishes like pasta with mussels, fried ice cream.

The Phoenix Restaurant (996-1441), 140 Huttleston Avenue. Open 11 PM– 2 PM (closed 3 PM–11 PM). Breakfast is the specialty here; try scrambled eggs with linguica and home fries. Cheese rolls, Portuguese and Greek specialties.

The Fairhaven Chowder House (996-4100), Sconticut Neck Road at Droun Boulevard. Open daily; a locally owned fish market with a modern, squeaky-clean dining room, seafood specialties. Serves wine and beer.

Tofu (990-2888), 9 Popes Island (US 6 on the New Bedford/Fairhaven causeway). Good Mandarin and Szechuan dishes (no MSG); we recommend the crispy whole fish and lunch and dinner buffets.

In Dartmouth and Westport

The Bayside (636-5882), 1253 Horseneck Road, Westport. Open 8 AM–8 PM, later in summer. Billing itself "the best dinky, socially responsible, environmentally aware, little restaurant in the Commonwealth," this family-owned oasis is a good reason to drive to this particularly inviting piece of the shore. The specialties are quahog chowder, codfish cakes, and johnnycakes, but you can get anything from a $1.95 hamburger to scallops Provençal or Cajun mussels served over linguine. Beer and wine are served.

Stone Soup, Elm Street, Padanaram Village. Open for breakfast and lunch, Friday night dinner. Carolyn Michaud's blackboard menu may list fish-and-chips, shepherd's pie, always soups, sandwiches, and chowders.

Joy's Landing Restaurant (992-8148), Water Street, South Dartmouth. Open daily 8 AM–9 PM, 24 hours on weekends. A shingled, waterside haven featuring fish-and-chips but also good for a linguica sandwich and kale soup for breakfast.

Ellie's Place (636-5590), 1403 Main Road, Westport. Open 7:30 AM–8 PM except Monday year-round. A friendly local eatery featuring stuffed quahogs and quahog chowder, johnnycakes with bacon, Portuguese-style fish broiled in a special marinade, fried smelts, and whiffleburgers (scrambled hamburger with onions, tomatoes, peppers, mushrooms, and melted cheese). Beer and wine are served.

ENTERTAINMENT

Zeiterion Theatre (994-2900), 684 Purchase Street, New Bedford. All-vaudeville theater. Its restoration has been a community effort, a symbol of the new New Bedford. The Zeiterion now has a professional summer and performing arts season, featuring musicals, jazz, dance, classical concerts, and children's performances. Call for seasonal schedule.

UMass Dartmouth (999-8000), Old Westport Road, North Dartmouth, stages cabaret theater July through August.

Heritage Concert Series at the Rotch-Jones-Duff House in July and August (Friday evenings). Guests are invited to picnic in the garden beforehand.

Note: A gambling casino, hotel, and theme park are in the permitting process in the Massachusetts legislature.

SELECTIVE SHOPPING

ANTIQUES SHOPS

Brookside Antiques (493-4944), 44 North Water Street, New Bedford, specializes in Pairpoint glass, other things local.

New Bedford Antique Co-op (993-7600), Coggeshall Street, an eclectic mix of good-quality antiques; represents 260 dealers.

Fairhaven Antiques Mart (991-2922) represents 100 dealers.

ART GALLERIES

Bierstadt Art Society Gallery (993-4308), 179 William Street, New Bedford. Hours vary. Area painters exhibit in changing shows.

Norton Gallery (997-9674), 330 Elm Street, Padanaram Village. Nautical prints, sculptures by locally known artists.

BOOKSTORES

Baker Books (992-3749), 69 State Road, North Dartmouth. Open Monday through Saturday 9–5, this large bookstore offers an exceptional range of titles including books of local, regional, and nautical interest as well as maps, guides, and children's books.

The Village Bookshop, 294 Elm Street, Padanaram Village. An extensive collection of yachting and children's books, greeting cards, a blue parakeet. A cheerful, welcoming store.

Barnes & Noble (997-0701), Dartmouth Commons off US 6, North Dartmouth. Open Monday through Saturday 9–9, Sunday noon–6. Huge and well stocked; general titles plus discount books, maps, guides, periodicals.

FACTORY OUTLETS

When petroleum replaced whale oil in the 1860s, New Bedford merchants put their money into cotton mills, which grew as whaling waned, reaching their peak prosperity in the 1920s. Then came a very long depres-

A favorite of visitors to New Bedford's Annual Portuguese Feast is fried linguica sandwiches.

sion for the city. "Factory Outlet Shopping" was supposedly invented here in the 1950s when clothing manufacturers opened a few square feet of factory floor space to the general public for direct sales. One outlet led to two and today there are relatively few "stand-alone" factory outlet shops. Most of them have gathered to form centers, usually in former mill buildings.

Howland Place Designer Outlet Mall (999-4100), 651 Orchard Street, is the only big outlet center in New Bedford itself: more than 20 outlets in three stories of a century-old mill. Stores include Calvin Klein, Escada, Arrow Shirts, and Libby Glass.

VF Factory Outlet (998-3311), 375 Faunce Corner Road (the road is an exit off I-195) in North Dartmouth. Open Monday through Saturday

9–9. This is a vast, hangarlike building filled with some of the best clothing outlets around. It was formerly known as "Kay Windsor," a line still carried in the large area that adjoins the Vanity Fair and Lee section (there are ample changing rooms and mirrors), with a great selection of jeans (including odd sizes) and sportswear for the whole family, all at 50 percent off. A dozen other outlets in the same complex include such popular brand names as Cape Isle Knitters, Van Heusen, American Tourister, and Bannister Shoes.

Bedspread Mill Outlet (992-6600), Mt. Pleasant Street, New Bedford. Open Monday through Saturday 9:30–5:30, Thursday until 8 PM. Blinds, balloon shades, drapes, sheets, comforters, blankets at 30 percent to 50 percent savings.

SPECIAL SHOPS

Davoll's General Store (636-4530), 1228 Russells Mills Road in the middle of Russells Mills village. You can buy coffee and cornflakes here, but also a variety of glass, metal, pottery lamps, antique and reproduction furniture, century-old quilts, handwoven woolen and cloth rugs, collectibles, and, most surprising of all, a selection of autographed children's books. Beyond the basic general store are five more rooms crammed with merchandise. Inquire about special events.

Salt Marsh Pottery (636-4813), 1167 Russells Mills Road on the edge of the village of Russells Mills. Open Monday through Saturday 10–6, Sunday noon–5. Housed in a vintage-1913 schoolhouse, the pottery employs some 20 artists producing handmade, hand-painted, decorative dishes, tiles, clocks, lamps, and tiled mirrors, all with wildflower impressions; distinctive magnets, seconds. Warning: It's difficult to leave without buying something.

Adriance Furnituremakers (997-6812), 288 Gulf Road, Padanaram Village. fine handcrafted Shaker and Colonial-style furniture.

Moby Dick Specialties (994-5024), 27 William Street, New Bedford. Open Monday through Saturday 8–5. An old chandlery, crammed from floor to ceiling with an eclectic mix of kitsch, basic marine hardware and camping gear, brass ornaments, and salty souvenirs. The shop is supplied by a warehouse full of similar treasures, a wholesale source of nautical decor for restaurants.

Bedford Merchant (997-9194), 28 William Street, New Bedford. Open Monday through Saturday 9–5. Quality gifts and home furnishings at modest prices; frequent sales and specials.

Gourmet Outlet (999-6408), 2301 Purchase Street, New Bedford. Call for directions and hours. An out-of-the-way specialty food store, the kind with nine varieties of fresh mushrooms, six kinds of fresh olives, five kinds of Russian caviar, daily fresh sourdough bread from San Francisco, and every conceivable spice.

Dorothy Cox's Candies (996-2465), 115 Huttleston Avenue (US 6), Fairhaven. Open daily 10–8, until 9 in summer. All recipes are made in small batches and cooked in heavy copper kettles. The specialties are buttercrunch and a variety of hand-dipped chocolates. In business since 1928; ships throughout the US.

SPECIAL EVENTS

Early May: Annual **WHALE Auction** at the Zeiterion Theatre, New Bedford—artwork and antique furniture to benefit the Waterfront Historic Area League.

Memorial Day: Probably the country's most moving day of the year in New Bedford. More than 300 names are read out at the harborside, each the name of a fisherman lost at sea since 1950. A bell is rung after each name, and families and friends throw flowers into the harbor.

June: **Padanaram Days**—sidewalk sale, trolley rides, music, Padanaram Village.

July: **Whaling City Festival** in Buttonwood Park, New Bedford, sunrise to sunset—giant flea market, car show, train rides.

Weekend after July 4: **Summerfest**—A waterfront festival featuring seafood, a tugboat rally, children's events, Blessing of the Fleet. **Art on the Waterfront** features southern New England painters to benefit restoration of the Lightship.

August, first weekend: The **Feast of the Blessed Sacrament,** music, dancing, and FOOD—"the world's largest barbecue" (you rent a skewer and brown your own meat over a pit). There are fava beans, baccalhau in a variety of sauces, linguica and other Madeiran delicacies, plenty of Madeiran wine. Midway at Madeira Field in the North End, New Bedford.

October: **Westport Harvest Festival,** the weekend after Columbus Day, at Westport River Winery, Westport.

December: Celebrations at the **Rotch-Jones-Duff House** (specially decorated for Christmas) and a downtown, outdoor **choral sing. First Night** celebration downtown, New Bedford.

FALL RIVER AREA

From its source in the Watuppa Ponds, the Quequehan River (said to mean "Falling Water") drops 132 feet in less than a mile. You can see the river in very few places today—it's been built over—but its effect has been dramatic. Fall River remains one of the state's outstanding monuments to the textile industry. Its mammoth, five- and six-story granite mills rise in tiers above Mount Hope Bay. Its first power loom was set in motion in 1817, and by the turn of the century, the city boasted more than 100 mills and 4 million spindles. In 1900 Fall River produced enough yardage to wrap the earth at the equator 57 times.

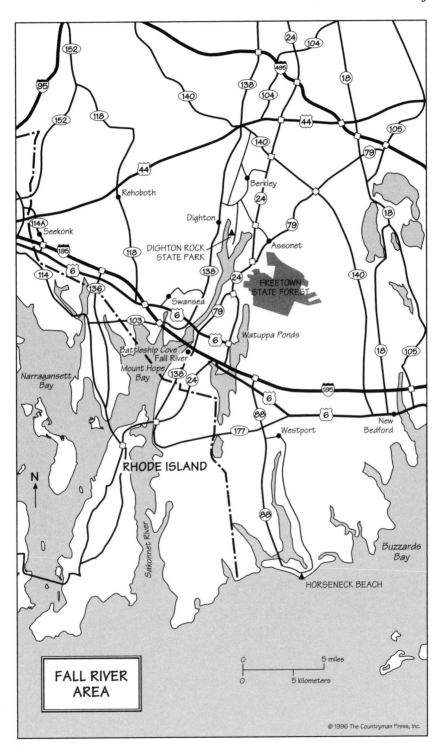

FALL RIVER
AREA

In 1927 the industry sagged. Over the next few years millions of square feet of factory space were abandoned, and fire wiped out the city's business core. Fall River went into receivership in the 1930s and was governed by a state-appointed finance board for a decade. The last mill shut down in 1965.

Today Fall River's mills are filled by "needle trades"—electronics and metals firms—and also by some 80 factory outlets and off-price stores. While the outlets draw bargain hunters, Battleship Cove draws families with its lineup of naval vessels, restored carousel, maritime museum, and Heritage State Park with exhibits and landscaped, riverside grounds.

The Fabric of Fall River, a film shown at the Heritage State Park Visitors Center, tells the story of how dozens of ethnic groups intermingled to form this unusual city. More than half of Fall River's residents are still classified as "foreign stock." The spires of St. Anne's Church (a symbol for French Canadian residents) tower above the factory domes, and Columbia Street is lined with Portuguese shops, bakeries, and restaurants. The city is still divided into the dozen ethnic neighborhoods that began as self-contained mill villages.

AREA CODE
508

GUIDANCE
The Fall River Heritage State Park (675-5759; 676-5773), Battleship Cove. Open year-round 9–4:30 daily except Monday; daily Memorial Day to Labor Day. Staff answer questions about local sights, restaurants, and lodging.
Bristol County Visitors Bureau (see the "New Bedford Region" introduction) maintains an information center (673-1311; 1-800-288-6263) in the Fall River Heritage State Park, Memorial Day through Labor Day.

GETTING THERE
By bus: The SRTA Bus Terminal (679-2335), 221 Second Street, Fall River, is served by Bonanza, connecting with Boston and New York, New Bedford, Padanaram Village, and Fairhaven.
By car: From Boston take MA 24 to MA 79; the Battleship Cove exit is not well marked. From I-195 it's Exit 4, just east of the Braga Bridge; from MA 79 South take the Davoll Street exit.

GETTING AROUND
Fall River is confusing. The three areas of interest—Battleship Cove, the Historical Society, and the factory outlets—are in three different parts of town. We suggest you begin at any of the sites in Battleship Cove and pick up a map and current pamphlet guides at the Heritage State Park (note that the excellent film here is shown only at 2 PM). The Portuguese restaurants and bakeries on Columbia Street are nearby. Get directions to the Historical Society (Lizzie Borden exhibits), which is in the fancy, mill-owned neighborhood set just above downtown, over-

looking the Taunton River. Most outlets are marked from I-95, Exit 8A.

MEDICAL EMERGENCY
Charlton Memorial Hospital (676-0431), 7363 Highland Avenue, Fall River.

TO SEE

MUSEUMS

✐ **Fall River Heritage State Park** (675-5759; 675-5773), Battleship Cove. Open year-round 10–4. The handsome, brick visitors center stands in an 8½-acre landscaped park, the scene of frequent concerts and special events; the adjacent boathouse offers rental paddleboats. *The Fabric of Fall River* is shown at 2 PM. The film traces the city's history vividly, dwelling on the rigors of immigrants working 6 AM–6 PM shifts and on the accidents and death suffered by child workers. It also dramatizes the vitality of the city in 1911 when President Taft visited for the Cotton Centennial. Exhibits include a loom and a variety of historical photo blowups. (Note the adjacent merry-go-round under *For Families.*)

✐ **Marine Museum** (674-3533), 70 Water Street, Battleship Cove. Open daily year-round; Memorial Day through October, 9–4 weekdays, noon–5 weekends; otherwise Wednesday through Friday 9–4, weekends noon–4. $3 adults, $2.50 seniors, $2 children. Housed in a former mill building of the American Print Works, once one of the world's largest textile mills, this museum holds a fascinating collection of ship models. It tells the story of the Fall River Line, from 1847 until 1937 the city's proudest advertisement. Exhibits include the 1880s Fall River Liner *Puritan*, which carried 1000 passengers and boasted electric lights, rich carpeting, mirrors, potted palms, and a full band to drown the thunder of paddle-wheels. Many passengers slept in open berths, but the 360 staterooms cost only $1 more. A four-course dinner, served on the boat's personalized china, included steak and lobster for $1.50; a glass of wine was $.15 extra. The minicruise was favored by business tycoons bound for Newport and New York, and by honeymooners and young swingers just for the live bands. On the northbound route, $4 bought steerage and a new life. In all there are more than 100 ship models on display, including the 28-foot *Titanic* built by 20th Century Fox for a 1952 movie. Special slide presentations on the Fall River Line and the sinking of the *Titanic* are shown regularly and available for groups.

Fall River Historical Society (679-1071), 451 Rock Street. Open April through December, Tuesday through Friday 9–4 (but closed for lunch); June through September, also weekends 1–5. $3 adults, $1.50 children aged 10–16. Built in 1843 for a mill owner near his mill, the building was moved in 1870 to this height-of-land, acquiring a mansard roof. The rich woodwork, elaborately carved doors, period chandeliers, and 14-foot ceilings in the front and back parlors are exceptional; displays

The Fall River Heritage State Park

fill 16 rooms and include exhibits on the mills and the Fall River Line and (what everyone comes to see) photos and descriptions of Lizzie Borden and her trial for brutally murdering her prominent parents in 1892.

FOR FAMILIES

USS *Massachusetts* (678-1100), Battleship Cove. Open year-round 9–5, until 7 PM in July and August. $8 adults, $4 children aged 6–14, admission to all the boats. The "Big Mamie" was saved from the scrap pile with $300,000 in nickels and dimes contributed by Bay State residents. Children now swivel the 40-millimeter gun mounts and clamber in and out of turrets. Women gawk at the 80-gallon stew pots. This one-time home for 2400 men has a soda fountain, three dental chairs, a sick bay, repair shops, and four mess halls. Groups (mostly Scout groups) can spend the night, September through June 1, for $33 per person. The World War II attack submarine **USS *Lionfish*** is moored next door. You can inspect the cramped living quarters for 120 men, the torpedo rooms, and conning tower. The destroyer **USS *Joseph P. Kennedy, Jr.*,** also here, is the official state memorial to the 4500 men and women who died in the Korean and Vietnam conflicts. There is also a gift store. Two World War II torpedo boats are also moored here.

Fall River Carousel (324-4300), Battleship Cove adjacent to the Heritage State Park. Open seasonally. A restored, vintage-1920 merry-go-round that stood for many years in the local amusement park to which trolleys ran for many decades from the city. Its 48 hand-painted horses and two chariots are now working again, housed in an elaborate pavilion with a snack bar.

HMS *Bounty* (676-8226), Battleship Cove. Open seasonally 10–6, until 8 on Friday, Saturday. Built specially for the MGM film *Mutiny on the*

Bounty, this 412-ton replica was launched from Lunenberg, Nova Scotia, and sailed to Tahiti for filming. Visitors are welcome to explore the three levels and 120-foot length of the vessel. $4 adults, $2 seniors, $2 children, free aged 4 and under.

Old Colony and Fall River Railroad Museum (674-9340), Battleship Cove at Central and Water Streets. Open late June through Labor Day daily 10–5, weekends 10–4. $1 adults; seniors and children $.50. Antique rail car exhibiting memorabilia, equipment, model trains, and steam engine.

Dighton Rock (822-7537) in Dighton Rock State Park, Bay View Road, Berkley. MA 24, Exit 10 West; left on Friends Street. Follow signs. The building that shelters the rock is closed. In 1677 Cotton Mather was impressed by the rock's significance but puzzled by its meaning and scholars have yet to agree on who drew the pictographs, still clearly visible. The most popular explanation in this heavily Portuguese region is that they were drawn by Miguel Cortereal, a Portuguese explorer who disappeared in 1502 while sailing to Newfoundland in search of his brother Gaspar, who had failed to return from a voyage the year before. Miguel's signature, the Portuguese cross, and the year 1511 are said to be clearly visible on the rock (it depends on how you look at it). There are picnic tables and a parking fee when someone is there to collect it.

TO DO

GOLF
Fall River Country Club (678-9374), 18 holes. **Fire Fly Country Club** (336-6622), Seekonk, 18 holes.

In Rehoboth: A number of former farms are now golf courses, among them: **Rehoboth Country Club** (252-6259) and **Sun Valley Country Club,** both with 18 holes.

SWIMMING
The big beach is **Horseneck** (see "New Bedford Region"). In Swansea visitors can also pay to swim at the town beach.

GREEN SPACE

Fall River's park system was designed by the firm of Frederick Law Olmsted in the 1870s. It includes Ruggles—North and South (now John F. Kennedy)—Parks (both include picnic space, tot lots, and wading pools), as well as the Durfee Green in the Highlands, Bradbury Green in the South End, and Northeastern Avenue.

Freetown State Forest (644-5522), Slab Bridge Road, Assonet. MA 24, Exit 10; bear left onto South Main Street. Follow signs. More than 5000 acres of woodland, a wading pool, hiking paths, picnic tables with fireplaces. As you pass through Assonet (a picturesque old village with a mill pond), note signs for **Profile Rock,** a wooded state reservation where paths lead to a striking profile of a Native American jutting out from an 80-foot-high pile of granite.

LODGING

INNS AND BED & BREAKFASTS

Perryville Inn (252-9239), 157 Perryville Road, Rehoboth 02769. An 1820s farmhouse enlarged and Victorianized in 1897, now offering five guest rooms, four baths. All are furnished in antiques and share two large sitting rooms. $65–85 for private bath, $50 for shared.

Colonel Blackington Inn (222-6022), 203 North Main Street, Attleboro 02073. An 1850 house situated on the Bungay River with 16 guest rooms, two small dining rooms, a sitting room, den, sun porch, and garden. $65–85 double, $42 single.

MOTEL

Johnson & Wales Inn (336-8700; 1-800-232-1772), MA 114A and MA 44, Seekonk 02771. A former standard motel has been transformed by one of the nation's leading culinary and hospitality schools. Of the 87 rooms, 26 are suites, most with whirlpool baths. Facilities include a restaurant (Audrey's) and access to the adjacent fitness center and 18-hole golf course.

WHERE TO EAT

DINING OUT

T.A. Restaurant (673-5890), 408 South Main Street, Fall River. Open 11–10 daily, Sunday noon–9. Parking (handy in this part of town) in the rear. "T.A." stands for "Tabacaria Acoreana," and you will hear more Portuguese than English spoken in this tastefully decorated restaurant. You might begin with kale soup and lunch on a chourico sandwich ($3.75) or marinated pork bits with steamed littlenecks and potatoes ($6.75), and dine on shrimp "St. Michael" style or steamed octopus. Most entrées are under $10. The Portuguese wines are reasonably priced. Service is formal and courteous, the kind you would expect in a far more expensive restaurant.

White's of Westport (675-7185; 993-2974), 66 State Road (US 6), Westport. Open daily 11:30–10. Overlooking Lake Watuppa, the large SS *Priscilla* dining room replicates the grand salon of the Fall River Line's most luxurious boat. Good for seafood dinners ($12 range) and for reasonably priced luncheons.

Sagres Restaurant (675-7018), 181 Columbia Street, Fall River. Open Monday through Thursday 11–10, Friday until 11 PM, Sunday noon–10. A family-owned place specializing in a mix of Portuguese and Spanish dishes. Come for the Fado singing on weekends. $6.50–13.

Venus de Milo (678-3901), US 6, Swansea. I-195, Exit 3. Open daily for lunch and dinner, noon–9. A long-established, family-owned restaurant that's known for its chowder and baked lobster. Excellent for seafood, but also good for prime rib and veal dishes. Entrées average $10.

Eagle (677-3788), 35 North Main Street, Fall River. Open daily for lunch and dinner. The gracefully curving, columned, vintage-1929 dining room is paneled in mahogany and studded with stained-glass windows. The extensive menu features pasta, seafood, steak; early-bird specials from $5.95. Sunday brunch buffet (10–2) features 20 dishes. Dining and dancing on weekends. Dinner $11–20.

Public Clam Bakes at Francis Farms (252-3212), Rehoboth. Ten summer Sundays and holidays, rain or shine (but call to check). The 125-acre farm dates from the 1820s, and the public clambakes, from the 1870s. Two pavilions can together accommodate around 1000 guests, and the clambakes are happenings done the traditional way, with lobsters, clams, corn, and so on. $21.75 adults, $7.75 children. Also inquire about Drovers Roasts and other special events; private clambakes can be scheduled anytime.

EATING OUT

Al Mac's Diner (679-5851), corner of President Avenue and Davoll Street, Fall River. Open most days 6 AM–3 AM. A '50s replica of an original diner, with a Formica counter, heavy coffee mugs, and plenty of chrome. Norman and Joyce Gauthier are known for French meat pie (sausage and hamburger) and hearty basics like American chop suey and turkey dinners, as well as three-egg omelets and great pies like blueberry cheese and banana cream.

Down Under Restaurant (672-6951), 91 Purchase Street, Fall River. Open daily for lunch and dinner. A big menu ranging from buffalo wings through pasta dishes to filet mignon. Full bar with imported draft beers.

Le Page's Seafood Restaurant and Market (677-2180), 439 Matine Street (US 6), Fall River. Open 7 AM–9 PM daily except holidays. Lebanese and local seafood dishes overlooking Watuppa Pond; outdoor terrace in-season.

SELECTIVE SHOPPING

BOOKSTORE

Partners Village Store (636-2572), 999 Main Road, Westport. Small but choice selection of books.

FACTORY OUTLETS

Only a couple of decades ago, "factory outlet" meant a small room selling half-price "seconds" in the actual factory in which the product was made. Fall River was the first New England town to augment these traditional outlets with other off-price stores, the first (long before bargain Kittery, Freeport, or North Conway) to cluster such stores for the

convenience of bus groups. Today Fall River remains a major shopping destination, with more than 70 stores gathered within a few blocks of each other just off MA 24 and I-195 in the **"Heart District"** (general information: 1-800-424-5519). The major complexes here are:
Tower Outlet Mill (674-4646). Daily 9–6, Friday until 8, Sunday noon–6. Includes the Burlington Coat Factory, Champion-Hanes, Izod-Monet sportswear, Luxury Linens, and Stetson Hats.
Wampanoag Mill Factory Outlet Center (678-5242), 9–5 weekdays, Friday until 8, Sunday noon–5. Includes Bay State Trading Co., the Curtain Factory Outlet, and Dress Express.
Quality Factory Outlets (677-4949) daily 9–6, Friday until 8, Sunday noon–6. Includes Bass & Co., the Book Warehouse, Carter's Children's Wear, Corning/Revere, Van Heusen, Swank jewelry, and the Farberware outlet.
Stafford Square has a glass and mirror factory outlet and a curtain factory outlet.

SPECIAL EVENTS

June: **Fall River Festival.**
Late June: **Santo Christo Feast,** Columbia Street, Fall River.
July: **Feast of St. Anne,** annual procession to the shrine of St. Anne. **Dighton Indian Council Somerset Pow-Wow** (phone: 401-941-5889).
August, second weekend: **Fall River Celebrates America**—waterfront festival includes parade, fireworks, live entertainment.

III. CENTRAL MASSACHUSETTS

The Nashoba Valley
The Central Uplands
Worcester
Blackstone River Valley
Old Sturbridge Village Area
Quabbin Area

City Hall in Worcester

JIM McELHOLM

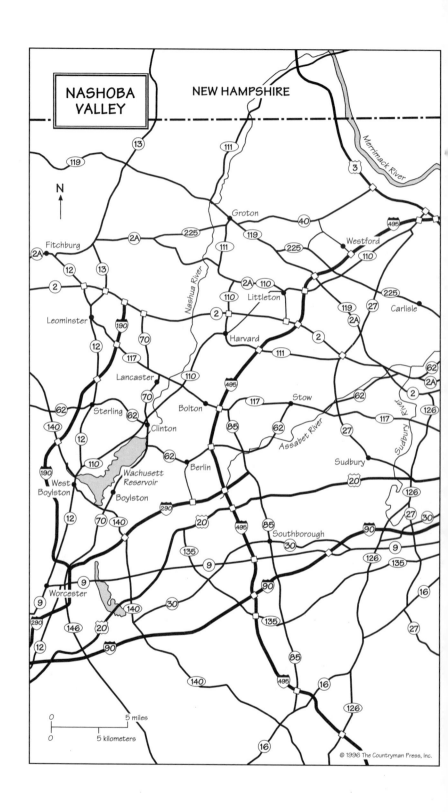

The Nashoba Valley

The heart of the Nashoba Valley is a wide swath of fertile farmland between the Nashua and Assabet Rivers, a landscape of lush green meadows, apple orchards, and villages clustered companionably around classic Commons. This area is one of those fortunate New England places that enjoy two distinct and equally beautiful foliage seasons. In mid-May its hundreds of thousands of apple trees blossom, and in mid-October the forested hillsides blaze with color. Verdant in summer, in winter the area abounds with the sort of snowy views and vistas beloved by Messrs. Currier and Ives.

Despite some creeping suburbanization, the valley remains a genuinely rural place, easily accessed from Boston via MA 2 to Harvard, and then onto country roads (great for bicycling) that meander south along the Nashua River to Wachusett Reservoir and north to Groton. In autumn Bostonians come to pick apples and view foliage, and in winter many return to cut Christmas trees.

A number of bed & breakfasts have opened in recent years—many in well-preserved Colonial-, Federal-, or Victorian-era houses—and the Nashoba Valley has become a destination: a convenient weekend getaway for Bostonians and a good base for visitors exploring Central Massachusetts.

AREA CODE
508
GUIDANCE
North Central Massachusetts Chamber of Commerce (840-4300), 110 Erdman Way, Leominster 01453. Publishes a seasonal guide that covers part of the area. There is no single information source for the rest.
GETTING THERE
The Nashoba Valley is an hour's drive from Boston. MA 2 runs east-west, while I-495 arcs south-north.
MEDICAL EMERGENCY
Clinton Hospital (365-4531), 201 Highland Street, Clinton; the emergency room is open daily around the clock.

VILLAGES

Harvard. This town's Common is often used for local festivities and is classically surrounded by white-steepled churches, a handsome library building, and a general store. The town's meandering rural roads, lined with orchards and gentlemen's farms, are ideal for bicycling. A Shaker community was established in Harvard in 1791 and lasted until 1919. The Shaker brothers and sisters rest under simple markers and in orderly rows in the old **Shaker Cemetery** on Shaker Road. A nearby nature trail leads to the top of Holy Hill, where in the mid-19th century the local Shakers held outdoor services at which they danced and sang ecstatically and claimed to glimpse paradise. All that can be seen from the hill today is the Nashoba Valley—maybe not heaven, but not bad either. Some of the community's buildings still stand on Shaker Road, but one of the original 1790s structures was moved to **Fruitlands Museums** (see *To See*) in the 1920s, restored, and now houses an extensive Shaker crafts collection.

Lancaster. The first town in Worcester County, Lancaster was founded in 1642 by Thomas King, who had a trading post on what is now George Hill Road. Native Americans sacked the town in 1676, during King Philip's War, and carried off a number of prisoners, including Mary Rowlandson, the minister's wife. Her gripping account of her captivity includes a vivid description of camping out with her captors under a rock on George Hill, now "Rowlandson's Rock." Burned twice more by Native Americans before the settlement finally took root, Lancaster today is a notably serene and peaceful place. Its **First Church of Christ,** designed by Charles Bulfinch and built in 1816 of local brick laid in Flemish bond, has a Paul Revere bell and preserves its handsome horse sheds, the venue of an annual fall crafts festival (see *Special Events*). One of Bulfinch's finest efforts, the church reflects the beginning of classical Greek influence on American architecture. The **Lancaster Library,** also on the Green, was built as a Civil War memorial, with a dome above its octagonal center and a luxurious 1920s children's room designed to look like a gentleman's study. Many of the old houses along Main Street belong to Atlantic Union College, operated by the Seventh-Day Adventist Church.

Groton. Founded in 1655, Groton was named for Puritan leader John Winthrop's ancestral home. Like so many other Nashoba Valley settlements, Groton was burned during King Philip's War; however, a Native American attack in 1694 was beaten off, and the town went on to prosper, as the elegant, tree-lined Main Street attests. In 1884 the Reverend Endicott Peabody, a Massachusetts Brahman who had been a preacher on the Wild West frontier, founded **Groton School**—and made the town a household name, at least in many well-to-do house-

Fruitlands Museum

holds. The prototypical elite American preparatory school, Groton was modeled after great British public schools. The campus complex, a quadrangle of ivy-covered buildings surrounded by playing fields, wouldn't look out of place in Sussex. Not as famous, but older by almost a century and more visible in town, is Groton's other prep school, **Lawrence Academy.** This school was founded in 1793 and named for its 19th-century benefactors, the wealthy industrialist brothers William and Amos Lawrence. The academy's attractive campus fronts on—and beautifies—Main Street (MA 119). Also on Main Street is the Old Groton Inn, now called the **Stagecoach Inn** (see *Lodging*). An inn has been at this spot, off and on, for more than 300 years. The present one incorporates the foundations of a tavern built in 1678.

TO SEE

MUSEUMS
Fruitlands Museums (456-3924), 102 Prospect Hill Road, Harvard. Open 10 AM–5 PM, Tuesday through Sunday and Monday holidays, from mid-May to mid-October. (Grounds and walking trails are open year-round, 10 AM–5 PM.) Admission $6 adults, $5 seniors, $3.50 students, $2.50 children. Fruitlands is a complex of four museums centered on the 18th-century farmhouse in which Bronson Alcott—Louisa May Alcott's father and the model for Dr. March in *Little Women*—and fellow transcendentalists attempted to create a "New Eden" based on absurdly high principles. The group was not just vegetarian but would only eat

"aspiring vegetables" that reached toward the sky (no carrots or potatoes), eschewed cotton (raised by slaves in the Deep South), and
wouldn't wear silk or wool (which would exploit helpless creatures).
Hungry, cold, and disillusioned, the group disbanded before the first
winter was over. The old farmhouse is now a museum on the transcen-
dentalist movement, with pictures, books, and relics of Alcott, Ralph
Waldo Emerson, and other leaders, as well as exhibits about the New
Eden experiment. Fruitlands was founded by Clara Endicott Sears, a
Boston grande dame who was a collector ahead of her time; she began
acquiring Shaker furniture and crafts, American portraits and landscape
painting, and Native American artifacts in the 1920s, well before they
were fashionable. Her remarkable collections are housed in separate
buildings and can be appreciated in their own context. The picture gallery contains outstanding portraits by itinerant, early-19th-century artists and Hudson River School–style paintings of New England scenes
by Thomas Cole, Albert Bierstadt, and E.F. Church, among others. The
Native American museum displays Henry David Thoreau's larger, personal collection of arrowheads and projectile points. There is also a
unique artifact recently recovered: King Philip's war club, stolen from
Fruitlands in the 1970s and found at a yard sale in 1995. Fruitlands has
beautiful grounds, and the view of the Nashoba Valley from Prospect
Hill is inspiring at any time but is spectacular in spring, when orchards
are in bloom, and during fall foliage season. There are picnic tables, a
gift shop, and a very pleasant tearoom and restaurant.

WINERY

Nashoba Valley Winery (779-5521), 100 Wattaquadoc Hill Road, Bolton
01740. Open year-round 10–5. A 45-acre orchard that produces a variety of delicious wines, including dry table wines from apples, pears,
peaches, plums, blueberries, strawberries, and elderberries. Visitors can
pick their own berries in summer and apples in fall. There is a tasting
room and gift shop as well as trails through the orchard groves for walking or cross-country skiing.

FOR FAMILIES

Toy Cupboard Theatre Museum and John Greene Chandler Museum (1-800-401-3694), 57 East George Hill Road (just off Main Street),
Lancaster. Admission is $3. Housed in a converted 200-year-old wood-
shed, this remarkable puppet theater has been entertaining children and
their parents since 1940. Buildings adjacent to the theater contain
founder Herbert Hosmer's large collections of dollhouses, antique toys,
and children's books, including editions of *The Remarkable Story of
Chicken Little* by Lancaster resident John Greene Chandler. Puppet
shows, based on classic children's stories, are presented Wednesday,
Thursday, and Saturday at 2 PM in July and August, once or twice a month
in spring and fall. Shows last about 30 minutes, and the ticket price includes
admission to the museums, open only by appointment at other times.

Farmland Petting Zoo (422-6666), Redstone Hill Road, Sterling. Open mid-May through October 31. The boast here is that the zoo contains one of North America's largest collections of endangered farm animals. Hayrides and pony rides.

TO DO

BICYCLING
Cyclists long ago discovered the beauty of the Nashoba Valley's winding country roads and sweeping views. **Friendly Crossways,** a youth hostel on the Harvard-Littleton line (see *Lodging*), has been catering to bikers since 1947 and is a good source for route information. Particularly scenic in apple blossom and foliage seasons are MA 110 in Harvard; MA 117 in Bolton; MA 62 through Sterling and Princeton; MA 70 through Boylston; and MA 119 through Townsend and Groton. The 17-mile loop around Wachusett Reservoir is also scenic and interesting.

CANOEING
Nashoba Paddler (448-8699), PO Box 385, West Groton. Located on MA 225 on the banks of the unspoiled Nashua River, Nashoba Paddler rents canoes, gives instruction, and has a tour program for a variety of New England rivers. Rentals are $28 a day; half-day and hourly rates are also available.

FISHING
Fishing is permitted in **Wachusett Reservoir** from April 1 through October 31. A state license is required. Access points are MA 70, Gates 6–16; MA 140, Gates 17–24; MA 12/MA 110, Gates 25–35; and Thomas Basin, West Boylston.

HORSEBACK RIDING
Bobby's Ranch (263-7165), off MA 2A in Littleton (behind Acton Mall). Open Wednesday through Sunday 9–6; $15 per hour weekdays, $20 on weekends and holidays. Trails are through a 2000-acre conservation area around Kennedy Pond.

CROSS-COUNTRY SKIING
Great Brook Farm State Park (369-6312), Lowell Road in Carlisle. Marked trails and winter rentals, instruction. There are trails at **Nashoba Winery** in Bolton and **Sterling Orchards** in Sterling (see *Lodging—Bed & Breakfasts*). (Also see *Green Space* and inquire locally about conservation land trails.)

DOWNHILL SKIING
Nashoba Valley (692-3033), Powers Road, Westford (between MA 2A/MA 119 and MA 110). Open late November through late March. A learners hill and local ski area, with only a 204-foot vertical drop but an extensive trail system, night skiing, and considerable lift capacity.
Lifts: Three triple chairs, one double chair, one bar, four tows.
Snowmaking: 100 percent.

Ski school: Strong.
Rates: Weekends $27 adults, $25 children; nights and weekdays $20 and $18.

GREEN SPACE

J. Harry Rich State Forest (597-8802), MA 119, Groton. An undeveloped 508-acre park with more than 6 miles of dirt roads, walking trails, canoeing.

New England Forestry Foundation properties in Groton include **Groton Place** (MA 225), a 54-acre former estate with a notable avenue of trees and walking and cross-country ski trails; and **Sabine Woods,** a 146-acre forest reserve with a nice swimming hole (adjoining Groton School and about 6 miles east of Groton village on MA 40).

Wachusett Reservoir (365-3272) in Clinton and Boylston was created in 1906 when a 206-foot-high dam was built across the south branch of the Nashua River. The reservoir has 37 miles of shoreline and a maximum depth of 120 feet. South Dike, which extends 2 miles out into the water and has a footpath, can be accessed from MA 70.

Note: Most Nashoba Valley towns have set aside conservation land with hiking, skiing, and sometimes bridle trails. Inquire locally about public land along the Nashua and Assabet Rivers.

LODGING

INNS

The Sterling Inn (442-6592), 240 Worcester Road (MA 12), PO Box 609, Sterling 01564. Closed the last week of July and every Monday. This Tudor Revival, turn-of-the-century inn has eight guest rooms (six with private bath) but is primarily a restaurant. Rooms are small and well kept but rather plain. $55–60 with continental breakfast.

Longfellow's Wayside Inn (443-1776), Boston Post Road, Sudbury 01776 (just off US 20). Although this inn is just east of the Nashoba Valley, we include the Wayside because it's handy to the area as well as being a rural roost from which to explore Boston. The inn has 10 rooms, beautifully furnished with antiques, but is better known as a restaurant. America's oldest operating inn and a national historic site, the Wayside is surrounded by a mini–New England village assembled by Henry Ford, who restored the place in the 1920s. (The Martha-Mary Chapel that Ford built is a popular wedding site.) The tavern dates back to the 1680s and was so creaky when Henry Wadsworth Longfellow visited it in 1861 that he dubbed it "Hobgoblin Hall." Longfellow grouped half a dozen characters around the hearth and gave each a story to tell, like Chaucer's Canterbury pilgrims. The hit of these *Tales of a Wayside Inn* was and remains the landlord's beginning: "Listen my children and you

shall hear of the midnight ride of Paul Revere." $96 for a double room with full breakfast. (Breakfast served only to inn guests.)
Chocksett Inn (422-3355), 59 Laurelwood Road (off MA 12), Sterling 01564. This 25-unit inn with one- and two-room efficiency suites opened in 1990. Quiet location and inoffensive neo-Colonial decor. Full kitchens and cable TV. Cocktail lounge and laundry facilities. $65–82 with continental breakfast.
Lyttleton Inn (1-800-433-4715), 423 King Street, Littleton 01460. A six-room inn in a handsome, 1860s house on the edge of the town Common. Pleasant, homey atmosphere. All rooms have private bath, telephone, air-conditioning, color TV, and refrigerator. $64–74 with full breakfast.
Stagecoach Inn (448-5614), Main Street (intersections of MA 40 and MA 119), Groton 01450. There has been an inn or a tavern on this spot for some 300 years, and the Stagecoach claims to have been "established" in 1678. The main building dates from early in this century, however, and has 17 comfortable but simply furnished units. The tavern attached to the inn serves breakfast, lunch, and dinner. An unusual amenity is a resident ghost, supposedly that of a Revolutionary War soldier, who is occasionally spotted by guests. $75–85 for rooms, $120 for suites, with full breakfast.
Stowaway Inn (897-1999), 271 Great Road, Stow 01775. An 1880s house with five guest rooms, all with private bath, telephone, and TV. Doug and Celia Hyde have been innkeepers since 1987. Rates are $65–70 with full breakfast.

BED & BREAKFASTS
Folkstone Bed and Breakfast Reservation Service (1-800-762-2751), Sears Road, Southborough 01772. This service places guests in some 35 homes, many historic, in central Massachusetts and northeastern Connecticut. $65–125, including breakfast.
The Rose Cottage (835-4034), 24 Worcester Street (MA 12), West Boylston 01583. A Gothic Revival (1850) house within sight of Wachusett Reservoir. Michael and Loretta Kittredge have been innkeepers since 1985. There are five guest rooms, all furnished with antiques. The Carriage House, moved to its present site when the reservoir was created, has a three-room apartment on the second floor and meeting space below. Rooms are $69.95 plus tax with full breakfast; the apartment is $325 a week.
Carter-Washburn House (365-2188), 34 Seven Bridge Road, Lancaster 01523. A classic Federal-style mansion built in 1812 for a local physician. Quite grand. Rooms are high ceilinged, and there are four connecting parlors guests can use. There is a sunny exercise room and a gazebo that overlooks tranquil little Angel Pond. The three large guest rooms all have fireplaces and are furnished with antiques and original artwork. $55–70 with full breakfast.
Sterling Orchards (422-6595), 60 Kendall Hill Road, Sterling 01564. Bob

and Shirley Smiley offer two suites, each with a sitting room and private bath, in the 1740 homestead of their 100-acre farm. There is a seasonal farm stand on the property and walking and cross-country ski trails. $65 with full country breakfast.

Polly Wilson's Bed and Breakfast (779-6955), 39 Long Hill Road, Bolton 01740. Only half a mile from the intersection of MA 117 and I-495, this B&B is remarkably rural in feeling. The house is relatively new but made of wood from old barns and has beamed ceilings and a massive Colonial-style fireplace. The two guest rooms are sunny and pleasant. The view is over West Pond. A herd of sheep graze in the meadow, and there is usually at least one saddle horse in residence. $60–70 with continental breakfast.

Ford's View Bed and Breakfast (838-2909), 179 Linden Street, Berlin. A 1750s house with two guest rooms sharing a bath. Swimming pool, TV lounge, and a fishing pond on the grounds. $60–70 with what owner Maria Ford calls a "full continental" breakfast.

Amerscot House (897-0666), 61 West Acton Road, Stow 01775. An elegant 1730s house with two guest rooms and a suite. Homey touches include fresh flowers and handmade quilts. Owners Jerry and Noreen Gibson, who was born in Scotland, often invite guests to join them for Scottish country dancing. $85 for rooms and $100 for the suite, which has a Jacuzzi. Included is a full breakfast, which often has Scottish touches such as Noreen's fresh-baked scones.

College Town Bed and Breakfast (368-7000 days; 365-5016 evenings), intersection of Old Common Road and MA 110, Lancaster 01523. Three rooms (one with private bath) and a large suite. The decor is California contemporary, and units all have private balcony or deck. The building is at a busy highway intersection, and the B&B shares the premises with the owner's floor-covering business. $45 for rooms; $100 for the suite.

YOUTH HOSTEL

Friendly Crossways Youth Hostel and Conference Center (456-3649), Whitcomb Avenue, Littleton (on the Harvard line) 01460. A large, comfortably furnished farmhouse set on a country road with a big barn and 50 acres of land. This has been an American Youth Hostel since 1947, and owner Anne Vensenka's knowledge of the area and its recreational options is encyclopedic. Hostelers are charged $10–15 for a night in dorms or semiprivate rooms. Other guests pay $20–25.

WHERE TO EAT

DINING OUT

The Sterling Inn (422-6592), MA 12, Sterling. Closed Monday, otherwise open for lunch and dinner. This is a popular eating spot and has an authentic 1920s atmosphere. Dinner entrées include Chicken Supreme, broiled filet mignon with mushroom sauce, and prime rib. There are daily lunch and dinner specials, daily baked desserts like Midnight Chocolate Cake and Indian pudding. Lunch is in the $4–7.50 range; dinner, $11–23.

Longfellow's Wayside Inn (443-8846), US 20, Sudbury. Open daily for lunch and dinner. Just east of the Nashoba Valley but too special (and near) to omit. Lunch is in the $8–12 range, and dinner, $16–21, but there are children's plates. Roast duckling, deep-dish apple pie, and Indian pudding; traditional New England cooking. (Also see *Inns.*)

EATING OUT

Johnson's Drive-in (448-6840), MA 119, Groton. Open 6 AM daily year-round, until 10 PM in summer, until 9 PM in spring and fall, until 3 PM in winter except Thursday, Friday, and Saturday, when it's open until 8 PM. This is a handy place to eat breakfast if you are setting out for a day of cross-country skiing or exploring; anytime for a basic burger or home-made ice cream. Also try the nightly specials like roast turkey or fried haddock.

4 Corners Restaurant (448-3358; 448-3359), junction of MA 119 and MA 225, Groton. Open daily for lunch and dinner. This Cantonese restaurant looks a little out of place in a Yankee woodscape but is a popular institution. The menu features chop suey, chow mein, and egg foo yong. Sweet-and-sour shrimp and a variety of meat and seafood dishes are in the $7–10 range; a Pu Pu Platter for two, $17.

The Stagecoach Inn Tavern (448-5614), Main Street (intersection of MA 40 and MA 119), Groton. Open for lunch and dinner. The inn's dining room is a popular local watering hole. Owner George Pergantis is Greek, but the menu has an Italian flavor with dishes like chicken Marsala, shrimp fettucine, and seafood scampi. Entrées in the $12–19 range.

Fruitlands Museums Tea Room (456-3924), Prospect Hill, Harvard. Open early May through late October. Lunch served 1–3. The dining area, both inside and out, is one of the most pleasant spots around; the menu includes some Shaker recipes. Lunch in the $7–10 range.

ENTERTAINMENT

Thayer Symphony Orchestra (368-0041) stages six concerts (three classical and three popular) over the October to May season. Concerts are in Machlan Auditorium on the campus of Atlantic Union College on Main Street (MA 70), South Lancaster.

Indian Hill Symphony Orchestra (486-9524) presents four classical concerts each season at the Groton Dunstable Performing Arts Center (the Middle School), MA 119, Groton.

Sunset Concerts at Fruitlands Museums (456-3924), 102 Prospect Hill Road, Harvard. Thursday at 7:30 PM in July and August.

Groton Center for the Arts (448-3001), Willowdale and Main Streets,

PO Box 423, Groton 01450, is an information source about children's and adult performances. (Also see the **Toy Cupboard Theatre** puppet shows under *To See*.)

SELECTIVE SHOPPING

BOOKSTORE
Village Books (597-5900), 18 Main Street, Townsend. General, Native American, children's books.
CRAFTS SHOP
The Museum Store at Fruitlands Museums (see *To See*) in Harvard sells Shaker and early American crafts reproductions.
ORCHARDS
Bolton Orchards (779-2733), junction of MA 110 and MA 117, Bolton, maintains a major farm stand featuring local produce and crafts.
Spring Farm (779-2898), 149 Main Street, Bolton, offers pick-your-own apples and pumpkins, a picnic area, and hot apple dumplings, home-made cider, and spice doughnuts.
Pick-your-own apples are available in-season at the following Harvard orchards: **Carlson Orchards** (456-3916), which operates a 150-acre orchard offering farm tours and has a large cider press at its roadside stand on MA 110 just north of MA 2; and **Phil's Apples,** 24 Prospect Hill Road, which also operates a cider press in September and October.
Deershorn Farm Orchard (365-3691), Chase Hill Road, Lancaster, off MA 62. Pick-your-own apples and strawberries, trailer rides through the orchards, picnic area. The farm stand on MA 62 sells native corn, pumpkins, vegetables, and cider, as well as apples.
George Hill Orchards (365-4331), George Hill Road, South Lancaster. Open Sunday through Friday in-season: wagon and pony rides, cider-press viewing, face painting, snack bar on weekends and holidays.
Hillbrook Orchards (448-3248), 170 Old Ayer Road, off MA 119, Groton. Open daily in-season, pick-your-own.
Chase Farm (486-3893), 509 Great Road, Littleton. A retail outlet selling local fruit and produce and open daily.
Nagog Hill Farm (486-3264), Nagog Hill Road, Littleton. Pick-your-own apples, peaches, and vegetables. Open daily in-season.
Honey Pot Hill Orchards (562-5666), 144 Sudbury Road, Stow. Mid-September to mid-October, daily for pick-your-own.
Also see Sterling Orchards under *Lodging—Bed & Breakfasts*.

SPECIAL EVENTS

May: **Spring Apple Blossom Festival,** held on the Harvard Common, usually on the second or third weekend of the month. **May Apple Blossom Festival,** Nashoba Valley Winery, Bolton. Usually coincides with the Harvard festival and includes music, crafts tables, and wine tasting. **Art Walk**—guided tours of the studios and galleries of Groton Center, mid-May.

October: **Horse Sheds Crafts Festival,** First Church of Christ, Lancaster, first weekend. **Three Apples Story Telling Festival**—a gathering of storytellers and musicians from around New England, the United States, and Canada. Harvard Town Common; first weekend.

December: **Artisans Exhibit**—a juried exhibition of the work of area artists and craftspersons at the Groton Center for the Arts. First weekend.

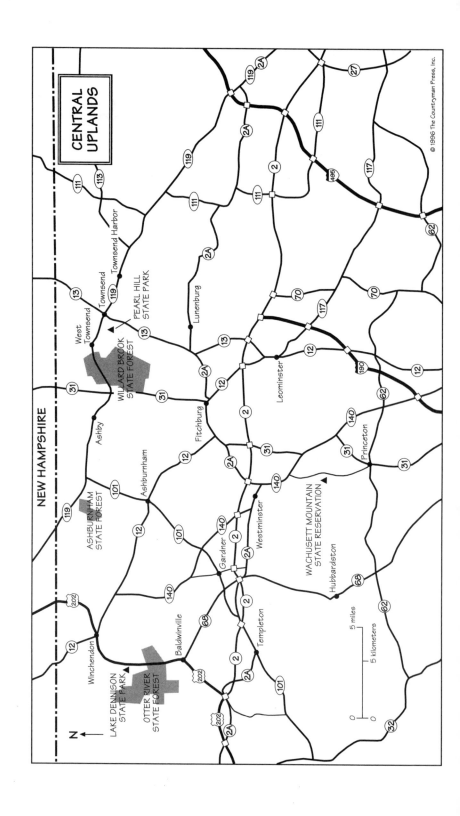

CENTRAL
UPLANDS

NEW HAMPSHIRE

N

Townsend Harbor
Townsend
West Townsend
PEARL HILL STATE PARK
WILLARD BROOK STATE FOREST
Lunenburg
Ashby
Ashburnham
ASHBURNHAM STATE FOREST
Fitchburg
Leominster
Westminster
Gardner
Princeton
WACHUSETT MOUNTAIN STATE RESERVATION
Hubbardston
Templeton
Baldwinville
Winchendon
LAKE DENNISON STATE PARK
OTTER RIVER STATE FOREST

5 miles
5 kilometers
0
0

The Central Uplands

The northern tier of Worcester County is a physical extension of New Hampshire's Monadnock region: hilly and forested with both classic villages and old mill towns.

The country's furniture industry was centered here in the 19th century because of a fortuitous combination of skilled labor, ample water, and great stands of hardwood trees. There is still some furniture manufacturing, but the great 1938 hurricane wiped out most of the hardwoods, and in subsequent decades many companies relocated to other parts of the country. The story of the local furniture industry's entrepreneurs, inventors, and artisans is well told at the Gardner Heritage State Park.

By the turn of the century, Gardner was known as "Chair City," exporting its cane-seated, stenciled, and bentwood rocking chairs throughout the world. The city has more the feeling of a bedroom community than a mill town these days, but there are still about a dozen furniture makers in the Greater Gardner area and many furniture outlets.

The eastern part of this region—the countryside around Fitchburg—is known as Montachusett, a name coined by a Fitchburg newspaperman from the area's three visible mountains: Monadnock (just over the New Hampshire line) and Watatic on the north, and Wachusett on the south. Sited beyond the Boston commuter belt (although accessible by rail), this area is genuine country, a fact evident in the size of the small cities of Gardner and Fitchburg as well as in the byways of Ashburnham and Townsend.

The area's many public forests and lakes offer camping and swimming, and its back roads are well known to wheelmen. The Mid-State Hiking Trail traverses the ridgeline that runs down the center of the region.

Fitchburg, like most other New England factory towns, contains considerable ethnic diversity, although French Canadians (mostly Acadians from New Brunswick) and Scandinavians are the major groups. There is also one of the oldest and largest Finnish communities in the country. Thanks to a tradition of philanthropy and a relatively healthy economy based on plastics and electronics, Fitchburg has found it easier to raise money for cultural causes than have most towns its size. It has a first-rate local library, an excellent small art museum, a

planetarium, and a civic-center complex frequently used for both amateur and professional sports and entertainment.

AREA CODE
508

GUIDANCE

Greater Gardner Chamber of Commerce (632-1780), 55 Lake Street,
Gardner 01440, open weekdays 9–4. Good for walk-in information and
print materials on Westminster, Winchendon, Templeton, Ashburnham, Barre, and Hubbardston, as well as Gardner. Puts out a useful
brochure listing the major furniture outlets in the area.

North Central Massachusetts Chamber of Commerce (343-6487), 110
Erdman Way, Leominster 01453. Open weekdays 9–5. Good for walk-
in as well as written information on Leominster, Fitchburg, Ashburnham, Townsend, Westminster, Ashby, Ayer, Groton, Harvard, Lancaster,
Lunenburg, Pepperell, Princeton, Shirley, and Sterling.

Gardner Heritage State Park (630-1497), 26 Lake Street, Gardner
01440. Walk-in information center open Tuesday through Saturday 9–
4, Sunday and Monday noon–4.

Department of Environmental Management, Region 3 (368-0126), can
furnish details about the area forests and reservations.

GETTING THERE

By train: **The MBTA Commuter Rail** (1-800-392-6100) extends to
Gardner on a limited basis, with more frequent runs to Fitchburg.

By bus: **Vermont Transit** (1-800-552-8737) serves Fitchburg, Gardner, and
Winchendon from the Greyhound Terminal, South Station, Boston.
Trailways–Peter Pan (1-800-343-9999) serves Fitchburg from the
Trailways Terminal at South Station, Boston.

GETTING AROUND

Montachusett Area Regional Transit (MART; 345-7711) serves Fitchburg and Leominster.

MEDICAL EMERGENCY

Burbank Hospital (343-5000), 275 Nichols Road, Fitchburg. **Heywood
Memorial Hospital** (632-3420), 242 Green Street, Gardner.

VILLAGES

Ashby, MA 31 and MA 119. The First Parish meetinghouse, now the Unitarian Church, has a Willard clock that has to be wound by hand. Also
note the Town Library, Grange Hall (old town hall), Congregational
Church, town pump, watering trough, and bandstand where the Ashby
Band, organized in 1887, holds forth on the Common, Wednesday evenings in summer.

Princeton, MA 31 and MA 62. The village frames an exceptional Common
at the southern foot of Mount Wachusett. The white-steepled Congregational Church dates just from 1883 but has a Paul Revere bell. The
ridge road from the village to Mount Wachusett is lined with 1890s

country mansions and former inns. (Also see Redemption Rock under *To See* and Wachusett Meadows and Wachusett Mountain State Reservation under *Green Space.*)

Townsend, West Townsend, and **Townsend Harbor,** MA 119. Townsend itself is a classic center with a steepled white church (built in 1731 with a slave balcony), brick mill, Victorian town hall, lineup of shops in 19th-century wooden buildings, and Common complete with bandstand. In West Townsend the Old Brick Store was constructed as a meetinghouse for the Universalist Restoration Society in 1849—with the meeting hall on the second floor, stores and post office on the street. The steeple is long gone, and the effect is unsettling but nice (the general store hasn't been fancied up). Townsend Harbor, east of Townsend, contains some unusually handsome houses. It's unclear whether the town's name stems from the fact that its three forts harbored settlers from 18th-century Native American attacks or from its status as a stop—and safe haven— on the Underground Railroad.

Winchendon is still known as "Toy Town," a name earned when it was a center for the wooden-toy industry and shipped its rocking horses all over the world. The toy factories are gone, but a giant wooden horse still dominates the small Common.

TO SEE

MUSEUMS
Fitchburg Art Museum (345-4207), 185 Elm Street, Fitchburg 01420. Open Tuesday through Saturday 11–4, Sunday 1–4. Closed Monday and major holidays. Admission $3 (students and children free). Founded by Fitchburg native Eleanor Norcross, who spent most of her life in Paris, the museum has a permanent collection of some 1000 American and European paintings, prints, drawings, and sculptures, including works by George Bellows, Edward Hopper, Rockwell Kent, Raoul Dufy, and Edouard Vuillard. A spacious new wing is used for changing exhibitions.

Gardner State Heritage Park Visitors Center (630-1497), 26 Lake Street, Gardner. Open daily 9–4, Tuesday through Saturday; noon–4 Sunday and Monday. Multimedia exhibits depict the history of furniture production, silversmithing, and the precision timing instruments invented and manufactured in town. There are also displays about the diverse ethnic groups—Swedish-speakers from Finland and French-speaking Acadians from New Brunswick, for instance—who made up the labor force. The Heritage Park includes Dunn's Pond on Pearl Street, about a half mile from the visitors center, which has a picnic area, swimming beach, and seasonal changing facilities.

Gardner Museum (632-3277), 28 Pearl Street, Gardner, housed in the town's former brick, Romanesque Revival library donated by furniture baron Levi Heywood. (The entrance was designed to resemble a chair.)

A small permanent collection and changing exhibits on local history and crafts. Open Tuesday through Friday 1–4.

Fitchburg Historical Society (345-1157), 50 Grove Street, Fitchburg. Open Monday through Thursday 10–4, Sunday 2–4. Closed summers. The collection includes a 300-year-old hurdy-gurdy and a rare 1777 "Vinegar" Bible, so called because of its misspelling of "vineyard."

Leominster Historical Society (537-5424), 17 School Street, Leominster. Leominster calls itself "Comb City" because of its long history of comb manufacturing, and the society has the country's largest comb collection. There are combs made of ivory, jade, silver, wood, and plastic, and some encrusted with rhinestones or precious gems. One particularly beautiful piece from China is shaped like a dragon.

WINERY

Afina Winery (827-4645), 203 Russell Hill Road, Ashburnham. Sited in the garage of a contemporary house but adjoining its own orchard and berry farm, this small, relatively new operation produces hard cider and blueberry wines. Tours and tastings by appointment.

HISTORIC SITE

Redemption Rock, MA 31 in Princeton, maintained by the Trustees of Reservations. In the pines sits a huge, flat table rock where, according to legend, King Philip's Native Americans agreed to ransom Mary White Rowlandson and her children. That event was in 1676, and Mrs. Rowlandson, wife of the first minister of Lancaster, wrote a best-seller about her kidnapping. The Mid-State Trail passes through this spot and continues south to the top of Wachusett Mountain.

FOR FAMILIES

Wallace Civic Center and Planetarium (343-7900), John Fitch Highway, Fitchburg. Open daily 9–5.

Whalom Park (342-3707), on MA 13 in Lunenburg (just east of Fitchburg). Open daily Memorial Day to Labor Day except Monday; weekends in spring and September. A family amusement area with a water slide, mini-train rides, some 50 carnival-style rides, and a beach and bathhouse on Whalom Lake. Admission $10.95 for all rides, $14.95 for rides and slide.

The Giant Chair, on Elm Street in Gardner in front of Elm Street Elementary School. The city's most photographed object, this item is a replica of the chair that stood by the railroad depot in Gardner's furniture-making heyday. Twenty feet, 7 inches high, it weighs 3000 pounds and is believed to be the world's largest chair.

TO DO

AERIAL LIFT

The **Skyride at Wachusett Mountain Ski Area** (464-2355) operates regularly in summer and fall. $4 round trip (you can hike either way, but you still have to pay for a round trip).

BICYCLING

MA 119, MA 12, and MA 31 are all popular, and there are endless possibilities along side roads.

BIRDING

Massachusetts Audubon Society properties include:

Wachusett Meadows Wildlife Sanctuary (464-2712), Goodnow Road off MA 62, west of the Common in Princeton. A 907-acre preserve with a boardwalk "swamp nature trail" and a variety of other walks through uplands, meadows, and woods. $2 adults, $1 seniors and children.

Flat Rock Wildlife Sanctuary in Fitchburg (537-9807); 315 acres with an excellent trail system. Enter from Flat Rock Road, the first right off Scott Road, which is off Ashby West Road.

Lincoln Woods Wildlife Sanctuary (537-9807), 226 Union Street, Leominster; a 65-acre site with several ponds and pronounced glacial topography.

Ashburnham State Forest (939-8962), 2000 acres accessible from MA 119 in Ashburnham, good for fishing, hiking, and hunting.

GOLF

Gardner Municipal Golf Course (632-9703), Eaton Road, 18-hole public course. **Grand View Country Club** (534-9685), Wachusett Street, Leominster, 18 holes. **Maplewood Golf Course** (582-6694) in Lunenburg, nine holes.

HIKING

The Mid-State Trail, utilizing and expanding a number of old trails, begins at Mount Watatic north of MA 119 in Ashby (you can park at the presently closed ski area). It follows the Waumpack Trail.

(Also note the trails mentioned in *Green Space.*)

SWIMMING

Dunn's Pond at the Gardiner Heritage State Park and **Whalom Lake** (see *To See* for both), as well as **Beaman Pond** in Ashby and **Wyman Lake** in Westminster, are all popular spots.

(Also see *Green Space—Parks and State Forests.*)

DOWNHILL SKIING

Wachusett Mountain Ski Area (464-2355), Mountain Road, Princeton. This is a privately operated ski area on a state reservation. A good mountain for beginners and for night skiing, with a vertical drop just under 1000 feet but facilities that include a nursery, rentals, and a ski shop.

Vertical drop: 990 feet.

Terrain: 18 trails.

Lifts: One quad, one triple, one double, one pony lift, one rope tow.

Ski school: SKIwee program for children aged 5–12 offered weekends and holidays.

Rates: Weekdays—$28 adults, $23 children aged 12 and under; weekends—$34 adults, $28 children; special rates for night skiing.

GREEN SPACE

(Also see the wildlife sanctuaries under *To Do—Birding.*)

PARKS AND STATE FORESTS

Willard Brook State Forest (597-8802), MA 119 in Townsend and Ashby, has 21 campsites and four year-round cabins; there's a sandy beach at Damon Pond. The miles of hiking and ski trails include one to Trapp Falls.

Lake Dennison State Park (297-1609), accessible from New Winchendon Road in Baldwinville, is part of the Otter River Forest. It offers 150 campsites in two distinct areas, a swim beach with bathhouse, 197 picnic tables and grills, fishing for bass and trout, and cross-country skiing on unplowed roads.

Otter River State Forest (939-8962), accessible from New Winchendon Road, Baldwinville, has 119 campsites; also offers picnicking and swimming and a summer interpretive program, centered on Beamen Pond.

Pearl Hill State Park (597-8802), accessible via New Fitchburg Road from West Townsend; 1000 acres with 51 campsites, swimming, fishing, picnicking, and hiking, ski touring trails.

WALKS

Wachusett Mountain State Reservation (464-2987), with a full visitors center. At 2006 feet, Wachusett Mountain is the highest point in Massachusetts east of the Connecticut River. In the late 19th century a road was built to the summit, site of a summer hotel until 1970. From the summit you can see Boston to the east and Mount Tom to the west, Monadnock to the north. This spot is a popular hiking goal for local Scout groups. There are 20 ways to the top, but most people favor the 1½-mile Jack Frost Trail. On the other hand, you can still drive or, better still, take the chair lift, which runs year-round from Wachusett Ski Area (386-6580). The 1950-acre reservation also includes 17 miles of hiking and cross-country ski trails, as well as picnic facilities. (Also see *Where to Eat* and *Downhill Skiing.*)

LODGING

HOTEL

Colonial Bed and Breakfast (630-2500), 625 Betty Spring Road, Gardner 01440. A 108-room, former Days Inn on a wooded road off MA 140. Indoor pool, lounge, and restaurant. $83 for a double with breakfast (often offers discount rates and special packages).

INN

The Harrington Farm Country Inn (464-5600), 178 Westminster Road, Princeton 01541. Accessed by a winding country road, the inn—a 1763 farmhouse—sits on the western slope of Mount Wachusett looking west toward the Berkshires, convenient to Mount Wachusett Ski Area and the hiking-trail system of the state reservation. Six pleasant rooms (three with private bath) and a comfortable, unfussy decor. Excellent restaurant (see *Dining Out*). $67–100 with continental breakfast.

BED & BREAKFASTS

Hawke Bed and Breakfast (632-5909), 162 Pearl Street, Gardner 01440. Two small, rather cluttered guest rooms on the ground floor of an old frame house. Bob and Nancy Hawke are the present owners, but part of the house dates to 1790 and was owned by chairmaker James Comee, who founded Gardner's furniture industry here in 1805. On a busy street but convenient to the Heritage State Park beach at Dunn's Pond. The only B&B in Gardner. Rates $40–50 with full breakfast.

John Adams Homestead (827-5388), 287 Russell Hill Road, Ashburnham 01430. A 1766 house in an idyllic country setting that so agreed with Adams, the first occupant, that he lived to be 104 years old. Owners Doug and Maria Quinn are avid ornithologists and gardeners, and the grounds are dotted with birdhouses and rose bushes. The three guest rooms are clean and pleasant if a tad overdecorated for some tastes. Rates are $70 with private bath, $50–65 shared. Continental breakfast usually includes Maria's homemade muffins.

☞ **Wood Farm** (597-6477), 41 Worcester Road (MA 113), Townsend 01469 (¾ mile from the Common). The oldest house in town: The old cape section dates from 1716 and has hardly changed since. Guests have the run of the 17-room house, in winter usually gathering around the fire in the keeping room, with its 8-foot-wide hearth. Owners Eric and Vi Stanway are hospitable and helpful. There are 13 acres with a stream running through them and a pond, good for both skating and swimming. There are bass in the pond, and the nearby Squanacook River is a famous trout stream. Three rooms share two baths. $45–65 with full, cooked-to-order breakfast.

☞ **Marble Farm** (827-5423), 41 Marble Road, Ashburnham 01430. Elizabeth and Dick Marble have restored the extended 18th-century farmhouse that's been in his family for five generations. It sits on 200 acres that include a pond good for fishing and swimming and is within walking distance of the Mid-State Trail. There are three rooms, one with private bath. $55–60 with "hearty country" continental breakfast.

MOTEL

Westminster Village Inn (874-5351), MA 2, Westminster 01473. Set back just a few hundred feet from the highway, this motel is a surprise. The main house welcomes you with a fireplace in winter and there is an attractive, reasonably priced dining room and a small counter, good for breakfast or soup and a sandwich. Amenities include both indoor and outdoor pools, and steam, game, and exercise rooms. There are 74 units, most in cottages, including efficiency suites. Sixteen rooms have fireplaces. The Mid-State Trail crosses MA 2 on a new overpass at this point and continues on the inn's property along a ridge and down to Redemption Rock in Princeton (see *To See*). $89–129 for a double, and guests receive discounts on dining there.

CAMPGROUNDS

Note the total of almost 250 campsites in the adjoining Lake Dennison, Otter River, Pearl Hill, and Willard Brook State Parks and Forests (see *Green Space*). Private campgrounds include **Howe's Camping** (827-4558) in Ashburnham, **Peaceful Acres** (928-4288) in Hubbardston, **Peaceful Pines** (939-5004) in Templeton, and **Pine Campgrounds** (386-7702) in Ashby.

WHERE TO EAT

DINING OUT

Old Mill Restaurant (874-5941), MA 2A, Westminster. Open for breakfast, lunch, and dinner. An area institution with an attractive old mill (a sawmill established in 1761) setting on a pond; small guests are given bread to feed the ducks. This is a busy, high-volume restaurant (very popular with wedding parties) but moderately priced, friendly, and welcoming. New England specialties include duck and prime rib. Entrées in the $12–18 range. Open weekdays, 11–10, weekends and holidays 8–10, Sunday brunch 11–2:30.

The Victorian House (827-5646), 16 Maple Avenue (off MA 12), Ashburnham. This elegant restaurant, operated by the Saccone family since 1987, has a devoted following. Occupying a redbrick, mansard-roofed, 19th-century building, the restaurant has a Victorian decor and an international menu. The menu changes with the season but often includes specials such as lobster Savannah and beef tournedos. Entrées are in the $12–35 range.

The Harrington Farm Restaurant (464-5600), 178 Westminster Road, Princeton; at the top of a twisty road up Mount Wachusett, but worth the trip. Open Wednesday through Sunday 5:30–9:30. Chef-owner John Bomba is a graduate of the Hyde Park Culinary Institute and a veteran of top hotel kitchens in Boston and Seattle; he creates his own dishes. A typical menu might include corn and lobster chowder with anise, grilled swordfish with white beans, and Savoy cabbage or sautéed venison loin with smoked sausage and pink and green peppercorns. Most entrées are in the $16–24 range. There are more than 100 selections on the wine list. The dining room is lovely (pink tablecloths and a great view) but only seats 45. Reservations required.

Slattery's Back Room (342-8880), 106 Lunenburg Street, Fitchburg. Open for lunch and dinner. A full menu from soup and sandwiches to lobsters and prime rib, casual atmosphere, reasonably priced.

Sully's Eating and Drinking Place (632-7457), 74–76 Parker Street, Gardner. A large family restaurant with adjacent pub. Extensive menu. Open daily for lunch and dinner. Live comedy acts on Saturday nights.

The Brass Pineapple (297-0312), MA 12, Winchendon. Open Wednesday through Saturday for lunch and dinner, Sunday for brunch. Intimate atmosphere, strong local following.

EATING OUT

Skip's Blue Moon Diner (632-4333), 102 Main Street, Gardner. An authentic Worcester Lunch Car Company diner, circa 1950, in mint condition with a dining room in back. Nice atmosphere, reasonable prices, traditional family diner menu (the meatloaf is reliable, and the pie, good).

Old Traveler's Restaurant (297-0740), 102 Front Street, Winchendon. Homestyle cooking and informal, friendly atmosphere.

Moran Square Diner (343-9549), 6 Myrtle Avenue (MA 2A), Fitchburg. A classic, much-photographed 1940s diner. Besides fried chicken, burgers, and joe, you can also buy diner T-shirts.

Coffee on The Common, in the Village Country Store, Princeton Common. Open 7 AM–3 PM, a cheerful small lunchroom with good soup, sandwiches, specials.

Jeanie's Lunch (939-8956), MA 2A/US 202 in Templeton. Breakfast from 6 AM on weekdays, from 7 on Saturday, and from 8 on Sunday, open until 2. Clean, cheerful, and reasonably priced.

ENTERTAINMENT

Theatre at the Mount (632-3856), La Fontaine Fine Arts Center, Mount Wachusett Community College, Gardner (MA 140). July and August productions of popular classics by a community theater group.

The Guild Players Touring Company (582-9041), The 50 Main Street Playhouse, Lunenburg. Adult and children's productions presented in this 100-seat theater during July and August.

High Tor Summer Theater (342-6888). From Fitchburg take MA 2A/MA 12 north on Main Street, then south on MA 31 for 100 yards; bear right at the Cumberland Farms and follow the sign. A long-established summer (July and August) theater presenting works ranging from Shakespeare to Molière, Ibsen, Chekhov, Miller, O'Neill, and more.

SELECTIVE SHOPPING

FACTORY OUTLETS

In Gardner

Chair City Wayside Furniture (632-1120), 372 East Broadway (MA 2A). This four-story, boxlike granite building with a giant ladderback chair out front is just as unusual as it looks. Ladderback chairs are crafted on the premises, with a craftsman weaving fiber seating as you watch. Also a selection of locally made bedroom and dining room furniture. Monday, Wednesday, Thursday, Friday 9–5; Tuesday 9–8; Saturday 9–4.

The Factory Coop (632-1447), 45 Logan Street, carries a variety of furniture. Open daily.

R. Smith Colonial Furniture (632-3461), 289 South Main Street. Colonial-style furnishings and accessories. Open daily.

Rome Sales Co. (632-1320), 74 Sherman Street. Contemporary, country, traditional furniture. New England's largest Canadian glider selection. Open daily.

Gardner Furniture Outlet (632-9661), 25 Kraft Street. Complete furniture line. Open daily.

Nothing but Seconds (630-1130), 45 Logan Street (the basement). Factory seconds from local and national manufacturers. Open daily.

In Winchendon

Ray's Furniture Warehouse, Inc. (297-3454), 1 High Street. Shaker, Colonial, traditional, contemporary, and country furniture. Open daily.

Winchendon Furniture Co., Inc. (297-0131), 13 Railroad Street. Furniture, lamps, and accessories. Adjacent discount warehouse. Open daily.

Pineault Furniture Corp. (297-0684), 290 Central Street. Discounted home furnishings in cherry, mahogany, maple, oak, and pine (closed Sunday in July and August).

In Baldwinville

Dan's Pine Shop (939-5687), 45 Elm Street (MA 302). A 14-room showroom with an extensive line of Colonial and country furniture and accessories.

In Templeton

Templeton Colonial Furniture (939-5504), 152 Baldwinville Road. Locally manufactured, traditional furniture in cherry, maple, and pine.

FARMS AND ORCHARDS

Flat Hill Orchards (582-6756), Lunenburg, is open daily August through December, selling its apples, peaches, plums, and nectarines.

Westfield Farm Goat Dairy (928-5110), 28 Worcester Road, Hubbardston, welcomes visitors year-round; eight different kinds of goat cheese are prepared for market.

SPECIAL EVENTS

June (first Saturday): **Johnny Appleseed Day**—Leominster's annual salute to native son John Chapman, the Swedenborgian missionary who planted apple trees everywhere.

July (early): The **Arthur M. Longsjo Jr. Memorial Bike Race,** a 50-mile event that attracts international participants, perpetuates the memory of a local Olympian who was both a cyclist and a speed skater.

Note: Inquire about summer and fall events at Wachusett Mountain.

Worcester

The acknowledged metropolis of central Massachusetts, Worcester, with a population of nearly 170,000, is the second largest city in both Massachusetts and all of New England.

Built on seven hills like Rome, Worcester has all the ingredients of a top-class city: eight colleges and universities (a major medical school and teaching hospital among them), a remarkable art museum, an excellent concert hall, a well-equipped convention center, good dining and shopping, and a diverse economy. Worcester, however, lives in the long shadow of Boston, an hour's drive away, and has serious "second city" self-image problems along with a lingering reputation for being more gritty than glamorous.

Compared to the confident founding of Boston by assertive Puritans, Worcester's start was rather shaky. Originally known by the Native American name Quinsigamond, Worcester was first settled in 1682 but later abandoned because of Native American raids. There were a few half-hearted attempts at returning to the area but no permanent settlement until 1713, when Jonas Rice established an enduring farm. Worcester was incorporated as a town nine years later, in 1722.

Because of its central location in the region, Worcester boasts that it is "The Heart of New England." That location didn't mean much at first, and Worcester was a placid, rural, inland outpost until the mid-19th century when improved transportation—notably the opening in 1828 of the Blackstone Canal, linking Worcester with the port of Providence, Rhode Island—set off a manufacturing boom. With the arrival of the railroad era, Worcester's easy accessibility to markets and raw materials enabled it rapidly to become an extraordinarily diversified manufacturing and commercial center.

The middle years of the 19th century were New England's Golden Age, characterized by a sunburst of Yankee ingenuity and creativity. Nowhere was the region's legendary breed of self-taught inventors and tinkerers busier than in Worcester. Within three years of each other in the mid-1850s, for example, Russell Hawes invented the first practical envelope-folding machine; George Crompton designed a revolutionary power loom; Thomas Blanchard developed a lathe for turning irregular forms; and Erastus B. Bigelow produced an improved carpet loom.

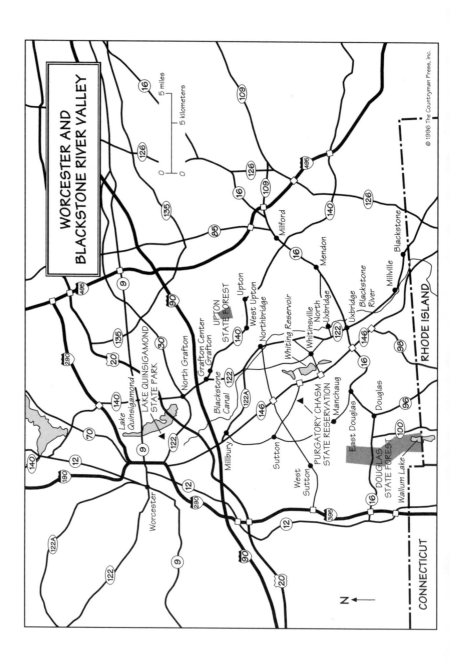

WORCESTER AND BLACKSTONE RIVER VALLEY

Factories based on these and other inventions sprang up around the city. Each factory center usually became a little world of its own, complete with bands, choral societies, sports teams, and ethnic social clubs. The factories had voracious appetites for labor, attracting workers from around the world to give Worcester an ethnic diversity unusual even by the polyglot standards of New England mill towns.

The carpet industry, for instance, employed Lebanese, Syrians, Turks, Assyrians, Albanians, Armenians (the first Armenian church in the country was in Worcester), Greeks, Romanians, and even Yorkshiremen. Swedes, not a major ethnic presence elsewhere in the state, once made up about a fifth of the population. Swedish immigrants began arriving in the 1860s, most going to work for the American Steel and Wire Company and Norton Company, one of the world's largest manufacturers of grinding wheels and abrasives.

Hispanics are the city's newest major ethnic group, arriving in large numbers only in the last 20 years or so. Like other immigrants before them, Spanish speakers have largely settled in tenement neighborhoods once home to other ethnic groups.

Shrewsbury Street is Worcester's prototypical immigrant neighborhood. Most of the workers who dug the Blackstone Canal, and later laid the tracks for the railroad that supplanted it, were Irishmen. When the Irish climbed up the economic ladder, other ethnic groups moved in along Shrewsbury Street, which follows the canal route. Shrewsbury Street eventually became Worcester's Little Italy and still has an Italian flavor, with a number of long-established pizzerias and Italian restaurants.

Ethnic bars and social clubs still anchor many Worcester neighborhoods. Older sections are also often dotted with "three deckers"—flat-roofed, three-story wooden tenements with porches at front and back—that were first built to meet the needs of large immigrant families. Worcester has one of the largest concentrations of this distinctively New England type of housing.

The old redbrick mills of another age also still loom large on the cityscape, but these days many have been converted to nonindustrial uses. Some are now office buildings, others, restaurants or lounges and, in one case, a huge bookstore.

Since World War II, Worcester has pioneered in the field of biological research: The birth-control pill was developed in the 1950s at the Worcester Center for Experimental Biology, now in neighboring Shrewsbury. Because of this activity, Worcester has attracted a number of biotech and health industry companies that may usher in a new era of dynamic innovation for the city. In fact, Worcester's largest employer today is the University of Massachusetts Medical Center. The center's neighbor on MA 9 is the innovative Massachusetts Biotechnology Research Park. A symbol of the high-tech "Massachusetts Miracle" when it opened in 1987, the park was the first fully operational one in the country devoted entirely to the biotech industry.

Worcester is now more of a service-oriented, white-collar town than a heavy industry, blue-collar one, but its central location is still important. Some 6 million people live within about an hour's interstate drive of the city, which makes it ideal for meetings, conventions, and major musical events. In fact, in recent years Worcester—once considered the squarest city in Massachusetts by many—has become the rock and pop music concert capital of New England, the regional venue of choice for the top bands and performers.

Most rock concerts take place in the Centrum, a modern, multi-purpose auditorium on downtown Foster Street. The Centrum is one of the busiest arenas in the country; it's so successful, in fact, that it recently (1995) had to be expanded. The restaurants and lounges that have sprung up to serve the Centrum crowds have also made downtown Worcester a much livelier place than it used to be.

Still, the traditional hub of the city remains the old colonial Common. Just off Main Street, the Common is wedged between the Italianate City Hall—modeled after the one in Siena, Italy—and the Worcester Center Galleria, an enclosed shopping mall. In the 1970s, the Common was modishly redesigned and given a reflecting pool mirroring City Hall, as part of a massive downtown renewal project of which Worcester Center was the keystone. Initially successful, the Worcester Center Galleria fell on hard times and for a period was virtually empty. In 1994, however, it was born again as Worcester Common Fashion Outlets, the country's first enclosed urban outlet mall.

The Common is a real link to Worcester's past, with both a Civil War monument and a fenced-in colonial burial ground. A monument in the middle of the graveyard marks the resting place of Timothy Bigelow, captain of the Minuteman company that marched to Cambridge in April 1775. One of Worcester's symbols is the Daniel Chester French sculpture of a boy riding a turtle that stands at the Salem Square corner of the Common.

The present City Hall is built on the site of the simple 18th-century meetinghouse that was the cradle of local government. It was here, on July 17, 1776, that the patriot printer Isaiah Thomas—whose newspaper, *The Massachusetts Spy,* is considered to be the country's first paper—read the Declaration of Independence to a large crowd assembled on the Common. This event was the first reading of the declaration in New England and one of the first in the country.

Thomas remained in Worcester after the Revolution, and his printing business grew until it was, for a period, the largest in the United States. A man of many interests, he also founded the American Antiquarian Society, today housed in a handsome neo-Federal building on Salisbury Street. The society's magnificent library contains an estimated

two-thirds of all the material printed in the country before 1820.
Close proximity to Boston has certainly had an inhibiting effect on
the city's cultural and social life, but Worcester tries hard to cultivate
the arts. There is a resident professional theater company, Worcester
Foothills Theater, and an orchestra, the Central Massachusetts Symphony. The Worcester Art Museum is one of the country's leading me-
dium-sized museums. The Worcester Music Festival, held each autumn
since 1858, is one of the country's oldest and attracts internationally
known performers and ensembles. Classical concerts are often held in
Mechanics Hall on Main Street, a graceful auditorium built in 1857.

AREA CODE
508

GUIDANCE
Worcester Area Chamber of Commerce and **Worcester County Con-
vention & Visitors Bureau** (753-2924; 753-2920), 33 Waldo Street,
Worcester 01608.

The Cultural Commission (799-1400). Call for daily cultural events and
programs.

Magazines: *Worcester Magazine* (755-8004); *Worcester Phoenix* (832-9800).

GETTING THERE
By car: Worcester is 40 miles from Boston via MA 9 or the Mass. Pike. Coming from Boston, take Exit 11 off the Turnpike. Use Exit 10 if approach-
ing the city from the south or west.

By bus: **Greyhound–Peter Pan Bus Lines** (754-4600; 1-800-237-8747)

By train: MBTA commuter Worcester-Boston service (722-3200; 1-800-
392-6099). The railway station is at 45 Shrewsbury Street.

GETTING AROUND
Worcester's attractions are widely scattered, and a car is necessary to see the
city properly.

PARKING
There is a 4300-car garage in Worcester Center (Worcester Common Fashion Outlets), and several large municipal lots and garages are located
downtown.

MEDICAL EMERGENCY
University of Massachusetts Medical Center (856-0011), 55 Lake Avenue North. **The Medical Center of Central Massachusetts,** Hah-
nemann Campus (792-8000), 281 Lincoln Street.

TO SEE

Massachusetts Avenue Historic District—a parkway off Salisbury
Street laid out in the late 19th century and lined with stately Victorian
and Edwardian homes built in Queen Anne and other period styles by
local business and professional men. Teddy Roosevelt paraded down
the avenue in an open carriage in 1902.

Goddard Exhibition (793-7572), Goddard Library, Clark University, 950 Main Street. Monday through Friday 10–4. The space age was born in 1926 when Dr. Robert Goddard, a physics professor at Clark, fired a rocket 41 feet in the air from a hilltop in Auburn, a Worcester suburb. Goddard's notebooks and patents, along with photos and rocket memorabilia, are displayed in the handsome library his alma mater named for him.

MUSEUMS

Worcester Art Museum (799-4406), 55 Salisbury Street. Open Tuesday through Friday 11–4, Saturday 10–5. Closed Monday, also Sunday in summer. $4 adults, $3 students and children. Marked from I-290, Lincoln Square exit. First opened in 1898, the museum ranks among the country's best with the region's second-largest permanent collection: more than 30,000 works of art spanning 5000 years. There are fine examples of Greek, Roman, pre-Columbian, Asian, Persian, European, and American art. The early-American paintings displayed are outstanding. The museum was one of the first to begin collecting photographs as fine art, and there are constantly changing exhibits of photographs from the Civil War era to the present. There is also a complete room from a 12th-century French monastery and a group of splendid Roman mosaics from Antioch. The museum has a gift shop, restaurant, and, in summer, garden café.

Worcester Historical Museum (753-8278), 30 Elm Street. Tuesday through Saturday 10–4, Sunday 1–4. Devoted to local history, the museum's handsome brick building is also headquarters of the Worcester Historical Society. There are interesting displays tracing the city's evolution from frontier village to industrial city and frequently changing exhibitions. The library has 10,000 volumes. A block away from the museum at 40 Highland Street is the **Salisbury Mansion,** residence of the prominent Salisbury family from 1772 to 1852. One of Worcester's few surviving 18th-century buildings, the mansion has been been restored by the historical society to re-create the home life of the Salisburys around 1830.

American Antiquarian Society (755-5221), 185 Salisbury Street. Open for guided tours Wednesday at 2 PM and to qualified researchers Monday through Friday 9–5. Founded by Isaiah Thomas in 1812, the society specializes in American printed material—books, newspapers, magazines, broadsides, and sheet music—from the mid-17th century through 1876. Thomas's original flatbread press and selections from the society's vast collection of Americana are displayed. The library is superb but open only to scholars working on specific projects.

American Sanitary Plumbing Museum (754-9453), 39 Piedmont Street. Tuesday and Thursday 10–2 (closed July and August). The only one of its kind in the country, this museum—the personal collection of a family in the plumbing business for several generations—has a unique per-

spective on American domestic life. Among its treasures are sections of one of 17th-century Boston's wooden water mains, a replica of the toilet at Mount Vernon, and a primitive 1920s prototype of the dishwasher called "an electric sink." Lots of plumbers' tools and fancy chamber pots, too.

FOR FAMILIES

Higgins Armory Museum (853-6015), 100 Barber Avenue, off Gold Star Boulevard. Tuesday through Saturday 10–4, Sunday noon–4. Located in an industrial section, this unusual museum is the result of the extensive research into ancient metallurgy of a local industrialist, John Woodman Higgins. While trying to rediscover the techniques that enabled medieval armorers to produce such fine steel, Higgins collected suits of armor—more than 100 of them. Dramatically displayed in a great hall, like that of a castle, the collection includes very rare and beautiful armor, such as the tournament armor of kings and special suits for children and dogs. Also on view are banners, swords, shields, battle axes, maces, and crossbows, along with period paintings, stained glass, wood carvings, tapestries, and a replica of an armorer's workshop. There is a gallery with armor reproductions that museum visitors can try on and also a gift shop selling all sorts of knightly memorabilia.

New England Science Center (791-9211), 222 Harrington Way. Monday through Saturday 10–5, Sunday noon–5. A museum and wildlife center set in a 60-acre park that includes a zoo complete with wolves, mountain lions, polar bears—and a miniature railroad. There are also science exhibits, an observatory, a planetarium, and nature trails.

TO DO

Providence and Worcester Railroad (755-4000). A working railroad that offers passenger excursions, most frequently in foliage season.

GREEN SPACE

Quinsigamond State Park (757-2140), off Lake Avenue on Lake Quinsigamond, consists of two areas: Regatta Point has a swimming beach, changing facilities, and sailboats; Lake Park has swimming and picnic areas as well as tennis courts and other sports facilities. The park is frequently the site of regional and national collegiate rowing competitions.

Rutland State Park (886-6333), a 1900-acre park on MA 122 in Rutland, has swimming and picnic areas on Whitehall Pond and fishing and boat-launching ramps on Long Pond.

Elm Park, off Park Avenue, established in 1854, is the oldest public park—as distinguished from town Green or Common—in the nation. Generations of Worcesterites have had their wedding photos taken on the ornate Victorian bridge over the pleasing pond.

Moore State Park (792-3969), off MA 31 in Paxton, is a 350-acre former estate with a 19th-century sawmill, fishing, and scenic walks.

Wachusett Mountain State Reservation (464-2987), Mountain Road, Princeton; a 1600-acre park dominated by Mount Wachusett. At an elevation of just over 2000 feet, the summit of the mountain is the highest point in Worcester County, with a view on a clear day that includes Mount Monadnock and the White Mountains. Hiking, cross-country skiing, and an alpine ski area, open for night skiing, that is the area's largest (see "The Central Uplands").

LODGING

HOTELS
Crown Plaza Hotel (791-1600; 1-800-628-4240), 10 Lincoln Square, at the junction of I-21 and MA 9. A 250-room hotel with indoor and outdoor pools, sauna, and exercise room. Single $135, double $155.

Beechwood Inn (754-5789), 363 Plantation Street. A distinctive, circular building with 58 deluxe rooms. Adjacent to the Medical Center complex and Biotechnology Park. Excellent restaurant with garden dining terrace. Single $139; double $149.

Holiday Inn (842-4000), 500 Lincoln Street. A 141-room hotel with indoor pool and restaurant. Single $85–110, double $95–120.

Clarion Suites Hotel (753-3512), 70 Southbridge Street. Downtown location and 100 one- and two-bedroom suites. Single $77, double $87.

BED & BREAKFASTS
See "The Central Uplands," "Old Sturbridge Village Area," or "Blackstone River Valley."

WHERE TO EAT

DINING OUT
Arturo's Ristorante (755-5640), 411 Chandler Street. Extensive northern Italian menu. Pleasant dining room. Open 11:30 AM–11:30 PM Monday through Saturday and 11:30 AM–10 PM Sunday. Arturo and Dianne Cartagenova have a winning touch with decor and with light but heavy-on-the-herbs-and-vegetables meat dishes and pastas. $10–16. If you don't want to go the whole three courses, the Pizzeria at Arturo's features a wood-fired oven for pizza or roast chicken. $6–9.
Beechwood Restaurant (754-5789), 363 Plantation Street, in the Beechwood Inn. Open 6:30–10:30 AM, 11:30 AM–2:30 PM, 6–10 PM for dinner. The long, elegant dining room and dining terrace are the setting for cuisine that's distinctly American with interesting international touches, such as linguine with smoked chicken in Cajun cream sauce, and ribeye steak served with demiglaze. $20–30.
Struck Cafe (757-1670), 415 Chandler Street, Worcester. Open Tuesday through Friday for lunch, Tuesday through Saturday for dinner. Simple decor, mismatched china, great food: soups and salads as well as light entrées at noon ($3–8) and an elegant a la carte dinner menu that changes every few months ($14-22). Reservations suggested for dinner.
El Morocco (756-7117), 100 Wall Street. Open 11:30 AM–10 PM Monday through Thursday, Friday to 10:30 PM, Saturday 4–11 PM, Sunday 4–9 PM for dinner. Although no longer under original ownership, "The El"—anchoring a hilltop in the old Lebanese neighborhood—remains a local institution, serving authentic Middle Eastern food. Lamb and beef kebabs are a particular specialty. Entrées $10–25.
Thai Orchid (792-9701), 144 Commercial Street. Located across from the Centrum, this is a moderately priced Thai restaurant very popular with locals as well as concertgoers. Specialties include Gai Chom Poo: chicken smothered with pineapple chunks, onions, green peppers, and tomatoes, served in a sweet-and-sour sauce. Open Monday through Friday 11:30 AM–3 PM, 5–9:30 PM; Saturday 4–10 PM; Sunday 4–9:30 PM. Dinner entrées $8–13.
Maxwell Silverman's Toolhouse (755-1200), 25 Union Street at Lincoln Square; housed in a 19th-century factory building and trendily decorated with old tools and machine parts. Open 11:30 AM–4 PM, 5–10 PM Monday through Friday, and until 11 PM Saturday; 4–9 PM Sunday. Dinner $11–20.

Mechanics Hall

EATING OUT
Once home of the Worcester Lunch Car Company, the country's leading diner manufacturer in its day, Worcester still has more than a dozen old-fashioned diners, more than any other city in the region. Two of the most popular are across from each other on Shrewsbury Street:

Boulevard Diner (791-4535), 155 Shrewsbury Street. Open 7 AM–4 AM. A classic and much-photographed 1930s diner, the Boulevard has a mostly Italian menu. The lasagne and meatball subs are particularly good.

Parkway Diner (753-9968), 148 Shrewsbury Street. Open Monday through Thursday 6 AM–9 PM, Friday and Saturday until midnight. A neighborhood institution serving traditional southern Italian dishes. Hot sausages or meatballs with eggs are a breakfast specialty.

East Park Grille (no phone), 172 Shrewsbury Street. Open Tuesday through Saturday 4–10 PM. Casual atmosphere, seafood the specialty. Cash only.

El Basha Restaurant (797-0884), 424 Belmont Street. Open Monday through Saturday 11:30 AM–10 PM. Distinctly unpretentious but noted for savory Lebanese cuisine.

LaPatisserie (756-1454), 252 Commercial Street. Weekdays 7 AM–3:30 PM; Sunday 8 AM–2 PM. Known for its homemade soups and sandwiches.

Weintraub's Deli (756-7870), 126 Water Street. Open 9 AM–8 PM Tuesday through Sunday, until 4 PM Monday. Still doing business in what was the city's first Jewish immigrant neighborhood. An authentic old-

style deli with great Romanian pastrami sandwiches. Cash only.
The Restaurant at Tatnuck Bookseller (756-7644), 335 Chandler Street.
Open for lunch and dinner, Monday through Saturday, Sunday 10–3.
Larger and far more serious about food than a bookstore café. Dinner
entrées usually include stir fries, and there are always specials.

ENTERTAINMENT

Centrum (755-6800), 50 Foster Street. A well-designed and centrally located auditorium that hosts more big-name rock and popular music
concerts than any other facility in New England.
Mechanics Hall (752-5608), 321 Main Street. Built in 1857, primarily for
lectures—Charles Dickens spoke here—the hall fell on hard times in this
century and was long used primarily for wrestling matches and roller der-
bies. Restored as a Bicentennial project, acoustically superb Mechanics
Hall is now used for concerts, balls, and theatrical presentations.
Foothills Theatre (754-4018), Worcester Center, 100 Front Street. The
city's resident professional theater company, it stages eight productions
during the September through April season.

SELECTIVE SHOPPING

There are a variety of shops along Main Street, but downtown Worcester's
shopping magnet is **Worcester Common Fashion Outlets** (798-
2581) in the impressively spiffed-up Worcester Center Galleria. Open
Monday through Saturday 10 AM–9 PM; Sunday 11 AM–7 PM. The nearly
120 stores in the enclosed, two-level atrium mall—most outlets for designer lines at discounts of 30 to 70 percent—include Saks Fifth Avenue, Polo Ralph Lauren, Filene's Basement, and Barneys New York.
There is a large food court and attached parking garage.
Spag's Supply (799-2570), MA 9, Shrewsbury. A no-nonsense, barnlike
place that carries everything from kitchenware and automotive supplies
to beauty aids and fishing tackle. Regionally renowned for its bargains
and hard-to-find items. Always crowded. Open Monday through Friday 9 AM–9 PM; Saturday 8 AM–9 PM; Sunday noon–6 PM.
Craft Center (753-8183), 25 Sagamore Road, Worcester. One of the
country's oldest crafts complexes. The center shop carries quality crafts
as well as craft supplies. Open Tuesday through Saturday 10–5.
Tatnuck Bookseller Marketplace (756-7644; 1-800-642-6657), 335
Chandler Street (MA 122), Worcester. Housed in a cavernous, brick,
former machine-tool factory, this is the largest independent bookseller
in Massachusetts. The more than 5 miles of bookshelves hold some
500,0000 volumes. There are separate departments for secondhand,
rare, foreign language, and children's books. Also candle, stationery, and
gift shops, and a café restaurant.

SPECIAL EVENTS

May: **Eastern Sprints Regatta,** intercollegiate rowing competition at Regatta Point on Lake Quinsigamond.

October: **Worcester County Music Association Festival**—held annually since 1858, the festival features major ensembles and internationally known artists.

December: **Handel's Messiah,** performed in Mechanics Hall by the Worcester Chorus and Orchestra. **First Night,** a community-wide cultural New Year's Eve celebration featuring mime, poetry readings, theater, dance, and music.

Blackstone River Valley

What fascinates historians about the Blackstone River Valley is the way it looks: woods and pastures spotted with 18th-century meetinghouses and early-19th-century mill villages, each carefully formed like a well-crafted bead strung along the thread of river.

America loves "firsts"; therefore, the vintage-1793 Old Slater Mill in Pawtucket, Rhode Island, the first place in which cotton was successfully spun by machine in America, has been a museum since the 1920s. More recently Congress has passed an act establishing a bi-state Blackstone River Valley National Heritage Corridor, recognizing that the Slater Mill was just the opening paragraph in the first chapter of America's Industrial Revolution, a chapter that's written all over the face of this 44-mile-long valley.

Park rangers at the Blackstone River and Canal Heritage State Park in Uxbridge explain that by 1810 an estimated 100 cotton mills were peppered along local rivers, most inspired by Slater's design, which is now known as the "Rhode Island System." In contrast to the mammoth mill cities that first appeared with Lowell in the 1830s (now known as the "Waltham System"), Blackstone Valley mills were usually run by the owner (rather than by agents and absentee investors), employed entire families for whom they provided housing (rather than mill hands for whom they built boardinghouses), and remained relatively small, compact, and on a human scale.

By the time the Blackstone Canal was completed in 1828 to link Worcester and Providence, dozens of small textile mills and several mill villages already lined the river, which drops 438 feet through innumerable rapids and falls. This uneven terrain necessitated no fewer than 49 locks on the canal.

In 1839 the fastest way to get from Worcester to Providence was aboard a 50-passenger canal barge. In 1847 the Providence and Worcester Railroad came along, reducing travel time from 12 to 2 hours, thus putting the canal out of business. Today only a half dozen of its original miles are still "watered."

The Heritage State Park in Uxbridge represents the most scenic and accessible stretch of the former canal. From the visitors center there, you can walk in one direction along a wooded millpond to high stone cliffs and, in the other, along a shaded towpath to the graceful Stanley Woolen Mill (built in 1851) in the middle of Uxbridge.

Some three dozen distinct mill villages survive within the valley. Other local attractions include New England's largest collection of wild animals and Purgatory Chasm, easier to explore than to explain.

AREA CODE
508

GUIDANCE

Blackstone Valley Chamber of Commerce (234-9090), 57 Church Street, Whitinsville 01588. Call weekday mornings. The best source of information before you come.

River Bend Farm Visitors Center at the Blackstone River and Canal Heritage State Park (278-7604), 287 Oak Street, Uxbridge. Open daily 10–6 in summer, 10–4 in winter. This is the logical place to begin exploring the Massachusetts segment of the valley: a staffed information center stocked with local tourist literature and furnished with interpretive exhibits and slide presentations. The center schedules walking tours, lectures, and educational programs on local nature and history, and holds special events.

Blackstone River Valley National Heritage Corridor (401-762-0250), One Depot Square, Woonsocket RI 02895. Monday through Friday 8–5. This is the National Park Service office for the valley, coordinating information for both the Massachusetts and Rhode Island segments of the corridor.

Blackstone River Valley Tourism Council (401-334-7773), PO Box 7663, Cumberland, RI 02864, serves the Rhode Island segment of the valley. Ask about the evolving museum of work and culture in Woonsocket, bike trails, and special events.

GETTING THERE

Less than an hour's drive southwest of Boston, the heart of this bi-state "National Heritage Corridor" (see *Guidance*) is Uxbridge, accessible from Boston via I-495 to Milford, then MA 16 West. To follow the canal from Grafton south to Blackstone, exit off the Mass. Pike at MA 122 in North Grafton. For Purgatory Chasm in Sutton, take the Mass. Pike to MA 146 South.

MEDICAL EMERGENCY

Milford-Whitinsville Regional Hospital (473-1190), MA 16, Milford.

VILLAGES

Grafton Center. Founded in 1654 as one of John Eliot's Praying Indian villages, it has a classic New England Common with a bandstand, surrounded by 19th-century homes, an inn, and commercial buildings (see *Lodging* and *Where to Eat.*)

East Douglas. A classic, sleepy crossroads with the two-story frame **E.N.**

The Blackstone River Valley National Heritage Corridor

Jenckes Store, preserved by the Douglas Historical Society (open weekends in June and August, 1–4 and by appointment; 476-7403), complete with a dry-goods section, ledgers, and crockery, and looking precisely the way it did in the 1890s.

TO SEE

Blackstone River and Canal Heritage State Park (278-7604), 287 Oak Street (marked from MA 16), Uxbridge. Open daily 10–6 in summer, 10–4 in winter (see *Guidance*). The farmhouse itself is fitted with interpretive exhibits on the history and other aspects of the valley, and from here you can walk a mile or so under arching trees to the Stanley Woolen Mill or walk north to the point at which the river and canal join at the graceful Stone Arch bridges. Muskrats and great blue herons are frequently sighted along the Goat Hill Trail, which continues another couple miles along the edge of Rice City Pond. A trail on the other side of the pond leads to King Philip's Rock, a high stone stage on which the 17th-century Native American chief should have stood even if he didn't. The view is off across rolling green hills and wetlands, punctured by just one smokestack in the distance. Inquire about lectures, walking tours, and special events. (Also see *Green Space.*)

Willard House & Clock Museum (839-3500), 11 Willard Street, Grafton. Signs point the way from Grafton's Common, also from MA 30 (it's just a half mile south). Open year-round Tuesday through Saturday 10–4, Sunday 1–5 for 1½-hour guided tours. $3 adults, $1 children aged 6–12. A classic saltbox built in 1718 by the grandfather of four clockmaking brothers who made some 5000 timepieces in the late 18th and early 19th centuries. Over 70 magnificent clocks are displayed in eight galleries, which include five original rooms in the house.

Southwick's Wild Animal Farm (883-9182), 9 Southwick Street, marked from MA 16, Mendon. Open May through Labor Day daily 10–5, limited hours in April, September, October. $8 adults, $6 for children over age 2. Given the lack of a first-rate public zoo in New England, this is the next best thing: the largest collection of animals in the region. Begun as a hobby on their 300-acre farm in the 1950s, the Southwicks now regularly care for 500 animals, representing more than 100 species: giraffes, rhinos, lions, tigers, bears, chimps, monkeys, camels, zebras, and giant tortoises. The petting zoo includes llamas, deer, and barnyard animals. Kiddie rides, a snack bar, and picnic tables are also part of the scene.

Quaker Meeting Houses. Many of the valley's first settlers were Quakers, and two of their 18th-century buildings survive. In Uxbridge, on MA 146A (south of town; across from the Quaker Motor Lodge), stands a 1770 meetinghouse (open July and August, Sunday afternoons 2–4) with its interior unchanged. The second is the **Chestnut Hill Meeting House** (open by appointment: 883-9409), Chestnut Hill Road between Southwick's Wild Animal Farm and Millville. Built in 1769 with a gallery and box pews, the building has been recently restored; a peaceful place.

SCENIC DRIVES

Mill Villages. Begin in North Uxbridge on MA 16 at the **Crown and Eagle Mill,** which looks more like a Yankee version of a Loire Valley château than a factory. Built in 1826 of local granite with clerestory monitor windows and a handsome bell tower, it spans the Mumford River and is set in formal parklike grounds. Burned by vandals in 1975, the mill has since been restored as housing for the elderly, and its village still includes a school, the original 1810 Clapp Cotton Mill, handsome brick housing, and a store.

A mile away, the mansard-roofed, brick **Linwood Mill,** built in 1870, overlooks a pond-shaped stretch of river. The mill housing is next door, and the ornate mill-owner's mansion, now the Victorian Inn and restaurant, is just up the road.

Another mile brings you to **Whitinsville** (pronounced "Whit-ins-ville"), a village built around three mills—a small vintage-1826 red mill with a weathervane on its belfry, a mid-19th-century granite mill, and the larger and later Whitin Machine Works around the corner. Mill-ponds stretch on and on both north and south of the village. **Purgatory Chasm** (see *Green Space*) is 2 miles up North Main Street through New Village, the valley's largest cluster of mill workers' housing. In Manchaug, less than 5 miles west of Whitinsville, the granite **B.B. Knight Cotton Mill** is another beauty with an ornate tower and wrought-iron balconies, across from an early dam and waterfall.

Farms and Fudge in Sutton. From MA 146 South take the Northbridge/Oxford exit and turn right onto Armsby Road at the Pleasant Valley sign. Just off MA 146 you pass **Vaillancourt Folk Art** (see *Selective Shopping*) and in a quarter mile come to the **Pleasant Valley Country Club,** home of the New England Classic Golf Tournament in July, an area landmark that's open to the public for lunch (see *Golf*). Continue across Boston Road to Burbank Road and, after another quarter mile, note **Eaton's Farm Confectioners,** a former dairy farm that's the source of great fudge and a sinful "Lust Bar"; this is also a good picnic site (box lunches available; see *Selective Shopping*).

From Eaton's take a right onto Burbank Road, keeping an eye out for **Freegrace Marble Farm** (on the right, at the second sharp curve in the road). This is a very special farm, little changed over the centuries and harboring a Native American burial ground. Owner Leona Dona (865-2406) has deeded it to SPNEA and is generally delighted to tell visitors about the Native American relics found on the property and the history of the farm itself. If you want to stop, be sure to call ahead.

Continue on Burbank Road until it intersects with Wheelock Road; turn left on Wheelock and follow it to the end. Take a left onto Singletary Road and follow it to the junction of Singletary and Boston Roads. The 1890s **Sherman Blacksmith Shop** (open by appointment: 865-2725) is on your left.

Purgatory and Heaven in Sutton. From MA 146 take Purgatory Road to Purgatory Chasm State Park (see *Green Space*), then continue along Purgatory Road to the Central Turnpike and take a left into West Sutton. There, make another left onto Douglas Road and, in a half mile, turn left again onto Waters Road. This road leads steeply uphill to **Waters Farm** (865-4886), a 1757 homestead, an 1840s barn, and 103 acres of land that have been conveyed to the town of Sutton and are being

The Stanley Woolen Mill, part of the Blackstone River and Canal Heritage State Park

developed as a living history center. It's worth stopping by just to enjoy the panoramic view of Lake Manchaug, but you might want to call ahead; the farm is the site of frequent special events ranging from bluegrass concerts to sleigh rallies.

TO DO

BICYCLING
The area's narrow country roads invite biking. From the Department of Environmental Management you might also secure a description of the **Southern New England Trunkline Trail,** a 22-mile bikepath-in-the-making that follows an old railbed from Franklin to Uxbridge and on into Connecticut.

BOAT EXCURSION
The Blackstone Valley *Explorer* (401-334-0837), a 49-passenger riverboat maintained by the Blackstone Valley Tourism Council, shifts its location throughout the summer. It is usually based in Uxbridge the first half of June.

CANOEING
"The Blackstone River Canoe Guide," a booklet available from all the guidance sources listed, divides the river into 15 segments of various lengths, 10 in Massachusetts. The most popular is the 6-mile segment through the Blackstone River and Canal Heritage State Park. Put in at Church Street in Northbridge. Canoes can be rented from **Fin & Feather Sports** (529-3901), MA 140, Upton Center.

GOLF

Pleasant Valley Country Club (865-4441), marked from MA 146 in Sutton. A highly rated 18-hole course, for many years host to the New England Classic Golf Tournament (July). It is private, but Dimples restaurant (lower level) is open to the public Tuesday through Friday for lunch. Tickets for tournaments must be purchased in advance.

SWIMMING

Wallum Lake, Douglas State Forest, Douglas (see *Green Space*), is exceptionally clear, sandy-bottomed with a beach large enough to absorb the weekend crowd; relatively empty midweek. Changing rooms, picnic tables. Nominal fee.

West Hill Recreation Area, Uxbridge. A glorified mud puddle, great for children. Older kids can swim right across the pond to the opposite beach. Changing rooms, picnic tables.

Breezy Picnic Grounds and Waterslide (476-2664), 538 Northwest Main Street, Douglas. Open weekends Memorial Day through mid-June, then daily through Labor Day. $3.50 adults weekdays, $4.50 weekends, $10 for use of waterslides as well as lake; less for children. Lake swimming, snack bar, picnic grounds, two 300-foot waterslides.

GREEN SPACE

Purgatory Chasm State Reservation (234-3733), Purgatory Road (off MA 146), Sutton. The chasm itself is a series of three 65-foot-deep ravines strewn with jumbles of granite boulders over which you pick your way, then follow a trail up through the pines along the rim, squeezing through "Fat Man's Misery" if you can. The 188-acre reservation includes a playground and picnic tables in the pines.

Douglas State Forest (476-7872), Wallum Lake Road, Douglas (off MA 16). Wallum Lake (see *Swimming*) is one of the state's outstanding swimming and fishing lakes. The recreation area includes a boat ramp, picnic tables and grills, changing rooms, and hiking trails. $3 day-use fee.

Upton State Forest (278-6486), off MA 122, Northbridge. A 2660-acre spread with hiking, snowmobiling, and biking trails; fishing in Dean Pond.

Blackstone State Forest (278-6486), off MA 122, Northbridge, offers canoeing and hiking.

West Hill Dam and Recreation Area, West Hill Road, Uxbridge. This is an Army Corps of Engineers project and includes the dam at the end of one road and a recreation area with swimming, picnicking, and hiking trails at the end of the other. Well-posted from MA 16.

Blackstone Gorge State Park. A Rhode Island state park but right on the line. Park in Blackstone near the wide, gently curving waterfall at Rolling Dam and walk south through the pines and maples above the river as it rushes through steep granite walls.

Blackstone River and Canal Heritage State Park (278-7604), 287 Oak

Street, Uxbridge. This 1005-acre park lies along some 6 miles of the river, including a dammed portion, Rice City Pond. River Bend Farm here serves as the information center for the Massachusetts segment of the valley (see *Guidance* and *Canoeing*).

LODGING

BED & BREAKFASTS

☞ **Charles Capron House** (278-2214), 2 Capron Street, Uxbridge 01569. A grand, Gothic, mill owner's mansion built in 1865 on a quiet, shady street; elegant but not stuffy. Ken and Mary Taft are genial hosts who have lived here more than 25 years, raising seven children. They offer three antiques-furnished guest rooms (Mary is a professional interior decorator), all with private bath. Common rooms include a gracious living room and sun porch. River Bend Farm is within walking distance. $70 per couple, $55 single includes breakfast.

☞ **Heritage House** (839-5063), 28 North Street, Grafton 01519. Coincidentally (see the Charles Capron House), Peg and John Koomey have also raised seven children in this gracious house, a vintage-1796 Federal beauty, on a maple-lined street, that meanders back along its garden. The three guest rooms, furnished in antiques, feature European featherbeds and share two large baths. Peg offers her guests terry-cloth robes (also alarm clocks and hair driers). Common spaces include the living room, music room, and sitting room, and breakfast is served either in the dining room or in the garden. $65 and up.

The Putnam House (865-9094), Putnam Hill Road, Sutton 01590. Dating from the 1730s, carefully restored with original paneling and walk-in fireplaces. Margaret and Martyn Bowdoen offer one large 20 by 20 room, with a working fireplace, and a small adjoining room sharing a bath can accommodate a family with up to three children. From $45 single to $75, breakfast included.

The Captain Slocomb House (839-3095), 6 South Street, Grafton 01519. Bob and Judy Maynard offer three attractive guest rooms: Aunt Mary's Room with its own sitting room, the Master Bedroom Suite with its own dressing room, and the West Room, all with private bath, in a fine 19th-century house just off Grafton Common. $60–70 includes a full breakfast. No children under 12, please.

The Fieldstone Victorian (883-4647), 40 Edgewater Drive, Blackstone 01504. Pleasantly sited overlooking a reservoir in South Blackstone; two rooms with private bath. $60–75.

WHERE TO EAT

DINING OUT

Note: Entrées at the first three of the following average $10.
Cocke'n Kettle (278-5517), MA 122 south of Uxbridge. Open for dinner

nightly except Monday. An imposing mansion, the local place to dine on veal *cordon bleu,* good early-bird specials ($8.95 for a complete meal).

New England Steak and Seafood (473-9787), MA 16, Mendon. Closed Tuesday, otherwise dinner from 5 nightly, lunch weekdays. A dependable steakhouse featuring live music and karaoke.

Ploughboy Pub at the Grafton Inn (839-5931), 25 Central Square, Grafton. Open daily 11–9, until 11 on Saturday.

The Victorian (234-2500), 583 Linwood Avenue, Whitinsville. Open for lunch Wednesday through Friday and dinner Wednesday through Sunday, but not always. Check. This extravagant but somewhat faded Victorian mansion is the setting for rather pretentious but generally fine dining; classics like escargots in puffed pastry and rack of lamb with rosemary and garlic. Entrées $18–30.

EATING OUT

Special Teas (839-7447), Grafton Common. Open Tuesday through Thursday 11–4, Saturday and Sunday 10–5, Thursday until 8. A tasteful tearoom serving lunch, weekend breakfasts, cakes, and desserts (to go, too).

Lowell's Restaurant (473-1073), MA 16, Mendon. Open daily 6:30 AM through dinner. A great family find, good for all three meals.

The Elmwood Club (476-2535), East Douglas. Open daily 7 AM–10 PM, good for fried seafood, sandwiches, Hershey ice cream.

Apple Tree Barn (476-2291), West Street off MA 16, East Douglas. Open for all three meals; rustic but good.

ENTERTAINMENT

A lingering '50s feel in the valley is evidenced by two of New England's last drive-in movie theaters: **Sutton Drive-In** (865-6525), MA 146, Sutton, and the **Mendon Drive-In,** MA 16, Mendon.

SELECTIVE SHOPPING

ANTIQUES SHOPS

David Rose (529-3838), MA 140, West Upton. Carries 18th- and 19th-century furniture and accessories.

Nipmuc Trading Post (634-8300), MA 16, Mendon. Open Tuesday through Sunday 10–5, Wednesday 10–8. A cooperative with varied quality antiques and collectibles.

Mendon Flea & Craft Market (478-5484), MA 16 (Hastings Street), Mendon. Open year-round Sunday 8–4. Look for the pink tractor. A weatherproof grab bag.

FARMS AND ORCHARDS

Wojcik Farm (883-9220), 65 Milk Street, Blackstone, sells fruit, vegetables, pick-your-own apples.

Douglas Orchard (476-2198), 36 Locust Street, East Douglas, offers pick-your-own apples and raspberries.

Cahills Farm (839-2990), Hartford Avenue, East Douglas, sells fruits and vegetables.

Lazy Acres Farm (839-2990), 109 Merrain Road, Grafton, sells vegetables and Christmas trees; and **K.C. Acres,** 11 George Hill Road, Grafton, offers pick-your-own blueberries.

Hawkhill Orchards (865-4905), 176 Charlton Road, Milbury, offers pick-your-own apples, peaches, plums, and apricots; and **Stowe Farm** (234-6711), 15 Stowe Road, Milbury, sells its apples and peaches.

Foppema's Farm (234-6711), 1612 Hill Street, Northbridge, offers fruit, vegetables, and pick-your-own strawberries.

Keown Orchards Farm Stand (865-6706), 9 McClellan Road, Sutton, is open mid-July through December 26, 10–6, selling (depending on the season) fruits, vegetables, herbs, flowers, pick-your-own apples and pumpkins, and Christmas trees. **Silvermine Farm** (865-5335), 96 Eight-lots Road, Sutton, offers pick-your-own strawberries, vegetables, and blueberries.

The Amato Farm (473-3819), 11 East Street, Upton, sells vegetables, fruits, baked goods, and pick-your-own raspberries and strawberries; and **Dick Kelly's Farmstand** (529-6258), 10 Gable Street, Upton, sells vegetables, peaches, strawberries, raspberries, and blueberries.

FACTORY OUTLET

Giovannio Ladies Hat Factory Outlet (839-9011), 308 Providence Road, South Grafton. Monday through Saturday 10–4:30; women's hats.

SPECIAL SHOPS

Eaton's Farm Confectioners (865-5235), Burbank Road, Sutton. Open weekdays 8–6, weekends 1–4. A former dairy farm, now a source of homemade fudge, hand-dipped chocolates and "bark candy," and baked goods.

Mendon Country Gift Barn (473-1820), 24 Hastings Street (MA 16), Mendon. Open daily. A source of gifts, dinnerware, candies, good for rainy-day browsing.

Vaillancourt Folk Art (865-9183), 145 Armsby Road, Sutton. Open Monday through Saturday 9–5, Sunday 11–5. Features collectible chalkware Santas and Father Christmases in limited editions; Christmas all year.

Grafton Country Store (839-4898), 2 Central Square, Grafton. Open Tuesday through Sunday 10–5. Assorted staples and gifts.

SPECIAL EVENTS

June: The excursion boat ***Blackstone Valley Explorer*** is based at the Heritage State Park in Uxbridge. **Canalfest** at the park, the first weekend, features music, guided tours. In late June, the **Waters Farm** (865-1730) is usually the site of a bluegrass and country music concert. Inquire about the **Native American Fair** at the Nipmuc Indian Reservation in Grafton, also in late June.

July: **Wednesday evening concerts** on the Common, Grafton. **Native American Indian Pow Wow,** Grafton Common.

August: **Wednesday evening concerts** on the Common, Grafton.

October: **Waters Farm Days,** open house at Waters Farm, first weekend.

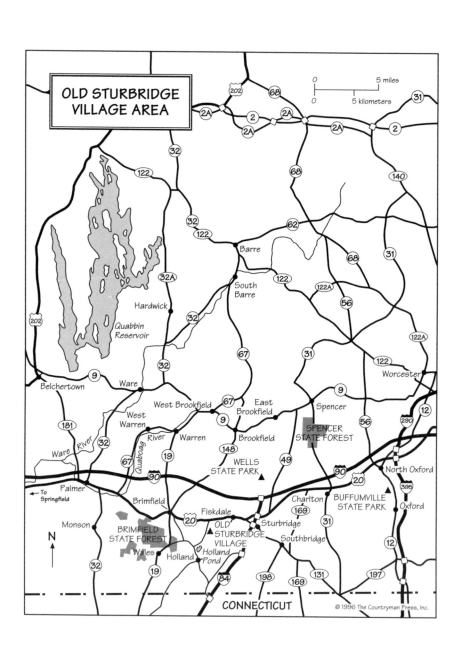

OLD STURBRIDGE
VILLAGE AREA

5 miles
5 kilometers

Barre

South
Barre

Hardwick

Quabbin
Reservoir

Belchertown

Ware

West Brookfield

West
Warren

West Brookfield

East
Brookfield

Spencer

SPENCER
STATE FOREST

Warren

Brookfield

WELLS
STATE PARK

Worcester

North Oxford

To
Springfield

Palmer

Brimfield

Fiskdale

Charlton

BUFFUMVILLE
STATE PARK

Oxford

Monson

BRIMFIELD
STATE FOREST

Wales

OLD
STURBRIDGE
VILLAGE

Holland

Holland
Pond

Sturbridge

Southbridge

N

CONNECTICUT

© 1996 The Countryman Press, Inc.

Old Sturbridge Village Area

Most Worcester County towns evolved between 1790 and 1830, an era during which churches, taverns, and stores still clustered around the Common, and, though not completely self-contained, each community was highly self-sufficient. Today most of these towns still retain their steepled old church and Common, much as a family preserves its formal head-and-shoulders portrait of a 19th-century forebear.

At Old Sturbridge Village, one of the country's finest museum villages, the portrait is full length, and you explore the mills, shops, homes, and farms that formed the body belonging to that 1830s face. Based on thorough and ongoing research, the museum village offers vivid insights into real life in this heavily romanticized era. Buildings straggle out from the Green along dirt roads. The farm animals seem hardier and less domesticated than the current norm, and it is difficult to believe that a family of nine once crowded into the working farm's small house. There is just one mansion in town: a square, Federal home where the leading member of the local gentry, the largest landowner, lives among his Boston-bought furnishings and passes the latest fashions on to his neighbors.

Although the more than 40 buildings in the village have been gathered from throughout New England, the story they tell is that of the surrounding countryside. We suggest that you allow a few days for the area: one at least for Old Sturbridge Village (an OSV admissions ticket is good for 2 days) and the shopping and attractions lineup just outside the gates along US 20. A day or two more can be pleasantly spent at local swimming holes, orchards, and antiques shops, as well as exploring the back roads of the Brookfields and Spencer, New Braintree, and Barre.

This is rewarding countryside almost any time of year. We actually prefer the village in winter when there are far fewer people and the Publick House inn stages its Yankee Winter Weekends, packages that offer period food and entertainment at off-season prices.

AREA CODE
508
GUIDANCE
Sturbridge Area Tourist Association Information Center (347-3362; 1-800-628-8379), 380 Main Street (US 20), opposite the entrance to Old Sturbridge Village. Open daily 10–5:30 in winter, 9:30–6 May

through October. Staff answer mail inquiries (the zip is 01566) and help walk-ins. This is an unusually welcoming center with wing chairs, racks of brochures, and a video directory that provides views of local inns, restaurants, and attractions, as well as information about them. Staff make lodging and restaurant reservations on request, sell bus tickets, and offer a wide range of advice about the entire area.

GETTING THERE

By bus: **Peter Pan Bus** (752-1717 for Sturbridge area) offers frequent service between Boston and Sturbridge.

By car: Sturbridge is at the junction of the Mass. Pike, I-84 to Hartford (and NYC), and US 20.

GETTING AROUND

King Courier (347-3660; 1-800-366-5466) offers 24-hour limo service to Bradley and Logan airports, also tours (reservations through the Sturbridge Information Center) to Quabbin Reservation and other local sites and to Sturbridge museums and restaurants.

Status Limousine (347-3660; 1-800-366-5466). Limo service around the clock to major airports and for tours and functions.

MEDICAL EMERGENCY

Harrington Memorial Hospital (765-9771), 100 South Street, Southbridge, marked from MA 131.

TO SEE

In Sturbridge

Old Sturbridge Village (OSV) (347-3362; hearing impaired 347-5383), US 20. Open daily year-round except winter Monday, Christmas, and New Year's Day. $15 adults, $7.50 for children aged 6–17. Admission ticket is good for two consecutive days. Special rates for groups of more than 15. Leashed pets welcome, but strollers not allowed in museum buildings.

A nonprofit museum, Old Sturbridge Village is one of the top attractions in New England. Expect to spend most of a day strolling the unpaved roads that wind around the Common and down to the Freeman Farm or through the covered bridge to the Mill Neighborhood. An orientation slide program sets the tone. Be sure to talk with the costumed "interpreters": the shoemaker and printer are delighted to describe their daily lives in the 1830s, and the minister's wife will tell you why she'd like a cookstove like her neighbor, Mrs. Towne. Three water-powered mills are important features, as well as the cider mill, which operates weekends in October.

Notice the care with which the Asa Knight Store has been stocked: English china, foreign fabrics, West India ginger and rum, tooth powder, and 2000 more items drawn from throughout the world. You learn that the storekeeper was the town's link with seaboard cities, the

OLD STURBRIDGE VILLAGE

Old Sturbridge Village

trusted middleman who exchanged his neighbor's produce for manufactured staples and the luxuries of life. There are countless such discov-
eries here.

In addition to the village buildings and a visitors center with changing exhibits, there is the adjacent T. Cheney Weeks Clock Gallery and
displays of glass, textiles, militia equipment, and lighting devices. In the
reference herb garden, more than 400 plants bloom between May and
October. There is a cafeteria and more formal dining in the Tavern and
an extensive gift shop. Frequent special events are staged, and there
are adult and family craft workshops and special theme programs, including hearthside cooking and dining in the parsonage as part of "Dinner in a Country Village" (winter only).

The story of how Old Sturbridge Village came to be is a typical
Massachusetts tale. It was founded through the philanthropy of Albert
Wells, a Southbridge optics magnate. His enthusiasm for antiques led
him to collect items in such quantities that they eventually outgrew his
home, so the family bought this 200-acre tract of meadow and woodlot
on the Quinebaug River. Since its 1946 opening the museum has
changed substantially, acquiring through dedication to authenticity (the
research library includes nearly 35,000 books, periodicals, and manu-
scripts relating to early-19th-century life in New England rural towns)
a life of its own. You come away with a genuine sense of not only how
this area not only looked but also how it smelled and felt in the early 19th
century.

Bethlehem in Sturbridge (347-3013), Stallion Hill. Continue on the road that runs off US 20 to OSV. Open from July 4 through Labor Day, 2–7 PM daily; at other times for groups by appointment. George Duquette has painstakingly crafted some 600 figures and buildings to re-create the Bethlehem nativity scene. Call before coming to make sure your visit doesn't coincide with a big bus group. No fee.

St. Anne's Shrine (347-7338). There are two century-old churches just off US 20—St. Anne's and St. Patrick's—and a museum building that houses a collection of 60 Russian icons, some more than 200 years old, acquired by priests of the Assumptionist order. There is also a picnic grounds and an open-air pavilion in which Mass is celebrated on summer weekends.

Beyond Sturbridge

Clara Barton's Birthplace (987-0498), 68 Clara Barton Road, off MA 12, North Oxford. Open April through October, Tuesday through Sunday 11 AM–5 PM; the rest of the year by appointment. A charming house on a back road tells the story of the founder of the American Red Cross and of her work during and after the Civil War. Note that the clapboard house is just up the road from North Oxford Mills (great for braided rugs; see *Selective Shopping*) and handy to Buffumville Federal Recreation Area (see *Green Space* and *Swimming*).

St. Joseph Abbey (885-3901), MA 31 in Spencer. This is a Trappist monastery, famed for the beauty of its Gregorian chants (available on tapes and CDs), for its jams, and as a place to find peace. Visitors are welcome in the side chapel. Daily Masses are at 5:45 AM, preceded by the singing of "lauds," a traditional choral service. Evening vespers are at 6:30 weekdays and 7 on Sunday, when they are preceded by a benediction service. For details about staying in the guest house, phone 885-3010.

WINERY

Mella Vineyard (943-6527), 108 Old Southbridge Road, Dudley. Open Memorial Day to December, Wednesday through Sunday 11–5. The specialty of this house is "Colonial Cuvee." No joke—Mella produces European-style wines from its own vineyards using French-American varieties. Visitors are invited to picnic.

TO DO

BALLOONING

The Balloon School of Massachusetts (413-245-7013), Balloonport at Dingley Dell, 69 Sutcliffe Road, Palmer, offers year-round rides, usually at daybreak. The $200 per person fee includes a postflight breakfast. The whole adventure takes less than 3 hours, with 1 hour in the air.

BICYCLING

This relatively flat, rural area has some little-trafficked back roads. *Short Bike Rides in Greater Boston and Central Massachusetts* by Howard Stone (Globe Pequot Press) suggests some specific routes. Westville Recreation Area offers good pedaling opportunities.

BOATING

Two flood-control dams have turned the Quinebaug into a chain of ponds and reservoirs, ideal for canoeing and sailboarding. A "Quinebaug River Canoe Trail Map" is available from the local state parks or forests (see *Green Space*). A canoe launch and fishing spot can be found in Brookfield, just before the railroad bridge on MA 148.

GOLF

Bay Path Golf Club (867-8161) in East Brookfield, nine holes. **Hemlock Ridge** (347-9935) in Sturbridge, nine holes. **Heritage Country Club** (248-3526; 248-3591) in Charlton, 18 holes. **Oxford Golf and Racquet Club** (892-9188), North Oxford, 18 holes.

HIKING

The Mid-State Trail passes through Charlton and Oxford. This long-distance trail is described in the *Massachusetts and Rhode Island Trail Guide* published by the Appalachian Mountain Club, 5 Joy Street, Boston 02108. A Mid-State Trail map is also available by contacting the Department of Environmental Management (see "What's Where").

HORSEBACK RIDING

Rocking M. Ranch (248-7075), 120 Northside Road (off US 20), Charlton, offers trail and pony rides. $16–18 an hour. Reservations recommended.

SWIMMING

Note under *Green Space* that Brimfield State Forest, Buffumville Federal Recreation Area, Lake Siago, and Spencer State Forest all have swimming areas. Other local swimming holes include the **Westville Recreation Area** in Southbridge (take MA 131 East to South Street), the **East Brimfield Dam** area at Long Pond in Sturbridge, the **Cedar Lake Recreation Area** in Sturbridge, and **South Pond** in Brookfield (small but free, with shade trees, off New Boston Road).

CROSS-COUNTRY SKIING

The local state parks and forests (see *Green Space*) have many miles of skiable trails.

GREEN SPACE

Brimfield State Forest, Dirth Hill Road, Brimfield. This area is a 4033-acre forest, but most visitors are interested only in the **Dean Pond Recreation Area** with its 100-foot-long beach and picnic facilities. Fishing, swimming, and boating are permitted, and the **Woodman Pond Group Camping Area** has three bunkroom buildings (for information call Wells State Park at 347-9257).

Buffumville Federal Recreation Area (248-5697), Charlton Street, Oxford. From the center of Charlton, turn left onto Muggett Hill Road; after 4 miles turn right onto Oxford Road, and the area is 2 miles on the left. There is a beach here, open 10 AM–8 PM in-season. Wildflowers bloom under the White Pine Observatory—lady's slippers and lilies of the valley; also picnic facilities and a self-guided nature trail. Fee.

Lake Siago (413-245-0116), Holland. From Sturbridge, turn west on US 20 to Holland. Take East Brimfield Road south 4 miles to Day Hill Road. A town-run recreation area with a swimming beach, picnic tables, barbecue grills, and a volleyball court. The pond is stocked with pike and is suitable for canoeing. Fee.

Streeter Point Recreation Area (347-9316), Sturbridge. Swimming beach, picnicking, and a boat-launch area. Pleasant but a bit marshy.

Spencer State Forest, Howe Pond Road, Spencer (for information call Rutland State Park at 866-6333). Swimming and picnicking at Howe Pond; trails used for hiking and horseback riding.

Wells State Park (347-9257), MA 49, Sturbridge. There are 59 campsites, $6 per night. Reservations for more than a week can be made 4 months in advance; less than a week, 3 months in advance. Swimming beach and picnic facilities.

WALKS

Tantiusques Reservation, Sturbridge, 1 mile west of MA 15 on a not-too-well marked dirt road. This 55-acre reserve includes a graphite or black lead mine granted by the Native Americans to John Winthrop in 1644. Several open cuts that followed the original veins are still visible. Owned by the Trustees of Reservations.

Norcross Wildlife Sanctuary (267-9654), Peck Road, Wales. Open year-round, Monday through Saturday 8–4; closed Sunday, holidays. Free. An exceptional visitors center displays pictures of flowers, ferns, and trees native to the Eastern Seaboard, and the sanctuary itself has been planted with specimens representing most of the species of this continent's vegetation, including rare wildflowers. Birds and animals, needless to say, are protected within the area. The 3000-acre preserve is a gift of Arthur D. Norcross, a Wales native who founded Norcross Greeting Cards.

LODGING

INNS AND BED & BREAKFASTS

Publick House (347-3313), PO Box 187, Sturbridge 01566. The proud white tavern was built in 1771 by Ebenezer Crafts, who gave everything to the Revolution. Impoverished by 1791 (a year after planting the elms that still grace the inn), he was forced to move north (150 neighbors went with him), founding the northern Vermont town of Craftsbury. Positioned at the junction of Boston and New York highroads, the inn prospered. Restored in the 1930s, it offers an extension of the Old Sturbridge Village atmosphere. Although shops, restaurants, and motels have proliferated to form a "strip" along US 20 outside the museum village entrance, the old inn has remained secure in its pristine setting on the original Sturbridge Village Common, complete with town hall and meetinghouse. Behind the inn stretch 60 acres of meadow. Though the Publick House is now known primarily for its dining rooms (see *Where to Eat*), there are 18 rooms upstairs and four suites, plus one room in neighboring Chamberlain House. All rooms are furnished with antiques, including wing chairs, four-posters, and canopy beds. There is also an adjacent 100-room motor lodge, nicely furnished with Colonial reproductions and small-print wallpaper. A pool, tennis court, and rental bicycles are available. $69–130 per room, $109–150 per suite in the inn; $55–89 per room, $85–130 per suite in the Country Lodge motel. Inquire about Yankee Winter Weekends, offered January to March—weekend packages that include 18th-century-style feasting, entertainment, and special tours of Old Sturbridge Village.

Colonel Ebenezer Crafts Inn (347-3313), Fiske Hill, Sturbridge 01566. Although it is owned by the Publick House, this 18th-century home is off by itself on a hilltop instead of in the middle of the village. There are gracious living and sun rooms and inviting spaces to linger, and tea or sherry is served in the afternoon. Rooms are beautifully paneled and furnished with antiques, and there is a secret panel downstairs behind which runaway slaves were once hidden. The inn has a pool, and guests have access to the Publick House tennis court. $109–130 for a double, $150 for a suite, less off-season.

Misty Meadows (413-245-7466), Allen Hill Road, RR 3, Box 3019, Holland 01521. A deceptively small-looking home that Ron Croke built some 30 years ago, truly delightful within, offering three rooms nicely furnished with Dot's family antiques—which include an iron bedstead and classic cottage furniture. The $48.48 double rate includes a full breakfast.

Spencer Country Inn (885-9036), 500 Main Street, Spencer 01562. An early country mansion, now primarily a restaurant, but with four guest rooms in the main house and six in an annex. $42 double with private bath.

Sturbridge Country Inn (347-5503), 530 Main Street, Sturbridge 01566. Handsome 1840s house extensively renovated. Each of the nine rooms has a fireplace, air-conditioning, cable TV, and private bathroom with whirlpool tub. There is a restaurant, the Fieldstone Tavern, on the premises. Live theater performances are held in the barn mid-June through October. Within walking distance of restaurants, shops, and OSV. Doubles are $69–159.

Avondo's Bed & Breakfast (413-267-5829), 26 East Hill Road, Monson 01057. There are four guest rooms sharing one bath in this pleasant, gambrel-roofed home, handy to Brimfield's antiques markets and to the Brimfield State Forest. $55–65 double.

Commonwealth Cottage (347-7708), 11 Summit Avenue, PO Box 368, Sturbridge 01566-0368. Conveniently located but just far enough off US 20 to distance it from the noise of the strip. An 1890s gingerbread house nicely restored by owners Wiebke and Bob Gilbert. The four guest rooms all have private baths (one also has an elegant black marble fireplace) and are comfortably but unfussily furnished with period antiques. $75–85 for a double, including full breakfast and afternoon tea.

The Birch Tree Bed and Breakfast (347-8218), 522 Leadmine Road, Sturbridge 01566. Built as a retirement home by Jim and Jane Fischer, the separate guest floor has two bedrooms (each with queen-sized bed and private bath) and an atrium TV lounge. Guests also have access to a private patio. In a quiet country area, about 5 miles from OSV, near Tantiusques Reservation. $65 per night, with full breakfast.

The Harding Allen Estate Bed & Breakfast Inn (355-4920), MA 122, Barre. This expansive white-pillared mansion, set on more than 2 acres of landscaped grounds just off Barre Common, opened its doors as a B&B in the summer of 1995. Shared space includes a paneled living room/library and a "morning room" with Italian marble flooring and a marble fountain; in fall and winter, hot tubs bubble in the old greenhouse. $65–85 double.

Jenkins Inn (355-6444), 7 West Street, Barre 01005. An attractive Victorian house with five guest rooms (three with private bath) and period decor. There is a restaurant-tea room on the premises. $70–100 with full breakfast. Bread and pastries are all homemade.

Hartman's Herb Farm (355-2015), Old Dana Road, Barre 01005. Three pleasant rooms (two with private bath) in a Colonial-style house (beamed ceilings and wide floorboards) built to replace the 200-year-old farmhouse that burned in 1989. Still a working herb farm. $60–70 with full breakfast.

Stevens Farm (355-2227), 749 Old Coldbrook Road, Barre 01005. This is the real thing: a 350-acre working hilltop farm in the same family for five generations. Irene and Richard Stevens raise heifers and keep pigs and chickens. There are walking and cross-country ski trails on the property, and Mount Wachusett and Quabbin Reservoir are nearby. Built in 1789, the farmhouse has five comfortable guest rooms sharing two baths, and there's a small swimming pool. $45–55 with breakfast.

Bethany Bed and Breakfast (347-5993), 5 McGregory Road, Sturbridge 01566. A modern house with four double guest rooms, two with private bath, the others sharing the same bathroom. Separate TV and sitting room. British-born hostess Colleen Box is an avid gardener, and there are flower arrangements in all the rooms. Full breakfast. Afternoon tea (or mulled cider in the chilly off-season), and tea in the garden can be arranged. $80–90 per room.

Elias Carter House (413-245-3267), The Common, Brimfield 01010. An 1809 house facing historic Brimfield Common and an easy walk from all dealer markets during the thrice-yearly Brimfield outdoor antiques shows. Four comfortable but plainly furnished rooms, all with private bath. Owner Carolyn Haley is a real estate agent, and much of the first floor of the house is given over to her business. The guest breakfast room and lounge is a small sun porch off the real estate office. Rates per room are $60 off-season, $80 in-season, and $115 on holidays and during antiques shows.

Zukas Homestead Farm (885-5320), 89 Smithville Road, Spencer 01562. A recently built post-and-beam house on a hilltop working farm. Pete Zukas raises heifers, and wife Lynn runs a baking and catering business from the house. The one rental unit is a three-room, top-floor suite with private bath and Jacuzzi, TV and VCR, and wonderful views. $85 per couple with a full breakfast that includes eggs from the farm's chickens and homemade jams and jellies.

(Also see "Quabbin Area" for the Wildwood Inn, Ware; Winterwood at Petersham; and Ingate Farms, Belchertown.)

MOTELS

Oliver Wight House and **Old Sturbridge Village Lodges** (347-3327), Sturbridge 01566. The Oliver Wight House is the only building on Old Sturbridge Village property that stands on its original site. In recent years the 1789 mansion has formed the centerpiece for a motel complex and has been restored, offering a genuine inn atmosphere in its 10 rooms (furnished with reproduction antiques from the period). The remaining 50 units are a notch above standard motel design (furnished in Colonial reproductions and Hitchcock chairs, bright chintz), scattered in clapboard-sheathed buildings. A continental breakfast is laid out mornings in the office. The inn and hotel (formerly the Liberty Cap) are owned by Old Sturbridge Village. $90–110 double in the Oliver Wight House, $70–90 double in the motel units; less off-season.

Check with the Sturbridge Area Tourist Information Center (see *Guidance*) for information about the many motels along US 20.

OTHER

Insight Meditation Society Center (355-4378), Barre 01005. This brick, former Catholic retreat now serves the same purpose for practitioners of the Southeast Asian school of Theavadin Buddhism. The emphasis is on simplicity of lifestyle and personal insights, the latter often gained by long meditative walks. Call ahead for a retreat schedule or to arrange a visit.

WHERE TO EAT

DINING OUT

Salem Cross Inn (867-2345; 867-8337), MA 9, West Brookfield. Open Tuesday through Friday 11:30–9, Saturday 5–10, Sunday and holidays noon–8; closed Monday. The original part of this handsome, four-square house was built in 1705 by the grandson of Peregrine White (the baby born on the *Mayflower*), and it still stands alone, surrounded by its 600 acres. This landmark was in sorry condition when the Salem family acquired it in the 1950s and began the daunting job of scraping away centuries of paint and restoring the 18th- and 19th-century woodwork. Specialties include old New England dishes such as baked stuffed scallops and broiled, herbed lamb steak. Dinner entrées in the $11–20 range. In winter, special Colonial-style "Fireplace Feasts" include mulled wine, chowder, prime rib (cooked on a rare, 17th-century "Roasting Jack"), breads, and pies, all cooked on the woodfire hearth ($39 per person). Sleigh rides are part of these Friday evening and Sunday (brunch) rituals. There are also outdoor hayrides and drovers' roasts in summer. The inn is worth visiting just to see the clutter of old tools, sleds, butter churns, and assorted antiques in the barn, as well as the collection of photos on the "Lost Towns" drowned to form the Quabbin Reservoir. "Salem Cross" refers to a traditional design on the inn's front door.

Publick House (347-3313), Sturbridge. Open Monday through Friday 7–10:30 AM and noon–8:30 PM; Saturday 7–11 and 4–9; Sunday 8–11 and noon–8:30. The original low-beamed, 18th-century tavern is now but one of six dining rooms in this grand old inn. Although 400 patrons can sit down to dine in these various spaces, the service is remarkably personal. There are cranberry muffins and pecan rolls at all meals as well as hearty, all-American fare, from deep-dish apple pie for breakfast to prime rib, stuffed shrimp, and individual baked lobster pies for dinner. Entrées in the $16–24 range. Children's plates. Special yule log dinners in Christmas season ($37).

The Whistling Swan (347-2321), 502 Main Street, Sturbridge. Closed Monday, otherwise open for lunch and dinner. Three formal dining rooms in a Greek Revival mansion are the setting for enjoying mussels maniere or frogs' legs followed by medallions of veal in three-mustard sauce or duckling *au poivre*, topped off by Russian cream with strawberries Romanoff or chocolate almond pie. Dinner entrées in the $15–24 range. Lighter (and cheaper) meals are served in the pleasantly informal Ugly Duckling Loft, which has a strong local following.

Spencer Country Inn (885-9036), 500 East Main Street (MA 9), Spencer. Closed Monday, otherwise open for lunch and dinner, Sunday brunch. A 19th-century mansion with five dining rooms, including the Hogshead Tavern; live music Saturday evenings. Dinner entrées run $13–18.

Charlie Brown's Steakhouse (347-9555), Haynes Street, Sturbridge. Open daily for lunch, dinner, and late supper, also Sunday brunch; children's menu. In the orchard of the Publick House complex, this is a happily unpretentious family restaurant. The decor is zany (chicken coops, stained glass, farm implements), and the prices are reasonable. House specialties, such as steak and prime rib, average $10–17.

Rom's (347-3349), MA 131, Sturbridge. Open daily for lunch and dinner, Italian specialties. Wednesday night buffet is $12.95; Thursday luncheon buffet is $6.25.

Le Bearn Restaurant Francais (347-5800), 12 Cedar Street, Sturbridge.

Owners Leon and Rose Marty are from the south of France and serve classic French cuisine with Provençal touches. Dinner served from 5 PM. Sunday brunch 11:30–2:30. Entrées average $17–20.

C.J.'s (413-283-2196), US 20, Palmer. Locals swear by this unpretentious place, noted for inexpensive, full lobster dinners.

Piccadilly Pub Restaurant (347-8189), 362 Main Street (US 20), Sturbridge. Open daily for lunch and dinner. Large, popular restaurant with extensive menu ranging from fish-and-chips to lobster pie, burgers to sirloin steaks. Usually busy, but service is fast and cheerful. All entrées under $10.

Admiral T.J. O'Brien's (347-2838), 407 Main Street, Sturbridge. Lively place in the midst of the Sturbridge strip. Mid-American cuisine with dinner entrées in the $8–15 range. Open for dinner Monday through Sunday 11:30–9. Live entertainment Friday and Saturday evenings.

"Dinner in a Country Village" at Old Sturbridge Village (347-3362) is offered Saturday nights, November through March, by reservation; $50 per person. Guests arrive at 5 and are ushered into one of the village homes, where they help prepare the dinner that they then consume. Recipes and atmosphere are as authentically 1830s as possible; limited to 14 per evening.

Col. Isaac Barre Restaurant (355-4629), The Common, Barre. Open Tuesday through Sunday. Quietly elegant, small restaurant with nice decorative touches (lots of dried flower arrangements) and a varied menu. Dinner entrées $13–18.

EATING OUT

The Sunburst (347-3097), 484 Main Street, Sturbridge (corner of US 20 and Arnold Road). Open daily 7–2. Home-baked muffins are the breakfast specialty—breakfast is served all day—and for lunch there are homemade soups, quiches and salads, fruit-flavored "smoothies," and more muffins. A dining deck is open May through October.

Woodbine Country Store and Restaurant (413-245-3552), US 20, Brimfield. A friendly, reasonably priced eatery in the middle of this classic New England village.

Kozy Cabin (355-6264), MA 122, Barre. A roadhouse exterior but comfortable and friendly family-style restaurant within. The extensive menu includes seafood and locally famous cream pies.

The Maine Dish (355-3416), Vernon Street, South Barre. The owner learned his trade in a Maine logging camp, and portions are lumberjack large. Breakfasts are locally renowned.

SNACKS

Westview Farms Creamery (413-267-5355), 111 East Hill Road (off US 20), Monson. A real working dairy farm (about 300 cows) with a great view of the Berkshire foothills. Its creamery serves homemade ice cream and light meals. Open daily April through November.

Hebert Candies and Ice Cream, River Road (Exit 2 off I-84), Sturbridge.

Old Sturbridge Village

One of the oldest roadside candy shops in the country, Hebert's has been in the same family since 1917. All candies are freshly made, without preservatives. The make-your-own sundae buffet offers 12 varieties of homemade ice cream and 18 different toppings.

SELECTIVE SHOPPING

ANTIQUES SHOPS

Brimfield Fair, US 20, Brimfield (7 miles west of Sturbridge). Three times a year—in May, July, and September—more than 4000 dealers gather in the meadows and open space just west of Brimfield Common. The antiques show has its own year-round, 24-hour information tape (413-283-6149) that tells you when the next antiques show will occur and gives directions to Brimfield. Information is also available at the Sturbridge Area Information Center (see *Guidance*) and the Quabog Valley Chamber of Commerce (413-283-2418). The shows are divided into 21 distinct markets, each with 50 to 500 dealers specializing in different kinds of furniture, clothing, jewelry, collectibles, and so on. The crowd usually tops 100,000, and it's a vivid scene that engulfs usually tranquil Brimfield. Stands serving surprisingly good finger food mushroom around the markets. For a booklet prepared by the local chamber of commerce, with detailed information about the shows, send $5 to QVCC, PO Box 269, Palmer, MA 01069.

Sturbridge Antique Shop (347-2744), about a mile east of OSV on US 20. Houses more than 70 dealers year-round; open daily.

Fairground Antiques Center (347-3926), 362 Main Street (US 20),

Sturbridge. A multidealer center with more than 75 booths and show-cases. Open Monday through Saturday 10–5; Sunday noon–5.

Quabog Antiques Center (413-283-3091), 10 Knox Street, Palmer. Open daily. More than 50 dealers.

Sunday Flea Markets are held regularly at the **Auburn Antique & Flea Market** on MA 12 in Auburn, at **Ye Old Brookfield Mill** in Brookfield, and in Spencer on MA 9.

FACTORY OUTLETS

Hyde Factory Shoe Outlet (867-7406), East Brookfield, is the area's sneaker and running shoe source. Also good for roller skates (made elsewhere by the parent company).

Wright's Mill Store (436-7737), MA 67, West Warren. A genuine old out-let in an old mill: trims, tapes, braids, lace, ribbon, and notions, penny sales in March and September.

North Oxford Mills (987-8521), MA 12, North Oxford. The place to buy braided rugs, all sizes, all shapes; also carpets, remnants.

Maurice the Pants Man (347-7859), US 20, Sturbridge. A discount store rather than a factory outlet, this is a great place to shop for Woolrich and other name-brand sportswear for the whole family.

ORCHARDS

This is apple country, and the orchards are in some of the most beautiful corners of it. Call ahead to make sure the following are open and set up for visitors.

Brookfield Orchards (867-6858), Orchard Road, off MA 9, East Brook-field. Set high on a hill, with picnic tables and children's play equip-ment, the Country Store sells jellies, gifts, and apple dumplings with an apple baked into each. Owned by the Lincoln family since 1918.

Breezelands Orchards Farm Stand & Cidermill (413-436-7100), Southbridge Road, Warren 01083. Pick-your-own peaches and apples, fresh cider. Petting zoo and tractor rides. Open daily from the end of July through autumn.

Cheney's Apple Barn (413-245-9223), Brimfield. Open daily in picking season: cider, fruit stand.

Cheney Orchards (413-436-7688), marked off MA 148 between Sturbridge and Brimfield. In the family since 1911, an 80-acre orchard and a country store selling 35 varieties of apples, peaches, pears (10 varieties), 8 varieties of honey, frozen apple pies, and more. Here you can also cut your own Christmas tree.

Fay Mountain Farm (248-7237), Stafford Street, Charlton. In the Gilmore family since 1910. Apples and fresh cider, raspberries, blueberries, strawberries, and peaches in-season.

Hyland Orchards (347-3416), Arnold Road, Sturbridge. Apples and cider in-season.

Baxter Echo Hill Orchard (413-267-3303), Wilbraham Road, Monson. Apples; shop selling gifts, antiques, and produce.

SPECIAL SHOPS

Sturbridge Yankee Workshop (1-800-343-1144), US 20, Sturbridge 01566. Catalog outlet for early-American furniture, home furnishings, and gifts.

The Shaker Shop (347-7564), 454 Main Street (US 20), Sturbridge. A restored 1830s house with 10 rooms of Shaker-style furniture, crafts, and accessories. Besides Shaker chairs and the like, the shop sells stencils for decorating walls and a line of milk-based paint, a biodegradable product ecologically minded Shakers invented in the 18th century.

Old Sturbridge Village Gift Shop (347-3362). Strategically positioned at the entrance to the museum village so that you don't have to pay the entry fee, this extensive emporium sells early-19th-century furniture, furnishings, a variety of gifts, and books. Same hours as OSV.

Hartman's Herb Farm (355-2015), Old Dana Road off MA 32 and MA 122, Barre. Open daily 10–6. Reasonably priced plants (175 varieties), dried herbs and teas packaged on the spot; also herb wreaths, potpourri, dried flowers, raffia dolls. You can walk through the gardens and browse in the barn where herbs dry in bunches on rafters and walls.

The League of American Crafters (347-2323), 559 Main Street (US 20), Fiskdale 01518. A permanent crafts show occupying the entire third floor of a renovated, turn-of-the-century cotton mill 1 mile west of OSV. More than 150 craftspeople represented.

SPECIAL EVENTS

Old Sturbridge Village publishes its own calendar, filled with events dictated by the seasons. The following notes only some of the highlights.

February: **George Washington's Birthday** is celebrated at OSV as it would have been in the 1830s. **Maple sugaring** at OSV.

March: **Hog butchering** at OSV.

April: **Annual Town Meeting** at OSV.

May: **Brimfield Flea Market. "Muskets, Music, and Merriment"** (Militia Day) and **"Shearing, Spinning, and Weaving"** (Wool Days) at OSV.

July: **Brimfield Flea Market. Independence Day celebrations** at OSV.

August: **Wales County Fair,** local exhibits and livestock, Main Street, Wales. **Hardwick Fair,** just off the Common.

September: **Brimfield Flea Market. Spencer Fair** (Labor Day weekend). **Antiquarian Book Fair** at OSV. Apple-picking and cider-pressing at local orchards.

November: **Thanksgiving** at OSV.

December: **Yule Log celebrations** at the Publick House. **Christmas shows** at Bethlehem in Sturbridge.

Quabbin Area

The Quabbin area is one of the most distinctive and interesting corners of Massachusetts, a place that invites and rewards leisurely exploration.

Possessed of extraordinary natural beauty, the area also has classic villages and town centers little changed in a century and old redbrick millyards where textile looms are giving way to antiques shops and discount clothing outlets. Here are also many poignant reminders of the once-flourishing villages and farms that were inundated to create the area's focal point: the vast Quabbin Reservoir.

The biggest body of fresh water in the state and one of the largest reservoirs in the world, Quabbin—a Native American name meaning "Land of Many Waters"—is 18 miles long and covers 39 square miles with an average water depth of more than 50 feet. Managed by the Metropolitan District Commission (MDC), the reservoir provides pure drinking water to the 2.5 million people of metropolitan Boston 65 miles away.

The reservoir and the watershed lands around it comprise a remarkable nature preserve. The woods and meadows of the 119,000-acre Quabbin reservation teem with deer and bird life, some species once rare or extinct in New England. Wild turkeys, bald eagles, and peregrine falcons, for instance, have all been successfully reintroduced by the MDC. The reservoir itself is open for fishing from April to October, and lake trout, bass, pickerel, and landlocked salmon are abundant.

Quabbin is unquestionably one of the state's great recreational and environmental assets, a haven for endangered wildlife and a boon for those seeking tranquillity and unspoiled nature. About 500,000 people visit it annually. Initially, however, the reservoir was widely seen as a social tragedy—an example of big-city imperatives overriding small-town rights—as much as a planning and engineering triumph.

Quabbin was first proposed at the turn of the century when it had become obvious that, unless new drinking water sources were found, Greater Boston's growing population faced a thirsty future. After surveying the state, engineers concluded that the steep-sided Swift River Valley was the natural location for a reservoir large enough to meet the metropolitan area's needs well into the 21st century.

For the residents of the valley, the price of metropolitan Boston's

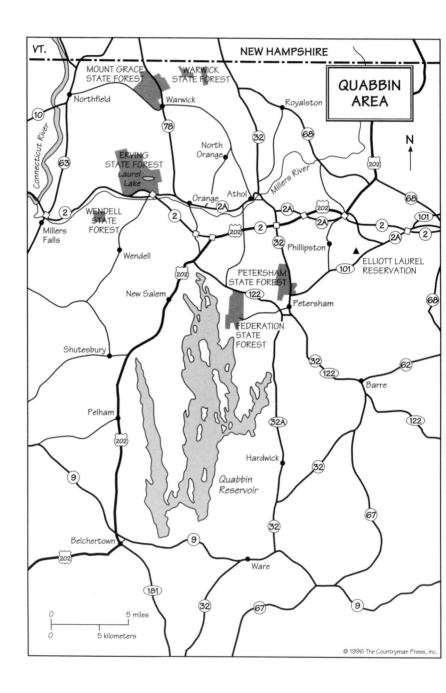

VT.   NEW HAMPSHIRE

MOUNT GRACE
STATE FOREST

WARWICK
STATE FOREST

QUABBIN
AREA

Northfield   Warwick   Royalston

N

10

Connecticut River

78

63

North
Orange

32

68

202

ERVING
STATE FOREST
Laurel
Lake

Millers River

Orange   Athol

2A

68

2

WENDELL
STATE
FOREST

2

2A

2A

202

101

Millers
Falls

202   2

2A

2

Wendell

32   Phillipston

ELLIOTT LAUREL
RESERVATION

202

101

New Salem

PETERSHAM
STATE FOREST

122

68

Petersham

Shutesbury

FEDERATION
STATE
FOREST

32

62

122

Barre

Pelham

202

32A

122

9

Hardwick

32

Quabbin
Reservoir

67

32

Belchertown

9

202

Ware

9

181

0   5 miles
0   5 kilometers

32   67   9

© 1996 The Countryman Press, Inc.

progress came high. Once the Swift River was dammed and the valley flooded, four entire towns would be inundated—Dana, Greenwich, Enfield, and Prescott—along with a number of villages in neighboring communities. The reservoir was bitterly opposed by the affected towns, who took their case all the way to the Massachusetts Supreme Court but lost. The state of Connecticut also sued Massachusetts, in the federal courts, charging that Quabbin would divert water rightfully meant to flow down to the Nutmeg State. After prolonged litigation, the US Supreme Court found in favor of Massachusetts.

The project got under way in 1926. Before actual construction could begin the MDC had to clear the site, a complex and painful process that involved displacing 2500 residents from 650 homes, exhuming 7500 bodies from 34 cemeteries, and taking up the tracks of the railroad that ran through the valley (trains stopped at so many villages and hamlets the railway was known as "The Rabbit Line"). Most buildings were demolished, but about 10 percent of the structures were moved to high ground off the MDC reservation, where many still stand.

Quabbin was completed in 1939, but it took 7 years for the reservoir to fill. Not until 1946 did it reach its maximum storage capacity of 412 billion gallons.

The Quabbin story is interestingly told with pictures, maps, models, and dioramas at the interpretive center in the Federal Revival, brick MDC administration building at Winsor Dam in Belchertown. Although there are many scenic views of Quabbin, the one from the observation tower overlooking the dam is perhaps the most impressive, the great artificially created lake stretching away to the northern horizon like a freshwater sea.

The MDC building is also headquarters for Quabbin Park, an 8500-acre reserve at the southern end of the reservoir that has picnic areas, scenic lookouts, 20 miles of hiking trails, and 13 miles of paved road. Also in the park is the Quabbin Cemetery, the final resting place of the deceased of Enfield, Dana, Prescott, and Greenwich.

With time, the painful memories surrounding the clearing and flooding of the valley have largely faded in the area, but the mystique of "The Four Lost Towns" is still strong. You certainly feel it in the Quabbin Cemetery, where each town has its own section, complete with Civil War monuments and other memorials that once stood in town Commons and parks. Also very moving is the Swift River Valley Historical Society museum in New Salem, where exhibits of household furnishings, tools, crafts, and photographs of valley people at work and play evoke a drowned world with painful clarity.

AREA CODE
508 east of the reservoir; 413 west of it.
GUIDANCE
Quabbin Park Visitors Center (413-323-7221), MDC administration

building, 485 Ware Road (MA 9), Belchertown. Maps and information on fishing, hiking, and wildlife. Open weekdays 8:30 AM–5 PM; weekends 9–5.

North Quabbin Chamber of Commerce (249-3849), 521 Main Street, Athol 01331. Brochures, maps, and tourist information about the nine towns around the northern end of the reservoir.

Franklin County Chamber of Commerce (413-773-5463), PO Box 790-W, Greenfield 01301. Maps and information on the area north and west of Quabbin.

GETTING THERE

The Quabbin Reservation is some 65 miles west of Boston, located between MA 2 and the Mass. Pike.

GETTING AROUND

The Quabbin area provides ample opportunities for hiking and biking, but you need a car to explore it properly. You can make a complete loop around the reservation on well-maintained and -marked state roads. MA 9 runs along the southern edge of the reservoir, where MDC headquarters, Quabbin Park, and the Quabbin Cemetery are located. MA 32 (which connects with the Mass. Pike to the south at Palmer) and MA 32A run up the eastern side. MA 122 runs along the northern end of Quabbin, between MA 32A and MA 122, the latter route paralleling the reservoir's western shore between MA 9 and MA 2.

MEDICAL EMERGENCY

Athol Memorial Hospital (249-3511), 2033 Main Street, Athol.

VILLAGES

New Salem. Although not wiped off the map by Quabbin like the four lost towns, New Salem was drastically affected by it. Today 80 percent of its original land area is owned by the MDC, and the town is almost eerily quiet, the essence of an off-the-beaten-path settlement. The old town center, just off US 202, is a gem, with an elliptical Common and streets lined with white clapboard 18th- and 19th-century houses. This was once a busy crossroads, but now Main Street, originally part of a major east-west thoroughfare, ends abruptly at a chain-link fence marking the Quabbin boundary. The area around the New Salem Common is a historic district that includes buildings like the granite **assembly hall** (once part of New Salem Academy), with its clock tower; the **Unitarian Church** (1794), now being restored as a cultural center; the old **Town House** (1838), now a public library; and the **Congregational Church** (1854). A plaque on the Common recalls the scene of April 20, 1775, when, summoned by ringing church bells, the patriotic men of New Salem marched off to Boston to fight the British.

North Orange. This village is a dignified gathering of old country homes near the **Community Church** of North Orange and Tully, built in 1781.

JOHN MARTIN

Town Hall and First Congregational Church on the Royalston Common

Goddard Park, in front of the rectory, is the scene of frequent church suppers and community events.

Petersham. Sited on a high ridge, Petersham (pronounced "Peter's Ham") has commanding views of the rolling, wooded central Massachusetts countryside. It's a beautiful place and a quiet one, with one of the state's lowest population density rates: 14 people per square mile. This combination of beauty and tranquillity has attracted a number of spiritual communities to Petersham. (At last count, five Roman Catholic orders were represented.) A thriving agricultural town in the 1830s, when fortunes made in sheep farming were spent on white-pillared mansions, Petersham was rediscovered as a summer resort in the 1890s. Architectural examples of both these eras of exuberant prosperity can be seen around the gracious town Common. The white-pillared **Country Store** (724-3245) has been purveying varied merchandise since 1842, making it one of the oldest general stores in the state, according to owner Charles Berube. The rambling **Nichewaug Inn** was Petersham's social center for more than half a century, then served as the Maria Assumpta Academy until 1973. Still the most imposing building on the Common, the old inn now has new owners who have renamed it "The Vintage" and plan to restore the place completely and reopen it as an inn and gourmet restaurant. A bronze plaque on the Common commemorates the winter morning in 1787 when state troops chased and captured the rebellious Daniel Shays and 150 of his followers.

Phillipston. This village center off MA 2A is small enough to fit into the snapshot it demands. The **Congregational Church,** built in 1785, is a beauty, the site of the annual June bazaar and October pumpkin weigh-in.

Warwick. This perfectly preserved old Hilltown is about as far off the beaten track as you can get in Massachusetts east of the Connecticut River. A three-sided marker notes that it's 20 miles from here to both Keene, New Hampshire, and Brattleboro, Vermont, and 8 (precipitously downhill) miles to Northfield. You seem a century from anywhere in this classic center, which includes a Unitarian Church, library, historical society building, fine old fountain, the Warwick Country Store, and the double-porched inn.

TO SEE

Swift River Valley Historical Society (544-6882), Elm Street (west of US 202), New Salem. Housed in the historic Whitaker-Clary House, this small museum contains photos and memorabilia of the lost towns. Open Wednesday afternoons in summer and by appointment. In front of the museum is a much-photographed, 1880s square "guide post" giving directions to three of the lost towns: Dana, Greenwich, and Enfield.

The Fisher Museum of Forestry (724-3302), on MA 32 between Petersham and MA 2. Open year-round weekdays 9–5, also Saturday 10–4

May through October. Call ahead to check if it is closed for a conference. Maintained by Harvard University, along with the 3000 acres in back (see *Green Space*), the museum contains a series of dioramas that dramatize the changes in the rural Massachusetts landscape over the past few hundred years. They depict the farms of the 1830s, when 75 percent of the land was cleared, the abandonment of the farms in the 1850s, and the succession of land-use practices to the present day.

Petersham Historical Society (724-3380), on the Petersham town Common. Open Sunday afternoons in summer and by appointment year-round. There is a permanent exhibit about the 18th-century farmers' rebellion led by Daniel Shays, so much a local hero that a highway is named after him.

The Stone House Museum (413-323-6573), Maple Street (US 202), Belchertown. Owned and operated by the Belchertown Historical Society, this 1827 Federal-style home contains examples of 18th- and 19th-century American furniture, china, and decorative accessories, much of it locally made. Particularly interesting is the collection of children's dolls, toys, and board games. Open mid-May through October, Wednesday and Saturday 2–5.

TO DO

FISHING
Quabbin Reservoir is open for fishing April to October. A wide variety of cold- and warm-water fish can be found, including landlocked salmon, bass, pickerel, perch, and trout. Boat and motor rentals and launching facilities are at Gate 31, off MA 122 in New Salem. All boating must be in conjunction with fishing. Contact the Quabbin Visitors Center (413-323-7221) for current regulations and restrictions.

GOLF
Petersham Country Club (508-724-3388), Petersham, nine holes. **Ellinwood Country Club** (508-249-9836), 1928 Pleasant Street, Athol, 18 holes. **Mill Valley Driving Range** (413-323-0264), Belchertown.

HIKING
There are 20 miles of hiking trails in 8500-acre Quabbin Park at the southern end of the MDC reservation. Trail maps are available at the visitors center. There are also very enjoyable trails in the northern section. From Gate 35, off MA 122 in New Salem, for instance, you can walk along an old railroad bed to the reservoir's edge. From Gate 30 in New Salem there is a self-guided nature walk. The former town Common of Dana is accessible by both foot and bike from Gate 40 off MA 32A in Petersham. (Also see *Green Space*.)

HORSEBACK RIDING
☞ **Ingate Farms** (413-253-0440), 60 Lamson Avenue, Belchertown. Trail rides are $16 an hour; lessons $15–25.

Quabbin Reservoir

SWIMMING
Laurel Lake in Erving State Forest (544-3939) is the most user-friendly place, with rest rooms, a pavilion, and a picnic area. There is also **Ruggles Pond** in Wendell State Forest (413-659-3797). Town beaches are found at **Lake Ellis** and **Silver Lake** in Athol, **Lake Mattawa** in Orange, **Queen Lake** in Phillipston, and **Moore's Pond** in Warwick.

CROSS-COUNTRY SKIING
Red Apple Farm (1-800-628-4851) in Phillipston maintains 10 miles of trails and roadways; the **James W. Brooks Woodland Preserve** on East Street, 1 mile east of the Petersham Common, offers superb ski touring along the east branch of the Swift River. Other trails are noted under *Green Space*.

GREEN SPACE

PICNICKING
Federation State Forest (939-8962), MA 122, Petersham. There are a couple dozen nicely sited picnic tables with fireplaces, from which unmarked trails lead to eight "wilderness" campsites.

STATE FORESTS
Petersham State Forest (939-8962), off MA 122. Fishing and canoeing on Riceville Pond.

Erving State Forest (544-3939). This 4479-acre spread offers swimming and boating on Laurel Lake, hiking on Overlook Trail, cross-country and skimobile trails in winter, and 32 campsites.

Royalston State Forest (939-8962). Just 776 acres of forested terrain in the western section of Royalston. Good for hiking, snowmobiling.

Warwick State Forest (544-7474), via Tully Road from Athol or Athol Road from Warwick. Shoemet Lake is a beautiful spot, created by Augustus Bliss in the mid-19th century as a millpond. There is a boat-launch ramp good for canoes and rowboats (no motors permitted). The lake is stocked with trout, but no swimming is allowed.

Wendell State Forest (413-659-3797). Take Wendell Road from Millers Falls. There is swimming and picnicking at Ruggles Pond, fishing and canoeing at Ruggles and Wickett Ponds. The miles of roads through this 7566-acre forest are used for the annual September fat-tire race; it's ideal for biking.

Orange State Forest (544-3939). Just 59 acres on the western end of Orange. Good for hiking, cross-country skiing.

WALKS

Quabbin Reservation. With 119,000 acres of wooded watershed, Quabbin is the biggest green space in the state. Much of it is off-limits or inaccessible, but that still leaves large areas, such as Quabbin Park, for public enjoyment. There are nine foot trails ranging in length from ½ to almost 2 miles.

Women's Federation Club State Forest (939-8962), marked from MA 122 near the Petersham/New Salem line. There are picnic tables, fireplaces, wilderness campsites, unmarked trails; also, trout fishing in Fever Brook.

Harvard Forest (724-3325), MA 32, Petersham. A 3000-acre property attached to the Fisher Museum (see *To See*). It includes a self-guided natural history trail and Black Gum Trail, which highlight the forest's features. Take the 4½-mile trail to Prospect Hill for a view of the area from a fire tower.

Mount Grace State Forest (544-7474), Winchester Road, Warwick. Mount Grace itself, a 1617-foot peak, has long attracted hikers, and for 20 years, beginning in the '40s, the state maintained a four-trail ski area here. There is still a great view from the top. The trail begins at the picnic area in a pine grove.

Elliott Laurel Reservation, Phillipston; off MA 101 just west of Queen Lake. Woodland paths follow stone walls through white pine and hardwood with an extensive understory of mountain laurel.

Bearsden Woods, entrance from Bearsden Road near Athol Memorial Hospital; 1000 acres maintained by the Athol Conservation Commission. From the parking lot, a dirt road continues to the Millers River. There are a total of 10 miles of hiking trails and nice views from Roundtop Mountain.

WATERFALLS

Bear's Den Reservation in North New Salem, off Elm Street, ¾ mile from US 202. This Trustees of Reservations site is a tiny grotto on the

Middle Branch of the Swift River with a sparkling waterfall. Local legend states that in 1675 King Philip met here with his chieftains to plan the attack on Deerfield.

Doane's Falls in Royalston, Athol Road at Doane Hill Road. Owned by the Trustees of Reservations, this site is a truly spectacular series of waterfalls. Lawrence Brook flows through a granite gorge crowned with pine and hemlock. A path leads down along the falls, worth following even in winter when the falls are an ice sculpture.

Spirit Falls, owned by Harvard Forest, is 1 mile west of Royalston Common but another mile hike via a forest road (north from Doane Hill Road) just east of a bridge across Tully River. The falls is also accessible from a forest road from MA 68; look for a small, unmarked turnout where a short footpath leads to a great view of the river.

LODGING

☞ **Bullard Farm** (544-6959), North New Salem 01355. A 1792 farmhouse on 400 acres, just a mile from Quabbin, that has been in Janet Krafts's family for many generations. The farm has its own walking and cross-country skiing trails and adjoins the Bear's Den Reservation and its waterfall. (Deer and flocks of wild turkeys from the reservation sometimes wander onto the farm.) The house offers four large and comfortable guest rooms with period furniture (sharing two bathrooms), and there is ample common space; also a meeting/function room in the former barn, good for weddings. Rates are $60 single, $74 double, with breakfast.

The Wildwood Inn (413-967-7798), 121 Church Street, Ware 01082. A turreted and shingled 1880s house, built during Ware's heyday as a textile manufacturing center. The house is filled with period antiques and brightly patterned quilts, and antique photographs (some scenes of the "lost towns") decorate the walls. There are nine rooms, seven with private bath, and guests have access to a large Victorian parlor with an ornate fireplace. Owners Fraidell Fenster and Richard Watson help visitors explore the area and will even lend them a canoe. Rooms are $60–80 with full "country" breakfast.

☞ **Ingate Farms Bed & Breakfast** (413-253-0440), 60 Lamson Avenue, Belchertown 01007. The B&B at Ingate Farms—a 500-acre horse farm—is a 250-year-old former bobbin mill moved from the Swift River Valley when Quabbin was created. There are four pleasant guest rooms, one with private bath and the others sharing two baths. Riding lessons and trail rides are available. Ingate Farms was formerly an equestrian camp (it can accommodate 100 horses), and amenities include an Olympic-sized swimming pool. Room rates with continental breakfast are $65–75 in-season and $50–60 the rest of the year.

WHERE TO EAT

DINING OUT

Also see Salem Cross Inn under "Old Sturbridge Village Area"—a destination restaurant with a display of photographs of flooded Quabbin towns.

Mark's New Salem Restaurant (508-544-6618), US 202, New Salem. Open for all three meals just Friday, Saturday, and Sunday. New chef-owner Mark Antsel has altered this popular little landmark to make it more of an intimate dining room, the setting for memorable meals that might commence with a cup of French vegetable soup with basic and white beans, and progress to grilled top sirloin steak with classic béarnaise sauce ($13.95), a fresh spinach tart with lentil pilaf ($12.95), or fresh salmon fillet with sorrel sauce ($13.95). Reservations suggested for dinner. Lunch might be a hearty Tuscan salad ($5.95), a roasted peppers and eggplant omelet ($4.55), or a quesadilla ($5.50).

The Homestead Restaurant (508-549-8949), US 202, Orange. Open daily. An established, very popular roadhouse-style restaurant, noted for its beef and seafood dishes and large portions. Most entrées in the $12–16 range. The "Homestead Hearty Platter" ($15.95) consists of more than 2 pounds of prime rib. Extensive wine list.

EATING OUT

Gouvin's Cafe (413-967-0308), old mill complex, Main Street (MA 9), Ware. An attractive café in an early-19th-century former textile mill. Serves a high tea in the afternoon for $3 with unlimited pastries.

Wendell Country Store (413-544-8646), Locks Village Road, Wendell. Light food served from 7:30 AM until 7 or 8 at night (depending on the day); tables inside and out. Inquire about monthly coffeehouses on the nearest Saturday to the full moon, held in the town hall.

(Also see Hamilton Orchards under *Selective Shopping.*)

SELECTIVE SHOPPING

The Common Reader Bookshop (544-3002), 8 Main Street on the Common, New Salem. May through October, Wednesday through Saturday 10–5, Sunday noon–5. Owner Dorothy Johnson has a large collection of general-interest old and used books. Women's history is a specialty.

Stonemill Antique Center (413-967-5964), MA 9, Ware. Located in a historic former textile mill, this large consignment store has a variety of antiques and collectibles. Open daily 10–5, Sunday noon–5. Hours are extended until 9 PM during Brimfield antiques fairs.

FARMS AND ORCHARDS

Hamilton Orchards (544-6867), US 202 and West Street, New Salem. Open weekends 9–5, March to Thanksgiving, but daily during apple harvest—Labor Day to mid-October. Closed in June. One of the nicest orchards around: 35 acres of trees yielding a variety of species that you can pick yourself in-season. Cider is also pressed in the fall, and you can pick raspberries from late August until mid-October, blueberries, earlier. Barb Hamilton makes the pies, which are for sale, and the snack bar serves hot dogs and hamburgers as well as the pies and pancakes with Hamilton-made syrup. The view is off across the Quabbin Reservoir, and nature trails meander across the property.

Red Apple Farm (1-800-628-4851), 455 Highland Avenue (marked from MA 2A), Phillipston. There is no pick-your-own; instead a farm store sells pears and peaches, many varieties of apples (shipped anywhere), and cider pressed in-season. Specializes in unusual species. There are also a bakery and retail shop, hayrides, and a Fall Festival. Visitors are invited to hike and cross-country ski.

Quabbin Lamb Farm, 1276 Patrill Hollow Road, Hardwick. Open year-round. A small sheep farm raising lambs and selling lambskins, yarn, knitted goods; cross-country skiing and birdwatching permitted on the property.

SPECIAL EVENTS

April: **Athol-to-Orange River Rat Race** (usually held on the third Saturday, but check). This is huge, usually attracting more than 300 canoes.

May: **May Day Morris Dancing** in North Orange.

June: **Phillipston Craft Fair** (last weekend); **Fly-in and Yankee Engineuity in Action steam engine show** at the Orange Municipal Airport; **Athol Summerfest** last weekend in June.

August: **Royalston Day,** North Orange Village Fair.

September: **New England Fat-tire Road Races** in Wendell State Forest. **Fall Festival** in downtown Athol, third Saturday.

October: **Columbus Day; Celebrate the Harvest** in Orange; **Phillipston Pumpkin Commission Weigh-in; Old Home Days** in Warwick, New Salem, and Wendell.

IV. WESTERN MASSACHUSETTS

The Pioneer Valley
The Hilltowns
The Berkshires

The Connecticut River Valley from Summit House

©KIMBERLY GRANT

The Pioneer Valley

Since 1811 the 50-mile, broad swatch of western Massachusetts flanking the Connecticut River has been divided into the three counties: Franklin, Hampshire, and Hampden. Since the 1940s this area has been known as "The Pioneer Valley." This name underscores the way settlement along the Connecticut River predated that of Berkshire County to the west and Worcester County to the east, but it also suggests that the entire area is a flat valley when, in fact, it includes country every bit as hilly as the Berkshires.

The distinction between the Connecticut River bottomland and its flanking hills is unusually sharp. The valley floor is a distinctive mix of farms, venerable towns, and cities, while the Hilltowns to the west (see "The Hilltowns") and gentler hills to the east (see "Quabbin Area") remain among the most rural landscape in New England. These towns were the last in Massachusetts to be settled, and the first to be all but vacated in the 1820s when residents moved west to easier farmland or to valley mill or rail towns. They are also far enough from major cities or resort areas to have changed little since.

The valley was carved by a series of glaciers, the last leaving 2-mile-deep Lake Hitchcock in its wake. Geologists have found that the lake was suddenly released, rushing to the sea all in one day—some 10,000 years ago. Just 5 miles wide up around the Vermont–New Hampshire line, the valley widens to 20 miles down around Springfield. Improbably, an abrupt chain of mountains march east-west across the middle of the valley (do they suggest a mammoth herd of dinosaurs to anyone else?), yielding views from ridge paths and from two especially famous peaks—Mount Tom and Mount Holyoke—on opposite sides of the Connecticut. Both peaks are accessible by car, and both overlook the oxbow and river loop.

New England's longest river, the Connecticut plays a far more obvious role as the boundary between New Hampshire and Vermont and, again, as the centerpiece for the state that bears its name than it does in its 69-mile passage through Massachusetts. Still, its role here has been far greater than you might think.

In the 18th and early 19th centuries Massachusetts's communities along the Connecticut—isolated from the state's coastal capital and

View from Mt. Holyoke, *by William Henry Bartlett, is in the collection of Springfield's Connecticut Valley Historical Museum.*

population centers—developed their own distinctive, valley-centered society, architecture, and, most interestingly, religion. In the 1730s and '40s Northampton-based Reverend Jonathan Edwards challenged the theology of Boston-based Congregationalism, trumpeting instead the message that everyone (not just the "elect") could be saved. Edwards's emotionally charged revival meetings launched a "Great Awakening" that rippled throughout New England.

In the valley itself, this fire-and-brimstone brand of Calvinism lingered on well into the 19th century, long after Boston had forgotten its Puritan horror of sin and embraced a more permissive Unitarianism. Puzzling on the themes of death and eternity in Amherst in the 1850s through '70s, poet Emily Dickinson was more a part of her time and place than is generally understood.

The valley's stern religion bred a concern for proper schooling. Deerfield Academy, founded in 1797, quickly attracted female as well as male students from throughout the area. Amherst College was founded in 1821 by town patriarchs and in 1837 Mount Holyoke College opened in South Hadley. Both contributed more than their share of Protestant missionaries.

Subtly but surely, education became a religion in its own right, and today it represents one of the valley's leading industries. Its heart is the "Five-College area," home to Smith, Hampshire, Amherst, and Mount Holyoke Colleges and the University of Massachusetts at Amherst. It represents one of the country's largest rural concentrations of students and certainly one of its liveliest rural music, crafts, art, and dining scenes.

Perhaps the valley's most striking feature for visitors is the way in which the many layers of its history—from dinosaurs to diners—are visible, far more so than in most other places. The dinosaurs left footprints, lots of them. Many were unearthed during construction of I-91 in the 1960s, and three-toed tracks can be seen in science museums in Springfield and at Amherst College and right in the ground at Smith's Ferry (US 5 north of Holyoke).

The valley's unusually rich soil—said to have been farmed in some places for 8000 years before the first white settlers arrived—is considered as sacred as the dino tracks by many local preservationists, and despite recent development pressures a number of farms survive. The story of the pioneer in this valley is vividly told in Old Deerfield, a village of 18th- and early-19th-century homes, 14 preserved as samplings of 18th-century rural life, one that was surprisingly rich and sophisticated.

This valley seems to have been a Yankee version of the Garden of Eden: rich soil bordering a waterway to the ocean. The Connecticut served as a highway on which new settlers continuously arrived and crops were exported. Flat-bottomed, square-rigged boats plied this thoroughfare, deftly negotiating a half-dozen patches of "quick water." In 1777 Springfield was chosen for the site of an armory. Skilled workmen flocked to the spot and speedily began turning out guns, paper cartridges, and cartridge boxes for the Patriot cause. These items went downriver too.

Today it is difficult to grasp the former importance of this waterway. In the 1790s transportation canals were built around the falls at Holyoke and at Turners Falls. A number of vessels were built on West Springfield's Common around 1800, and at the height of the subsequent canal-building craze, a canal system linked Northampton with New Haven.

With the dawn of the industrial revolution in the 1820s, the waterfalls that had been obstacles in the canal era were viewed as the valley's biggest assets. In the 1820s Boston developers began to build textile mills at Chicopee Falls and in the '30s and '40s developed Holyoke from scratch—a planned, brick town, complete with factories, 4½ miles of power canals, workers' housing, and mill owners' mansions. Meanwhile Springfield was booming thanks to its own home-bred inventors and investors, a breed initially drawn to the area by the armory.

Although working and living conditions in the mill towns were dreadful (and well publicized by *Springfield Union* editor Edward Bellamy), the 1890s–1920—the period from which most buildings in its towns and cities still date—was obviously the valley's most colorful and exuberant era. In Springfield public buildings like the magnificent City Hall and Symphony Hall, the soaring Florentine-style campanile, and the quadrangle of museums all conjure up this era. So do exhibits in the Holyoke Heritage State Park—dramatizing Sunday picnics on Mount Tom and suggesting the extent of trolley lines that webbed the valley. Also during this period volleyball was invented in Holyoke (look for exhibits in the Children's Museum complex), and basketball (a three-story Hall of Fame tells the story), in Springfield.

The valley today is distinguished by its number of extensive, manicured parks, its elaborate stone and brick public buildings, and its private school and institutional buildings designed in every conceivable "Revival" style—all gifts of 19th-century philanthropists who refused to be forgotten (each bears the donor's name). Mount Holyoke itself now stands in vast Skinner Park, donated by a family who made its fortune producing satin in the country's largest silk mill. Northampton's 200-acre Look and 22-acre Childs Parks were both donated by the industrialists whose names they bear, and Stanley Park in Westfield was created by Stanley Home Products founder Frank Stanley Bevridge. Although Springfield's 795-acre Forest Park isn't named for its principal benefactor, it does harbor New England's most elaborate mausoleum, built by ice skate tycoon Everett H. Barney.

As early as the 1820s, sophisticated tourists came to view the valley's peculiar mix of factory and farmscape, bottomland and abrupt mountains. In 1836 Thomas Cole, one of America's most celebrated landscape artists, painted the mammoth work *The Oxbow: View from Mt. Holyoke, Northampton, Massachusetts, after a Thunderstorm*, now owned by New York's Metropolitan Museum. The oxbow subsequently became the "motif number one" of western Massachusetts, and the small Mountain House on the summit of Mount Holyoke was soon replaced with a more elaborate hotel (a portion of which still survives), accessed from riverboats and a riverside train station by a perpendicular cog-and-cable-driven railway. Other hotels appeared atop Mount Tom and Sugarloaf Mountain in South Deerfield.

Even before the Civil War, Old Deerfield's mile-long street of 18th- and early-19th-century houses was already drawing history buffs. An 1848 crusade to save the so-called "Indian House" (still bearing the marks of a tomahawk embedded in it during the 1704 raid) is now cited as the first effort in this country to preserve a historic house. The door, at least, survived and was displayed, along with the first "period room" in America, in Memorial Hall, a museum that opened in 1880. Over the next few years the village's 18th-century tavern was restored as a center and showcase for an arts and crafts movement dedicated to reviving traditional handicrafts—not unlike those for which the area is currently known.

Still linked both physically by I-91 (which superseded old north-south highways US 5/MA 10, which in turn had upstaged the railway, which had replaced the river) and culturally with Connecticut's cities and Brattleboro (Vermont) more than with Boston, the valley remains a place unto itself. It's little touristed in the usual sense but rewards anyone willing to explore college and city museums, to walk ridge paths, or to drive to the top of mountains on winding roads designed for carriages. Though it's liveliest during the academic year, in summer the valley still offers music in Northampton coffeehouses, on college campuses, in historic house gardens, and on top of Mount Holyoke.

The Connecticut itself is, moreover, recapturing some of its old status as the region's focal point. It has made a dramatic comeback since the federally mandated Clean Water Act began to take effect in the '70s. Now swimmable and fishable, it has been further improved through the protection of more than 4000 riparian acres in Massachusetts. A 52-mile Riverway State Park is in the works.

On summer weekends hundreds of powerboats emerge from marinas sited on the deep lakelike stretches of the river above the power dams at Holyoke and Turners Falls, but two particularly beautiful stretches of the river—the dozen miles below Turners Falls and above French King Gorge—are too shallow for power boating and particularly appealing to canoeists. The easiest way onto the river is aboard *Quinnetukut II,* a snappy riverboat cruising back and forth through the gorge between Barton Cove and Northfield Mountain. The sleepy old roads along both sides of the river are also becoming increasingly popular with bicyclists.

One of the state's most popular bike paths follows an old railbed, linking Northampton and Amherst, two towns that together represent one of the state's largest and most interesting concentrations of shops and restaurants. Lodging ranges from tents within sight of the eagles at Barton Cove to convention hotels in Springfield and includes both long-standing inns and a burgeoning number of B&Bs.

GREENFIELD/DEERFIELD AREA

The northern reach of the Connecticut River Valley in Massachusetts is narrow, rural, and scenic. The big sight to see in this area is the village of Old Deerfield. The mile-long march of 18th- and early-19th-century brick and wood buildings, 45 built before 1825, are set starkly against a thousand acres of cornfields. Although no museum village in the usual sense, Old Deerfield does include 14 Historic Deerfield buildings open to the public, plus Memorial Hall (an exceptional town historical museum) and the 1890s Deerfield Inn. The Historic Deerfield houses are open year-round, as rewarding to visit in January as they are in July.

Old Deerfield's serene good looks belie its ups and downs during the 19th and 20th, as well as the 17th and 18th, centuries. Founded on a lush plain in 1663, the first settlement here was deserted in 1675 after

King Philip's Native Americans killed most of its young men in an ambush that's remembered as the "Bloody Brook Massacre." Seven years later, however, the proprietors of Deerfield were back, harvesting crops and listening to Sunday sermons in the square, tower-topped meetinghouse (reconstructed on a smaller scale as the present post office). Then one blustery February night in 1704, Frenchmen and Native Americans swarmed over the stockade, carrying more than 100 villagers off to Montreal. Within three years of this widely publicized event, many of the same families were back again. Today visitors are amazed by the richness and sophistication of life as it was lived here during and after the Revolution—as judged from the quality of the architectural detailing, furniture, silver, and furnishings on view. Ironically, having been wiped out twice, Old Deerfield survives today as a unique sampling of life in the late 18th and early 19th centuries.

By the 1820s, however, Deerfield had been upstaged by Greenfield as the local commercial center. Already it had become the place to come to school (Deerfield Academy was founded in 1797) and to visit "historic" sites. In 1830 an elaborate granite obelisk replaced a vintage-1720s memorial on the North Main Street (in South Deerfield) site of the Bloody Massacre, and in 1848 a campaign was mounted to save the Indian House, which still bore the mark of the hatchet implanted in it during the 1704 raid. Though the campaign failed, it is now cited as the first effort in this country to preserve a historic house; the door was acquired by a Boston antiquarian, which so outraged local residents that he had to return it.

Deerfield's zeal for self-preservation was fanned by George Sheldon, a self-appointed town historian given to raiding his neighbors' attics. Sheldon organized the Pocumtuck Valley Memorial Association in 1870 and a decade later acquired a striking, three-story brick building designed by Asher Benjamin (it had been the original Deerfield Academy building). The society filled this Memorial Hall with local relics ranging from the Indian House door to colonial-era cooking utensils, displayed in what is now recognized as the first "period room" to be seen in any American museum.

Sheldon also enticed his cousin C. Alice Baker back to town. Born in Deerfield, Baker had become a teacher and noted preservationist in the Boston area (she was involved in the campaign to preserve the Old South Meeting House) and was familiar with the then-current attempts to restore colonial buildings in and around the village of York, Maine. Back in Deerfield, Alice Baker acquired the Frary Tavern, restored it, and went on to found two societies dedicated to reviving colonial-era crafts such as weaving, hearth cookery, pottery, and basketry. Visitors came. They came by rail and later by rural trolley, stayed in local farms and several now-vanished hotels (including Jewitt House atop Mount Sugarloaf), and shopped for arts and crafts in local homes and studios.

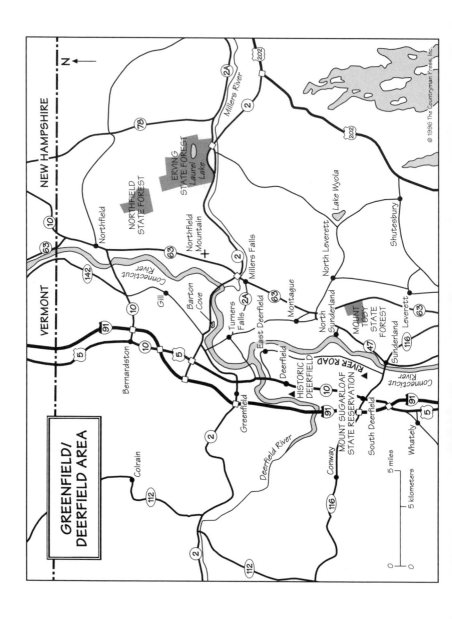

By the 1920s Deerfield was again forgotten. The 1937 WPA *Guide to Massachusetts* described it as "the ghost of a town, its dimness almost transparent, its quiet almost a cessation, [but] it is essential to add that it is probably quite the most beautiful ghost of its kind, and with the deepest poetic and historic significance to be found in America."

This time it was Deerfield Academy headmaster Frank Boyden who came to the rescue of the old houses, persuading Deerfield Academy alumnus and parent Henry Flynt and his wife, Helen, to buy a number of decaying Old Deerfield buildings. The Flynts subsequently restored a number of buildings, incorporating them as the nonprofit Heritage Foundation (now Historic Deerfield) in 1952. The entire town of Deerfield has been remarkably lucky in preserving no less than 5900 acres of cultivated land. Although tract housing sprouted in several fields in the late 1980s, a Deerfield Land Trust was subsequently established and is now dedicated to preserving local farmland.

The commercial strip along US 5/MA 10 in Deerfield has become an attraction in its own right. Yankee Candle, with its Bavarian Village, counts more than 1½ million customers a year (compared to Historic Deerfield's ¼ million visitors). The village of South Deerfield, 4 miles south of Old Deerfield, offers a surprising number and range of restaurants and a view down the valley—from the top of Mount Sugarloaf.

Greenfield remains the commercial hub of this upper end of the Pioneer Valley. It's the county seat of Franklin County and blessed with one of the state's more interesting Main Streets. It recently fought WalMart and won, and it retains a 1950s feel (the landmarks are Wilson's Department Store, the Garden Movie Theater, and Famous Bill's Restaurant), with a peppering of New Age galleries, shops, and cafés.

The area's other fine old river towns—Sunderland, Whately, and Northfield—also preserve their early-19th-century architecture and farmland. Bicycle or drive up River Road through farmland along the Connecticut and through Whately and Deerfield. Above Turners Falls the river itself is accessible by excursion boat as well as by rental boats and canoes.

AREA CODE
413

GUIDANCE
Franklin County Chamber of Commerce (773-5463, daily, 24 hours), PO Box 790, Greenfield 01302. The chamber's office at 395 Main Street serves as a walk-in information center year-round. Weekdays June through foliage season an information center at the I-91, MA 2 rotary is also open.

GETTING THERE
By bus: From New York City, **Greyhound** (1-800-231-2222) and **Vermont Transit** (1-800-552-8737) serve Greenfield on north-south routes, and **Peter Pan** (413-781-3320) comes from both Boston and New York.

By car: MA 2 is the east-west access, and I-91 runs north-south.
MEDICAL EMERGENCY
Franklin Medical Center (772-0211), 164 High Street, Greenfield.

VILLAGES

Deerfield. We've already discussed Deerfield in the introduction, but we
should add that the largest property holder in Old Deerfield is **Deerfield Academy,** and that there are two more private schools—
Eaglebrook and **Bement School**—in the village. Also in Old Deerfield: **The Brick Church,** built in 1824, has arched doorways and a
closed wooden cupola. It's the scene of frequent special events as well
as regular (Unitarian) services. **The Old Burying Ground** (walk along
Albany Road) has many 18th-century stones. Sited as it is at the
confluence of the Deerfield and Connecticut Rivers, the town enjoys
an unusual amount of water frontage (see *Green Space*), and many of
the farms that welcome visitors (see *Selective Shopping*) are on river
roads, which are good for bicycling. Also see *Lodging, Where to Eat,*
and *Special Events.*
Greenfield. This proud old town of 18,000 is sited at the confluence of the
Deerfield and Connecticut Rivers, and also at the junction of MA 2 and
I-91. Main Street is distinguished by a number of interesting buildings
in a wide variety of styles, several by native son Asher Benjamin, the
unsung hero responsible for the architectural look of much of rural New
England. In the 1790s, a period when much of western Massachusetts
and northern New England was quickly settled, Benjamin was keenly
aware of the need for a "do-it-yourself" guide to the new architectural
styles being introduced in Boston by Charles Bulfinch. In 1796 Benjamin wrote *The Country Builder's Assistant,* followed by six more
books that resulted in the construction of thousands of homes and hundreds of churches—the distinctive three-story houses and high-steepled
churches that remain the pride of New England villages. The **Greenfield Public Library** (772-1544), 402 Main Street, said to be the first
building designed by Asher Benjamin, has an exceptional children's
room and an interesting historical collection. The **Greenfield Historical Society** (774-3663), 3 Church Street (by appointment), offers eight
rooms filled with furnishings, portraits, early Greenfield artifacts, and
photos. Also check *Lodging, Eating Out,* and *Selective Shopping.*
Northfield, bisected by the Connecticut River and bounded on the north
by both Vermont and New Hampshire, has an unusually wide and long
Main Street lined with many houses built during the heyday of river
traffic and sheep farming. Northfield is best known today for the two
college-sized campuses of **Northfield Mount Hermon,** founded as
two distinct prep schools by evangelist Reverend Dwight Moody in the
late 19th century. Although there is no trace of Moody's grand old sum-

mer hotel, there is a summer Youth Hostel (AYH began here in 1934) and two bed & breakfasts representing the town's two most notable eras. The trails at **Northfield Mountain** and rides aboard the excursion boat *Quinnetukut II* also attract visitors, and both golf and bicycling options are outstanding. Stop by the **Northfield Historical Society** (498-5565) to learn more about Dwight Moody and the Stearns brothers, and don't miss Rua's (see *Eating Out*).

Sunderland is a classic, 18th-century river town with most of its homes strung along Main Street, flanking a brick town hall that was built in 1867 to double as the town school. From MA 2 we like to approach Deerfield via MA 63 and MA 47, past Mount Toby and tobacco barns rather than around rotaries and down the interstate.

Montague harbors no fewer than five villages, most notably **Montague Center,** off MA 63 near the junction with MA 47; its standout Common has a Congregational church designed by Asher Benjamin and a brick town hall that serves as a summer theater. The Book Mill Cafe, a major gathering center for the valley, is just down Greenfield Road. **Turners Falls,** an 1860s mill village built around a cutlery factory by the falls, is just off MA 2; its Shea Community Theater offers live entertainment, and the fish ladder in the Great Falls Discovery Center is well worth a trip in spring to see fish climbing.

Leverett is included in this chapter because it lies within Franklin County, but it's really a bedroom town for Amherst. Hidden away along its heavily wooded roads are some rewarding historic and natural sites—notably colonial-era charcoal kilns, shallow caves known as "beehive huts," and a spectacular ravine known as "Rattlesnake Gutter"—that are worth searching out.

TO SEE

MUSEUMS AND HISTORIC HOMES

Historic Deerfield (774-5581), in Old Deerfield, marked from US 5, six miles north of Exit 24 off I-91. Open all year 9:30–4:30 daily except Thanksgiving, Christmas Eve, and Christmas Day. $10 adults, $5 children aged 6–17. Tickets (good for 2 consecutive days) are sold in the **Hall Tavern** (be sure to see the upstairs ballroom). Guided tours are presently offered of 13 buildings displaying a total of some 20,000 objects made or used in America between 1630 and 1850. An introductory film helps you decide which buildings you may wish to tour. We have already described Historic Deerfield in the chapter introduction and under *Villages;* historic houses we recommend include:

The Wells-Thorn House (sections built in 1717 and 1751) shows the dramatic changes in the lifestyles in Deerfield through two centuries. **The Ashley House** (1733), with its elegantly carved cupboards and furnishings, depicts the lifestyle of the village's Tory minister (note his 1730s

Yale diploma). **Asa Stebbins House** (1799/1810) is the first brick home in town, grandly furnished with French wallpapers, Chinese porcelains, and Federal-era pieces. **The Wright House** (1824), another brick mansion, is a mini-museum of early furniture and china. **Sheldon-Hawks House** (1743) is furnished almost exclusively with pieces from the Connecticut River Valley and Boston and is still filled with the spirit of George Sheldon, the town's colorful first historian. **Frary House/Barnard Tavern** (1740/1795), is my favorite because of its classic tavern look, ballroom, and 1890s restoration by C. Alice Baker. **Ebenezer Hinsdale Williams House** (1750s, rebuilt 1816–20), opened in 1993 after 12 years of painstaking restoration, seems surprisingly light and airy, with touches like the light-toned rag stair rug, "glass curtains," and brightly patterned wallpapers.

Memorial Hall (774-7476), Memorial Street and US 5/MA 10, Old Deerfield. Open May through October 10–4:30 weekdays, 12:30–4:30 weekends. $2.50 adults, $1.50 students, $.75 children aged 6–12. This brick building was designed by Asher Benjamin in 1797 for Deerfield Academy and purchased by the Pocumtuck Valley Memorial Association in 1878 to house the wealth of things collected by town historian George Sheldon. The most famous piece is the vintage-1698 "Indian House Door" with a tomahawk hole in its center. Exhibits in 19 rooms on three floors include the first "period room" in any American museum (see chapter introduction), an extensive collection of Native American relics, early paintings and quilts, and priceless Hadley chests. This is also the place to savor the town's 1890s–1920s revival—through paintings, photographs, clothing, and the world's largest collection of "Deerfield Society of Blue and White needlework." Inquire about the society's semiannual crafts festivals and other special events. The Old Indian House, reconstructed in 1929 and owned by Memorial Hall, is open for special events and can be rented for parties and weddings.

FOR FAMILIES

Yankee Candle Company (665-2929), US 5/MA 10, ¼ mile north of I-91 Exit 24, South Deerfield. In 1969 Michael Kittredge used his mother's kitchen to make his first candles. Now the largest handcrafter of its kind in the country, Yankee Candle is a vast, ever-growing complex that includes a Bavarian Village complete with year-round falling snow and make-your-own-country-kitchen candles; it lures more than a million visitors a year. Attractions include a castle courtyard and waterfall, nutcracker castle, year-round Santa's toy factory, giant toy machine, and its own Chandler's Tavern (all three meals).

Northfield Mountain Recreational and Environmental Center (659-3714), MA 63 in Northfield. April through October bus tours take you to the upper reservoir and underground powerhouse of Northeast Utilities' unusual pumped storage hydroelectric plant. A film about the construction and operation of the plant can be viewed in the visitors center.

JOHN MARTIN

The Dwight Barnard House on Old Deerfield's Main Street

The project utilizes water from the Connecticut, draws it up into an artificially created lake on top of the mountain, and uses the stored water to generate power during high-use periods. The powerhouse itself is hidden in a cavern as high as a 10-story building, as wide as a four-lane highway, and longer than a football field. The center also houses superb displays dramatizing the story of the river's 18th- and early-19th-century flat-bottomed sailing barges for which canals were constructed in the 1790s. The story of steamboating and the advent of the railroad is also told, along with subsequent industrialization, logging, and the present hydro uses of the river's "white gold." The center also offers a series of lectures and workshops on the area's flora and fauna. Check under *To Do* for June through mid-October cruises on the Connecticut aboard the *Quinnetukut II.*

Turners Falls Fish Ladder (863-3221), off MA 2 in Turners Falls. Mid-May through July be sure to stop by to view the fish ladder through a glass wall. Shad, striped bass, and salmon are the ladder patrons. A small display also depicts the natural and industrial history of the falls, and Unity Park here offers picnicking facilities and a playground.

SCENIC DRIVES

River Road runs along the Connecticut all the way from Hatfield north to the confluence with the Deerfield, and it's lined with farms, tobacco sheds, and fields. It's flat except for the monadnock, Mount Sugarloaf, which thrusts up all alone (be sure to drive to the top). See *Selective Shopping* for farms along this road, and note the old headstones in Pine Nook Cemetery some 4 miles north of MA 116. (*Note:* Finding River Road south from MA 116 is difficult because it isn't marked, but it is

there; just take the road nearest the river.) River Road south from the landing (off MA 63) at Northfield Mountain to MA 2 is also beautiful.
Montague Center to Greenfield. From Amherst or Sunderland the quick and scenic route to Greenfield is up MA 63, then into Montague Center (see *Villages*). Turn left past the Book Mill, and continue on Greenfield Road; take a left on Montague City Road, which crosses the river, and a right on Mountain Road, which climbs to the Poet's Seat (see *Green Space*). Take any road downhill to MA 2A (High Street) and Main Street, Greenfield.

TO DO

AIRPLANE RIDES
Pioneer Aviation (863-9391) offers scenic flights from Turners Falls Airport.

BICYCLING
At this writing the Franklin County Bicycle Path is evolving along the Connecticut River between South Deerfield and Northfield, and local bicycle shops can advise you on a number of scenic loops. Mountain biking is also popular in summer on the 40 miles of trails at Northfield Mountain. Rentals as well as advice are available from:
Northfield Bicycle Barn (498-2996), Main Street, Northfield. Look for Al's Convenience Store; the "Barn" is behind the neighboring house. **Basically Bicycles** (863-3556), 88 Third Street in Turners Falls. **Bicycles Unlimited** (772-2700), 322 High Street, Greenfield.

BOAT EXCURSION
The Quinnetukut II (659-3714) cruises the Connecticut from the Riverview Picnic Area at Northfield Mountain 6 miles downstream to the Turners Falls dam. Departures are from two to four times per day during late May through mid-October. Call for reservations. $7 adults, $3 children under 14, $6 senior citizens. Inquire about special children's cruises.

CANOEING
A 52-mile Riverway State Park is, at this writing, still in the works. Phone 586-8706 or send a self-addressed, stamped envelope to DEM, 136 Damon Road, Northampton 01060, for a copy of "A Connecticut River Water Trail," an excellent pamphlet guide to the 12 miles of river (too shallow for power boats) below Turners Falls.
Northfield Mountain Recreation and Environmental Center (659-3714) is the source for information about canoeing sites that Northeast Utilities maintains for public access: **Captain Kidds' Island** (also good for picnicking), **Munn's Ferry Campground** (with Adirondack shelters and tent sites, accessible only by boat), and **River View,** a float dock, picnic tables, and sanitary facilities on the river across from the entrance to Northfield Mountain.

Excursion Boat The Quinnetukut II *from Northfield Mountain*

At **Barton Cove** (863-9300), Northeast Utilities maintains tent sites, rents canoes and rowboats, and offers shuttle service to put-in places in Northfield. There is also a state boat-launch site on the Connecticut at Pauchaug Brook in Northfield, and below Turners Falls dam you can put in at the Montague City Bridge (off Poplar Street). There is also an informal access point at the MA 116 bridge on the Sunderland side, at a small park in Whately, and at Elwell State Park, the start of the Norwottuck Rail Trail in Northampton (see "Five-College Area").
Taylor Rentals (773-8643) in Greenfield rents aluminum canoes.
Outdoor Centre of New England (659-3926) in Millers Falls specializes in whitewater instruction and expeditions.

FISHING

The State Fisheries and Game Division operates hatcheries in Montague (367-2477) and South Deerfield (665-4680). The little-controlled, shallow section of the Connecticut River south of the Turners Falls dam offers good trout fishing.
Note the Turners Falls fish ladder (see *For Families*) and Thomas & Thomas Rod Makers, also in Turners Falls (see *Selective Shopping*).
Red-Wing Meadow Trout Hatchery (367-9494), 528 Federal Street, Montague. Open for fee fishing April through November. $2 adults, $5 per family, plus $4.25 per pound for fish you catch. Picnic tables. Pole rentals.

GOLF

Crumpin-Fox Golf Club (648-9101), MA 10, Bernardston, 18 holes; the front 9 were designed by Robert Trent Jones himself and the back 9 by his firm. This is a destination golf course with lodging, the neighboring Fox Inn (see *Motels*), and dining at hilltop Andiamo (see *Dining Out*). **Thomas Memorial Golf Club** (863-8003), Turners Falls, nine holes. **Mohawk Meadows Golf Club** (773-9047) in Greenfield, nine holes. **Greenfield Country Club** (773-7530), 18 holes. **Oak Ridge Golf Club** (863-2010) in Gill, nine holes, par 36. **Northfield Country Club** (498-5341), Northfield, nine holes.

HIKING
See *Green Space*.

SKYDIVING
Massachusetts Sport Parachute Club (863-8362), Turners Falls Airport. Skydiving instruction with three different methods: static line, tandem, and accelerated free fall.

SWIMMING
Lake Wyola (367-2627) in Shutesbury is a privately maintained, sandy public beach on a wooded lake; there are also picnic tables and campsites. The **Greenfield Town Beach** (772-1553), Nash's Mill Road (2 miles from MA 2), is open Memorial Day weekend through Labor Day weekend (parking fee). See also Erving and Wendell State Forests in "Quabbin Area.")

TENNIS
The **Club Tennis & Fitness Center** (582-9073), MA 116 in Sunderland, has three indoor and two outdoor clay courts, and four racquetball courts.

CROSS-COUNTRY SKIING
Northfield Mountain Ski Touring Center (659-3714) offers 40 kilometers of double-tracked trails. Touring equipment and snowshoes can be rented here and at the **Northfield Bicycle Barn** (see *Bicycling*). (Also see *Green Space*.)

GREEN SPACE

PICNICKING
Mount Sugarloaf State Reservation off MA 116 in South Deerfield. A road winds up this red sandstone mountain (said to resemble the old loaves into which sugar was shaped) to a modern observation tower on the summit, supposedly the site from which King Philip surveyed his prey before the mid-17th-century Bloody Brook Massacre. There are picnic tables and a great view down the valley.

WALKS
Poet's Seat Tower and **Rocky Mountain Trails**. Off High Street (MA 2A) on Rocky Mountain stands a medieval-looking sandstone tower with an American flag on top. Local 19th-century poet Frederick Goddard Tuckerman liked to sit near this spot, and you understand why when you see the view. A Ridge Trail (blue blazes), good for cross-country

skiing as well as hiking, loops along the top of this abrupt hill, commanding valley views on both sides.

French King Bridge (MA 2 west of Millers Falls) spans a dramatically steep, banked, narrow stretch of the Connecticut, 140 feet above the water. Park at the rest area and walk back onto the bridge (there's a pedestrian walk) for the view. Note the mouth of the Millers River just downstream. The bridge is named for French King Rock below. The king was Louis XV, and the rock was reportedly named by one of his subjects in the mid-1700s. It's funny how some names stick.

Mount Toby, off MA 47, almost 1 mile south of its junction with MA 63 in Montague. Follow Reservation Road to a small parking area and take the trail to the fire tower, which commands an incredible view of the valley and beyond. It's a 3-hour round-trip hike.

Channing Blake Meadow Walk in Old Deerfield. A half-mile path through the village's north meadows and a working 700-acre farm begins at the northern end of Deerfield Street; inquire at Historic Deerfield about special family tours and nature activities.

Pocumtuck Ridge Trail, South Deerfield. Take North Main Street to Hillside Drive (across from Hardigg Industries), to Stage Road. Turn left at the top of the hill onto Ridge Road for the trailhead for paths through Deerfield Land Trust's 120-acre preserve.

Barton Cove Nature and Camping Area, MA 2, just east of Turners Falls in Gill. An interpretive nature trail meanders along a rocky ridge overlooking the Connecticut River, and there's a picnic area in addition to tent sites. Canoe and boat rentals available.

Northfield Mountain, MA 63, Northfield (see *For Families.*)

Bennett Meadow Wildlife Management Area, also maintained by Northeast Utilities, maintains space to park by the west side of the river in Northfield.

LODGING

INNS AND BED & BREAKFASTS

Deerfield Inn (774-5587), Deerfield 01342. Open year-round. A newcomer by Old Deerfield standards (it opened in 1884), the antiques-filled inn is dignified but not stiff. It is *the* place to stay when visiting Historic Deerfield, enabling you to steep and sleep in the full atmosphere of the village after visitors have gone. There are 23 rooms, all with private bath, 12 in a new annex added since the 1979 fire (from which townspeople and Deerfield Academy students heroically rescued most of the antiques). Rooms feature wallpapers and fabrics from the Historic Deerfield collection, and furnishings are either antiques or reproduction antiques; some canopy beds, attention to details, phones. Some annex rooms are quite spacious. $122 includes a full breakfast; lunch and dinner are also served. Inquire about the resident ghost.

The Brandt House (774-3329; 1-800-235-3329), 29 Highland Avenue, Greenfield 01301. Phoebe Compton's expansive, 16-room Georgian Revival house is set on more than 3 acres and offers seven exceptional guest rooms, all with private bath. Common rooms include a tastefully comfortable living room, the garden-view dining room, a game room with a full-sized pool table, a wicker-furnished porch and patio, and an upstairs sun room stocked with local menus, a microwave, and TV; there's also a clay tennis court. Rooms #9 and #1 both have working fireplaces, and all guest rooms are furnished with antiques and bright florals; the top floor harbors a two-room suite. $85–135 includes a full breakfast.

☞ **Northfield Country House** (498-2692; 1-800-498-2692), 181 School Street, Northfield 01360. The house was built in 1901 on 16 acres along "the ridge" above town as a summer mansion for a prominent Boston family, one among many who attended Dwight Moody's summer Northfield Conferences. Andrea Dale is a hospitable, helpful host. Her dining room is richly paneled and has a quartz-studded mantel to match that in the living room. The latter has a grand piano, an Estey (made in nearby Brattleboro, Vermont) organ, Oriental rugs, and inviting reading nooks. The seven upstairs rooms vary in size, but all are nicely furnished with comfortable antiques. Three have working fireplaces, but just two have private baths. The house is hedged in hydrangeas and set in landscaped grounds, complete with pool. Breakfast is a production. $50–80 per room. No children under 10, please.

Centennial House (498-5921), Northfield 01360. Built in 1811 and formerly the headmaster's house for Mount Hermon School, this handsome old home was designed and built by the town's premier builder, Calvin Stearns. There are six guest rooms, a gracious parlor and dining room, and, the best part, an expansive view of the river valley. The house sits right on Northfield's long, wide Main Street, which invites strolling. $60–70 including breakfast.

☞ **Sunnyside Farm** (665-3113), River Road, Whately 01093. Mary Lou and Dick Green welcome visitors to the big, yellow, turn-of-the-century farmhouse that's been in their family since it was built. It stands on 50 acres of farmland that grew tobacco and is now leased in part to the neighboring strawberry farm. All five rooms overlook fields. Two spacious front rooms with small TVs face River Road, and there's a small but appealing corner double and a back room with a king-sized bed; baths are shared. Guests have full access to the downstairs rooms, which include a comfortable living room and a dining room in which everyone gathers around a long table for breakfast. Don't miss the porch swing. $50–80.

Yellow Gabled House (665-4922), 307 North Main Street, South Deerfield 01373. Overlooking Bloody Brook (now tamed to a small stream) and the obelisk-shaped memorial to the 1675 massacre on the site, this Gothic Revival house is both snug and elegant, with three carefully furnished upstairs guest rooms, all with fans and air-conditioning, two front rooms (we like the one with the spool bed) sharing a bath, and a back room with a canopy bed and private bath. Host Edna Julia Stahelek is a cartographer and local historian. $75–105, including breakfast served in the elegant dining room.

Orchard Terrace (665-3829), 124 North Main Street, South Deerfield 01373. Host Phyllis Whitney describes the house in which she has raised her children as "gracious and comfortable," and it is. It's set back from the street up a shady drive, with twin porches on each end and a kidney-shaped swimming pool in the spacious yard. There's a formal living room and a family room with TV; upstairs one big room offers a private bath, working hearth, and color TV, and another with twin beds has a Jacuzzi as well as a working fireplace. Rooms run $90–125, and an efficiency suite in the Carriage House is $110–130 depending on the season; weekly rates available.

The Hitchcock House (774-7452), 15 Congress Street, Greenfield 01301. Betty and Peter Gott's Victorian-style house sits on a quiet residential street within walking distance of downtown Greenfield. The five second-floor guest rooms are all immaculate, two with private baths. Guests are welcome to try out the electric organ in the living room. Breakfast features freshly made fruit cocktail and homemade muffins. $60–85.

MOTELS

☞ **Fox Inn** (648-9101), MA 10, Bernardston 01337. An unusually attractive motel just off I-91 Exit 28, but with an out-in-the-country feel; rooms all overlook greenery. Request one with peaked ceilings. $54–64 double.

In Greenfield at the junction of I-91 and MA 2 you can also choose from a 100-room **Howard Johnson** (774-2211), a 60-unit **Super 8** (774-5578), and the 45-room **Candlelight Motor Inn** (772-0101).

CAMPGROUND

Barton Cove Nature and Camping Area (for reservations prior to the season phone 695-3714; otherwise 863-9300), MA 2, Gill. This is an unusual facility maintained by Northeast Utilities on a peninsula that juts into the Connecticut River. Wooded tent sites are available. $15–20 per night.

OTHER

Rebecca Tippens (624-5140), 68 Van Nuys Road, Colrain. Although Colrain is technically in the western Hilltowns, this end of town is so easily accessible from the valley that it belongs here: a spectacular round-house designed as a performance center. Becky Tippens is a professional storyteller who also orchestrates theatrical performances and gives movement classes. A dozen couples can be accommodated in built-in bunks up on the third floor, but baths are on the second floor. Inquire about workshops and rental of the entire space. The house is perched on a hillside with dramatic valley views and a good deal of fine detailing.

American Youth Hostel (498-3505 in-season; 498-5983 off-season) at Highland Avenue and Pine Street, Northfield 01360. Open only late June to late August. Named for Isabel and Monroe Smith, founders of AYH, who opened America's first hostel in Northfield in 1934 in "The Chateau," a stone mansion (since leveled). The current hostel offers 14 beds, both private and dorm-style rooms, in a Victorian house with a large yard, good for volleyball, croquet, and barbecues. Tennis courts, a pool, golf, and mountain biking are all nearby. $16 per person for non-members, $13 for members.

WHERE TO EAT

DINING OUT

Sienna (665-0215), 6 Elm Street, South Deerfield. Dinner Wednesday to Sunday, reservations a must. An unpretentious storefront is the setting for this chef-owned restaurant that's generally ranked among the best west of Boston. Jonathan Marohn's menu changes frequently and always features local produce. The five first-course choices ($6 and $7) might include chili relleno (fresh-roasted poblano chili filled with Vermont chevre and mushrooms, pan-fired in beer batter, fresh salsa) and seafood sausage (grilled salmon and shrimp sausage with basil, black beans, and grilled radicchio), and the seven main-course choices might range from spinach empenata with white cheese on a saffron vegetable broth ($15) to grilled BBQ duck breast served with a chili and bean strudel and apple-cranberry chutney ($19). There's a separate dessert menu.

Deerfield Inn (774-2359), The Street, Old Deerfield. Open daily for lunch, dinner nightly. This is a formal dining room with white tablecloths, Chippendale chairs, and a moderately expensive lunch menu. At dinner you might begin with house smoked salmon ($8) or wild mushroom hash ($7), then dine on breast of chicken wrapped in puff pastry filled with creamed spinach and goat cheese and served with roasted shallot demiglaze ($18), or on jumbo shrimp sautéed with fresh herbs and orzo pasta ($18). Wine is available by the glass (from $3.50), and the wine list itself is extensive. Inquire about late-afternoon carriage rides as part of the dinner package.

Steeplejacks (665-7980), Amherst Road, center of Sunderland. Open daily for lunch and dinner. An attractive, dependable place to dine on entrées like gingered Cornish game hen ($10.95).

Andiamo Ristorante (648-9107), Huckle Hill Road, Bernardston. Open for dinner. A glass-faced, hilltop building with the best views of any restaurant in the valley. Classic Italian dishes like chicken or veal Florentine, *alla romano,* parmigiana. Specialties include calamari in a spicy marinara sauce and *bistecca alla Pepe* (a 12-ounce New York cut, broiled or sautéed with peppercorns, brandy, and cream). Entrées from $9.95 for pasta to $17.95.

Bricker's (774-2857), MA 2/I-91 rotary, Greenfield. Open daily for lunch and dinner. This large restaurant has a number of attractive dining areas (bricks figure in the decor) and a large, moderately priced menu. A favorite place for business lunches, meetings, and wedding receptions. Entrées $8.95–16.95.

Turnbull's Sunny Farms (773-8203), MA 2/I-91 rotary, Greenfield. Open daily for lunch and dinner. Not a particularly fancy place, this restaurant is our family's favored waystop, good for quiche, sandwiches, or seafood and steaks, great salads; liquor served, moderately priced.

Whately Inn (665-3044; 1-800-WHATELY), Chestnut Plain Road, Whately Center. The dining room in this chef-owned, white clapboard, center-of-town inn is large and rather funky, but the food is reputedly good, service slow. Entrées are priced from $11.95 for broiled stuffed scrod to $19.95 for lamb dijonaise; roast crisp duckling bigarade ($15.95) is a favorite.

Falls River Inn (648-9904), Main Street, Bernardston. Open weekends for lunch, Wednesday through Sunday for dinner. This restaurant is in a classic, century-old, three-story inn; under its current ownership by Kathleen Kerber, the food is reputedly good, but it was closed when we stopped by. Let us know what you think.

EATING OUT

Green River Cafe (773-3312), 24 Federal Street, Greenfield. Open Tuesday through Friday for lunch, Saturday and Sunday brunch (9–2:30) and dinner (6:30–9). A worker-owned business, with organically produced vegetarian specialties, this is a lively gathering spot. The burgers are made of marinated tempeh, and the veggie pastas, burritos, and soups are tasty. Regulars tend to go with the daily specials.

Famous Bill's Restaurant (773-8331), 30 Federal Street, Greenfield. Open daily 11–11. This friendly, traditional restaurant sports a menu that's the antithesis of the Green River Cafe; liquor served. Lunch from $3.95, dinner from $6.95, a children's and senior's menu.

French King Restaurant (659-3328), handy to MA 2, Millers Falls. A family restaurant, open daily for lunch and dinner, breakfast in summer.

Fourleaf Clover Restaurant (648-9514), US 5, Bernardston. A solid family restaurant within minutes of I-91 Exit 28B.

Brad's Place (773-8460), 353 Main Street, Greenfield. Open 6 AM until midafternoon, closed Sunday. Fast, friendly, local eatery with booths in back.

☞ **Shady Glen Restaurant** (863-9636), 7 Avenue A, Turners Falls. Open Monday through Saturday 5 AM–9 PM, Sunday 5:30–11:45 AM. A real find: good home cooking, great pies and atmosphere, just off MA 2, a great waystop.

The Main Street Cafe, Main Street, Northfield. Open Tuesday through Sunday for breakfast and lunch, Tuesday night (when Rua's across the street closes) for dinner. The breads and muffins are all freshly baked in this storefront café; service is quick and friendly and most patrons along the counter and in the booths know each other. The one-person tables are an unusual, much-appreciated feature.

Rua's, Main Street, Northfield. Open 5:30 AM–8 PM except Tuesday, when closing time is 2 PM. This place serves as the center of town, where news is traded along a yellow Formica counter with eight stools; there's also a small, pine-paneled space with red vinyl booths. The soup of the day is $1.50, and a great chicken-salad sandwich on whole wheat is $1.95; coffee comes in solid mugs, and the service is warmly efficient.

Book Mill Cafe (367-0200), 440 Greenfield Road, Montague. Open Monday through Wednesday 10–6, Thursday through Saturday 10–8 in summer, otherwise 10–6. An attractive café in a vintage riverside gristmill with lunch specials like salad with roasted summer vegetables in balsamic vinaigrette, soups and sandwiches made to order, coffees, desserts, and Bart's Ice Cream. Also see *Entertainment* and *Selective Shopping.*

Greenfield Corner Cupboard (774-2990), Main Street, Greenfield. Owned by a former chef at a well-known New York restaurant, a popular local gathering spot known for good food.

Wolfie's (665-7068), 106 South Main Street, South Deerfield. Open 11 AM–10 PM, Monday through Saturday. An appealing little family restaurant in the middle of town, good for sandwiches like a Deerfield Reuben (sliced kielbasa loaf, sauerkraut, Swiss cheese, and mustard on rye) or a Wolfieburger. Dinner begins at $6.95 for barbecued ribs, and there are daily specials; full liquor license.

The Filling Station, US 5/MA 10 just off I-91 Exit 24. This is a classic chrome diner, open 24 hours, adjacent to a gas station/truck stop. The homemade meatloaf is $5.65.

Green Fields Market (773-9567), 144 Main Street, Greenfield. This natural-foods cooperative occupies a former JC Penney and includes a tempting deli and a "from scratch" bakery with attractive seating space near the windows.

Herm's Restaurant (772-6300), 91 Main Street, Greenfield. Open daily for lunch and dinner until 10:30. The decor is assorted memorabilia, advertising signs, and stained glass, and the menu is also a casual mix, of salads, sandwiches, pastas, and all-American entrées.

Howard Johnson's (774-2314), at the MA 2 rotary, Greenfield. Serving all three meals and known locally for good food; a lively sports bar.

SNACKS

The Coffee Club (774-3841), 286 Main Street, Greenfield. A good selection of coffees, teas, pastries; lunch tables.

ENTERTAINMENT

Book Mill Cafe (367-9206), corner of Greenfield and Depot Roads, Montague. Poetry readings, concerts, and other live entertainment are offered every weekend.

Arena Civic Theatre (773-9891) presents musicals and comedies, mid-June through August, in various Franklin County locations.

Shea Community Theater (863-2281), 71 Avenue A, Turners Falls. Call Tuesday through Friday between noon and 3. Inquire about performances by the resident community theater and visiting professional theater companies.

Old Deerfield Productions presents periodic summer performances; for details: 774-7476.

SELECTIVE SHOPPING

ANTIQUES
This is a particularly rich antiquing area. First, there are two active auction houses: **Douglas** (665-2877), US 5, Deerfield, Friday auctions; and **Ken Miller** (498-2749), Northfield, auctions on Monday night (6:30) in summer and fall, on Saturday (10–5) in the off-season, and also runs a flea market on Sunday, mid-April through October, 7–3.

Along US 5/MA 10 in Deerfield: **Antique Center of Old Deerfield** (773-3620). **Lighthouse Antiques,** specializing in New England items; **Yesterdays Antique Center** (665-7226), 27 dealers, displaying everything from books to major furniture pieces.

BOOKSTORES
World Eye Bookshop (772-2186), 60 Federal Street, Greenfield. A well-stocked book and gift store serving a wide upcountry area.

Montague Book Mill & Book Mill Cafe (367-9206), Greenfield and Depot Roads, Montague. Housed in an 1842 gristmill overlooking the Sawmill River, some 50,000 used and discount books are on two floors. Also see *Eating Out,* for the café, and *Entertainment.*

CRAFTS SHOPS
Note the **Old Deerfield Crafts Fairs** under *Special Events* in June and September: major showcases of work by local craftspeople and artists. You might also request a current copy of the "Regional Guide of Artists & Craftspeople" (see *Guidance.*)

Leverett Crafts and Arts (548-9070), Leverett Center. Take Bull Hill Road off MA 63 and follow signs to Leverett Center. A number of studios are housed in an 1875 box factory; the Barnes Gallery with changing exhibits of arts and crafts is usually open 1–5, but call ahead.

ArtSpace Gallery (772-6811), 7 Franklin Street, Greenfield. Open Wednesday through Friday noon–4, Saturday 10–4. Changing craft shows representing area artisans.

Joel McFadden Designs (772-1003), 24 Miles Street, Greenfield. A master goldsmith, McFadden is known for the settings he designs for brilliant stones. His attractive gallery is also the scene of changing exhibits for a variety of area craftspeople and artists.

Upcountry Massachusetts (665-3220), US 5/MA 10 in South Deerfield.

Open Wednesday through Saturday 10–5, Sunday noon–5. This deceptively small looking shop showcases a wide variety of locally crafted and produced quality items.

The Northfield Carriage House (498-2925), 158 Birnam Road, Northfield. John Nelson, working primarily in clay but also in other media, is the anchor artist in this studio, which is also home to three potters, a photographer, and other artisans. Call ahead.

Tom White Pottery (498-2175), 205 Winchester Road, Northfield. Sited at the corner of Pierson and Winchester Roads, this studio is a source of wheel-thrown, porcelain production work that's obviously been influenced by traditional Chinese forms and glazes. Call ahead.

Lunt Silversmiths (774-2774), 298 Federal Street, Greenfield. A major gallery featuring Lunt's own table and gift silver as well as products by its subsidiaries (which include Buckland-based Lamson and Goodnow), also demonstrations and products by local craftspeople, is due to open spring of 1996. A café is also planned. Long established in Greenfield, Lunt is one of just a half-dozen large-scale silversmiths in the United States.

FLOWERS

Blue Meadow Farm (367-2394), 184 Meadow Road, Montague Center. Open April 15 through June 15, daily 9–6, closed at 5 and on Tuesday in summer. This is one of New England's truly outstanding flower farms, featuring perennials, ornamental grasses, woody plants, annuals, and herbs. The display garden is itself worth a trip.

Baystate Perennial Farm (665-3525), US 5/MA 10, Whately. Open daily 9–6.

FARMS

Nourse Farm (665-2650), River Road, Whately. Billed as the state's largest strawberry farm. Pick-your-own strawberries mid-June to early July; farm stand by the river.

Greenwood Farm (498-5995), MA 63, Northfield, just north of Northfield Mountain. Antique varieties of apples, apple cider, apple butter, cider jelly, and syrup.

Little Creek Farm (367-9921), 66 Sunderland Road (MA 47), Montague. Fall farm stand; home-grown organic beef and hay sold.

Waldrich Farm (659-3497), Mineral Road, Millers Falls. Sweet corn is sold from August through mid-September.

Pekarski's Sausage (665-4537), MA 116, South Deerfield. Homemade Polish kielbasa, breakfast sausage, smoked ham and bacon.

The Deerfield Land Trust (628-4696) publishes a handy pamphlet map/ guide to 18 Deerfield farms, among them:

The Bars (773-5004), Mill Village Road, Deerfield, a family farm since 1820, open daily 9–6 selling sweet corn, peppers, blueberries, vegetables, freezer lamb, pick-your-own tomatoes. **Clarkdale Fruit Farm** (772-6797), Upper Road, West Deerfield. Open daily August 1 through April 1. Peaches, pears, plums, squash, pick-your-own apples, cider. **Fox**

The Antique Car Show is held in Old Deerfield each summer.

Hollow Farm (665-2663), 153 Conway Road, South Deerfield. Open daily mid-April to mid-June: bedding plants, vegetable plants, geraniums, hanging baskets. **Ripka's Farm** (665-4687), US 5/MA 10, Deerfield. Open daily, pick-your-own strawberries, farm stand.

SUGARHOUSES

Maple producers who welcome visitors include **River Maple Farm** in Bernardston (648-9676); **Williams Farm Sugar House**, US 5/MA 10 in Deerfield; **Brookledge Sugarhouse** (665-3837) and **Fairview Farms** (665-4361) in Whately; **River Maple Farm** (648-9767), 250 Brattleboro Road, Bernardston.

Ripley's Sugarhouse (367-2031), 195 Chestnut Hill Road, Montague. Gary and Cathy Billings produce and sell maple syrup, hard and soft sugar, available year-round, will ship.

OTHER SPECIAL STORES AND ENTERPRISES

The Museum Store, Historic Deerfield. The J.G. Pratt store is a trove of books, crafts, museum reproductions, gifts, and souvenirs. Open museum hours.

Wilson's, 258 Main Street, Greenfield. The town's long-established, dependable department store with four floors of general merchandise, clothing, housewares, jewelry, books, cards, and gifts.

Thomas & Thomas Rod Makers, Inc. (863-9727), 2 Avenue A, Turners Falls. Fine fly rods are made and sold; visitors welcome.

Berkshire Brewing Co., Inc. (665-6600), 12 Railroad Street, South

Deerfield. Chris Lalli and Gary Bogoff produce a variety of tasty brews, notably Steel Rail Extra Pale Ale; tours and tastings are offered Saturday at 1 PM, but call ahead.

SPECIAL EVENTS

June (last weekend): **Old Deerfield Summer Crafts Fair** at Memorial Hall; more than 250 exhibitors.

July: **Old Fashioned Independence Day** in Old Deerfield. **Upcountry Balloon Festival,** a mid-July spectacle, sponsored by the Franklin County Chamber of Commerce, at Greenfield Community College.

September: **Franklin County Fair**—always the Friday through Monday following Labor Day, Greenfield. **Old Deerfield Autumn Crafts Fair** on the last weekend in September on the lawn of Memorial Hall Museum; more than 250 exhibitors.

October: **Greenfield Fall Festival,** Main Street, Columbus Day weekend—craftspeople, music, children's entertainment, sidewalk sales.

FIVE-COLLEGE AREA

The five colleges of Amherst, Smith, Mount Holyoke, Hampshire, and the University of Massachusetts at Amherst together enroll some 30,000 students on campuses within an 11-mile radius of each other. In cities, such academic concentrations are less noticeable. Here, against a backdrop of cornfields, apple orchards, and small towns, the visible and cultural impact of academia has been dramatic, especially since the '70s. Between 1961 and 1972, the UMass enrollment tripled, and five 22-story dormitories plus one of the world's tallest libraries appeared above surrounding fields. Innovative Hampshire College opened in an Amherst apple orchard, and the Five-College Consortium evolved from a concept into a reality.

Free buses now circulate constantly (residents and visitors welcome) among the campuses. Five thousand students annually take courses at the other institutions, and all share a lively calendar of plays, concerts, and lectures. Increasingly, too, graduates have opted to stay on in the valley, establishing the crafts and arts studios, restaurants, and coffeehouses for which the area is now known.

With more than two-thirds of the area's students, you would assume the town of Amherst would be a local hot spot. Not so. Amherst retains an appealing but small-town look and feel. The outsized Common, framed by the Amherst College campus and 19th-century shopfronts, remains its centerpiece, connected to the UMass campus (curiously invisible, despite the high-rises, unless you go looking for it) by one long street of shops and restaurants that offers plenty of good

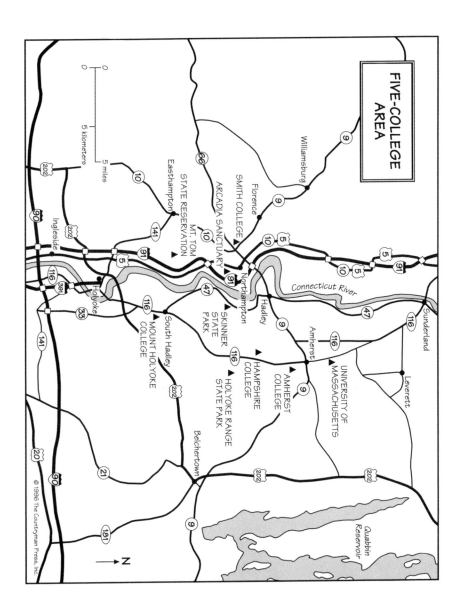

eating, shopping, and book browsing but remains low-key.

Downtown Northampton is, on the other hand, the Harvard Square of western Massachusetts. Less pressured by high rents than urban and resort areas, it offers a better range of quality, independently owned galleries, shops, bookstores, coffeehouses, and restaurants than in any four blocks in New England. Northampton is, besides, an architecturally interesting old county seat, with an outstanding art museum (at Smith College), the country's oldest and most ornate municipal theater, a presidential library (within the public library), and an elaborate little four-story Museum of Words & Pictures founded by a creator of the Teenage Mutant Ninja Turtles.

Mount Holyoke in South Hadley is the country's oldest women's college and arguably has the most beautiful of the five campuses, an 800-acre spread designed by the firm of Frederick Law Olmsted with two lakes and majestic trees.

The fact that each of the five "colleges" is so different adds, of course, to the beauty of their mix—a phenomenon best experienced during the academic year. Summer is, however, increasingly interesting in the valley. Entertainment options include theater at Mount Holyoke College, concerts at the Summit House atop Mount Holyoke and in the garden at Forty Acres, and Jazz in July at UMass. Hiking trails run along the ridge of the Holyoke Range and through many miles of conservation land, a bike trail follows the old railbed between Northampton and Amherst, and canoes can be rented to paddle down the Connecticut River.

We include the small brick mill city of Holyoke in the Five-College area because it's physically—improbably—here, designed from scratch by Boston developers in the 1840s, a foil to the nearby ivy-covered communities. Industrial-architecture buffs will be intrigued by canalside mill buildings, and shoppers, by genuine galleries and outlets. Families will appreciate the attractions conveniently grouped around the Holyoke Heritage State Park: the children's Museum, a working antique merry-go-round, and an excursion train. Mount Tom, furthermore, offers great views, a wave pool, and water slides.

Thanks to the excellent bus service, both to NYC and Boston and among the campuses, the Five-College area is accessible without a car, and, thanks to the recent proliferation of bed & breakfasts, especially in and around Amherst, it's a genuinely appealing destination.

AREA CODE
413

GUIDANCE

Amherst Area Chamber of Commerce (253-0700), 11 Spring Street (side entrance of the Lord Jeffery Inn), Amherst. Monday through Friday 9–3:30. Information booth on the Common open May through mid-October.

Greater Northampton Chamber of Commerce (584-1900), 62 State Street, Northampton. A seasonal information booth is maintained in a brick box of a building across from the Hotel Northampton (US 5 North), Memorial Day through Labor Day, Thursday through Sunday 9–5.
Holyoke Heritage State Park (534-1723), 221 Appleton Street, Holyoke. Open Tuesday through Sunday noon–4:30. 1-800-884-0053 (9–5).
Holyoke Chamber of Commerce (534-3376), 177 High Street, Holyoke. Open weekdays 9–5.

GETTING THERE
By air: Bradley International Airport; see "Springfield."
By bus: **Peter Pan–Trailways** (1-800-343-9999) connects Amherst, South Hadley, and Holyoke with Boston, Springfield, Bradley, and points beyond. The local departure points are: in Amherst, 79 South Pleasant Street (256-0431); in Northampton; 1 Round House Plaza (586-1030).
By train: AMTRAK (1-800-872-7245). Local shuttlebus service connects with AMTRAK in Springfield; car rentals are available at the train station as well as at the airport.

GETTING AROUND
The Pioneer Valley Transit Authority, or PVTA (586-5806), connecting Northampton, Amherst, and South Hadley, is free and frequent, circling among the five campuses from 6:45 AM until 11:35 PM weekdays during the academic year, less frequently on weekends and in summer.

PARKING
In Northampton: The big parking garage ($.25 an hour) is on South Street behind Thornes Market; parking lots are scattered through town with major areas just south of Main Street, accessible from Pleasant Street and from Hampton Avenue.
In Amherst: In addition to metered street parking there are four downtown lots. The Boltwood lot (access from Main Street) is the handiest, with access to North Pleasant Street shops. Behind the CVS on North Pleasant Street is another lot, and there are also small lots on Spring Street (adjacent to the Common) and Amity Street (across from the Jones Library).
In Holyoke: The downtown parking garage is on Dwight Street, one block from the Heritage State Park.

MEDICAL EMERGENCY
The Cooley Dickinson Hospital (582-2000), 30 Locust Street (MA 9), Northampton. **Holyoke Hospital** (534-2500), 575 Beech Street, Holyoke.

TO SEE

THE COLLEGES AND THEIR MUSEUMS
Amherst College (542-2000), Amherst 01002. Founded in 1821 to educate "promising but needy youths who wished to enter the ministry,"

Amherst is today one of the country's most selective colleges. It enrolls some 1500 men and women, offers a B.A. and, in cooperation with the four other colleges, a Ph.D. The campus is handsome and nicely sited, its oldest buildings grouped around a Common overlooking the valley to the south and the Holyoke Range beyond. Amherst maintains two museums on campus:

Mead Art Museum (542-2335), September through May, Monday through Friday 10–4:30, Saturday and Sunday 1–5; June through August, Tuesday through Sunday 1–4. The building was designed by McKim, Mead, and White, and although exhibits change there is always the Rotherwas Room, an ornately paneled, vintage-1611 English hall. The college's 9000-piece collection includes paintings by Thomas Eakins, Winslow Homer, Marsden Hartley, and Childe Hassam.

✐ **The Pratt Museum of Natural History** (542-2165), September through May, weekdays 9–3:30, Saturday 10–4, Sunday noon–5; summer; Saturday 10–4, Sunday noon–5. This is a terrific, very old-fashioned museum with displays ranging from local "track ways" (dinosaur tracks) to the skeleton of a woolly mammoth, the skeletal legs of an 87-foot-long *diplodorus*, and an 800,000-year-old human skull.

Hampshire College (549-4600), 893 West Street (MA 116), Amherst 01002. Opened in 1970, this liberal arts college is predicated on cooperative programming with the other four colleges. Its 1200 students design their own programs of study. Inquire about current exhibits at the three campus galleries and events at the Performing Arts Center.

Mount Holyoke College (538-2000), South Hadley (MA 116) 01075. Founded in 1837, Mount Holyoke is the country's oldest women's college. The 800-acre campus features two lakes and outstanding plantings (it was designed by the firm of Frederick Law Olmsted) and ivied buildings in a number of Revival styles, home to some 1800 women from throughout the world. The adjacent Village Commons, a complex of restaurants, shops, and a theater, was designed by Graham Gund. In summer a tent houses the Mount Holyoke Summer Theater, good for both adult and children's productions. The Musicorda music festival attracts internationally known musicians who offer free summer concerts. Mount Holyoke offers three interesting sights to visitors:

Mount Holyoke College Art Museum (538-2245). Open Tuesday through Friday 11–5, Saturday 1–5. One of the oldest collegiate art collections in the country but housed in a modern building. Permanent holdings range from ancient Asian and Egyptian works to some outstanding 19th-century landscapes; changing exhibits.

✐ **The Talcott Arboretum** (538-2116). Open weekdays 9–4, weekends 1–4. This is an exquisite little Victorian-style greenhouse filled with a jungle of exotic flora, special late winter and spring flower shows.

✐ **Skinner Museum** (538-2085), MA 116. Open May through October, Wednesday and Sunday 2–5. Housed in the 1846 church that once stood in the town of Prescott (flooded by Quabbin Reservoir), this holds a trove of 4000 items ranging from Native American artifacts to medieval sets of armor.

Smith College (584-2700), Northampton 01062. Founded in 1875 for "the education of the intelligent gentlewoman," Smith currently enrolls some 2800 women. The 125-acre campus includes 97 buildings, an eclectic mix of ages and styles. Don't miss Paradise Pond. Two places are worth seeking out at Smith:

Smith College Museum of Art (585-2760), Elm Street (MA 9, just beyond College Hall). Open July and August, Tuesday through Sunday noon–4, Thursday until 8; September through June, Tuesday, Friday, and Saturday 9:30–4, Wednesday and Sunday noon–4, Thursday noon–8. This is the standout collection of art in the entire valley, housed in an unobtrusive but spacious three-story museum. Usually on view are works by Picasso, Degas, Winslow Homer, Seurat, and Whistler, sculpture by Rodin and Leonard Baskin. We've returned time and again to see Rockwell Kent's *Dublin Pont*, Marsden Hartley's *Sea Window*, and two starkly realistic oils by Edwin Romanzo Elmer evoking 19th-century scenes from the nearby Hilltowns.

Lyman Plant House (585-2740). Open daily 8–4:15. Known for its spring and fall flower shows; adjacent arboretum and gardens.

University of Massachusetts (545-0111), Amherst 01003. Founded in the mid-19th century as the state's agricultural college, the university doubled its size and suddenly skyrocketed both physically and academically in the 1960s and '70s. It now includes nine undergraduate schools and colleges, also graduate schools, in more than 150 buildings on a 1200-acre campus. Some 5500 courses are offered by 1300 faculty members to 23,000 students. Sights to see at UMass include:

Fine Arts Center and Gallery (545-3670). Changing exhibits.

William Smith Clark Memorial. A half-acre memorial at the eastern entrance to the campus (off North Pleasant Street) dedicated to the first president of the university and his work in Japan, where he founded Sopporo Agricultural College, now the University of Hokkaido. The unusual memorial encompasses two circles linked by a spiral walk and twin steel walls depicting Clark's Amherst home and the Agricultural Hall at Hokkaido. Clark is widely revered in Japan, and many youth clubs are still dedicated to his memory. The memorial garden is sited on a hill with views extending across the campus to the river and hills.

Durfee Gardens and Durfee Conservatory. The conservatory (545-5234; open weekdays 8:30–4:30) dates from 1867 and houses tropical plants like banana, coffee, and papayas divided by a 40-foot pool with an ornamental bridge and fountain. Five interlocking garden spaces offer benches, paths, and trellised wisteria and morning glories.

MUSEUMS AND HISTORIC HOUSES

Emily Dickinson Homestead (542-8161), 280 Main Street, Amherst.

GABRIEL A. COONEY

Mount Holyoke College Campus

Open only by appointment May through October, Wednesday through Saturday 1:30–3:45; also spring and late fall Wednesday and Saturday (same tour times). Closed December 15 through February. $3 admission. Emily Dickinson was born here, and her second-floor bedroom has been restored to look the same as during the years (1855–86) when she wrote her finest verse. The only objects known to have belonged to her, however, are the sleigh bed, a hat box, and the white dress she wore after her father's death in 1874. The garden Dickinson tended remains a pleasant place to sit, and a path still leads next door to her brother Austin's house, The Evergreens, an ornate period piece that, through a curious sequence of events, still retains its 1870s decor and feel; hopefully it will one day soon be open to the public. More than 5000 visitors each year come to Amherst looking for a sense of the poet behind the pithy, ragged-edged lines like:

> *"Hope" is the thing with feathers,*
> *That perches in the soul,*
> *And sings the tune without the words*
> *And never stops—at all.*

Unfortunately her presence in Amherst today is as elusive as it was when she lived there as a recluse. The best display on her life and work is at the **Jones Library** (256-4090), 43 Amity Street; open Monday, Wednesday, Friday, and Saturday 9–5:30, Tuesday and Thursday 9–9:30, closed Sunday. A recent wing includes a handsome research facility with seven panels depicting Dickinson's life (1830–86) in Amherst and original handwritten poems; the collection here includes 8000 items. Also inquire about the **Robert Frost** collection (Frost lived in Amherst from 1931 to 1938 and returned in the '40s to teach at Amherst College).

In **West Cemetery** on Triangle Street, walk or drive through the gate and bear left on the path. Look for an ornate black iron fence near the center rear of the cemetery. It marks the Dickinson plot in which Emily lies surrounded by her grandparents, parents, and sister Lavinia. Note that on the Saturday nearest May 15 (the anniversary of her death) visitors are invited to meet at the Homestead and walk to the cemetery. Inquire about periodic workshops held to coincide with this event.

The Amherst History Museum at the Strong House (256-0678), 67 Amity Street. Mid-May to mid-October, Wednesday through Saturday 12:30–3:30; otherwise Thursday 12:30–3:30 or by appointment; inquire about crafts workshops, talks, special events. $2 adults, $1 children, students, and seniors. This 1750s, gambrel-roofed house features decorative arts, clothing, textiles, fine art, period rooms, and changing exhibits from the late 18th to early 20th centuries. The 18th-century garden is maintained by the Amherst Garden Club.

Porter-Phelps-Huntington Historic House Museum (584-4699), 130 River Drive, Hadley (MA 47, two miles north of the junction of MA 9 and MA 47). Open May 15 through October 15, Saturday through Wednesday 1–4:30. Wednesday Folk Traditions (ethnic folk music) at 7 PM in June and July. A Perfect Spot of Tea, Saturday in July and August (pastries and music at 2:30 and 3:30); also a Fall Foliage Festival (crafts, a barn dance, storytelling, children's games) on a mid-October weekend. Also known as Forty Acres, this aristocratic old farm was built right on the banks of the Connecticut River in 1752, and there have been no structural changes since 1799. The furnishings have accumulated over six generations of one extended family.

Mourning Picture (1890), *by Edwin Romanzo Elmer, is set in Ashfield; the painting can be found in the Smith College Museum of Art.*

The Farm Museum, MA 9 and MA 47, Hadley. Open May through October 12, 10–4:30, Sunday 1:30–4:30, closed Monday; free. The 1782 barn from Forty Acres was moved in 1930 to its present site near the First Congregational Church and white-pillared Town Hall. It houses old broom-making machines (broom corn was once the town's chief crop), hay tedders and other old farm implements, pottery, an old stagecoach from Hardwick, and other assorted mementos of life in the valley.
Historic Northampton (584-6011), 46–66 Bridge Street (MA 9), Northampton. Open for tours March through December, Wednesday and Sunday noon–4. The Parsons House (1730), the Damon House (home of architect Isaac Damon), and the Shepherd House (a mid-19th-century home), reflect lifestyles over three generations. $2 admission.
Coolidge Memorial Room in the Forbes Library (584-8399), 20 West Street, Northampton. Open Monday through Wednesday 1–5 and by appointment. The only presidential library in a public library, this room contains all of Calvin Coolidge's papers from his years as governor, vice president, and president. The Amherst College graduate (1895) studied law and first hung out his shingle in Northampton. He became city solicitor, met his wife (Grace Goodhue was teaching at the Clarke School for the Deaf in Northampton when she met fellow-Vermonter Cal), was elected a state representative, then mayor of Northampton

DAVID STANSBURY PHOTOGRAPHY

(two terms). He became state senator, then governor, then vice president, and, when Harding died suddenly (August 3, 1923), president (for 6 years). The Coolidges returned to Northampton, dying here in 1933. Personal belongings on display include an electric horse.

Wistariahurst Museum (534-2216), 238 Cabot Street, Holyoke. Open Wednesday, Saturday, Sunday 1–5. A late-19th-century, 26-room mansion built for the Skinner family (owners of the world's largest silk mill). Period rooms feature turn-of-the-century furnishings and decorative arts; also changing exhibits in two galleries.

FOR FAMILIES

Holyoke Heritage State Park (534-1723), 221 Appleton Street (follow the signs for downtown), Holyoke. Open Tuesday through Sunday noon–4:30. Its design suggests a 19th-century roundhouse, and the brick visitors center adjoins tracks on which rail excursions run in summer. Inside exhibits tell a remarkable story: In 1847 Boston investors formed the Hadley Falls Company, buying 1000 acres with the idea of utilizing the water power from the magnificent falls here. The company, and its dam, went bust but was soon replaced by the Holyoke Water Power Company, until recently the city's major political and economic force. You learn that Holyoke is a classic, planned mill city. Its 4½ miles of canals rise in tiers past dozens of mills. The commercial area is set in a neat grid above the mills. Housing changes with the altitude—from 1840s brick workers' housing on "The Flats" near the river, through hundreds of hastily built, late-19th- and early-20th-century tenements, to the mill owners' mansions above, and above that the parkland on Mount Tom. A short film conveys a sense of the city's late-19th-century vitality, of the era in which immigrants turned neighborhoods into "Little" Ireland, Poland, France, and a half dozen more bastions. If the film were remade today it would note the last two decades' influx of Puerto Ricans, a group first drawn in the 60s to work in the nearby tobacco fields. Specialty papers, from college bluebooks to hospital johnnies, remain Holyoke's most notable product. Inquire about guided and leaflet walking tours and frequent special events. Mill architecture buffs will appreciate the beauty of the canalside Graham Mill (Second Level Canal near the MA 116 bridge), and will locate both outlets (see *Selective Shopping*) and artists studios and galleries (inquire at the park for open hours) in many of the mills.

The Holyoke Heritage Park Railroad (534-1723) departs weekends, June through October, from the Heritage State Park on 20-mile round-trip excursions to Westfield, stopping at the Holyoke Mall at Ingleside. The antique cars are from the Holyoke & Westfield Railroad, which ceased operation in 1982. Phone for hours and inquire about shorter excursions, murder mysteries, and other special events.

Merry-Go-Round (538-9838), next to the Holyoke Heritage State Park Visitors Center. September through May, weekends noon–4; June through Labor Day, Tuesday through Sunday 11–5. $1 per ride. This vintage-1929 carousel with 48 hand-carved steeds, two chariots, and 800 lights was built for Mountain Park, an old-fashioned amusement park that closed in 1987. It was restored and moved to this handsome pavilion at a total cost of $2 million. Also available for private parties.

Children's Museum (536-KIDS), 444 Dwight Street (across from the Heritage State Park Visitors Center), Holyoke. Open Monday through Friday 9:30–4:30, Sunday noon–5. $3.50 per person. A stimulating space with a Main Street that simulates downtown Holyoke's shops and enterprises (the favorite is a working TV station). There is also usually a large, dramatic exhibit in a lower-level museum (additional admission), a gift store, and a café.

Volleyball Hall of Fame (536-0926). Housed in the Children's Museum complex. Open Tuesday through Friday 10–5, Saturday noon–5. Invented in Holyoke in 1895, volleyball is commemorated in a series of interpretive panels.

Words & Pictures Museum (586-8545), 140 Main Street, Northampton. Open Tuesday through Sunday noon–5. $3 adults, $2 students and seniors, $1 under 18. Founded by the Teenage Mutant Ninja Turtles cocreator Kevin Eastman, this nonprofit museum has transformed a former Main Street commercial building into a four-story happening— with changing exhibits and a permanent collection in a classic museum on the top floor. You enter through a cave (note the cave paintings) and beam up through the age of hieroglyphics and ancient Chinese illustrations into the world of superheroes. Exhibits change frequently, but cartoons are always featured and would-be cartoonists can always test their skill in a number of satisfying hands-on ways.

SummerSide at Mount Tom (536-0416), US 5, Holyoke. Open 10–8 beginning weekends Memorial Day; daily in July and August. $15.95 admission. This ski area has replaced its Alpine Slide with Alpine Falls (two tube rides), a huge wave pool, and a water slide. Slopeside café.

Robert E. Barrett Fishway (536-9428), Holyoke Dam, Holyoke. Just off MA 116 at the South Hadley Falls Bridge. Open in mid-June, Wednesday through Sunday 9–5. Viewing windows and an observation platform overlook American shad and Atlantic salmon as elevators help them bypass the falls on their trip upriver to spawn.

Dinosaur Footprints Reservation, Smith's Ferry on US 5, 1 mile south of Mount Tom, Holyoke. Look for a small, unmarked turnout on the river side of the road. An 8-acre stretch of three-toed tracks, each 15 inches long and belonging to a 20-foot-long dinosaur (*Eubrontes giganteus)* who lumbered by 200 million years ago, is visible. Smaller tracks and other fossils have also been preserved.

McCray Farm (533-3714), 55 Alvord Street, South Hadley. Open daily, year-round, with a dairy bar open spring through fall. A petting zoo, wagon and sleigh rides depending on the season, maple breakfasts in March, and pick-your-own pumpkins.

TO DO

BICYCLING

Rentals are available from **Peloton Sports** (584-1016), 15 State Street in Northampton, and at **Valley Bicycles** (256-0880), 319 Main Street, Amherst.

The Norwottuck Rail Trail, an 8.5-mile bike path, links Northampton, Hadley, and Amherst along the former Boston & Maine Railroad right-of-way. Parking is available at Elwell State Park on Damon Road in Northampton, at Mountain Farms Mall on MA 9 in Hadley, and at Station Road in South Amherst. The path crosses the Connecticut on an old rail bridge and passes through open farmland, with views to the Holyoke Range on the south and to Mount Toby and Mount Sugarloaf on the north.

BOATING

Wildwater Outfitters (586-2323), MA 9, Hadley, rents canoes and kayaks.

Elwell State Park, a former junkyard just north of MA 9 at the Northampton end of the Coolidge Bridge, is now a state-of-the-art boat dock, handicapped accessible.

Arcadia Nature Center and Wildlife Sanctuary (584-3009), marked from US 5, Easthampton, but on the Northampton-Easthampton line in Northampton, is a great place for novice canoeists to explore quiet waters. Inquire about guided canoe trips.

River information: For a copy of the brochure "A Connecticut River Water Trail," detailing information about canoeing the Connecticut, send a self-addressed, stamped envelope to the **Mass. Dept. of Environmental Management,** 136 Damon Road, Northampton 01060; to inquire about guided river trips, phone 586-8706. **The Connecticut River Watershed Council** (529-9500), One Ferry Street, Easthampton, publishes a canoe guide to the entire river and offers periodic guided canoe trips.

Sportsman's Marina (586-2426), MA 9 at the Coolidge Bridge, Hadley, rents boats April through October (weather permitting): canoes, aluminum outboards, and pontoon boats. Bring a picnic and head for an island. **Brunelle's Marina** (536-3132) in South Hadley has a restaurant and launch area. There is also a state access ramp almost 1½ miles north of Hatfield Center, and another is off US 5 at the Oxbow in Easthampton. The 16-mile stretch of the Connecticut River above the Holyoke Dam is heavily used on summer weekends by water-skiers, fishermen, and powerboat owners as well as canoeists.

FISHING

Red-Wing Meadow Trout Hatchery (367-9494), 528 Federal Street, Montague. Open for fee fishing April through November. $2 adults, $5 for a family, $4.25 per pound for fish you catch. Pole rentals available. Picnic tables are scattered around the ponds.

GOLF

Hickory Ridge Country Club (256-6638), West Pomeroy Lane, Amherst, is an 18-hole championship course with a clubhouse and snack bar; **Cherry Hill** (253-9935), Montague Road, Amherst, is a public nine-hole course in North Amherst. Also check out **Pine Grove Golf Club** (584-4570), and Wilson Road, Northampton; **Holyoke Country Club** (534-1933), 18 holes, clubhouse.

✐ **Western Massachusetts Family Golf Center Practice Range and Miniature Golf** (586-2311), MA 9 in Hadley.

HIKING

In addition to the trails described under *Green Space*, the long-distance Metacomet-Monadnock Trail traverses the ridge of the Mount Holyoke Range, continuing north through Warwick to Mount Monadnock in New Hampshire and south to Mount Tom and on into Connecticut (the logistics of getting across the Connecticut and I-91 are a bit fuzzy).

HOT TUBS

East Heaven Hot Tub Company (586-6843), 33 West Street, Northamption, offers rooftop hot tubs. Open daily.

SWIMMING

In Amherst the unofficial swimming hole is **Factory Hollow Pond** (better known as **Puffer's Pond**); also check **West Memorial Pool** in the Upper Mill River Conservation area, and **Lake Wyola** in nearby Shutesbury.

CROSS-COUNTRY SKIING

See Mount Tom and the Holyoke Range under *Green Space*.

DOWNHILL SKIING

Mount Tom (536-0416), US 5, Holyoke. This is a teaching and, frankly, locally geared mountain with Christmas and February vacation ski camps for area youngsters.

Vertical drop: 680 feet.

Terrain: 15 trails.

Lifts: Four chairs, one J-bar.

Night skiing: Nightly.

Snowmaking: 100 percent.

Facilities: Base lodge, ski shop, large ski school.

Rates: $29 adult weekend, $25 junior, less midweek; half-day tickets also available.

ICE SKATING

Mullins Center, UMass campus (545-0505). Olympic-sized skating rink open to the public; rentals; call for hours.

GREEN SPACE

The Holyoke Range State Park (253-2883), MA 116, Amherst. Visitors center open daily 9–4 except Tuesday and Wednesday in winter. This dramatic east-west range rises abruptly from the valley floor. It is the most striking feature of the area, visible everywhere from Belchertown to Northampton. Mount Holyoke at its western tip (see Skinner State Park) is the only summit accessible by road, but a trail traverses the entire 9-mile-long ridgeline. From the visitors center at "the Notch" on MA 116, a trail leads east to Mount Norwottuck (connecting with trails to Mount Toby in Sunderland and Mount Monadnock in New Hampshire). Ask about the Horse Caves below Mount Norwottuck in which Daniel Shays and his men supposedly sheltered after raiding the Springfield Armory (the caves are actually so shallow that two Boy Scouts and a pony would have trouble fitting in).

Skinner State Park (586-0350), MA 47, Hadley. Summit Road open mid-April to mid-November, Summit House open mid-May to mid-October. "The Paradise of America" is the way Swedish singer Jenny Lind described the view from the top of Mount Holyoke in 1850—the same view of the Connecticut River oxbow, surrounding towns, and distant hills that Thomas Cole popularized in his 1836 painting. One of the first mountaintop inns to be built in New England (the first inn opened in 1821) and the only one preserved in any shape today, the **Summit House** (also known as Prospect House) is accessible by an auto road and hiking trails. In 1938 Joseph Skinner donated the Summit House and the surrounding 390 acres to the state. It's the setting for sunset concerts in summer.

The Amherst Conservation Commission (Amherst Town Hall, 256-4045) maintains some 1450 acres scattered in 45 distinct holdings, with 60 miles of trails for walking, birding, ski-touring. It's worth stopping by the town hall or local bookstores to pick up printed maps or guides. The most popular (and most heavily used) areas include: **Upper Mill River and Puffer's Pond,** State Street off Pine, good for swimming and picnicking. Trails, including one designed for handicapped access and blind walkers, lead upstream from the pond along the Cushman Brook's cascades.

Hitchcock Center for the Environment (256-6006) at the **Larch Hill Conservation Area,** 1 mile south of Amherst center on MA 116. The 25 acres include hiking trails, formal gardens, and ponds. The center offers a variety of lectures and workshops; it also exhibits local artwork.

Mount Pollux, off South East Street, is a favorite spot from which to watch the sunset, a gentle slope to climb through old apple orchards to a summit with a 365-degree view. **Amethyst Brook,** Pelham Road, is a great spot to walk or ski through woods and fields; the **Robert Frost Trail** continues 33 miles north to Mount Toby and Cranberry Pond.

Arcadia Wildlife Sanctuary (584-3009). Grounds open dawn to dusk except Monday (unless a holiday); the office is staffed 9–3 Tuesday through Friday, 1–4 on Saturday. Accessible from Northampton (take Lovefield to Clapp Street) and MA 10 (off US 5) in Easthampton. This

Massachusetts Audubon Sanctuary owns more than 500 acres of field, woodland, and marsh on the Connecticut River Oxbow. Walk out the Cedar Trail and along the Mill River to look out over the Arcadia Marsh from the observation tower. Duckling Trail is a short loop for children. The Conservation Center offers a full program of guided walks, canoe trips, and campouts.

Northampton Conservation Areas include **Robert's Hill** in Florence, overlooking the Lower Leeds reservoir; **Fitzgerald Lake** in Florence; **Childs Park,** 30 acres off Elm and Prospect Streets; and **Look Memorial Park** (584-5457), MA 9 in Florence. The latter includes 150 acres with picnicking, swimming and wading pools, pedal boating and canoeing on Willow Lake, a playground, a small zoo with native deer, peacocks, pheasants, and raccoons, the Pines Outdoor Theater (summer concerts and theater), the Picnic Store, and a miniature replica of an 1863 train that circles the zoo. Open Memorial Day through Labor Day.

Mount Tom State Reservation (527-4805), Holyoke. Access from US 5 or from MA 141, Easthampton. This 1800-acre mountaintop woodland contains 30 miles of trails, picnic tables, a lookout tower, and the Robert Cole Museum (open May 30 through Labor Day) with nature exhibits. Goat Peak has a spectacular view across the valley. In winter the road isn't plowed, but you can ski or snowshoe in. Lake Bray offers fishing in summer.

LODGING

HOTEL AND INNS

Hotel Northampton (584-3100), 36 King Street, Northampton 01060. Built in 1927, this is a proud, redbrick, 76-room, five-story downtown hotel, handy to all the town's shops and restaurants. The lobby has a hearth, wing chairs, and a soaring ceiling. The glass-fronted Coolidge Park Café serves light lunches and dinners, and Wiggins Tavern Restaurant (see *Dining Out*) is a valley landmark. The one suite (#500) we've seen is a beauty, complete with Jacuzzi and a view of Mount Holyoke, but most of the standard rooms, though furnished nicely with reproduction antiques, wicker, and duvets, are small. Rates include continental breakfast, parking, and use of the exercise room. $93–175 per couple; packages available.

Lord Jeffery Inn (253-2576), 30 Boltwood Avenue, Amherst 01002. Built in 1926 by the same architect who designed the matching Colonial Revival Jones Library across the Common. College owned and obviously college geared, this is more of a small hotel than an inn. All 50 rooms have private bath, phone, and cable TV, and 12 have (theoretically at least) a working fireplace; a number also have balconies overlooking the garden. All rooms have been recently refurbished but look much as we remember them 30 years ago. Dining options include the informal

Holyoke Heritage State Park

Boltwood Tavern and the more formal main dining room (see *Dining Out*). You can picture Robert Frost sitting in the big old parlor with its huge hearth and worn books or rocking on the porch. $68 (for an economy double, low season) to $138 for a large suite in high season; standard doubles are $78–88.

Yankee Pedlar (532-9494), 1866 Northampton Street (US 5, handy to I-91), Holyoke. An 1870 Victorian mansion that's been a popular restaurant (see *Dining Out*) and inn since the 1940s. Most of the 40 guest rooms are in neighboring clapboard annexes; all have private bath and are furnished in a mix of antiques and reproductions. By far the most attractive are the suites with French doors separating the bedrooms from sitting areas. Continental breakfast is included in $55–70 for standard rooms, $75–95 for suites and efficiencies.

BED & BREAKFASTS

Allen House Inn (253-5000), 599 Main Street, Amherst 01002. Peacock feathers in chinoiserie vases, ornate Victorian-era wallpaper on ceilings as well as walls, and antimacassars on intricately carved Eastlake chairs don't usually turn us on, but the Allen House does. This 1880s, stick-style Queen Anne home is a genuine period piece that's never really been on the market. The rush matting is as original to the house as the Eastlake fireplace mantels. Each of the five bedrooms (all with private baths) is papered in hand-silkscreened copies of William Morris, Walter Crane, and Charles Eastlake, and all are furnished with appropriate antique beds and dressers bought locally; they range in size from the back "scullery" to a large front room with three beds. Alan Zieminski first became intrigued with the house while lodging here as a student and secured first option when it came up for sale. Ann Zieminski is a warm hostess and known for spectacular breakfasts like Swedish pancakes, stuffed French toast, homemade fruit sauces, quiche, and fruit compotes. They're served at the dining room table, but all guests need not gather at the same time. $45–95.

Hannah Dudley House (367-2323), 114 Dudleyville Road, Leverett 01054. Built handsomely in 1797 on a rise surrounded by fields and woods, the house offers four guest rooms, two with working fireplaces. Our favorite is the lemon-colored "Dragon's Lair" ($143), and the Kitty Korner suite ($184) is ideal for a couple with a youngster in tow. Windows are tall, sunny, and uncurtained. Furniture is comfortable rather than antique. Breakfast, served at 8:30 in the square little dining room, includes homemade granola, muffins, pastries, and fresh fruit. Facilities include a guest fridge in the game room, an in-ground pool, landscaped grounds with two ponds, and hiking trails through the woods. Lake Wyola and Rattlesnake Ravine are also nearby. The house is 12 miles north of Amherst. $119–184.

Black Walnut Inn (549-5149), 1184 North Amherst Street, North Amherst 01059. The most imposing house in North Amherst, right in the middle of the village (at the traffic light), this Federal brick house meanders back through an 18th-century wing to a Victorian carriage house. Marie and Ed Twohig have been forced to rebuild much of the house from the floors up (note the natural mahogany in the dining room) thanks to what seem unreasonable demands by Amherst building inspectors. (You have to wonder why, for instance, they had to install large institutional "exit" signs over what are obviously external doors.) Still, the integrity of the rooms survives, furnishings are handsome (we especially like the Mulberry Room), quilts are handmade, and baths, private. Breakfast always includes hot apple pie as well as hot dishes like crêpes suzette, three-cheese quiche, or Belgian waffles. Three rooms were complete when we visited, and four more were in process. $95–115.

☞ **Lincoln Avenue B&B** (549-0517), 242 Lincoln Avenue, Amherst 01002. This spacious, casual, turn-of-the-century home just a couple of blocks from everything is home for Bonnie and Larry Navakov-Lawlor, two typical Amherst residents. Larry is a lighting specialist, set designer, and artist, and Bonnie offers acupressure and yoga classes (the reason the living room is so sparsely furnished). Guests tend to gather in the comfortable dining room overlooking the garden. Breakfast is self-service: muffins, granola, and coffee. The guest rooms—two on the second floor (shared bath, robes in room) and several more under the eaves on the third floor—are all attractive, very much what you would expect to be offered by friends if you were visiting. Children welcome. $60–75.

Amherst Bed & Breakfast (256-6151), 132 Farmington Road, Amherst 01002. "This is just our house," Ann Gross explained as she gave directions to the suburban-style development in which it sits. The two pleasant twin-bedded rooms share a bath. Breakfast in the gracious dining room features popovers and muffins. Ann and Bob Gross lived in Amherst College faculty housing for decades and delight in tuning guests in to the area.

The Knoll (584-8164), 230 North Main Street, Florence 01060. An English Tudor–style home set on 17 acres 3 miles west of downtown Northampton, within walking distance of Look Park. Lee and Ed Lesko offer three rooms, two with double and one with twin beds, sharing two baths. Breakfast is included in $50–55. No smokers and no children under 12.

Ingate Farms (253-0440), 60 Lamsen Road, Belchertown 01007. B&B accommodations are in a 250-year-old bobbin factory moved here from land flooded by Quabbin Reservoir. There are three double rooms (two with queen-sized beds, one with twins) and a two-room suite with private baths; two rooms have working fireplaces. $50–75 includes continental breakfast. The B&B adjoins the farm's Equine Center; inquire about trail rides (insurance is an issue at this writing). Facilities also include an Olympic-sized swimming pool.

Berkshire B&B Associations (413-268-7244), 106 South Street, Williamsburg, is a long-established reservation service that offers bed & breakfast in some 30 private homes scattered throughout this area, from $55 per couple.

(Also see Bullard Farm under "Quabbin Area," Sunnyside Farm in "Greenfield/Deerfield Area," and Outlook Farm in "Hampshire Hills.")

MOTELS

Autumn Inn (584-7660), 259 Elm Street, Northampton 01060. This is a splendidly built and maintained 30-room motel, built for and geared to the parents of Smith students. Rooms are large with double and single beds, TV, phones, and private baths. Breakfast and lunch are served in the coffee shop with a hearth, and there's a landscaped pool. $68 single, $92 double, two nonsmoking efficiency suites, $110; $12 per extra adult, $6 for children aged 11 and under.

Campus Center Hotel (549-6000), Murray D. Lincoln Campus Center, University of Massachusetts, Amherst 01003. A high-rise building with 160 rooms (each has a double and single bed and color TV). $65 single, $76 double, $84 for three or four.

The Inn at Northampton (1-800-582-2929), junction of US 5 and I-91, Northampton 01060. The good bet if you have children along: 125 rooms, an indoor and an outdoor pool, sauna, game room, and lighted tennis court; also a restaurant and lounge. $75–115.

Holiday Inn (534-3311), Holidrome and Conference Center, junction of

I-91 and the Mass. Pike at Ingleside, Holyoke. A 219-room, four-story complex featuring a tropical recreational area with 18-foot-high palm trees, a pool, full spa, and, of course, a volleyball court. $86–95 per couple.

WHERE TO EAT

DINING OUT
Green Street Cafe (586-5650), 62 Green Street, Northampton. Open 7 AM–10 PM daily. Owner-chef John Sielski is a valley native who operated a restaurant in Brooklyn before opening this elegant storefront bistro that plays several roles. Students are welcome to sip coffee and read in the casual outer room and garden, and there are homemade pastries and lunch (noon–2; see *Eating Out*). For dinner the plum-colored rooms, hung with original art, take on a more formal air, and on weekends there's frequently music. The handwritten menu might include such appetizers as sun-dried tomato, leek, and chevre tart ($3.95) or wild mushroom bisque ($4.95), with entrées such as salmon baked *en papillote* with potato soufflé ($16.95) or chicken with apples and hazelnuts ($13.95); half portions of pasta dishes like spicy noodles with shrimp and vegetables ($7.95) are also available. Inquire whether liquor is served. If the seasonal license isn't in effect, it's BYOB.

North Star Seafood Restaurant and Bar (586-9409), 25 West Street, Northampton. Open 5:30 PM–9 PM weekdays, 5:30–10 weekends, Sunday 4:30–9. Sushi is a specialty, as is bouillabaisse ($17.95). The menu might include salmon roasted with a red; green, and yellow pepper sauce ($14.95), veal stuffed with artichokes, and a range of vegetarian dishes like penne ($12.95) or tofu grilled with oriental barbecue sauce ($9.95). There's outdoor dining in summer, and dinner jazz on Friday and Saturday.

Cafe DiCarlo (253-9300), 71 North Pleasant Street, Amherst. Open 11:30 AM to midnight or 1 AM, Sunday from 1:30 for brunch. Choose from a formal dining room or informal downstairs café. The menu features northern Italian dishes ranging from sandwiches (like smoked turkey with mozzarella and prosciutto) to *bistecca alla Florentina*, and there's an extensive wine list. Live jazz and blues on Thursday and Friday; a garden patio in-season. Dinner $12.50–17.50.

Seasons Restaurant (253-9909), 529 Belchertown Road, Amherst. Open Sunday through Thursday 5–9:30, Friday and Saturday 5–10, Sunday buffet brunch 10:30–3. A restored post-and-beam barn with a deck overlooking hills. Hugely popular locally. Specializes in prime rib, Italian dishes, and seafood; plenty of pasta. Dinner entrées $9–17, but sandwiches and lighter fare available.

Carmelina's at the Commons (584-8000), 96 Russell Street, Hadley. Open for dinner nightly from 5 and for Sunday brunch. Huge portions

279 The Pioneer Valley 279

of standout Italian cuisine at reasonable rates make this a big area favorite; there may be lines on weekends, and it's always busy. Full liquor license. Entrées $10.50–15.95.

Spoleto (586-6313), 50 Main Street, Northampton. Open Monday through Thursday 5–10, Friday and Saturday 5–11, Sunday 4–9. Recently expanded and moved to this prominent site, featuring Spoleto Festival posters and creative "fine Italian" dishes like penne alfredo with grilled chicken; freshly made pasta and steak are specialties. Entrées $8.95–15.95. Full bar.

East Side Grill (586-3347), 19 Strong Avenue, Northampton. Open Monday through Saturday 11:30–2:30, dinner 5–11, Sunday 4–10. A popular place with a pleasant, multi-level dining room (try for a booth) and an enclosed porch. Known for Cajun dishes like "Crawfish Enchiladas" (Louisiana crawfish tails, jack cheese, chilis, peppers, and onions baked in flour tortillas and topped with a tomato salsa: $6.95). Dinner options are huge, ranging from Cajun burgers to blackened prime rib. Full bar. Dinner entrées $8.50–14.95.

Wiggins Tavern Restaurant (584-3100), 36 King Street, Northampton. Open Wednesday through Saturday 5:30–9:30, Sunday 3–8. An authentic low-beamed, 18th-century tavern with a large hearth that was incorporated into the hotel when it was built. Traditional New England fare ranging from Yankee pot roast ($11.95) to roast rack of lamb ($21.95).

The Lord Jeffery Inn (253-2576), 30 Boltwood Avenue, Amherst. Open daily for breakfast, lunch, and dinner. Admittedly we haven't dined here lately, but our survey reveals that the food in this formal main dining room has improved vastly in the past couple of years and is now fully commensurate with prices like $18.95 for grilled duck breast and $19.95 for seafood *le creme Dijon* (lobster, scallops, shrimp, sea clams, and mussels sautéed in a roasted garlic white wine cream sauce with mushroom, scallions, and a touch of Dijon on linguine). Specials change daily; dinner entrées begin at $13.75.

Yankee Pedlar Inn (532-9494), 1866 Northampton Street (US 5 near I-91 Exit 16), Holyoke. The big dining room here is J.J. Hildreth's, a glass-walled area that's popular with local businesspeople at lunch and packs few surprises in its dinner menu. Entrées range from baked scrod or pasta primavera ($11.95) to roast filet mignon or seafood Alfredo ($18.95). Sunday champagne brunch (10–5) is in the more ornate Opera House dining room, and the most attractive room, the richly paneled Oyster Bar, is open from 11:30 AM for deli sandwiches as well as libations.

The Delaney House (532-1800), US 5 at Smith's Ferry, Holyoke. Open Monday through Saturday from 5 PM, Sunday from 4. A large, popular, special-occasion place, newly renovated at vast expense, with four different dining rooms and an extensive menu that usually includes bouillabaisse ($17.95) and salmon and dill (also $17.95). A favorite dessert is fresh strawberries in maraschino cream served in a pastry shell with candied violets; specialty drinks are featured. Children's menu.

Johan's Dutch Inn (527-2911), MA 10, Easthampton. Open Tuesday through Thursday 4–9, until 10 Friday and Saturday, Sunday noon–9. Known to Springfield diners from his 26 years in the kitchen of that city's most famous restaurant (The Student Prince), Dutch-born Johan DeVries and his wife, Leslie, have opened their own place. Formerly the Gold Mine, this large restaurant has elaborate dining rooms, which seem to be the rule in this area. The specialties are Dutch/Indonesian as well as German, and the specialty of the house is *sambal oedang*, hot and spicy shrimp prepared tableside. $8.50–15.

The Log Cabin (536-7700), Easthampton Road, Holyoke. Open daily for lunch and dinner. A valley landmark that now features Swiss as well as American and continental dishes. Set high on a flank of Mount Tom with a great view and seasonal "Alpine Cafe" outdoor terrace overlooking the valley. Dinner entrées $11–20.

Windows on the Common (534-8222), 25 College Street, Village Commons, South Hadley. Open Monday through Saturday for lunch and dinner, Sunday 10:30–2 for a brunch buffet ($10.95). This is the most formal place to eat in the Village Commons, an interesting mix of shops and restaurants designed for this college town by one of New England's best-known architects, Graham Gund. Decor is contemporary elegant, and the menu, large; early dinner specials (5–7) are $7.99–9.99, otherwise you're talking $9.50–16.95.

(Also see Sienna restaurant in "Greenfield/Deerfield Area.")

EATING OUT

In Northampton

Green Street Cafe. We never list restaurants under both *Dining* and *Eating Out,* but this case has to be the exception, because the $6.95 all-you-can-eat luncheon buffet is certainly the best value in the valley. The day we sampled it, choices included gingered duck, moist salmon, a spiced lentil or tossed salad, and mussels. Of course you can also have soup and a sandwich.

La Cazuela (586-0400), 7 Old South Street. Open Monday for dinner from 5, Saturday and Sunday for brunch 11–3. Housed in the rambling old hotel known as a semilegal watering hole to generations of students, this cheerful place (note the seasonal patio dining) offers outstanding spicy Mexican and southwestern fare, including plenty of vegetarian dishes. Try the spinach enchiladas or pollo verde. Entrées $6–10. Full bar.

Fitzwilly's (584-8666), 23 Main Street. Open daily, 11:30 until midnight. One of New England's first fern bars: brick walls, plenty of copper, antiques, hanging plants. It all works, including the immense menu and sandwiches. Dinner entrées average $9.

Curtis & Schwartz (586-3278), 116 Main Street. Open Monday through

Wednesday 7:30–3, Thursday until 10, Friday and Saturday until 11, Sunday 8–2. An art deco café decor that's especially popular for Sunday brunch.

Paul & Elizabeth's (584-4832), 150 Main Street. Open Sunday through Wednesday 11:30–9 or 9:30, Friday and Saturday until 10. The town's oldest natural foods restaurant, specializing in vegetarian dishes, seafood, homebaked breads and pastries. No smoking. Dinner entrées average $10. Beer and wine.

India House (586-6344), 45 State Street. Open Monday through Saturday for lunch and dinner, Sunday 4–9. Decorated with Indian prints and featuring background sitar music, Tandoori cooking, many vegetarian dishes; the valley's original Indian restaurant. Entrées from $7.95.

J.C. Pullman's at the Depot (586-5366), 125 Pleasant Street. Open daily 11:30–9 or 10:30. Housed in the splendid old depot.

The Northampton Brewery (584-9903), 11 Brewer Court. Open Monday through Saturday 11:30–11, Sunday 1–11. The area's only microbrewery, housed in a 19th-century livery stable. A pleasant, multilevel space serving sandwiches, pizzas, burgers, steaks, seafood, and stir fries. Beer changes daily; live music on Wednesday and Sunday evenings.

Miss Florence Diner (584-3179), 99 Main Street, Florence (Northampton). Open for early breakfast through late dinner, 3 miles west of downtown Northampton. Known locally as "Miss Flo," this is the most famous diner in western Massachusetts, in the same family since the '40s. Forget the banquet addition and stick to the stools or booths. Unexpected specialties like clam and oyster stew ($4.94) and baked stuffed lobster casserole ($10.95), a soup and salad bar, and full liquor license. On our last visit we had a great beef barley soup ($1.50). Try the coconut and macaroon cream pudding.

Bluebonnet Diner (584-3333), 324 King Street. Open Monday through Friday 5:30 AM–midnight, Saturday 6 AM–midnight. A classic diner with "homecooking." Full bar. Smoking section. Dinners average $6.95.

Look Restaurant (584-9850), 410 North Main Street, Leeds (Northampton). A landmark with a '50s look and menu, "homestyle cooking," breakfast available all day. Fresh-made breads, muffins, and pies.

In Amherst

Judie's (253-3491), 51 North Pleasant Street. Open Sunday through Thursday 11:30–11, Friday and Saturday until 11:30. This cheerful, glass-fronted restaurant seems to be everyone's favorite: casual, friendly, and specializing in oversized, overstuffed popovers (we recommend the lime chili chicken with mushrooms, peppers, onions, and tomatoes), creative salad and pasta dishes, and sinful desserts. Dinner entrées include a salad and popover and run from $12.95 for vegetarian primavera pasta to $14.95 for broiled New York sirloin tip bordelaise. Full bar.

Amber Waves (253-9200), 31 Boltwood Walk (facing the parking lot). Open

Monday through Saturday 11:30–10:30, Sunday 12:30–9:30. Geared to takeout (with a small sit-down area), but so good we predict it will soon expand to larger premises. Remarkably reasonable in price, with interesting Thai, Vietnamese, Chinese, and Japanese noodle soups and stir fries. Plenty of vegetarian dishes.

El Acuna, Boltwood Walk. A fun and funky place with Tex-Mex food and decor. You can sit on saddles and munch a grilled papaya cilantro burrito at a table that's an upturned washtub. The bucket lanterns have real bullet holes to let the light shine through.

Top of the Campus (549-6000), Murray D. Lincoln Campus Center, UMass. Open weekdays for lunch. Inquire about dinner. A pleasant, 11th-floor dining room with a moderately priced, ho-hum menu and a spectacular view.

Classé Café (253-2291), 168 North Pleasant Street. Open Monday through Saturday 7 AM–10 PM, Sunday brunch 7 AM–3 PM. Kids eat free on Wednesday. A college hangout known for decent burgers (including veggieburgers) and excellent fries. Local artwork, wine and beer, no smoking from 2–8.

The Pub (549-1200), 15 East Pleasant Street, Amherst. Open Monday through Saturday 11:30–9:30, Sunday brunch 11–3 and dinner to 9:30. The name says it all: a classic college-town pub with a 10-page menu featuring everything from burgers to broiled scrod; a wide choice of beer. Most dinner entrées are under $10. There's dancing, too.

Panda East Restaurant (256-8923), 103 North Pleasant Street. Open 11:30–10:30 daily. This is part of an excellent local chain specializing in traditional Hunan-style Chinese food. Full bar.

Atkins Farms Fruit Bowl (253-9528), corner of MA 116 and Bay Road in South Amherst. Open daily, hours vary. Probably the fanciest farm stand in New England, this handsome redwood building sits amid thousands of fruit trees on the 190 acres that the family has farmed for generations. There is a first-rate deli, but for some reason it's on the opposite side of the building from the bakery (everything is baked on the premises), where there's attractive seating.

El Greco-Mykonos Greek Restaurant (253-9239), 460 West Street (MA 116 South in South Amherst). Open Monday through Saturday 11–2, dinner Monday through Sunday 5–10. Your basic, friendly Greek restaurant with an unusual number of vegetarian dishes (like Armenian pumpkin with lentils) and pasta dishes, plus the predictable moussaka and shish kebob; most entrées are well under $10. Beer and wine.

Amherst Chinese (253-7835), 62 Main Street. Open daily for lunch and dinner. A mural in the dining room depicts the restaurant's nearby farm, source of the vegetables in its dishes. Known fondly as "AmChin," this is a local favorite. Note the luncheon specials from $4.25 and the $5.75 weekday dinner specials; no MSG.

Elsewhere

Marfrans Turkey Ranch & Restaurant (467-7440), 55 Taylor Street, Granby. Open Wednesday through Sunday 11–8:30. Well worth finding, this valley landmark should be far better known than it is. The two cheerful rooms are in a restaurant that Marion and Frank (hence Marfran) Nugent built, part of a 25-acre farm that they bought in 1963. With their six children they rebuilt the "pole barns" and have been raising quality, grain-fed birds ever since. There's also a slaughtering house and a retail store (where you can buy a turkey fresh or cooked), and the dinner turkey plate ($9.50) is about as good as it can be. Turkey pot pie, turkey croquettes, and turkey liver with onions are also specialties, but the menu ranges from haddock to baked ham to fried clams and lobster Newburg. At lunch you can have a lobster and crab roll as well as a turkey club or turkey burger. Full liquor license.

Bub's Bar BQ (548-9630), MA 116, Sunderland. Known as the best barbecue (try the hickory-smoked ribs) in the valley, with a fixin's bar that includes collard greens, yams, salads, and more; eat inside or (weather permitting) out.

Fernandez Family Restaurant (532-1139), 111 High Street, Holyoke. Open daily. A short walk from the Heritage State Park complex, this clean, cafeteria-style restaurant specializes in roast pork, BBQ ribs, and Puerto Rican–style meat pies. It helps if you speak Spanish.

Woodbridge's (536-7341), South Hadley Common. Open daily for lunch and dinner, well-spaced tables, casual atmosphere. Dinner entrées might include poached salmon ($11.25) or seafood pie ($13). Daily blackboard specials, early-bird specials 4–6, and Sunday brunch ($9.95).

Gohyang, 111 Russell Street (MA 9), Hadley. Open Tuesday through Sunday. Jihuyan and Chongyol Kim have run the adjoining Kim's Korean market for many years and in '94 opened the area's first Korean restaurant. "Gohyang" means "hometown," and the restaurant includes a "waiting area," a hardwood floor, and stacks of cushions on which guests are invited to sit and talk, Korean style. Korean cuisine features leafy vegetables and more boiled than fried dishes.

Harvest Valley Country Store (532-1664), MA 141 near the Mount Tom Reservation entrance, Easthampton. Open Monday through Saturday for lunch (11–4) and dinner (4–9) and Sunday brunch. The impressive thing here is the view—out across the valley and west to the Hilltowns. Good sandwiches, quiche, and pies like apple pecan. The dining room is glass-sided, and there's a sun deck.

SNACKS

Black Sheep Deli and Bakery (253-3442), 79 Main Street, Amherst. A genuine coffeehouse/deli with exceptional deli sandwiches, baked goods; the best source in town for picnics. Folk music on weekends. Periodic poetry readings.

Bart's in Amherst (103 North Pleasant Street) and Northampton (249 Main Street). Open Sunday through Thursday until 11 PM, Friday and Saturday until midnight. Since 1976, milk from local cows is used for great ice cream in 100 flavors like mud pie, blueberry cheesecake, and orange Dutch chocolate.

McCray Farm (533-3714), 55 Alvord Street, South Hadley. The dairy bar, open spring through fall, features homemade ice cream. This working dairy farm is near the river, with a small petting zoo; maple breakfasts during sugaring season.

ENTERTAINMENT

For the academic year consult the *Five-College Calendar of Events,* published monthly and available at all campuses. A typical month lists more than 27 films, 30 lectures, 19 concerts, and 32 theatrical performances. Visitors welcome.

Academy of Music Opera House (584-8463), 274 Main Street, Northampton. This renaissance-style, century-old theater with a balcony, even graceful men's and women's lounges, shows, art films, and first-run movies; also a schedule of live entertainment.

Mullins Center (545-0505). A 10,500-seat sports and entertainment arena with a year-round schedule of theater and concerts as well as sports.

Fine Arts Center, University of Massachusetts (545-2511). Performing arts series of theater, music, dance.

Northampton Center for the Arts, New South Street. Theater, dance, art exhibits.

MUSIC

Summer music series include the **Amherst College Early Music Festival** (542-2000), **Bright Moments Music Festival** (also known as Jazz in July) at the University of Massachusetts (545-3530) in Amherst, and **Musicorda** (532-0607), Chapin Auditorium, Mount Holyoke College, South Hadley (string festival presenting distinguished guest artists and faculty on Friday, students on Sunday, Wednesday, and Thursday, July through August).

The Mount Holyoke Summit House (586-8686) is the scene of a sunset concert series (folk, jazz, barbershop), 7:30 Thursday; and in Northampton **Look Park Sunday Concerts** are held Sunday, 4 PM, late June through mid-August.

THEATER

Mount Holyoke Summer Theater (538-2632), in the Festival Tent at Mount Holyoke College, South Hadley, a professional summer stock company performing late June through mid-August; also children's theater.

Hampshire Shakespeare Company (253-2576). Shakespeare Under the Stars summer festival June through August. Performances on selected nights in the garden of the Lord Jeffery Inn, Amherst.

NewWORLD Theater performances at the Fine Arts Center, UMass (545-1972). This outstanding series, presented during the academic year, features ethnic and minority themes.

FILM

Tower Theaters (533-2663), 19 College Street, South Hadley. First-run and art films; seats may be reserved.

Pleasant Street Theater (586-0935). 27 Pleasant Street, Northampton. Independent, foreign, and art films, one theater upstairs and the well-named Little Theater in the basement.

Amherst Cinema (253-5426), 30 Amity Street. First-run films nightly.

Hampshire 6 Theaters (584-7550), Café Square, Hampshire Mall, MA 9, and **Mountain Farms 4 Theaters,** Mountain Farms Mall, MA 9, Hadley.

NIGHT LIFE

The Iron Horse (584-0610), 20 Center Street, Northampton. Live folk, jazz, and comedy, plus 50 brands of imported beer; dinner served. According to *Billboard* magazine, the Iron Horse "boasts one of the richest musical traditions in the country."

Pearl Street (584-7771), 10 Pearl Street, Northampton. Dancing nightly, live music several nights a week. DJ.

Live music can also be heard frequently in Northampton at the **Green Street Cafe** and at neighboring **North Star** (see *Dining Out*), and at the **Fire & Water Coffee House** (586-8336) on Old South Street (also the place for Wednesday night poetry readings). In Amherst live entertainment is found at the **Cafe DiCarlo** (*Dining Out*) and **Black Sheep Deli** (*Snacks*). (Also see the Montague Book Mill Cafe in "Greenfield/Deerfield Area.")

SELECTIVE SHOPPING

ANTIQUES SHOPS

Northampton has become a good place for antiques in the past few years since a half-dozen shops have opened along and around Market Street. The largest is the **Antique Center of Northampton** (584-3600), 9½ Market Street. Open five days 10–5, closed Wednesday, Sunday noon–5. A multidealer shop on three levels. **American Decorative Arts,** 3 Olive Street, has become something of a mecca for collectors of early-20th-century furniture. **Hadley Antique Center** (586-4093), MA 9, Hadley, is open 10–5 except Wednesday. Ninety dealers in antiques and collectibles.

ARTISANS

Some 1500 craftspeople work in the valley and nearby Hilltowns, and Northampton is their major showcase, known particularly for hand-crafted jewelry, pottery, and furniture. One Cottage Street in Easthampton, for instance, is a former mill building that's now home for over 100 artists. Tours and open houses are scheduled periodically throughout the year. Check with the chamber of commerce.

Pinch Pottery (586-4509), 179 Main Street, Northampton. A combination shop with varied crafts and a gallery specializing in functional works of art, particularly ceramics. The gallery mounts frequently changing exhibits of work by well-known artists. Inquire about studio tours.

Skera Gallery & Crafts (586-4509), 221 Main Street, Northampton. A long-established gallery featuring a variety of American crafts, known for textiles and wearable art.

Silverscape Designs (586-3324), 3 Pleasant Street, Northampton; also 264 North Pleasant Street, Amherst (253-3324). The Northampton store (open weekdays 10–6, Saturday until 9, Sunday noon–5) is a beauty, the Tiffany's of the valley—a former bank building with art deco detailing and a glorious stained-glass skylight. The old tellers' windows are still in place; there's also a cascading fountain. A wide variety of jewelry and accessories.

Don Muller Gallery (586-1119), 40 Main Street, Northampton. One of the original quality crafts stores (established way back in 1978) in Northampton, displaying a spectrum of work by 60 craftspeople, always exhibiting local glass artist Josh Simpson's hand-blown glass orbs.

Peacework Gallery (586-7033), 263 Main Street, Northampton, specializes in the fine arts and crafts of Native Americans and the Southwest.

Alexander's Jewelry (586-9552), 207 Main Street, Northampton. New, estate, and antique jewelry and vintage Rolex wrist watches.

Sutter's (586-1470), 233 Main Street, Northampton. A long-established custom jeweler exhibiting work by some 20 designers as well as John Sutter's own work.

Artisan Gallery (586-1942), Thornes Market, 150 Main Street, Northampton. A quality selection of jewelry, pottery, woodwork, and glass; kaleidoscopes are a specialty.

Hart Gallery at the Guild Art Centre (584-1207), 102 Main Street, Northampton. Fine art, featuring regional artists.

Bill Brough Jewelry Designs (586-8985), 18 Main Street, Northampton. Original jewelry designs in gold, diamonds, pearls, and special stones.

R. Michelson Galleries (586-3964), 132 Main Street, Northampton (and 25 South Pleasant Street, Amherst). Represents top New England artists including Leonard Baskin, Barry Moser.

The Canal Gallery (532-4141), 380 Dwight Street, Holyoke. A 19th-century mill building houses some 20 artists' studios. Shows and gallery hours vary.

BOOKSTORES

Book browsing is a major pastime in this area.

In Northampton

Beyond Words Bookshop (586-6304; 1-800-442-6304), 189 Main Street. The city's largest bookstore featuring books for inner development; also music, stationery, gifts. **Broadside Bookshop** (586-4235), 247 Main Street. A general trade bookstore with a strong emphasis on fiction and literature as well as personal advice. **Globe Bookshop** (584-0374; in New England: 1-800-464-0374), 38 Pleasant Street. New, used, and publishers' overstocks. **Bookends** (585-8667), 93 Main Street, Florence; nine rooms of quality used books. **Third Wave Bookstore** (586-7851), 90 King Street; new, used, and rare feminist and lesbian books, periodicals, and music, jewelry, cards, bumper stickers. **Metropolitan Books & Records** (586-7077), 93/4 Market Street; specializes in used poetry and art books. **Pride and Joy** (585-0683), 20 Crafts Avenue, featuring books for lesbians, bisexuals, and gays. **Raven Used Books** (584-9868), 4 Old South Street, specializing in scholarly, women's studies, and philosophy.

In Amherst
Jeffery Amherst Bookstore (253-3381), 55 South Pleasant Street. A full-service bookstore with a strong children's book section, specializing in Emily Dickinson. **Atticus/Albion** (256-1547), 8 Main Street, has a wide selection of new and used books. **Book Marks** (549-6136), 1 East Pleasant Street (Carriage Shops). A wide selection of used books specializing in art, poetry, photography, and Emily Dickinson. **Food for Thought Books** (253-5432), 106 North Pleasant Street, featuring gay and lesbian, progressive political, and African American titles. **Laos Religious Book Center** (253-3909), 16 Spring Street, an ecumenical bookstore with both Christian and Jewish titles. **The University Store** (545-2619), Lincoln Campus Center, University of Massachusetts. A full-service college bookstore specializing in academic, technical reference, math, physics, and chemistry. The store also carries a large selection of UMass gift items. **Wooten's Books** (253-2722), 19 North Pleasant Street. A used bookstore specializing in art, poetry, fiction, philosophy, and cultural studies.

In South Hadley
Odyssey Bookstore (534-7307; 1-800-540-7307), Village Commons, 9 College Street. One of the largest and most attractive bookstores in the valley.

CLOTHING
No longer bastions of humdrum tweed, Northampton stores that are on the cutting edge of rural chic include: **Cathy Cross** (586-9398), 151 Main Street; **Bloomingals** (584-8049), 273 Main Street; **Country Comfort, Ltd.** (584-0042), 153 Main Street; **Square One Presents** (585-1118), 24 Pleasant Street; **Bibi Stein Handweavings** (584-7455), 225 Main Street, second floor; **25 Central** (586-8017), 150 Main Street; and **Serendipity** (584-6528), 126 Main Street.
Zanna (253-2563), 187 North Pleasant Street, Amherst, the largest in a three-shop chain (the others are in Williamstown and Brattleboro, Vermont).

FACTORY OUTLETS
Pick up a brochure at the Heritage State Park. These entries are real factory

outlets housed in factories in Holyoke. They include **ES Sports** (534-5634), 47 Jackson Street (gym bags, sweatshirts, sportswear); **Deerfield Woodworking Factory Store** (532-2377), 420 Dwight Street (wooden curtain rods and brackets, bookcases, quilt racks, shelves, nightstands); **Becker Jean Factory Store** (532-5797), 323 Main Street (Becker, Levi, and Lee jeans); and **Riverbend Woodworks** and **Lady Bugs Ltd.** (533-8809), 380 Dwight Street (dried flowers, wreaths, baskets, hats).

SHOPPING AREAS
Thornes Marketplace, 150 Main Street, Northampton. An incubator for many Northampton stores: a five-story, 40-shop complex with high ceilings, wood floors.

The Village Commons in South Hadley. A whimsical, white-clapboard complex of shops designed by Boston architect Graham Gund to fit compactly into a corner of the South Hadley Common while providing all the amenities for the college community: a pizza place, coffeehouse, movie theater (two screens), Chinese restaurant, and pub. It also includes boutiques and specialty shops ranging from Stonebrook Saddlery to Neuchatel chocolates. Appropriately, the anchor store is a splendid bookstore (Odyssey Bookshop).

Holyoke Mall (536-1440) at Ingleside (I-91 Exit 15, and Mass. Pike Exit 4), open Monday through Saturday 10–9:30 and Sunday noon–6. The single biggest mall in western Massachusetts, with Filene's, Lord & Taylor, JC Penney, Macy's Close-Out, and Sears as anchors.

SPECIAL SHOPS
A₂Z Science and Learning Store (586-1611), 150 Main Street, Thornes Market, Northampton. Three floors of intelligent toys, gadgets, and gifts for children of all ages.

Atkins Fruit Bowl (253-9528), 1150 West Street, Amherst. Open daily except major holidays 8–6, later in summer. "The farms aren't all gone from the valley," says Howard Atkins, the entrepreneur who has put his grandfather's orchards to good use. He harvests fruit from more than 25,000 trees on 290 acres and has built New England's fanciest fruit stand, a redwood building housing aisles of vegetables, fruits, and flowers, plus a deli and bakery (see *Eating Out*). Pick-your-own peaches mid- to late August and apples September through mid-October; scarecrow workshops Saturday and Sunday late October until Halloween.

SPECIAL EVENTS

Note: Northampton maintains an events listings number: 1-800-A-FUNTOWN. Farmers' markets are held spring through fall on Saturday in Northampton (on Gothic Street) and Amherst (on the Common), and in Holyoke on Thursday afternoons (2:30–5:30; Hampden Park off Dwight Street).

March: **St. Patrick's Day Parade,** Holyoke (Sunday after St. Pattie's Day).

May: **Taste of Amherst, Community Fair,** and (the Saturday nearest the

14th) **Emily Dickinson's World Weekend. Western Massachusetts Appaloosa Horse Show,** Three-County Fairgrounds, Northampton.
June: **Crafts night** in Northampton.
June through August: **"Hot Summer Nights,"** Wednesday night concert series on the Common, Amherst.
July: **Amherst Crafts Fair** (July 1). **Fireworks** (July 4), Amherst. **Morgan Horse Show,** Northampton.
August: **Amherst Teddy Bear Rally** (first weekend). **Taste of Northampton** (second weekend). **Three-County Fair** at the Three-County Fairground.
Weekend before Labor Day: **Celebrate Holyoke** (four-day, multicultural music festival, food, dancing at Heritage State Park).
October: **Book and Plow Festival,** Amherst—three days honoring local writers and farmers. **Paradise City Arts Festival** (584-9017), Northampton.
December: **First Night,** Northampton.

SPRINGFIELD

Springfield is a 33-square-mile city of 157,000 people with high-rises, shops, and major museums, all conveniently grouped within a few blocks of each other. Known locally as Springfield Center, this downtown rewards everyone who stops long enough to find the stately old Court Square, the Quadrangle of art, science, and history museums, and the Springfield Armory museum.

Founded in 1794, the armory became a magnet for skilled technicians during the industrial revolution. During the War of 1812 it turned Springfield into a boomtown, and during the Civil War the population once more doubled as the armory produced more than half the guns for the Union cause, while nearby Smith and Wesson turned out 110,000 revolvers and the Ames Sword Company in Chicopee made 150,000 swords. During the late 19th century Springfield continued to prosper as a rail, industrial, and commercial center and became known for an impressive array of inventions: the first gas-powered car and first motorcycle, pioneering vacuum cleaners, airplanes, and steel-bladed ice skates, to name a few. Although 19th-century philanthropists bequeathed the Quadrangle museums and grand public spaces like Forest Park, they never established a museum to dramatize all those inventions, so the only "first" anyone remembers is basketball, memorialized in a splendid, three-story Basketball Hall of Fame.

Most of the turn-of-the-century downtown theaters, hotels, department stores, and shops are now just memories, supplanted by the sterile if impressive Baystate West complex (a 29-story office tower and hotel with parking and shopping) and the Civic Center (a sports arena and convention center). In recent decades many old buildings have been restored, a Riverfront Park has opened the downtown to the Con-

SPRINGFIELD

necticut, and the area has become known for good eating.
Springfield is also the birthplace of Dr. Seuss. Born Theodor Geisel
to the son of a park commissioner in 1904, the artist grew up following his
father around the city's splendid Forest Park, a landscape now known to a
world of children. After viewing the displays in the Quadrangle, visit the
park itself.

AREA CODE
413

GUIDANCE
Greater Springfield Convention and Visitors Bureau (787-1548; 1-800-
723-1548), 34 Boland Way, Springfield 01103. Open 8:30–5 weekdays.
Request the "Official Guide to Springfield and the Pioneer Valley."
Springfield Hospitality Council (732-7467), 338 Worthington Street,
Springfield. Open weekdays 9–5.

GETTING THERE
By air: **Bradley International Airport** (203-292-2000) is 18 miles south
of Springfield in Windsor Locks, Connecticut. It is served by most national and regional carriers and major car rentals. **Airport Service of
Springfield** (739-9999) also connects Bradley with the city.
By train: **AMTRAK** (1-800-USA-RAIL; 785-4230) connects Springfield
with Hartford, New Haven, New York City, Philadelphia, Baltimore,
Washington, DC, and Chicago. There is frequent service from New York
(change in New Haven). The bus depot is right around the corner from
the train station.
By bus: **Peter Pan–Trailways** (781-2900), based in Springfield (with its
own terminal at 1776 Main Street), connects with the airport, Boston,
Hartford, Cape Cod, Albany, and New York City. **Vermont Transit**
(1-800-552-8737) stops en route from New York and Albany to Vermont, New Hampshire, and Montreal.
By car: The route is trickier than you might think. From NYC and points
north you obviously take I-91 (Exit 4). From Boston take Mass. Pike to
Exit 6, I-291 (a cross-town connector); from Holyoke, I-391 is another
connector.

GETTING AROUND
Pioneer Valley Transit Authority (781-7882) serves Springfield-Holyoke.
By taxi: **Diamond Cab** (739-9999), **City Cab** (734-8294), and **Yellow Cab**
(732-1101).

PARKING
Because downtown Springfield is such a relatively small, congested area of
one-way streets, it's best to park as quickly as possible and walk. Reasonably priced parking lots can be found under I-91, in the Baystate
West complex (Boland Way), and in the Civic Center Garage (enter
from E. Court or Harrison Street).

MEDICAL EMERGENCY
Baystate Medical Center (784-3233), Chestnut at Spring Street. Also dial
911.

HISTORICAL MONUMENT OF THE AMERICAN REPUBLIC.

Historical Monument of the American Republic (1876), by Erastus Salisbury Field, can be viewed at Springfield's Museum of Fine Arts.

TO SEE

MUSEUMS

The Quadrangle (739-3871), corner of State and Chestnut Streets, Springfield. A unique cultural Common: four museums and the city's main library assembled around a grassy Green. The museums are open Thursday through Sunday noon–4; $4 adults, $1 children 6–18, under 6 free; includes admission to all four museums. The Quadrangle Cafe is open summers, and there are frequent special events. June through August the Connecticut Valley Historical Museum offers Friday morning tours of the Quadrangle-Mattoon Historic District and downtown Springfield, departing 11 AM. Year-round the bronze *Puritan* by Augustus Saint-Gaudens stands in Merrick Park at the entrance, welcoming visitors to each of the following four museums:

The Museum of Fine Arts (732-6092). A 1930s art deco building with a central court, the museum houses a collection ranging from ancient through medieval to modern, with paintings by Winslow Homer, John Singleton Copley, and several by Erastus Field. The latter was a Leverett portrait painter whose *Historical Monument of the American Republic* is a huge, absorbing fantasy depicting 10 elaborate towers that represent American history, culminating with the triumph over slavery (note Abraham Lincoln rising to heaven in a fiery chariot near the top of the central tower). Completed in 1876, the painting was found behind a Leverett pigsty in the 1940s and is now enshrined at the center of the museum court. Also note Field's compelling primitive portraits and *The Newsboy,* a moment in 1889 captured by George Newhall, Springfield's leading late-19th-century artist. Be sure to locate *New England Scenery* by Frederic Church. The '20s and '30s are also well represented; note *Church Supper,* by Paul Sample, depicting a small town in 1933. Changing exhibits.

George Walter Vincent Smith Art Museum (733-4214). The first museum on the Quadrangle (1896), this is a one-man collection housed in a magnificent palazzo. G.W.V. Smith (always called by his full name locally) amassed a fortune in New York and married Springfield's Belle Townsley, retiring here at age 35. The couple devoted the remainder of their lives to collecting ancient Japanese swords, armor, and art; Islamic rugs, the largest Western collection of cloisonné, and 19th-century landscape paintings. Like Boston's Isabella Stewart Gardner, the Smiths stipulated that the collection not be altered after their deaths; their ashes are interred in the museum. The couple's portraits are just off the entry hall, surrounded by portraits of stern past captains of valley industry.

Connecticut Valley Historical Museum (732-3080). A Colonial Revival mansion built in 1927 (note the replicated Connecticut Valley front door) houses an excellent genealogical library and increasingly interesting exhibits on Springfield inventions, personalities, and institutions. Our favorite is the "Valley Faces" room, with exhibits on Steigers (the department store that marked the center of Main Street from 1893 to 1994), the Breck girls (the J.H. Breck Company shampoos were made here), and Theodor Geisel (Dr. Seuss). Exhibits on Springfield inventions include an early vacuum cleaner and fire hydrant. There are also changing exhibits.

Science Museum (733-1194). Dinosaur buffs will find a 20-foot-high model of *Tyrannosaurus rex* and the tracks of much smaller dinosaurs. Exhibits also include a vintage-1937 Gee Bee monoplane made in Springfield, a hands-on Exploration Center, an impressive African Hall full of animals, some great old-fashioned dioramas, Native American artifacts, a new Eco-Center featuring live animals in realistic habitats—lifelike vegetation, fish that walk on land, turtles that look like leaves, and an Amazon rainforest. The planetarium is open weekends for shows at 1 and 2 ($1).

Springfield Armory National Historic Site, Armory Square (enter from Federal Street near the corner of State Street). Open Tuesday through Sunday 10–5. Billed as the world's largest collection of firearms, exhibits include an array of weapons used in every war since the Revolution; also a film with footage from old, wartime-era newsreels. The museum building dates from just before the Civil War in 1847. The handsome brick complex, which occupies more than 15 acres of bluff above the city, was demilitarized in 1968 and is now Springfield Technical Community College.

Basketball Hall of Fame (781-6500), 1150 West Columbus Avenue, Springfield. Open daily 9–6 in summer, 9–5 September through June. A three-story building just off I-91 (the one site that's well marked from the interstate) tells the story of how Dr. James Naismith first threw a soccer ball into a peach basket in 1891. Exhibits include a basketball court, multi-image presentations of the game, and a hall depicting its greats. Newcomers are inaugurated each spring. $7 adults, $4 seniors and students, free under age 7.

Storrowton Village Museum (787-0136), 1305 Memorial Avenue in West Springfield, at the Eastern States Exposition grounds (MA 147). Open mid-June through Labor Day, Monday through Saturday 11–3:30. The gift shop and the Old Storrowton Tavern are open year-round (closed Sunday). Donated to the Exposition in 1929 by Mrs. James Storrow of Boston (the same family for whom Storrow Drive is named), this grouping of 13 restored 18th-century buildings makes up one of the first museum villages in the country. All buildings were moved here from their original locations. $5 adults, $4 for children.

Springfield Indian Motocycle Museum and Hall of Fame (737-2624), 33 Hendee Street, Springfield. Open daily March through November 10–5 and December through February 1–5. From downtown Springfield take I-291 East to the St. James Avenue exit, then turn right onto Page Boulevard until you see the "Historic Springfield" sign. The museum is a brick, garagelike building in an industrial complex. The collection includes a wide variety of vehicles, from old Columbia bikes to motorized toboggans. You learn that Indian was the first commercially marketed, gasoline-powered motorcycle manufacturing company in the US; manufacturing ceased in 1953. $3

HISTORIC HOMES AND SITES

Court Square, bounded by Court and Elm Streets. Springfield's "Municipal Group" recalls the city's golden era. Completed in 1913, the monumental, many-columned, Greek Revival **City Hall** and **Symphony Hall** buildings are separated by a soaring, 300-foot Italianate campanile. The City Hall's interior is graced by 27 kinds of marble and fine wood paneling and includes a Municipal Auditorium seating 3000. Symphony Hall is equally elegant and known for its acoustics. In the white, columned **Old First Church** (737-1411) check out the art gallery (open Monday through Friday 9:30–2:30 or by appointment), topped with a rooster shipped from England in 1749. The park here, created in 1812 to complement the first Hampden County Courthouse, is the scene of frequent events. Note the Victorian-era Court House designed by Henry Hobson Richardson.

Storrs House (567-3600; 567-5500), 697 Longmeadow Street, Long-

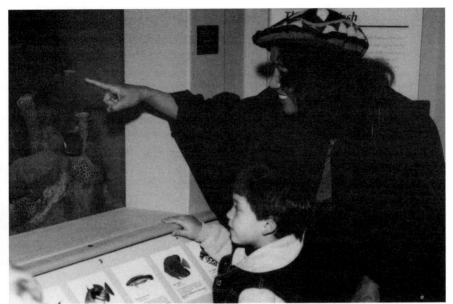

Monsanto Eco-Center, the new aquarium and live animal center at the Springfield Science Museum

meadow. Open Wednesday and Thursday 9–noon and by appointment. Originally the parsonage for the First Church of Christ, now headquarters of the Longmeadow Historical Society, furnished with Connecticut Valley furnishings; 18th-century-style grounds.

Josiah Day House (734-8322), 70 Park Street, West Springfield. Open Saturday and Sunday 1–5. Built in 1754 and billed as "the oldest saltbox in America," it houses the collection of the Ramapogue Historical Society.

Historic Springfield Neighborhoods. In the late 19th century Springfield became known as the "City of Homes," reflecting the quality of the thousands of wooden homes—single- and two-family houses instead of the usual tenements and triple deckers for the working class, and truly splendid houses for the middle and upper classes. Unfortunately, with the flight of families to the suburbs, several once-proud neighborhoods are now shabby, but still well worth driving through. **Forest Park,** developed almost entirely between the 1890s and 1920, is filled with turreted, Victorian shingled homes, many built by the McKnight brothers for whom the **McKnight District,** boasting some 900 of these homes, is named. Right downtown the **Mattoon Street Historic District** is a street of 19th-century brick row houses, leading to the 1870s Grace Baptist Church designed by Henry Hobson Richardson.

FOR FAMILIES

Riverside (786-9300), 1623 Main Street (MA 159), Agawam. Open weekends mid-April through May, daily June through Labor Day, weekends in September; hours vary. Largest amusement park in New England; over 50 rides, including the Cyclone roller coaster and three more coasters, a flume ride, midway, arcades, food outlets, live entertainment. $21.99 adults for all rides and shows, $11.99 for juniors under 54 inches tall. Stock-car races on NASCAR speedway on Saturday nights March through Labor Day; some off-season races ($10.99 and up).

TO DO

GOLF
In Springfield check out the **Franconia Municipal Golf Club** (734-9334) and the **Veterans Municipal Golf Course** (787-6449).
HIKING
See *Green Space*.
SWIMMING
See Forest Park and Chicopee Memorial State Park under *Green Space*.
J.C. Robinson State Park (786-2877), North Street, Agawam, also offers swimming and picnicking.

GREEN SPACE

Forest Park (787-6440). Three miles south of the center of Springfield, just east of I-91, also off MA 21 (Sumner Avenue). Open year-round. Free for walk-ins, $1 per car ($2 for out-of-state) weekdays, $2 ($3 for out-of-state) weekends. The 795 acres include a wild animal zoo (deer, bear, woodland animals) and a petting zoo (open mid-April to mid-November; admission $3 adults, $2 seniors and aged 5–12). The park also offers paddleboats, 21 miles of nature trails, tennis courts, picnic groves, swimming pools, and summer concerts at the Barney Amphitheater. A magnificent, columned mausoleum built by ice skate tycoon Everett H. Barney (his mansion was destroyed to make way for I-91) commands a great view of the Connecticut.
Stanley Park (568-9312), Westfield, open mid-May to mid-October, 8–dusk. Endowed by the founder of Stanley Home Products, the 100-acre park is known for its extensive rose garden (over 50 varieties), mini–New England village, 96-foot-high carillon tower, Japanese Garden with Tea House, arboretum, and large fountain. Sunday evening concerts range from singing groups to the Springfield Symphony Pops.
Laughing Brook Education Center & Wildlife Sanctuary (566-8034), 789 Main Street, Hampden (from I-91 in Springfield take Exit 4, MA 83, to Sumner Avenue, then 3.6 miles). Off any main route to anywhere, this is a popular destination for families drawn by the one-time home of storyteller Thornton Burgess. The house is now part of a 259-acre preserve owned by the Massachusetts Audubon Society, which includes

hiking trails, fields, streams, and a pond, caged animals, a picnic pavilion, and a "touch-and-see" trail.

Chicopee Memorial State Park (594-9416), Burnett Road, Chicopee. A 574-acre park with two human-made lakes and the Chicopee and Morton Brook Reservoirs. There is a beach and bathhouse at Chicopee Reservoir; also four separate picnic areas and a 2-mile paved bicycle path. Day-use fee in summer.

Riverfront Park, foot of State Street, Springfield. A 6-acre, riverfront park offers a view of the Connecticut, which is otherwise walled from access by rail tracks and highway. This is the site of summer concerts.

LODGING

The downtown convention hotels include the 264-room high-rise **Springfield-Marriott Hotel** (781-7111) and the 304-room **Sheraton Springfield Monarch Place** (781-1010), both right at the downtown I-91 exit, both with indoor heated pools and full health clubs. Marriott rates are $135 per couple and Sheraton's are $89–160. A 12-story, 252-room, relatively new **Holiday Inn** (781-0900; 1-800-465-4329), 711 Dwight Street (I-291, Exit 2A), has an indoor pool and rooftop restaurant. $90–115 double, but inquire about specials.

Berkshire Bed & Breakfast Homes (268-7244), PO Box 211, Williamsburg 01096. This reservation service offers bed & breakfast in a number of Springfield homes. We were delighted with the one we stayed at; our host, a life-long Springfield resident and enthusiast, insisted on giving us a tour of Forest Park. $45–150.

WHERE TO EAT

DINING OUT

Student Prince & Fort Restaurant (734-7475), 8 Fort Street (off Main), Springfield. Open 11–11, Sunday noon–10. Sandwiches served all day. The Springfield business community's favorite spot since 1935: a grand old downtown beer hall with stained-glass windows, hung with beer steins. Serves imported wine and draft beers and offers a large menu of hearty German specialties: sauerbraten, Jaeger schnitzel and wiener schnitzel, hunter's pie, and Hungarian goulash. Seasonal specialties include a February wild game menu (where else can you try young bear or buffalo in wine sauce with spaetzle). Lunch runs $4.50–12.95; dinner, $8.25–21.

Cara Mia (739-0101), 1011 East Columbus Avenue, Springfield. Open Tuesday through Saturday 4–10. An upstairs place with welcoming red velvet decor but surprisingly, delightfully nonstuffy. Jackets not mandatory, but the food is elegant. The veal and lamb dishes are particularly good; several daily specials. Live music Saturday nights. Entrées run $9.95–22.

Michael's Restaurant (532-2350), 85 Montcalm Street, Chicopee. Open Wednesday through Saturday 5:30–10. Attached to a long-established local function facility (Chateau Provost), this French restaurant gets good reviews. Both the menu and nightly specials are ambitious. You might begin with a pâté or baked Brie in puff pastry, dine on roast lamb, and finish with crêpe suzette. $14.95–22.95. A good wine list.

Hofbrauhaus (737-4905), 1105 Main Street, West Springfield. The dining room features murals of German landscapes, and the atmosphere is quite formal but fun. Try deep-fried sauerkraut balls or goulash soup, a selection of good veal dishes, and a sparkling German wine. Be sure to leave room for a torte. Dinner entrées average $10.

Federal Hill Club (789-1267), 135 Cooper Street, Agawam. Open for dinner by reservation Tuesday through Saturday 4:30–9:30. The atmosphere and history here are that of a private club, but one that has been open to the public for a couple of decades now. The setting is the dignified dining room of a mansion and the extensive menu is recited, not printed. Five courses are the rule, and the wine list is quite impressive. $15.50–32.

Old Storrowton Tavern (732-4188), Eastern States Exposition Grounds, West Springfield (on MA 147). Open daily except Sunday 11:30–10. Built as the John Atkinson Tavern in Prescott (one of the towns drowned by the Quabbin Reservoir), it has a traditional Yankee menu, good for chicken pot pie and seafood, veal, and beef dishes. Entrées $10 for lunch, $15–22 for dinner.

EATING OUT

Tilly's (732-3613), 1390 Main Street, Springfield. Open 11:30 AM–9 PM Monday through Wednesday; open later through Saturday; Sunday noon–8. Great homemade soups, deli sandwiches, quiches, breads and desserts, daily specials, full dinners. Try the Black Forest pie. A popular meeting place for lunch and after work.

Blue Eagle (737-6135), 930 Worthington Street, Springfield. Open from 11:30 daily, until 9 Sunday through Thursday, until 10 on weekends. Diner fans should drive (though not far from Main Street, this isn't a walking neighborhood) up Worthington Street to this popular place with '40s touches like round windows in the door and glass-block windows. The menu is large and better than basic, ranging from a BLT to surf-and-turf, including lamb shish kebob and fried seafood dinners.

Mom & Rico's Market (732-8941), 899 Main Street, Springfield. Open Monday through Friday 8–5:30. A great Italian deli/grocery with a self-service buffet that usually includes lasagne, sausage and peppers, eggplant Parmigiana (better than your mother's). Pay by the pound or order from the large choice of grinders. This is headquarters for local bocci fans. For cappuccino and a cannoli, step next door to the **Cafe La Fiorentina** (883 Main Street).

Frigo's (731-7797), 1244 Main Street, Springfield. Open Monday through

Friday 8–5, until 6 in summer. The blackboard menu features take-out specialties like pizza rustica, veal Parmigiana, large and interesting sandwich combinations; a favorite with the downtown lunch crowd. If you have time, step around to Frigo's Market at 90 Williams Street, a cheese lover's mecca, also Italian coldcuts and takeouts.

Lido (736-9433), 555 Worthington, Springfield. Open Monday through Saturday 11–11. Drive (don't walk) to this Italian favorite, good for the basics like lasagne and eggplant Parmigiana and hot or sweet sausage. Best garlic bread in town.

Mex Italia (781-6101), SIS Center, 1441 Main Street, Springfield. Open for lunch and dinner. Basic and not-so-basic Mexican and Italian dishes—tacos, burritos, and pastas—in a fiesta atmosphere. The all-you-can-eat Mexican buffet is (at this writing) $4.99.

Sitar (732-8011), 1688 Main Street, Springfield. Open Monday through Saturday for lunch and dinner, Sunday for dinner 5–10. Sampler platters and luncheon specials help the uninitiated choose from a large menu of Indian and Pakistani dishes.

Tavern Inn (736-0456), 91 West Gardner at West Columbus Avenue, Springfield. Open Monday through Friday 11:30–2:30 and again from 4:30 for dinner. Saturday open for dinner only. Handy to the Basketball Hall of Fame, a solid local eatery with no-nonsense service and menu and very reasonable prices. A turkey-stuffed pepper dinner is $4.50, and a chicken Parmigiana dinner, $5.50.

Restaurant Latino (733-6599), 1696 Main Street, Springfield. Open Monday through Saturday from 11 for lunch and dinner. A Caribbean/Central and South American menu, prepared with pride in a welcoming atmosphere. Soups are particularly imaginative. The local Latino station is broadcast from speakers.

Montori & Company (733-4511), 5 Dwight Street, Springfield. Open for lunch. Handy to the Quadrangle museums, a blackboard deli menu with hearty soups, salads, Styrofoam cups and paper plates (but good food, pleasant atmosphere).

ENTERTAINMENT

StageWest (781-2340), 1 Columbus Center, Springfield. Professional theater, November through May. StageWest Summer Series includes concert, dance, and comedy.

Springfield Civic Center and Symphony Hall (787-6610; box office 787-6600), 1277 Main Street, Springfield. This complex, across from Court Square, stands on the site of the courthouse that Daniel Shays and his friends besieged after the Revolution. It includes a 7500-seat Grand Arena that also serves as a theater, as a basketball court for the NCAA Division II Championship Playoffs, and, with a coat of ice, as the home of the Springfield Indians hockey team and scene of the annual Ice

Capades. There is also a Little Arena, scene of a variety of live presentations. Symphony Hall, the classic, columned music hall on Court Square itself, is the home of the **Springfield Symphony Orchestra** (733-2291). It also stages top-name performers, Broadway shows, children's theater, and travelogues.

Paramount Performing Arts Theater (734-5874), 1700 Main Street, Springfield. A '20s movie palace staging pop, rock, and country music concerts as well as comedy and children's shows.

Bing Theater (733-4273), 716 Sumner Avenue, Springfield. Second-run films at bargain prices.

Palace Cinema (781-4890), 895 Riverdale, and **Showcase Cinemas** (733-5131), 864 Riverdale, West Springfield; both show first-run films.

Zone Arts Center (732-1995), 395 Dwight Street, West Springfield. Exhibitions, readings, films, and concerts, as well as art exhibits.

SELECTIVE SHOPPING

Baystate West, 1500 Main Street, Springfield, an indoor mall harboring 70 shops and restaurants; the complex is currently slated for a remake as an outlet center.

Johnson's (732-6222), 1379 Main Street, Springfield. A two-floor bookstore that's got whatever you're looking for.

ART GALLERIES

Thronja Art Gallery (732-0269), 260 Washington Street, Springfield. Open Monday through Friday 9:30–2:30 or by appointment. A private gallery displaying original art. (Also see the Zone Arts Center under *Entertainment* and the Old First Church gallery under *Historic Homes and Sites* [Court Square]).

SPECIAL EVENTS

Note: For event information call **Downtown Happenings Hotline** (734-2745) or **Spirit of Springfield** (733-3800).

February: **Spring Flower Show** at the Civic Center, Springfield.

May: **Peach Basket Festival,** includes enshrinement of newcomers to the Basketball Hall of Fame, Springfield.

June: The **American Crafts Council's Fair** at the exposition grounds in West Springfield. **Laurel Week** in the Westfield River Valley.

June through August: **Summer Sounds** (free outdoor concerts Saturday evenings in Riverfront Park, Springfield).

July through August: Sunday performances by Springfield Pops in Stanley Park, Westfield. Theatrical and musical performances in Forest Park, Sunday evenings.

Fourth of July: The Symphony Orchestra performs, there's an arts festival and fireworks in Court Square, Springfield.

Mid-August: **Harambee Festival of Black Culture,** Winchester Square, Springfield.

September: **Glendi**—Greek festival with folk dances, crafts, food at the Greek Cultural Center, Springfield. **Kielbasa Festival**—Polish music, dance, and food at Fairfield Mall, Chicopee. **Eastern States Exposition** ("The Big E"; 732-2361), West Springfield, the biggest annual fair in the East—livestock shows, horse shows, giant midway, entertainment, avenue of states; always runs 12 days including the third week in September. **Quadrangle Weekend** (737-1750)—outdoor festivities, films, lectures, crafts demonstrations, Springfield. **Mattoon Arts Festival**—an outdoor fair on a downtown street lined with brownstones, gaslights, Springfield.

October: **Chicopee Octoberfest.**

November: **Fall Color Festival** in Springfield, day after Thanksgiving.

December: **First Night,** New Year's Eve celebration, centered in the Quadrangle.

The Hilltowns

The 500-square-mile swath of rolling terra incognita between the Connecticut River Valley and the Berkshires is known simply as "the Hilltowns." Physically this area is one of the hilliest parts of the state, the extension of the Taconic and Berkshire ranges. It looks the way much of Vermont did a couple decades ago: Valleys are steep, alternately wooded and patched with open fields. Relatively few homes have been built in this century.

In winter, cross-country skiers drive from Boston and Hartford to take advantage of the highest, most dependably snow-covered trails south of Vermont. Early spring brings sit-down breakfasts in sugarhouses and tours of the sugarbush (there are more maple producers here than in all the rest of the state put together). In late spring whitewater rafters begin converging on the Deerfield River, and nationally ranked whitewater canoeists compete on the Westfield. Fishermen find trout in both rivers. In summer, back roads throughout this region beckon bicyclists, farms offer horseback riding, and hikers follow trails to hilltop lookouts and deep-in-the-woods waterfalls. In fall the Mohawk Trail is thronged with leaf peepers, but the region's web of back roads receive surprisingly little use.

Although the fertile bottomland along the Deerfield and Westfield Rivers was settled in the mid-18th century, this area was mostly an outpost until after the Revolution, and many hill farms were deserted as early as the 1820s, when the Erie Canal opened the way to greener, less stony, western pastures.

Too far from population centers to be bedroom towns and too far from Boston or New York to attract second-home owners in serious numbers, the Hilltowns are home to an unusual number of artists, craftspeople, and musicians. You'll find a poet laureate reading his works in a country church, a former director of Dublin's famed Abbey Theater producing plays in a village town hall, and world-class pianists performing in a defunct country academy. The biggest events are still country fairs.

The Hilltowns have a long tradition of welcoming summer people (witness William Cullen Bryant's summer home and the 19th-century hotel, now affordable housing and schoolrooms, in Ashfield), and

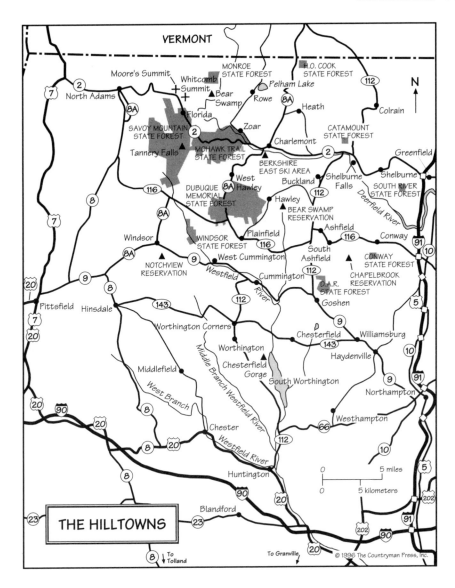

throughout the past century many farms took in summer boarders. In 1916 the Mohawk Trail—38 miles of up-and-down paved road (in an era when the country boasted relatively few paved miles) through the northern, hilliest part of this region—was inaugurated as New England's first formal "Tourist Route." Thousands of "tourists" came to drive it in their first cars. Hopefully the trail's surviving observation towers, Indian trading posts, and old motor courts will be preserved as historic (the way similar roadside icons from that era are in other parts of the country) before they disappear.

Though the Hilltown area may all look much the same to visitors, locals will tell you that the region is clearly divided along county lines. Conway, Ashfield, Hawley, and the towns to the north all fall into "West County" (of Franklin County), whereas the towns along MA 9 and south consider themselves the "Hampshire Hills," a name coined a dozen years ago by the area's bed & breakfast association.

Present lodging options in the Hilltowns include roughly three dozen widely scattered B&Bs, a small resort, and a rustic lodge or two, plus several farms with rental units and a half-dozen motels and campgrounds. At present, however, the only information center in this entire area is in Shelburne Falls, the most obvious waystop on the Mohawk Trail; it serves just its immediate area.

Nowhere else in New England is such a beautiful, easily accessible and yet unspoiled area as underpromoted. We predict this situation won't last forever and suggest you explore it now, before the word spreads.

WEST COUNTY/MOHAWK TRAIL

"Peaks of one or two thousand feet rush up either bank of the river in ranges, thrusting out their shoulders side by side. . . I have never driven through such romantic scenery, where there was such a variety and boldness of mountain shapes as this," observed Nathaniel Hawthorne about the view that you can now enjoy from the truncated, wooden observation tower at Whitcomb Summit.

The tower is one of three period pieces still staked along the original Mohawk Trail, that 38-mile stretch of MA 2 between Greenfield and North Adams that was formally dedicated in 1916. Although it shadows an ancient Native American path through the mountains, the Mohawk Trail in its present incarnation was designed specifically for "auto touring." In the era it was inaugurated, the quickest way to North Adams was by train. This route was the one Bostonians drove with their first cars to explore the most dramatic, least populated part of the state. The Indian trading posts, with their plastic buffalos and wooden Indians, and the '30s and '40s tourist cabins now look a bit funky and worn, but they still smack of a romantic era.

East of the Hoosac Range the Mohawk Trail follows the Deerfield River through a narrow valley, hemmed by abrupt hills. Charlemont, the old crossroads community here, offers motel rooms and campsites, attracting fishermen in spring, whitewater rafters spring through fall, and both downhill and cross-country skiers in winter. But in recent years Shelburne Falls, 8 miles east, has become the most popular waystop on the "Trail." Long known for its Bridge of Flowers and "glacial" potholes, Shelburne has become one of the better places in western Massachusetts to shop for a surprising range of things, from art glass to fine cutlery to medieval armor. It's also a good place to eat.

The one problem with any "trail" is the implication that it is a route that leads to something. We present it, instead, as simply the northern-most spine of "West County." Venture north off MA 2—up the roads to Zoar and Rowe, Heath or Colrain—and you will find a mix of dairy farms and orchards, backed by spruce-forested hills, harboring any number of surprises: memorable places to stay, whitewater rafting, a winery, and a lively café in a former church, for starters.

South of MA 2 the hills are gentler and still patterned with open meadows, fields, and orchards. Valley roads link the classic village centers of Ashfield, Conway, and Buckland, and bed & breakfasts are scattered along the old roads that web the hills.

AREA CODE
413

GUIDANCE
Franklin County Chamber of Commerce (773-5463; daily, 24 hours), PO Box 790, Main Street, Greenfield 01302. Note the information booth at the MA 2/I-91 rotary.

Shelburne Falls Village Information Center (625-2544), 75 Bridge Street, PO Box 42, Shelburne Falls 01370. A friendly, well-stocked information source for the surrounding area as well as the village, in a former fire station at the center of town.

The Mohawk Trail Association (664-6256), PO Box J, Charlemont 01339, publishes a pamphlet guide.

GETTING THERE
From Boston the obvious way is MA 2, which technically becomes the Mohawk Trail in Orange but is not evident as a tourist route until you hit the first observation platform just west of Greenfield. From points north and south, take Exit 26 off I-91 at Greenfield. Coming from the Five-College area take MA 116 North from Amherst or MA 9 North to MA 112 from Northampton.

MEDICAL EMERGENCY
Franklin Medical Center (772-0211), 164 High Street, Greenfield.

VILLAGES

Ashfield. This unusually spirited town of some 1700 people publishes its own paper. A large, former summer hotel (now the Ashfield Rest Home) still stands in the middle of the village but most traffic now stops at Elmer's Store—which carries the *New York Daily News* and a large selection of wines. The pride of Ashfield remains the Wren-style steeple on its town hall (built as a church in 1814) and its unusual number of both maple producers and craftspeople, most of whom exhibit at the annual Fall Festival. Ashfield is the birthplace of movie director

Cecil B. deMille (his parents happened to be staying at the hotel) and has been home for a number of artists and writers, making for an unusually interesting **Ashfield Historical Society** (open Saturday and Sunday in July and August, 2–5, or call 628-4541). The historical society also features the glass-plate photos of New England towns and working people taken by the two Howes brothers of Ashfield around the turn of the century. In summer there is swimming at the small town beach (transients discouraged), right in the village on Ashfield Lake, and there are two outstanding Trustees of Reservations properties (see *Green Space*).

Buckland. Buckland's town hall stands just across the Bridge of Flowers in the heart of Shelburne Falls (the town's northern boundary is the Deerfield River). The village of Buckland is, however, a gathering of a classic little church, a historical society, a small brick library, and aristocratic, 18th-century homes (one of them now a bed & breakfast), all set high on a hill a dozen miles south and off MA 112. The **historical society** (open Sunday in summer, 2–5; 625-6472) has exhibits about Mary Lyon, the Buckland woman who pioneered education for women in the early 19th century and is remembered as the founder of both Mount Holyoke College in South Hadley and Wheaton College in Norton, Massachusetts. In the four-square, four-chimneyed **Major Joseph Griswold House** you can inspect the third-floor ballroom in which Ms. Lyon began her first female academy in 1824. The space has been restored to look as it did then, complete with appropriate books (open Tuesday in summer, but call ahead: 625-2031). The way to the site of Mary Lyon's birthplace is marked from MA 112, but following it is like finding your way to the bellybutton of the earth.

Charlemont. The Deerfield River rushes down from Vermont, then slows, widens, and turns east in Charlemont, creating fertile floodplains that clearly have been farmed since the mid-18th century (judging from the age of several proud brick and clapboard farmhouses). Today the year-round population of Charlemont hovers around just 1500, and this town is the only one in New England known for both alpine skiing (Berkshire East is across the Deerfield River from the village) and whitewater rafting (see *To Do*). Rafting has introduced many visitors to the high backcountry north of MA 2. **Bissel Covered Bridge,** rebuilt in 1951 and presently in danger of being deep-sixed, spans Mill Brook just off MA 2 on MA 8A. The **Charlemont Historical Society Museum** in the town hall is open June through September, Saturday 1:30–4.

Colrain. This town boomed with sheep raising, cotton mills, and an iron foundry in the mid-19th century. The old foundry is still in Foundry Hollow, and a covered bridge sits by the North River (waiting to be put back on its pilings). Catamount Hill, site of the first schoolhouse to fly the American flag, has old cellar holes, a monument, and a small lake. **The Colrain Historical Society Museum** is housed in the former

First Methodist Church in Colrain Center (open Sunday 1–4).

Conway. Turn off MA 116 and stop long enough at the triangular Green to admire the domed **Marshall Field Memorial Library** (369-4646), gift of the native son who founded a Chicago department store. There's a marble rotunda and elaborate detailing within; the historical collection is open selected days. Also note the covered bridge across the South River off MA 116.

Shelburne Falls. Usually rivers divide towns, but in this case the Deerfield has united the 19th-century shopping and depot areas of two towns to form Shelburne Falls, one of the most unusual and lively villages in western Massachusetts. Instead of a Common there's a bridge—an abandoned trolley bridge (now reserved for foot traffic) that local garden clubs keep flooded with flowers as a war memorial. An iron bridge also links the main drags (Bridge and State Streets) on both sides of the river. An aberration from its rural setting, this totally Victorian shopping center has become a showcase for the fine craftswork produced in the surrounding hills. It's a place to get out and walk around. The "Potholes" at the foot of Salmon Falls (Deerfield Avenue, off Bridge Street) are no longer considered "glacial," but they are still unusual, worth a look. The **historical society** in the **Arms Academy Building** (corner of Maple and Church Streets) is open fairly regularly (check with the information center). Mill buffs should cross the river to see the **Lamson & Goodnow Cutlery** wood and brick complex, dating back more than 150 years.

Rowe (population 378) is known chiefly as the former home of New England's first atomic energy plant (1961–93), which has had obvious effects on the town's budget for civil amenities. Instead of the usual town dump, Rowe has a landscaped "Refuse Garden." Plaques label the sites of buildings that stood in town when it bustled: the Foliated Talc Mill (1908–22) and Eddy's Casket Shop (1846-1948), for example. The **Browning Bench Tool Factory** has been restored and moved to the shore of Pelham Lake, where it serves as an arts and community center. There are picnic tables in 1000-acre **Pelham Lake Park,** and a gazebo ornaments the Common. The **Rowe Historical Society Museum** (open weekends July 4 through Columbus Day, 2–5) has an unusually extensive collection, including records and artifacts from 18th-century Fort Pelham (the site is marked).

TO SEE

SCENIC DRIVES
The Mohawk Trail. Every autumn the AAA and other leaf-peeping pundits advise the world to take this route—which is blessedly little used the rest of the year. If you do drive it during foliage season, be sure to come midweek. Whenever you come, shift back mentally to the 1920s

Along the Mohawk Trail

to '40s auto-touring era. Note that the first "must" stop—the "Highest Steel Observation Tower in Massachusetts" at the **Longview Gift Shop**—is sited not just to take advantage of the "five-state view" but also to water and cool the engines of the early automobiles making the steep climb from Greenfield. The original tower and a similar tower at the western end of the summit were built by two enterprising sisters as added attractions to their tea rooms. **The Mohawk Trading Post,** with its huge buffalo outside, is the first trading post you see. The second, just beyond the turnoff to Shelburne Falls (see *Villages*), is the **Big Indian Shop,** because a 28-foot-tall wooden Indian guards its door. There were plenty of Indians on hand to greet 1920s tourists: Shopkeepers imported Indians to sell baskets and beadwork by the road. The largest of the half-dozen "trading posts" that survive is **Indian Plaza** in Charlemont (see *Villages*), site of periodic **Indian Pow Wows** spring through fall. **Mohawk Park** in Charlemont is the official centerpiece of the trail, site of the bronze statue placed in 1932 to commemorate the five Native American nations that regularly used this trail, chiefly for raiding purposes. The arrowhead-shaped tablet at the base of the statue reads: "Hail to the Sunrise—In Memory of the Mohawk Indian." There is a wishing pool with 100 inscribed stones from the various tribes and councils from throughout the country. MA 2 climbs steeply west from here, following the river, and then travels over Florida Mountain. **Florida,** incidentally, is one of the coldest towns in the state, but it was named in 1805 just as the United States was purchasing

Florida from Spain. The next landmark is **Whitcomb Summit,** site of a motel, snack bar, cluster of vintage cottages, bronze elk (placed here by the Massachusetts Elks in 1923), and the second tower (much reduced in height) from which you look back down the narrow Deerfield Valley. A path leads off to **Moore's Summit** (2250 feet), the highest point on the Mohawk Trail. Continue on to the **Western Summit,** site of the third lookout tower with its "three-state view" and of the Wigwam gift shop and cottages. From this point on MA 2 the well-named Hairpin Turn zigs and zags down the Western Summit into North Adams.

River Road to Whitcomb Summit is a slight but worthwhile deviation from the Mohawk Trail. Take the road marked "Rowe" just west of the village of Charlemont, but bear left at the fork (marked by a dead tree with numerous signs tacked to it) along River Road. Follow it along the river, by a picnic grove. Continue along the river as the valley walls steepen, and go past Whitcomb Summit Road, over the railroad tracks. Look here for the eastern portal of the Hoosac Tunnel, opened in the 1870s by blasting through granite. Continue a little more than 3 miles until you reach the Fife Brook Dam; in another mile you will see the **Bear Swamp Visitors Center** (424-5213). It's open Memorial Day weekend through Columbus Day, except Tuesday and Wednesday, 9–5. Displays explain how underground pumps generate power from the Deerfield as it flows from the upper to lower reservoirs. The Dunbar picnic area with rest rooms and swings is another mile up the road, across from the trailheads for hiking in the **Monroe State Forest.** Return to Whitcomb Road and follow it up to MA 2 at the Whitcomb Summit.

TO DO

BICYCLING
Bicycles Unlimited (772-2700), 322 High Street, Greenfield, rents mountain bikes and can advise about good routes through this region's maze of back roads.

CANOEING
Zoar Outdoor (1-800-532-7483), MA 2 in Charlemont, rents canoes for use on several stretches of the Deerfield; also offers shuttle service. Canoeing and whitewater clinics offered.

FISHING
The stretch of the Deerfield River in Charlemont lures fishermen from throughout the Northeast. There is a catch-and-release section in the village of Hoosac Tunnel. Beware of the changing depth of the water throughout this area due to releases from the dam. Fly-fishing clinics on the Deerfield River are offered by **Points North Fly Fishing Outfitters** (743-4030).

GOLF
Edge Hill Golf Course (628-6018), Barnes Road in Ashfield; a former

dairy farm that's now a nine-hole course with the golf shop/snack bar and lounge in the former barn overlooking a pond.

SWIMMING

See Mohawk Trail and Savoy Mountain State Forests; ask locally about swimming holes in the Deerfield River.

WHITEWATER RAFTING

"When I first approached New England Electric they said 'No. You can't raft the river,'" Bruce Lessels recalls, adding that over the next few years the power company became increasingly cooperative. In 1989 the company began releasing water from Fife Brook Dam with a regularity that makes rafting possible on most days April through October on a 10-mile stretch of the river—from Florida, through steep, green-walled, boulder-strewn Zoar Gap, and on down to Charlemont. Lessels, a former member of the US whitewater team, now heads up **Zoar Outdoor** (1-800-532-7483), based in a 1750s house with 80 acres on MA 2 in Charlemont. The complex presently includes a bathhouse with changing rooms and hot showers, an orientation pavilion, and a campground.

Crab Apple (1-800-553-7238), an outfitter with a larger base on Maine's Kennebec River, has been offering raft trips on the Deerfield since 1989 and is now also based in a former riverside motel and restaurant in Charlemont (open Wednesday through Sunday). Although Zoar Gap is admittedly not as visually and viscerally exciting as parts of Maine's Kennebec or Penobscot Rivers, it offers a great introduction to rafting. The day we ran it, a third of our group was under age 16 (minimum weight: 50 pounds). The Upper Deerfield Dryway, a stretch of water above the Fife Field Dam, is also a rafting and kayaking possibility on specific days.

CROSS-COUNTRY SKIING

Stump Sprouts (339-4265), West Hill Road, West Hawley 01339. High on the side of a mountain, this 450-acre tract offers some memorable cross-country skiing on wooded trails at 1500- to 2000-foot elevations. Snacks and rentals are available in the warming hut, which is part of Lloyd and Suzanne Crawford's home. There are 25 km of trails, lessons, and guided tours. (Also see *Lodging.*)

(Also see *Green Space* for trails in the Savoy Mountain and Kenneth Dubuque Memorial State Forests.)

DOWNHILL SKIING

Berkshire East (339-6617), South River Road, Charlemont. This is an unusually challenging mountain for its size.

Vertical drop: 1180 feet.

Terrain: 25 trails, 40 percent expert, 40 percent intermediate.

Lifts: Four chairs, two bars.

Snowmaking: 90 percent of terrain.

Facilities: Nursery, two base lodges, ski school, shop; open daily; night skiing Wednesday through Saturday.

GREEN SPACE

PICNICKING

Gardner Falls, Shelburne Falls Recreation Area. Follow North Street along the river until you see the sign. The old power canal here is a great fishing spot, and it's a great place for a picnic (go past the picnic tables, down by the river).

STATE FORESTS

Savoy Mountain State Forest (663-8469). From MA 2 in Florida take Shaft Road south to the supervisor's headquarters; the more direct approach is from MA 116 in Savoy. You can swim in North Pond and camp (45 sites) at South Pond. **Tannery Falls** is past the camping area: At a Y in the road fork right, cross the bridge, and turn left at the sign; continue until you reach the picnic area on your left; park and take the short trail to the head of the falls. At the campground there are toilets, showers, picnic sites, and three log cabins. There are 24 miles of hiking trails, two ski-touring loops, and a "crooked forest" of deformed trees. The waters are stocked with fish.

Monroe State Forest (339-5504) covers 4000 acres in the towns of Florida and Monroe. Access is on Monroe Road off MA 2 (just east of Whitcomb Summit; see River Road under *Scenic Drives*). Nine miles of hiking trails and several "pack-in" campsites are on the Dunbar Brook Falls Trail. The Roycroft Lookout takes in a panorama of the Deerfield River Valley.

Mohawk Trail State Forest (339-5504), MA 2, Charlemont, covers 6457 acres, offers more than 50 campsites and four log cabins, and allows swimming in an artificially formed pool, complete with bathhouse, scattered picnic tables, and many miles of hiking trails.

Catamount State Forest (339-5504), MA 112, Colrain. Fishing is the big attraction in this 1125-acre forest in southwestern Colrain and eastern Charlemont. Streams and a 27-acre lake are stocked. There are also hiking and riding trails.

H.O. Cook State Forest (258-4774), MA 8A, Colrain. The lure here is fishing for trout in more than 5 miles of streams. There are also hiking and riding trails. Access is off MA 8A on State Farm Road in northeastern Heath, ½ mile south of the Vermont line.

Kenneth Dubuque Memorial State Forest, also known as Hawley State Forest (339-5504), northwest of Plainfield on MA 8A, offers a fine loop hike starting at **Moody Spring,** a genuine mineral spring with a metal pipe spouting water. A sign proclaims: "This water has proven helpful in cases of sore throat, stomachache, intestinal disorders, rheumatism and all scrofula diseases." Not far from the spring, just off East Hawley Road, stands a well-preserved charcoal kiln. The forest's many miles of dirt roads make for fine winter ski touring and summer dirt biking.

WALKS

Bear Swamp Reservation, maintained by the Trustees of Reservations, is in Ashfield on the Hawley Road (less than 2 miles west of the junction of MA 116 and 112). It has 171 acres with roads and trails and is known for wildflowers: lady's slippers, painted trillium, cowslips, marsh marigolds, blue gentian, wild azaleas, and flowering dogwood.

High Ledges, Shelburne. A 300-acre preserve with superb views of the surrounding countryside. This Massachusetts Audubon Sanctuary is still maintained by the family that donated it. For directions, check with the Shelburne Falls Information Center (see *Guidance*).

WATERFALLS

Chapelbrook Reservation, maintained by the Trustees, is in South Ashfield. (Where MA 116 doglegs east, continue south on the Williamsburg Road for 2¼ miles.) Turn left to find the series of shallow falls that spill into a deep pool, perfect for sliding down. Across the road the Chapelbrook Ledges offer long views.

LODGING

BED & BREAKFASTS

☞ **1796 House** (625-2975), Upper Street, Buckland 01338. Janet Turley's 18th-century home on Buckland's classic Green is a standout. The front parlor and dining room retain their original paneling and are filled with antiques; fairly formal, but guests enter through the big country kitchen and tend to start chatting there and settle in on the ample screened-in porch. Of the three upstairs rooms our favorite is the front one with Bermuda prints, a four-poster, and a dressing room leading to the bath. Breakfast is substantial and tasty but best of all is the welcome you get from Janet, a motherly host who obviously enjoys her guests. $60–75 includes a very full breakfast.

Bull Frog Bed & Breakfast (628-4493), MA 116, South Ashfield, 01330. Lucille Thibault's home was the first bed & breakfast in Ashfield (a number have come and gone since). This 200-year-old Cape sits back from MA 116 south of South Ashfield, with a lovely back garden, a frog pond, and five kinds of berry bushes—the source of fresh berries and jams that are part of the full country breakfast. $75–85.

☞ **Penfrydd Farm B&B** (624-5516), 105 Hillman Road, Colrain 01340. Thom and Ceci Griffin offer far more than a B&B. Penfrydd Farm consists of 160 rolling acres, ringed by hills. Resident animals include sheep, llamas, and a number of horses. Riding vacations with or without your own horse can be arranged, and guests are invited to hike with the llamas along paths through woods and meadows. There are three guest rooms, two sharing a bath ($55 per couple); the third and the most popular has a whirlpool ($65).

Parson Hubbard House (625-9730), Old Village Road, Shelburne 01370.

Open May through October only. Dick and Jean Bole pride themselves on preserving the beauty of this 200-year-old parsonage that has been their own home for more than 25 years. Choose from three rooms sharing one and a half baths. The view is off across fields. Note the mossy maple out front. It dates from the 1750s. $45–55 per couple.

The Farm at Ashfield (628-4067), 1084 Cape Street (MA 112), Ashfield 01330. Bunny Tavares and John Bos have both held high-powered jobs in Washington, DC, among other places, and their 1790s house is a beauty, a blend of comfort and interesting pieces. Common spaces include a hospitable country kitchen and music/TV room as well as a parlor with a fireplace; the master bedroom has its own wood stove. $45–55 includes a full country breakfast.

Maple House Bed and Breakfast (339-0107), Middletown Hill Road, Rowe 01367. A 200-year-old farmhouse that took in summer boarders a century ago, Maple House sits high on a hill surrounded by fields. Becky and Michael Bradley have young children of their own and welcome families. Common rooms are comfortable rather than fancy, and the four guest rooms are on the renovated third floor, with pine floors and exposed posts and beams; they range from a double with private bath to a family suite. Full breakfasts feature homemade syrups (blueberry and raspberry as well as maple). Guests can swim in Pelham Lake. $45 single, $50–55 double.

The Merriams (369-4052), Conway 01341. This 1767 center-chimney classic house could easily fit into the lineup in Old Deerfield. Its paneling is exquisite, and a formal parlor is hung with forebear portraits. The upstairs former ballroom is still used as common space. A full breakfast is served in the formal dining room. Guest rooms include two doubles ($65) and one single ($50), divided between the main house and "The Barn." Bob Merriam taught English at Deerfield Academy for 25 years and now maintains an antiquarian bookshop here. Mary Merriam is a noted quilter and gives workshops.

MOTELS

The Oxbow (625-6011), Mohawk Trail, Charlemont 01339. A 24-room motel with a dining room, air-conditioning, TV, tennis, and a pool and fitness center. Breakfast served in the restaurant on weekends. $39–59.

Hilltop Motel & Cabins (625-2587), Shelburne Falls 01370. A small motel with cottages and kitchenettes; $45–50 double.

Whitcomb Summit Motel (662-2625), MA 2, North Adams 01247. Open May through October. Actually located in the town of Florida at the highest point on the Mohawk Trail, it was closed in April when we stopped by. A two-story building with balconies for each unit overlooking the view back east down the Deerfield Valley. Motel rooms are $75–85; funky old cottages for $35 (one room) to $50 (three rooms in fall).

CAMPGROUND

Springbrook Family Camp Area (625-6618), 32 Tower Road, Shelburne

01370. We rarely list private campgrounds, but this one is a standout, set high on a hillside with a great view as well as recreational lodge, lawn games, and a big pool. $20–22.

OTHER LODGING

☞ **Stump Sprouts Guest Lodge** (339-4265), West Hill Road, Hawley 01339. Lloyd Crawford has built the modern, hilltop lodge almost entirely with his own hands, from timbers he found standing on this 450-acre spread. He has also built the bunks and much of the furniture inside. A maximum of 20 can be accommodated in seven rooms, sleeping from two to five, and the common spaces are on many levels (there are lofts and corners to sit in with skylights and stained glass). Windows maximize the view of tier on tier of wooded hills. The former barn is a great rec room with table tennis, pool, and a piano; the ceiling drops down for warmth in winter and can be raised to allow even more space (the old silo is a great aerie) in summer. There's a wonderful view from the sauna, too. Vegetable gardens supply the table, which Suzanne Crawford sets family style, or you can cook for yourself. It's possible to come singly or in couples, but it's most fun to come as a group. In winter there are the cross-country ski trails for which this place is well known (see *To Do*), and in summer the trails are still there to walk or bike. Unfortunately, most weekends are now booked from year to year by returning guests, but there is usually plenty of room midweek. $109 per person per weekend includes six meals; $29 per person midweek if you cook.

Rowe Conference Center (339-4954), Kings Highway Road, Rowe 01367. The Unitarian-Universalist center consists of a farmhouse and assorted camp buildings on a quiet back road. On most weekends throughout the year there are speakers (many of them well known) on topics ranging from "Writing from the Heart," to "Herbs, Holiness, and Menopause," to "Gardening: Making and Keeping a Private Eden." Seven summer weeks are also reserved for school-aged, adult, and family camps.

Open Hearth Home Hostel (625-9638), Box 16, RR1, Shelburne 01370. Open for arrivals 6–9 PM. An affiliate of Hosteling International; bring-your-own linens, kitchen use. We have not checked this out personally but hear good things. $12 per night for HI members, $15 for nonmembers; a private room is more.

Blue Heron Farm (339-4045), Warner Hill Road, Charlemont 01339. Bill and Norma Coli offer a choice of lodging options on their 100-acre organic farm. Two self-contained cottages and the attractive apartment attached to the sugarhouse are all good for families. Overall this place is great for families; pony-cart rides, berry picking, and helping with the horses and goats are encouraged. $100 per night, $250 for three nights, $550 per week, based on four people.

Hall Tavern Farm (625-9008), MA 2, Shelburne Falls 01370. This is the state's oldest privately owned tree farm. A two-bedroom cottage is tucked into meadowland on the banks of the Deerfield River. Prices on request.

WHERE TO EAT

DINING OUT
Copper Angel Cafe (625-2727), 2 State Street, Shelburne Falls. Open daily 11:30–9, Sunday 9–8. Gail Beauregard and Nicol Wander have created a very special place in this dining room that seems suspended over the river, with the best view in town of the Bridge of Flowers. There are plenty of vegetarian dishes like Thai fried noodles, but if you must there's a cheeseburger platter (admittedly it's ground turkey). Dinner specialties include crabcakes served with the house tartar sauce ($10.95) and ham-wrapped scallops with maple mustard cream ($12.95), as well as lentil cutlets with gravy ($6.50); brunch includes veggie eggs Benedict. The "Kids Menu" choices are under $3. Wine is served along with a variety of organic coffees.

EATING OUT
Green Emporium (624-5122), MA 112, Colrain. Open daily 8–4. Michael Collins, a New York chef, and Pacifico "Tony" Palumbo, a well-known neon artist, have transformed the former (150-year-old) Methodist Church into a coffeehouse/gallery with tables in the former sanctuary at which patrons can lunch on the soup and sandwiches of the day; inquire about special concerts. The space doubles as an antiques shop/gallery with upended pews serving as shelves on which locally made and environmentally correct gifts are displayed.

10 Bridge Street Cafe & Restaurant (625-2345), 10 Bridge Street, Shelburne Falls. Open Monday through Thursday 6:30 AM–9 PM, Friday and Saturday 7 AM–10 PM, Sunday 7 AM–9 PM. The restaurant is closed some days, but the café is the lively center of town, good for a variety of burgers (the Whately Burger features locally grown onions), a selection of hearty sandwiches, soups, quiches, and salads; liquor served.

McCusker's Market & Deli (625-9411), 3 State Street, Shelburne Falls. Open weekdays 6 AM–8 PM, weekends 7 AM–8 PM.

Countrypie Pizza Company (628-4488), 343 Main Street, Ashfield. Open Wednesday through Sunday 11–9. Good pizza with plenty of veggie varieties, including eggplant, broccoli, artichoke hearts, feta, and a "Garden Delight" (featuring fresh spinach, mushrooms, and so forth). Plenty of grinders.

Buckland Bar & Grill (625-2588), 15 State Street, Shelburne Falls. Open 10 AM–midnight. Known affectionately as "The Hole," this is the alternative to the neighboring sprouts and lentils menus. The subterranean room features a long bar and booths, hometown style, and reasonably priced sandwiches and dinners like liver and onions, hot turkey, and fried fish.

Gould's Sugar House (625-6170), MA 2, Shelburne. Open March through October except May, daily 8:30 AM–2 PM. A great roadside stop for breakfast or lunch, featuring maple specialties.

Charlemont Inn (339-5796), Main Street, Charlemont. Open daily 6 AM through dinner, best known for live entertainment on weekends. The big, informal room has a lively bar.

Charlemont Pizza (339-4472), Main Street, Charlemont. Open at 11 daily, noon Sunday, until at least 9. The pizza is good, really good. Try the kielbasa with mushrooms and extra cheese.

Pine Hill Orchards (624-3325), Greenfield Road, Colrain. Open weekdays 7 AM–5, 6 on Friday, weekends from 8 AM. A counter and tables, home-baked items. The property also includes a petting zoo, picnic tables, and West County Winery (see *To See*).

Ashfield Lake House, off Main Street by the lake. Open 4–11. Better than it looks.

ENTERTAINMENT

Mohawk Trail Concerts (625-9511), 75 Bridge Street, Charlemont. Having celebrated its 25th season in 1994, this series of chamber and choral music concerts only seems to get better. Concerts are Friday at 7:30 PM, Saturday at 8 PM during July and August, in the 225-seat, acoustically fine Federated Church on MA 2.

SELECTIVE SHOPPING

ANTIQUES SHOPS
The Shelburne Falls information center (see *Guidance*) publishes a list of local dealers.

BOOKSTORE
Boswell's (625-9362), 1 State Street, Shelburne Falls. Open daily. A full-service bookshop with new and used books, audio and video rentals, and pleasant reading corners.

CRAFTS SHOPS
Salmon Falls Artisans (625-9833), 176 Ashfield Street, Shelburne Falls. Open April through December, daily 10–5, Sunday noon–5; January through March, Wednesday through Saturday 10–5, Sunday noon–5. This is an exceptional gallery showcasing much of the best work crafted in this area as well as farther afield and featuring the distinctive, widely acclaimed glass orbs by Shelburne-based Josh Simpson.

Bald Mountain Pottery (625-8110), 28 State Street, Shelburne Falls 01370. Open Tuesday through Saturday 10–5, Sunday noon–5; closed Monday through Wednesday off-season. The distinctive, functional pottery is made in the riverside studio, which also displays work by several other local potters.

Mohawk Trail concerts

North River Glass (625-6422), Deerfield Avenue, Shelburne Falls. Watch glass being blown; the deeply colored resulting vases, bowls, perfume bottles, and art glass are displayed in the adjacent gallery.

Mole Hollow Candles (625-6337), Deerfield Avenue, Shelburne Falls. Open daily 10–5, later in summer. Overlooks the potholes in the Deerfield River; candles are made on weekdays. The shop also sells gifts and cards.

Textile Arts (625-8241), 6 Bridge Street, Shelburne Falls. A small shop in which Susie Robbins repairs sewing machines but also displays work by local weavers like Rebecca Ashenden (wool blankets and shawls, cotton placemats and tablecloths).

FARMS

Donovan Farm (339-4213), Forget Road, Hawley. The state's largest organically certified farm, with sweeping views and five kinds of potatoes; it produces its own hand-cooked, organic potato chips.

Hall Tavern Farm (625-9008), MA 2, Shelburne Falls. The state's oldest privately owned tree farm produces timbers and lumber for its sawmill and offers a variety of kiln-dried wood products, including wide pine flooring, paneling, and wainscoting as well as ash, cherry, maple, and oak flooring from its 500 acres. (Also see *Lodging.*)

Penfrydd Farm (624-5516), Colrain. The Farm Store on the 160-acre farm off the byways of Colrain features hand-dyed yarns, handwoven blankets, knitted garments, sheepskins, and other farm products. Also see *Lodging.*

Burnt Hill Farm (337-4454), Burnt Hill, Heath. Pick-your-own blueberries in-season on top of a mountain with a 50-mile view.

Long Hill Farm (339-4336), Long Hill Road, Heath. Open Tuesday through Saturday 10–5; farmers' market Saturday during the season.

Wool is processed in the farm store, a former Unitarian meetinghouse (1830–60); the farm includes a picnic area, hiking trails, a sugarhouse, a cider press, lambs, and hay.

Walnut Hill Farm (625-9002), 104 Ashfield Road, Shelburne Falls. Open daily 7:30 AM–7 PM. A dairy farm and vegetable stand welcome visitors. The world's largest ox, weighing 4700 pounds, was raised here at the turn of the century.

SUGARHOUSES

As already noted, the Hilltowns are the prime source of Massachusetts's maple sugar, and the sugaring season—which can begin as early as late February and extend well into April—draws locals and visitors alike to sugarhouses and to pancake breakfasts featuring the new syrup. A brochure detailing information about the sugaring process and each producer is available from the Massachusetts Maple Producers Association, Watson-Spruce Corner Road, Ashfield 01330. During sugaring season you can call the Massachusetts Maple Phone (628-3912) to get an overall view on whether the sap is flowing and producers are "boiling off."

The following sugarhouses are geared toward visitors more than most, but it's still a good idea to call before coming. All also sell their syrup from their farms year-round.

In Ashfield, **Gray's Sugarhouse** (625-6559) has a dining room open on weekends during sugaring, as does **South Face Farm** (628-4493), which also exhibits antique maple-sugaring equipment.

Puringtons' Maple (625-2780), Buckland, still use horses to collect sap.

Blue Heron Farm (339-4045), Charlemont, welcomes visitors with rental units attached to its sugarhouse; the farm also features dairy goats, Norwegian Fjord horses, and organic produce.

Boyden Brothers, right on MA 116 in Conway, is the big producer here, but a number of other producers using wood-burning evaporators are scattered through the hills.

Girard's Sugarhouse (337-5788) in Heath has been operating over 90 years.

In Shelburne, **Gould's Sugar House** (625-6170), right on MA 2, features locally made syrup on waffles; also homemade sausage and sugar-on-snow among its other items (see *Eating Out*). **Davenport Maple Farm** (625-2866), set high above the valley with a splendid view, operates a restaurant during sugaring season and sells syrup from the house year-round (a good excuse to drive up).

APPLE ORCHARDS

Mohawk Orchards (625-2874), ¼ mile north of MA 2 on the Colrain-Shelburne Road. Open year-round, daily. Pick-your-own apples Labor Day through Columbus Day, otherwise a farm stand sited in the middle of the orchard, picnic tables, small farm animals for petting.

Pine Hill Orchards (624-3324), 248 Greenfield Road, Colrain. Open year-round daily. Pick-your-own apples in-season, also bakery/restaurant (see *Eating Out*), sugarhouse, farm animals for petting.

SPECIAL SHOPS

McCusker's Market (625-9411), 3 State Street, Shelburne Falls. Aside from carrying gourmet and ecologically correct lines, McCusker's is the only outlet for **Lamson & Goodnow Cutlery,** manufactured in town for more than 150 years. Exceptional in quality, the cutlery ranges from a $16 bar/fruit knife to a $40 "slicer," and there are frequent sales on individual pieces and sets.

Green Emporium (624-5122), MA 112, Colrain Center. Open Wednesday through Friday 1–3:30, weekends 8–4. Handmade crafts, antiques, paintings, and sculpture displayed in a former church that's also a café (see *Eating Out*).

Bear Meadow Farm (663-9241), Whitcomb Summit, MA 2, Florida. Quality preserves and condiments sold here are made at a neighboring farm.

WINERY

West County Winery (624-3481) at Pine Hill Orchards, Colrain (turn at the Duck Pond Restaurant on MA 2). Open May through December, Thursday through Sunday 11–5, and Friday through Sunday the rest of the year. Six hard ciders, dry to sweet, with alcohol 4 to 5 percent, are produced from local fruit, available for sampling in the tasting room.

SPECIAL EVENTS

May: **Indian Pow Wow** at Indian Plaza, Charlemont. **Memorial Day Parade,** Shelburne Falls.

June: **Riverfest**—day-long festival along the street and river in Shelburne Falls. **Indian Pow Wow,** Indian Plaza, Charlemont.

July: **July 4th Indian Pow Wow,** Charlemont. **Parade** in Shelburne Falls.

August: **Bridge of Flowers 10K road race** and **Bridge of Flowers Festival. Heath Fair** (mid-month).

September: The big event comes the last weekend with the **Conway Festival of the Hills,** one of New England's most colorful foliage festivals. The **Colrain Fair** is mid-month.

October: The **Fall Foliage Festival in Ashfield** on Columbus Day weekend is not to be missed. Shelburne Falls also stages a fall foliage festival with sidewalk sales, music, and trolley rides the first weekend.

November: **Midnight Madness** the day after Thanksgiving; tree lighting, caroling, and special sales in Shelburne Falls.

HAMPSHIRE HILLS

This 225-square-mile spread of rolling hill and woodland is even farther off the tourist map than the West County Hilltowns to the north. It's been blessedly bypassed by the Mass. Pike (there are no exits for the 30 miles between Westfield and Lee).

During the decades before income taxes, when wealthy Americans were building themselves summer palaces around Stockbridge and Lenox, a number of old farms around Worthington and Cummington became "gentlemen's farms." William Cullen Bryant Homestead and Swift River Inn are the most obvious surviving examples, but there are many more.

For much of this century, however, this area was just a nameless region to pass through. You could count the number of commercial lodging places on your fingers. Then in 1982 the Hilltown Community Development Corporation placed an ad in local papers asking people with spare rooms to consider the bed & breakfast business. The results were spectacular in a low-key way. In short order a dozen or so households responded, forming the Hampshire Hills Bed & Breakfast Association and publishing a descriptive brochure. Seemingly overnight the "Hampshire Hills" became a destination with a name and a choice of places to stay.

Not much has changed since 1982. The number of B&Bs has increased and now includes several in Hamden County to the south. Although there are no information centers or phone numbers, B&B hosts direct their guests to local swimming holes, antiques shops, craftspeople, hiking trails, and waterfalls. Perusing the listings here you will note that there's only one entry under *To See* and relatively few restaurants, but an unusual number of places under *Green Space*, several genuine old general stores that can supply picnic needs, and some outstanding craftspeople worth locating both for the quality of their work and for the backroad-beauty of their settings. Generally speaking, the hills are less steep here than in the Hilltowns to the north, more conducive to bicycling.

The Miniature Theater of Chester and the Sevenars concerts in South Worthington are both widely acclaimed, but most events—auctions, agricultural fairs, and town homecomings—are promoted only locally.

AREA CODE
413

GUIDANCE
Hampshire Hills Bed & Breakfast Association, write: Box 553, Worthington 01098.

Hilltown Community Development Corporation (296-4536), PO Box 17, Chesterfield 01012. Though it is not funded or geared to deal with tourism, this group is presently the only source of general information about the area.

GETTING THERE
Part of the beauty of this area is in its approach. Few places in this region are much more than a half hour's drive from I-91 or the Mass. Pike, but you are quickly on back roads. The principal east-west roads—MA 9

and MA 66/US 20—follow the river valleys, while MA 57 to the south is a high old byway. The major north-south routes, MA 112 and MA 8, also follow rivers.

MEDICAL EMERGENCY

Worthington Health Center (238-5511), Old North Road, Worthington.

VILLAGES

Chesterfield. A white-clapboard village with an 1835 Congregational Church, 1848 town hall, and the Edward Memorial (historical) museum near the library. But the big attraction is Chesterfield Gorge (see *Green Space*).

Cummington. The classic village center is posted from MA 9 and worth a stop to see the **Kingman Tavern** (open Saturday 2–5 in July and August), a lovingly restored combination tavern, fully stocked general store, and post office. There are a dozen period rooms filled with town mementos like the palm leaf hat and cigar once made here. There is also a barn full of tools and a shed full of horse-drawn vehicles. The big annual event is the **Hillside Agricultural Society Fair,** the last weekend in August. Cummington has nurtured a number of poets over the years and is the longtime home of America's former poet laureate Richard Wilbur.

Middlefield (population 392), a town in which the main road (one of the few that's paved) is known as the Skyline Trail because it follows the edge of a 1650-foot-high plateau, offers spectacular views west to the Berkshires. The only specific site to visit here is **Glendale Falls** (see *Green Space*), but everywhere you walk or drive is rewarding.

Plainfield. This beautiful old farming town has a population of 466, which swells to 2000 in summer. Roads are lined with stone walls and avenues of maples, and the center has its mid-19th-century white Congregational church and town hall. **The Shaw-Hudson House** (634-5417), open by appointment, was built in 1833 by Dr. Samuel Shaw, medical partner and brother-in-law of William Cullen Bryant. The personality of the house, especially the medical office with its drug case and books, is worth a stop.

Williamsburg. The easternmost of the Hilltowns, this village is something of a bedroom town for Northampton. The two-street center straddles the Mill River and invites you to stroll, munching something you've bought at the General Store; the **historical society** (268-7332), housed in the 1841 town hall, exhibits photographs of the 1874 flood that burst a dam 3 miles above the village, killing 136 residents, collapsing buildings, and wiping out most of the mills. Note the Brassworks mill in Haydenville, rebuilt since the flood and recently renovated.

Worthington. The village at the heart of this town, known locally as Worthington Corners, is a classic, mid-19th-century crossroads with its general store and surrounding old homes along roads that radiate in every direction. Note the general store, golf course (vintage 1904), B&Bs, cross-country ski center, and auctions and crafts store.

TO SEE

William Cullen Bryant Homestead (634-2244) in Cummington, south of MA 9 off MA 112. Open for guided tours from the last week in June through Labor Day, Friday, Saturday, Sunday, and holidays 1–5; until Columbus Day, weekends and holidays. Admission charged. This graceful mansion is filled with the spirit of an obviously tough-minded and original individual and with a sense of the era in which he was thoroughly involved. William Cullen Bryant was born in Cummington in 1794 and is remembered for his early nature poems, "Thanatopsis" and "To a Waterfowl," and for his impact as editor and part owner for a half century (1829–1878) of the *New York Evening Post*. Bryant successfully advocated causes ranging from abolitionism, to free trade, to the creation of Central Park. He returned to his boyhood home at age 72, buying back the family homestead, adding another floor, and totally transforming it into a 23-room Victorian summer manse set atop 246 acres of farmland. The acreage has since been reduced to a mere 189 acres, but the expansive view of hills and meadows remains. The house has been beautifully preserved (painted in its original chocolate browns) by the Trustees of Reservations to look as it did during Bryant's last summer here in 1878.

SCENIC DRIVES

In the Hilltowns the drive that is not scenic is the exception. You almost can't lose, especially if you turn off the main roads in search of the waterfalls, swimming holes, crafts studios, or maple producers described in this chapter. Several drives, however, are particularly noteworthy.

The Skyline Trail, accessible from MA 143 in Hinsdale and from US 20 in Chester, follows the edge of the Berkshire Plateau through the middle of Middlefield. It's possible to make a loop from Chesterfield through Middlefield, stopping at **Glendale Falls** and the **River Studio** and returning via Chester Hill (another high point), but it's best to ask directions locally.

Ireland Street, Chesterfield to South Worthington. A mile or so west of the village of Chesterfield turn left off MA 143 at the bridge. This is Ireland Street and best known as the way to **Chesterfield Gorge** (0.8 mile from MA 143 at River Road; see *Green Space*). Be sure to stop, then continue along Ireland Street, which is a straight, high ridge road. Stop at **Ireland Orchards** for the view, if for nothing else. Continue on to South Worthington, stopping by **Stonepool Pottery** (see *Selective Shopping*). If you feel like a swim, **Gardner State Park** (see *Swimming*) is just down MA 112.

Get Lost. Seriously. If we try to direct you from **Plainfield** to **Buckland** via the web of back roads that begin with Union Street north from the middle of Plainfield, you will have us to blame. But this is high, largely, open countryside that was obviously far more populated a couple of hundred years ago than it is now. Bring a camera and compass.

TO DO

BALLOONING
Paul Sena (238-5514) offers champagne flights May to November from a variety of local sites (including local B&Bs); sunrise and sunset flights geared to couples. $350 for a 1½-hour flight in multicolored "Thunderbuster."

BICYCLING
Swift River Inn (634-5751; 1-800-632-8038) rents mountain bikes for use on its cross-country ski trails in summer.

FISHING
All three branches of the Westfield River are good for fishing; the Swift River Inn (see *Lodging*) offers occasional fly-fishing workshops.

GOLF
Chesterfield Chip & Putt (296-4767), 223 South Street. A par-three, 18-hole course open daily 9–dark. Children must be 9 years old to play. **Beaver Brook Golf Club** (268-7229), 191 Haydenville Road (MA 9), Williamsburg, and the **Worthington Golf Club** (238-9731) are both nine holes.

HORSEBACK RIDING
Pleasure Horse Paso Fino Barn (848-2214), 43 Russell Road, Blandford. This place is really a bed & breakfast catering to people who are interested in horses. You can bring your horse with you or work with a resident mount; lessons are offered in hunt seat, western, dressage, and paso fino. Hourly trail rides are available by appointment.

SWIMMING
The West Branch, Middle Branch, and Westfield River proper all weave their ways through this area, offering countless swimming holes to which B&B hosts can direct you. More formal, public swimming spots like Plainfield Pond tend to be restricted to residents.
D.A.R. State Forest (268-7098), Goshen, maintains a swimming area on Upper Highland Lake (see *Green Space*).
Windsor State Forest (684-9760), River Road, West Cummington, has a swimming area on a dammed portion of the river (see *Green Space*).
Gardner State Park, MA 112, Huntington. Probably the best-known swimming hole on the Westfield River. A great spot to bring small children; an old-fashioned picnic pavilion in the pines.

CROSS-COUNTRY SKIING
Swift River Inn (634-5751; 1-800-632-8038), 151 South Street, Cumming-

ton. The 23 km of groomed trails meandering through hardwoods and firs represent one of the oldest, best-known cross-country systems around, revived under current ownership. The center offers at least 1 km of lighted trail covered by snowmaking, a large, open-timbered lodge with a massive hearth, a ski shop with rentals, cafeteria-style food service, and a pub. Open 9–9. Note: Packages are offered in conjunction with the Swift River Inn (see *Lodging*).

Hickory Hill Ski Touring Center (623-5535), Buffington Hill Road, Worthington. Open Friday through Monday in-season. In contrast to Swift River's sleek lodge and multi-tiered staff, the lodge here is an old potato barn with a bar and snack bar (both featuring homemade pretzels) and a staff of three, all related. "It's kind of funky, but people like it," observes Paul Sena, the man who cut as well as grooms the 24 km of trails on his family's 500-acre farm, a largely wooded spread. Snowfarming is Paul Sena's obsession. When we last visited, there had been virtually no new snow for more than a week, and freezing rain had glazed the landscape. Sena was in his Snowcat, a large alpine groomer, chewing the surface to bits—to be subsequently smoothed with a powder-maker and ultimately tracked. Trails climb through maples, birches, beeches, and firs, skirting a large field or two, and follow several streams to an altitude of more than 1800 feet. Although a track is kept carefully groomed for skating and free-style skiing, the majority of the trails are tracked for traditional recreational skiing.

Maple Corner Farm (357-6697), Beech Hill Road, Granville. Twelve miles of trails; lessons, lodge with fireplace, moonlight tours.

Notchview Reservation (684-3722), MA 9, Windsor. The highest cross-country trails in Massachusetts are found on this 3000-acre Trustees of Reservations property. Admittedly, it takes a new snowfall to work your way up to the summit of 2297-foot-high Judges Hill, but frequently there is snow up on the former lawns of the General Budd Homesite. The panoramic view from this open area includes the notch in the hills cut by the Westfield River, for which the preserve is named.

ICE SKATING

The **Swift River Inn** offers an outdoor skating rink with lights and music for night skating. Skate rentals.

GREEN SPACE

PICNICKING

South River State Forest (268-7098; 339-5504), north from Conway Village on the Shelburne Falls and Bardwells Ferry Roads, offers picnic tables and grills scattered along the gorge of the South River to its confluence with the Deerfield. Near the parking area notice the South River Dam, once used to power the trolley line that carried passengers to and from the New York–New Haven and Hartford Railroad, which crossed South River here over the highest trestle in the state (you can see the railbed and the remains of the trestle).

STATE FORESTS

D.A.R. State Forest (268-7098), Goshen, provides more than 50 campsites, each with a table and fireplace. The swimming area at Upper Highland Lake. complete with bathhouses and lifeguards, also has a boat ramp (no motors allowed). Trails lead to Moore's Hill, just 1697 feet high but with an extensive view.

Windsor State Forest (684-9760). Follow signs from MA 9 in West Cummington, via River Road. There are 24 campsites. You can swim in the dammed section of the river; there are bathhouses, picnic tables, and grills here. A road across from the recreation area on River Road leads to **Conway State Forest** (268-7098), West Whately Road, south from the eastern edge of Conway Village. This 1946-acre forest is good for hiking, ski-touring, and snowmobiling.

East Branch State Forest (268-7098), River Road, Chesterfield, offers some good fishing.

WALKS

Notchview Reservation (684-0148). The Budd Visitor Center on MA 9 in Windsor (1 mile east of the junction with MA 8A), is open daily yearround. There are picnic tables and trail maps for the 25 miles of hiking and cross-country trails (see *Cross-Country Skiing*) on this former 3000-acre estate maintained by the Trustees of Reservations. This is a good place for birding.

Windsor Jambs in Windsor State Park is a ¼-mile-long gorge with sheer cliffs, topped with hemlocks above the rushing water. A trail leads along the edge. Unfortunately, picnicking is not permitted here, but it's a beautiful walk (there's a railing). The state dams the river for swimming, and there are bathhouses, 80 picnic tables, and grills. This stretch of the Westfield River is a popular spot for whitewater canoeing. There are also many miles of hiking trails.

Petticoat Hill Reservation in Williamsburg (up Petticoat Hill Road from the village). A trail leads to the summit of Scott Hill. Stone walls and cellar holes hint that this spot was the most populated part of town in the 1700s, but it's now forested, a good spot for wildflowers.

Devil's Den Brook in Williamsburg is a rocky gorge off Old Goshen Road (turn right on Hemenway Road at the western fringe of the center, branch left onto Old Goshen). If you take the next left, up Brier Hill Road, you come to 70 acres of wooded trails, good for cross-country skiing and hiking. Ask locally about Rheena's Cave.

WATERFALLS

Glendale Falls, Middlefield (off the Skyline Trail Road onto Clark Wright Road—which is closed in winter—some 3½ miles southeast of the village). Glendale Brook drops more than 150 feet over rocky ledges. There are 60 surrounding acres.

Chesterfield Gorge. Turn off MA 143 at the West Chesterfield Bridge, 1 mile south on River Road. A deep canyon was carved by the Westfield River, walled by sheer granite cliffs topped with hemlock, ash, and yellow birch. Swimming is not allowed, but the Trustees of Reservations provide picnic tables.

LODGING

INNS
Swift River Inn (634-5751; 1-800-532-8022), 151 South Street, Cummington 01026. The rooms, 22 in all, are hollowed out of former dairy barns, part of a 600-acre gentleman's estate built by a Northampton merchant in 1919. The property has had a checkered history since and is still fondly remembered by many as "Cummington Farm" (1973–84), one of New England's first cross-country touring centers. Now substantially upscaled, it is owned by Peter Laird, co-creator of the Teenage Mutant Ninja Turtles. Laird has built New England's most elaborate ski-touring lodge and a 25-km trail system that includes 5 km with snowmaking. In summer the trails are used for mountain biking (rentals available), and the lodge is the site of periodic concerts. Rooms in the inn are attractive, many split-level suites, all with private bath, phone, and TV. Management, however, has changed frequently over the past few years, and the inn has yet to acquire a reputation for hospitality. Facilities include a restaurant serving all three meals (but check) and an outdoor pool. $69–169 without meals depending on the day and season.

The Whale Inn (263-6246), MA 9, Goshen 01032. Built as a parsonage in 1799, this landmark became an inn in 1923 and is known as a place to dine, but upstairs are six rooms with private bath. $35 single, $55 double includes continental breakfast.

BED & BREAKFASTS
☞ **Windfields Farm** (684-3786), 154 Windsor Bush Road, Cummington 01026. Open daily except in March and April. We put this at the head of the Hilltown listings because it was one of the first and remains among our favorites based on its location and the hospitality of its hosts. There are just two rooms (one with an exquisite, early-19th-century canopy bed), and these share a bath; but just behind this Federal (1830) house is a swimming pond, blueberry pastures, organic gardens, fireplace, and solar greenhouse. You can ski or walk up the road to the falls at Windsor Jambs or hike through the 200-acre property itself. Carolyn and Arnold Westwood (Arnold is a retired Unitarian minister who is still frequently called upon to perform marriages in the area) are, moreover, consummate hosts, and Carolyn's maple syrup has won top honors at the Cummington Fair. Breakfast is an event, featuring the farm's eggs, raspberries, breads, and jams, as well as maple syrup. Facilities include

a fully equipped guest kitchen. Two-night minimum on most weekends. $70 per couple, $50 single, midweek discounts.

The Worthington Inn (238-4441), at Four Corners Farm, Old North Road (MA 143), Worthington 01098. A striking, vintage-1780 house with wide floorboards, five fireplaces, and fine paneling, restored in 1942 by the architect responsible for much of the Old Deerfield restoration. The three bedrooms are sparely, tastefully furnished with antiques and down comforters and have private baths. The house is beautifully sited on its own 15 acres but on the edge of a photogenic village. Hickory Hill Ski Touring Center is also less than a mile away. Children and horses are welcome. Debi Shaw is a hospitable, helpful host. $70–90.

☞ **The Seven Hearths** (296-4312), 412 Main Road, Chesterfield 01012. An 1890s house that has been renovated to look older, set in the middle of the historic district of Chesterfield's picturesque village. Doc and Denise LeDuc make you feel welcome in the comfortable living room, and they serve memorable multicourse breakfasts (maybe stuffed French toast prefaced by a fruit-stuffed melon) in the formal dining room. The common rooms and two of the three guest rooms have working fireplaces; the larger guest room offers sitting and writing space and a private bath. Facilities include a hot tub. $60–65.

☞ **Twin Maples** (268-7925), 106 South Street, Williamsburg 01096. This graceful house is vintage 1806, set in its own 27 acres and surrounding farmland on a back road not far from the center of Williamsburg. It's been home to Eleanor and Martin Hebert for more than 30 years, and for more than a decade now the couple have welcomed B&B guests. Eleanor also operates the Berkshire Bed & Breakfast, a reservation service for much of western Massachusetts; in other words, she's a pro. The three bedrooms and shared bath are clean and crisp (we like the blue room with the iron bed), and the welcome is genuine. During March you can watch sap turn into syrup in the sugarhouse, and any season you can meet the farm animals, which included, at latest count, two sows and a boar, a flock of Rhode Island Red hens and roosters, and a number of sheep. The dog's name is Charlie. $60–65. One-night surcharge, $5.

☞ **Cumworth Farm** (634-5529), 472 West Cummington Road (MA 112), Cummington 01026. This is a splendid but comfortable 18th-century, hip-roofed farmhouse, and Ed McColgan, a former state representative, still does serious farming, producing some 600 gallons of maple syrup and raising berries and sheep. The McColgans' seven children are grown and have left five spare rooms, all furnished with antiques. Amenities include a hot tub in the gazebo and breakfasts that are full farm. $60 double, $40 single.

Strawberry Banke Farm (623-6471), 140 Skyline Trail, Middlefield 01243. Middlefield is the kind of place where you might expect to find a bed & breakfast like Strawberry Banke Farm, a 1780s farmhouse surrounded by flowers, painted (inside and out) and whimsically furnished by artist/host Judy Tavener Artioli, whose own paintings (Chagall is monotone by comparison) are displayed in the adjacent studio. The guest room with private bath is on the first floor, and two more rooms upstairs share a bath. The breakfast specialty of the house is Belgian waffles. $75 double, $70 single.

Baird Tavern (848-2096), 2 Old Chester Road, Blandford 01008. This vintage-1768 house retains its original paneling and wide floorboards and conveys a sense of comfort. Host Carolyn Taylor is a local caterer, and breakfasts can as easily be quiche as blueberry pancakes. One bedroom is a double, and the other has twins and an add-on space suitable for a family. A cot and crib are available, and at least a couple of Persian Angora cats (which Carolyn raises) are usually on hand. $60 double, $50 single, $10 for a crib.

Carmelwood (667-5786), 8 Montgomery Road, Huntington 01050. Handy to the Sevenars concerts just up the road, also to swimming in the Westfield River. This is a handsome Victorian house with a grand piano in the living room, an ample front porch, and the gardens that are Katheryn Corrigan's pride. Breakfast features home-baked breads and pastries and locally grown fruit. There are three double bedrooms, two with double beds, one with twins. $50–70 double.

The Hill Gallery (238-5914), 137 East Windsor Road, Worthington 01098. A modern home, designed and built by owner Walter Korzec, offers two rooms with private baths (cots available). The multilevel home doubles as a gallery for Korzec's prints and paintings and also showcases local pottery. $60 double, $50 single; a small cottage is also available.

Outlook Farm (527-0633), MA 66, Westhampton 01027. From downtown Northampton you climb a dozen miles west, up onto a plateau that's still farm country. Outlook Farm is best known for its farm stand, really a country store (see *Selective Shopping*), but it offers two double guest rooms and a single, all sharing one basic bath. Though the house is right on MA 66, it is surrounded by apple, peach, and pear orchards and more than 200 acres that include a swim pond and hiking trails. Mary Lee Morse is an exceptional baker, and $50 per night ($40 single) includes a full breakfast.

Pleasure Horse Farm (848-2214), Russell Road, Blandford 01008, features horseback riding; all rooms have single and double beds, shared bath. $40 per person.

Note: The following additional B&Bs are described in the leaflet guide available by writing: Hampshire Hills Bed & Breakfast Association, PO Box 553, Worthington 01098. We do not describe them here individually only because no one was home when we tried to visit this past year; this fact in no way reflects their quality. In Worthington: **Inn Yesterday** (238-5529), **The Franklin Burr Homestead** (238-5826), **The Heritage** (238-4230), and **Tamarack Lodge** (238-4449). In Plainfield: **Rolling Meadow Farm** (634-2166). For lodging in Becket see "South County."

OTHER LODGING

Remington Lodge (634-5388), West Cummington 01026. Jo and Ken Cyr offer old-fashioned, no-frills hospitality to hikers, bikers, whitewater canoeists, skiers, hunters, anyone willing to bring his or her own sleeping bag and sleep in a room with 4, 6, or 16 other people. The food is fine (the lodge is open to nonguests Friday evenings by reservation), and $50 weekend packages include Saturday dinner, Sunday breakfast, and a brown-bag lunch. Ask about the hot tub.

WHERE TO EAT

DINING OUT

The Squires' (268-7222), the Brassworks on MA 9, Williamsburg. Open Wednesday through Sunday from 5 PM; call for reservations. The menu borrows from a number of cultures, but all dishes are smoked or grilled with a wood fire. Specialties include Fava duck, Moroccan-style chicken, and "Blues ribs"; entrée prices are $13.95–28. The special might be a mixed grill of elk and wild boar sausage with sage ($16.95). Liquor, as well as wine and beer, is served.

Historic Williams House (268-7300), MA 9, Williamsburg. Open daily for lunch and dinner; Sunday brunch 9–1. David and Carol Majercik, who own the neighboring Williamsburg General Store, have rejuvenated this old landmark with its low-beamed dining room and large hearth. Hearty luncheon sandwiches run $4.15–6.95, and dinner entrées range from "fancy fettucine" to prime rib ($8.95–16.95). There are daily specials and full wine and liquor lists; patrons are also welcome simply for espresso and dessert.

Little River Cafe (238-5837), corner of MA 112 and Ireland Street, South Worthington. Open Wednesday through Sunday 5–9:30. Nothing fancy but very pleasant, with a screened porch set above the Little River, handy to Sevenars (see *Entertainment*) concerts. Entrées range from bean burritos ($6.95) to seafood linguine ($13.95) and steak *au poivre,* pan-fried in sherry and sweet butter, served flambéed ($16.95). There's also an extensive pub menu, wine and beer lists.

The Restaurant at Swift River Inn (634-5751), 151 South Street, Cummington. Theoretically open for breakfast weekdays, Sunday brunch buffet, lunch Monday through Saturday, and dinner (5–9) nightly, but check; reservations required for dinner. The dinner is traditional New England fare in the $10–17 per entrée range. The decor includes brass and quilts; it's pleasant.

The Whale Inn (268-7246), MA 9, Goshen. A large traditional restaurant open daily for lunch and dinner with dance music on Friday and Saturday evenings.

EATING OUT

Woodside Restaurant (268-3685), Main Street (MA 9), Williamsburg.

Open 6 AM–8 PM; until 2 PM Monday, 9 PM Friday and Saturday. Clean, welcoming, a counter as well as several tables, homemade soups, daily specials.

The Old Creamery (634-5560), corner of MA 9 and MA 112, Cummington. Open daily 7:30–7:30, from 9 on Sunday. A spiffed-up general store with a deli, wine selection, and several tables.

Howe's Cafe (634-5454), MA 9, Cummington. Open from 6 AM weekdays, from 7:30 Sunday. We frankly prefer this local gathering place with its heavy crockery and homemade soups to the Creamery. *Note:* It can be smoky.

ENTERTAINMENT

Miniature Theatre of Chester (667-8818), PO Box 487, Huntington 01050. The season runs from early July through Labor Day weekend. Vincent Dowling, a former artistic director and still an associate director of Dublin's famed Abbey Theatre, first came to Chester to fish and swim in the Westfield River and has since built himself a house while staging a summer program of plays—a mix of lesser-known classics and original works, performed in Chester's town hall (150 seats). Casts are limited to just one or two professional actors and are generally outstanding.

Sevenars Music Festival (238-5854), MA 112 between Huntington and Worthington. Concerts are Friday evenings (at 7:30) and Sunday afternoons (at 5), mid-July through August. The seven "R"s stand for the seven Schrades, who include Robert (longtime soloist with orchestras and a member of the faculty at the Manhattan School of Music), his wife Rolande (a concert pianist in her own right and composer of more than 1000 songs), Robelyn, Rorianne, and Randolf Schrade (all with impressive degrees and concert careers). The twins Rhonda-Lee and Rolisa don't perform but Robelyn's husband, well-known New Zealand pianist David James, and their 9-year-old daughter, Lynelle, do. Concerts are staged in a double-porched, 19th-century academy just off MA 112 by the South Worthington Cascade. The old-fashioned hall is walled in tongue-in-groove paneling, literally papered with posters advertising worldwide performances by members of the family and their guests. Like many Hilltown artists the Schrades were originally drawn to the area by the price as well as the beauty of its land. Back in 1964, soon after their fifth child was born, the Manhattan-based family bought the old South Worthington Inn as a summer home for $1000 down. In time, after a number of local concerts-by-demand, they acquired and stabilized the neighboring academy. Recently they have also rehabbed an adjacent former blacksmith's shop, a showcase for some exceptional work by members of the Hilltown Artisans Guild, that's open, unfortunately, only on Sevenars concert days.

SELECTIVE SHOPPING

ANTIQUES SHOPS

Sena Auctions (238-5813), Worthington. Since the 1950s auctions have taken place on Tuesday, but check to make sure. Held in the former potato barn that serves in winter as a ski-touring center.

Chesterfield Antiques, MA 143, Chesterfield, has a good selection.

CRAFTS SHOPS

The Basket Shop (296-4278), 513 Main Road (MA 143), Chesterfield. The shop itself is special, built by hand by Ben Higgins with an open basket-weave ceiling, woven cabinet doors, dovetailed drawers, and a variety of timeworn tools. Ben specialized in the rare art of weaving ash baskets, a skill his son-in-law Milton Lanford carries on using a variety of wooden molds, some over 100 years old. The baskets are striking and unusually durable. Call before making a special trip; inquire about "Open Days."

Sheepgate Handwovens (848-0990), Otis Stage Road, Blandford. Open Sunday 11–5. The sheep are at the door, and the weaver is working her hand looms, selling one-of-a-kind clothing, shawls, bedding, pillows, sheepskins, buttons, and jewelry.

Stonepool Pottery (238-5362), Conwell Road, Worthington, just up Ireland Street from the old academy in South Worthington (take the next left). Open daily, year-round. Distinctive. Functional work by three potters is displayed in a small gallery near a studio and above the house now owned by potter Mark Shapiro, an old homestead in which the Reverend Russell Conwell was born. Conwell later added an unusual "stone pool" and built the nearby academy, but he is better known as the founder of Philadelphia's Temple University.

Judy Tavener Artoli (623-6481), Skyline Trail, Middlefield. You don't have to stay at Strawberry Banke Farm in order to view the original bright oils, acrylics, pastels, handpainted floor cloths, and clothes displayed in the studio here.

River Studio (238-7755), River Road, Middlefield. Open July, August, and September, Thursday through Saturday 1–6, or year-round by appointment. The internationally acclaimed dancing statues of Andrew deVries are a find in their own right—especially set as they are on a meadow stage in a particularly obscure and lovely corner of Middlefield.

Storybook Hill (238-5548), Buffington Hill Road, Worthington. No set hours, just ring the bell on the shop door behind the house. Florence Chamberlin takes several days to sew each of the stuffed animals for which she has become widely known over the past 30 years. Rabbits are her trademark, rabbits with beguiling faces and amazing clothing. All the creations, each one unique, are sturdy and washable. To complement the dolls Florence's husband, Edward, builds dollhouses, also among the 1000 items for sale in the shop.

FARMS

Roberts Family Blueberry Farm, 223 South Street, Chesterfield.

Ireland Street Orchards (296-4014), Ireland Street, Chesterfield. April through November, open 10–6. Pick-your-own apples, flowers, a farm stand with local produce and crafts, and horse-drawn hayrides on weekends during harvest season. Annual apple festival the first weekend in October.

Outlook Farm (529-9338), MA 66, Westhampton. Open weekdays 6–7, weekends 6–6. You can pick your own apples and find seasonal fruit and produce here, but the real specialties of the roadside store are homemade sausage, smoked hams, bacon, and ribs (although the pigs are no longer raised here the way they used to be, the USDA-certified slaughterhouse and smokehouse continue to operate). Sandwiches and daily specials are served. Hayrides available.

Gran-Val Farm/Scoop, MA 189, Granville. Open mid-April to mid-October, 11–9:30. This is a dairy farm with an ice cream stand serving at least 24 flavors of homemade ice cream. There's also a petting zoo with goats, sheep, a donkey, rabbits, chickens, and a heifer barn.

Robert's Hillside Orchards (357-6696), South Lane Road, Granville. Open July 15 through December 24. Pick-your-own blueberries, peaches, and apples; a cider mill, hiking trails.

Cumworth Farm (634-5529), MA 112 between Worthington and Cummington. Pick-your-own blueberries and raspberries, also sells jam, syrup.

Minority Mountain Farm (634-5404), 133 Plainfield Road, Cummington. This is a dairy operation with home-grown vegetables, maple syrup, jams, jellies, and pickles at the farm stand.

Splendorview Farm (634-5528), 160 Bryant Road, Cummington. A sheep farm with a nice view. Tours offered.

Sunscape Gardens (667-5786), 8 Montgomery Road, Huntington. Gifts for gardeners, from gardens, and inspired by gardeners. Features work by local artisans, books, a schedule of workshops, garden tours, in-season farm stand.

GENERAL STORES

Granville Country Store (1-800-356-2141), Granville, just off MA 57. Open daily 7–6:30, Sunday 7:30–5:30. A typical village store but with a difference: a store cheese (regular and sharp cheddar) that's been sold here since 1850; will ship anywhere. Lucy and Rowland Entwiestle are only the third proprietors.

The High Country General Store (258-4055), MA 57, Tolland. Open daily 8–6:30, Sunday 9–5. Not particularly picturesque but claims to be "the biggest little store in the country" and serves breakfast and lunch.

Huntington General Store (667-3232), MA 112 north of the village, Huntington. A bit hokeyed up but known for its baked goods and soups; ice cream and assorted gadgetry, local crafts are also sold.

Middlefield General Store, Skyline Trail, Middlefield. Sweeping views from the store's front door, an oasis selling good coffee as well as picnic basics.

Williamsburg General Store (268-3006), 3 Main Street, Williamsburg. Local maple products, grinders, soups and salads, fresh fruit, local crafts.

The Corners Grocery (238-5531), Worthington Center. A double-porched, extremely photogenic store in the middle of a matching village; picnic makings.

SUGARHOUSES

As already noted, the Hilltowns are the prime source of Massachusetts's maple sugar and sugaring season—which can begin as early as late February and extend well into April. Locals and visitors alike are drawn to sugarhouses and pancake breakfasts featuring the new syrup. A brochure detailing information about the sugaring process and each producer is available from the Massachusetts Maple Producers Association, Watson-Spruce Corner Road, Ashfield 01330.

The following sugarhouses welcome visitors during sugaring-off, but call before coming. All also sell their syrup from their farms year-round:

In Chester: **High Meadow Sugar Shack** (667-3640) on the Skyline Trail offers spectacular views. **Lyman Farm Sugarhouse** (667-3463) is a 200-year-old farm. **Misty Mountain Farm** (354-6337) has a covered bridge and chapel. Sugar is collected by horses and oxen on weekends.

In Chesterfield: **Bisbee Family Maple** (296-4717) has a hand-built sugarhouse sited in the apple orchard; hot coffee and picnic tables; maple creams a specialty. **Krug Sugarbush** (549-1461), South Street; nature walks offered through the sugarbush.

In Cummington: **Cumworth Farm** (634-5529) is between Worthington and Cummington on MA 112; Ed McColgan is a longtime producer and, with his wife Mary, welcomes guests (see *Bed & Breakfasts*) in their 200-year-old farmhouse. **Tessiers Sugarhouse** (634-5022), 60 Fairgrounds Road, is ½ mile south of MA 9.

Hillwood Farm (268-7036), MA 9, Goshen, 3 miles west of Williamsburg Center, uses Clydesdale horses to gather sap.

East Branch Sugarhouse (667-3995), Knightville Dam Road off MA 112, Huntington; open evenings and weekends with free samples for kids.

Thatcher's Sugarhouse (634-5582), 1 mile south of Plainfield Center or 3 miles north of MA 9; the sugarhouse is set behind dairy barns.

In Westhampton: **Hanging Mt. Farm** (527-0710), just off MA 66. **Bridgmont Farm** (527-6193), a 200-year-old dairy farm; call for directions.

Paul's Sugar House (268-3544), MA 9, 1 mile west of Williamsburg. Open March through mid-April; maple candies, also apple, cherry, and blackberry syrups.

In Worthington: **Cook's Maple Products** (238-5827) in West Worthington

The work of sculptor Andrew deVries is on display in his Middlefield sculpture garden.

has a sugarhouse accessible via a marked trail; picnic tables. **High Hopes Sugarshack** (238-5919) displays work by local artists and features an "all-you-can-eat" pancake buffet. **The Red Bucket Sugar Shack** (238-7710) features pancakes, French toast, wagon rides, and snowshoeing. **Windy Hill Farm** (238-5869) also offers a dining room with a full maple menu in-season.

SPECIAL EVENTS

March: **Chester Hill Maplefest.**
April: **Westfield River race,** Huntington.
May: Beginning mid-May through Columbus Day weekend, **Hilltown Farmers' Market,** Huntington Town Common, Saturday 9 AM–1 PM.
July: **Jacob's Ladder Days,** Chesterfield, first weekend. **Goshen Flower Show.**
August: **Littleville Fair** (first weekend). **Middlefield Fair** (second weekend). **Hillside Agricultural Society Fair** in Cummington (last weekend).
September: **Blandford Fair** on Labor Day weekend. **Worthington Country Music Festival and Picnic** (second weekend).
October: Columbus Day weekend—**Chester Hill Harvest Festival.**

The Berkshires

SOUTH COUNTY

The quiet southwest corner of Massachusetts has its own distinctive beauty and pace. The Housatonic River is slower, and the roads are more heavily wooded, winding through classic old villages, by swimming holes, and past hiking paths that lead to waterfalls.

Everyone agrees that the hub of "South County" is Great Barrington, but where to draw its northern boundary is less clear. The Mass. Pike is generally considered the dividing line, and we have included Lee—which straddles the Mass. Pike—in this more laid-back part of the county. This corner of the state lies beyond the cultural activity often associated with the Berkshires—Tanglewood, Edith Wharton's home ("The Mount"), and Jacob's Pillow.

Stockbridge, admittedly, is the exception. As aristocratic as Lenox and known for its summer Berkshire Theater Festival, Stockbridge is unquestionably part of the cultural circle. It nevertheless draws far less traffic than Lenox during Tanglewood season and does little to encourage more tourism, especially since the area's biggest draw—the Norman Rockwell Museum—has relocated to a hilltop of the village. The other resort villages in this area are South Egremont (blink and you're through), with its clutch of restaurants and antiques shops, and Sheffield, synonymous with antiques dealers. Great Barrington itself is a workaday western Massachusetts town, a place to buy a book or a bolt, to see a doctor, or to go to the movies. Of course the movies are shown at the Mahaiwe Theater, a restored vaudeville stage with occasional live entertainment, and any night of the week you can eat exceptionally well in town. In recent years an eclectic mix of boutiques have also appeared.

AREA CODE
413
GUIDANCE
Southern Berkshire Chamber of Commerce (528-1510), 362 Main Street at the southern edge of Great Barrington (MA 23/US 7). Open

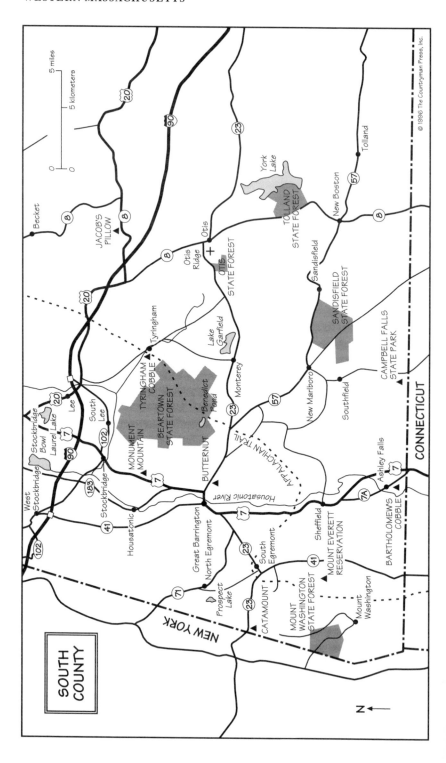

year-round Tuesday through Saturday 9:30–4:30, daily in summer, until 6 except Monday (10–4) and Sunday (11–3).

Stockbridge Information Booth. A kiosk-style booth on Main Street is open daily in summer months (but just noon–2 on Sunday). The **Stockbridge Chamber of Commerce** (298-5200) is good for help by phone weekdays, 8:30–2:30. The **Stockbridge Lodging Association** publishes its own pamphlet brochure (write: Box 224, Stockbridge 01262) and operates a lodging hotline: 298-5327.

The **Lee Chamber of Commerce** (243-0852) office is open Monday, Wednesday, and Friday 9–noon. A seasonal wooden booth is conveniently positioned in the town hall parking lot on Main Street, open May through September, Monday through Saturday 11–5.

(Also see "Central Berkshire" for general Berkshire information.)

GETTING THERE

By rail and air: See "Central Berkshire."

By bus: From Boston **Peter Pan–Trailways** (1-800-343-9999) serves Lee; bikes are permitted as baggage. From NYC **Bonanza** comes up US 7, stopping in Great Barrington (Bill's Pharmacy: 528-1590) and in Lee (McClelland Drugs: 243-0135).

By car: One route from Boston is the Mass. Pike to Lee (2 hours on the button), but a more scenic route through South Berkshire is the turnpike to Westfield (Exit 3) and either MA 10/US 202 to MA 57 West through Granville and Tolland to New Boston and New Marlboro or US 20 to MA 23 West through Otis and Monterey. From NYC the obvious approach is the Major Deegan Expressway or the Henry Hudson Parkway to the Saw Mill River Parkway, then to the Taconic Parkway; take the South Berkshire exit "Hillsdale, Claverack, MA 23."

MEDICAL EMERGENCY

Fairview Hospital (528-0790), Great Barrington; or dial **911**.

VILLAGES

Stockbridge. Stockbridge didn't even begin like other towns: In 1734 it was founded to contain and educate the local Mohegans. Just four white families were permitted to settle, theoretically to "afford civilizing examples to the Indians." But predictably these multiplied, and the Native Americans dwindled. After distinguishing themselves as the only tribe to serve in the Revolution and the first to be given US citizenship, the Stockbridge tribe was shipped west, eventually to Wisconsin, where a few hundred descendants still live.

Stockbridge has always been the county aristocrat, spawning the Laurel Hill Association—the country's first village-improvement society. Residents will tell you that the same number of notables have been summering in town for the past century; only the faces change periodically. The rambling, wooden **Red Lion Inn** forms the heart of the vil-

338 WESTERN MASSACHUSETTS

lage, a short walk from the **Mission** and **Merwin** houses. **Naumkeag** is just a short way up the hill, and the **Berkshire Theatre Festival** is on the northern fringe of town. The village Green is actually west of the MA 102/US 7 junction, and many visitors miss it entirely. Here stand the imposing brick **Congregational Church** (1824), the pillared **Old Town Hall** (1839), and the **Field Chime Tower,** which marks the site of the original Native American mission. The **Indian Burial Ground** is nearby—the large mound topped by a stone obelisk and overlooking the golf course. The **Village Cemetery,** across from the Green, contains the remains of John Sergeant, Native American chief John Konkapot, 19th-century tycoons like Joseph Choate, and town aristocrats like the Fields and Sedgwicks.

Sheffield. This town was the first to be chartered in the Berkshires; its wide main street (US 7) is lined with stately old homes. Its **Colonel Ashley House** (1735) is the oldest in the Berkshires, and the town boasts the greatest number of antiques dealers of any town in the Berkshires. The 1770s brick **Dan Raymond House** (open Friday 1:30–4) in the center of town is maintained by the historical society to reflect the lifestyle of this prosperous merchant, his wife, and their nine children. The 1760 **Old Parish Church** is a beauty, the oldest church in Berkshire County and the site of the annual 3-day Sheffield Antiques Fair, always the second weekend in August.

Tyringham. Hemmed in on three sides by mountains and not on the way to anywhere else, this village was the site of a Shaker community from the 1790s until the 1870s (a group of privately owned Shaker buildings still stands on Jerusalem Road near Shaker Pond). The village then began attracting prominent summer residents, including Samuel Clemens. A number of 19th-century writers eulogized Tyringham but the reason most people visit today is to see the **Tyringham Art Galleries** (243-3260), rebuilt by sculptor Henry Hudson Kitson in the 1930s. The building is also known as the Gingerbread House because it resembles a fairy-tale witch's house. In the village itself note the Greek Revival (1844) **United Church of Christ.** Local historian Mimi MacDonald tells us that Tyringham is the birthplace of the New England maple-syrup industry: It was here that the Mohegans took missionary John Sergeant into the "sugarbush" and showed him the art of tapping maple trees in spring. (See also Tyringham Cobble under *Green Space.*)

Egremont. There is no village of Egremont; instead there's **North Egremont** and **South Egremont,** divided by **Baldwin Hill.** South Egremont is the livelier village, one of the few in Berkshire to retain its original, rambling old inn, and though there's no longer a general store or gas station, there are plenty of antiques shops, galleries, and restaurants. Note the "Egremont Fan Window" in the Congregational Church and the town hall in the southern village. Don't miss Baldwin Hill, with

The Gingerbread House in Tyringham

©KIMBERLY GRANT

its surviving farms and sense of serenity, and North Village, with its
general store, inn, and lakeside campground.

Monterey. Much of this town has been absorbed into Beartown State Forest, and it is largely a second-home community (Lake Garfield is ringed
with summer homes, and its beach is private). The General Store,
though, is well worth a stop any day (you can lunch or snack at tables in
the rear), and the **Bidwell House** on Art School Road (open Memorial
Day to mid-October, Tuesday through Sunday and holidays, 11–4; $4
adults, $2 children) is an appropriately furnished 18th-century home.
This was once a dairy center producing more cheese than any other
location in the county, and Ranson Brook goat farm still produces the
county's best cheese.

Mount Washington looms like a solitary green island above the valleys in
three different states. The town is the southwesternmost, the highest,
and one of the smallest in Massachusetts. Best known as the home of
Bash Bish Falls, the state's most dramatic and photographed cascade
(see *Green Space*), it is also the site of the second highest peak (Mount
Everett) and the highest lake (Guilder Pond) in Massachusetts. The
community is also arguably the oldest in Berkshire County (settled by
the Dutch in the 1690s). It's strange how almost everything about
Mount Washington is a superlative ("highest," "smallest") and yet how
little known it really is. Actually a high table of land, it sits more than
1500 feet above its neighbors—Sheffield on the east, Salisbury, Connecticut, on the south, and Copake, New York, on the west—with peaks
rising to 2239 feet (Alander Mountain), 2365 feet (Mount Race), and

2602 feet (Mount Everett). Bear Mountain, part of the same massif but just over the line in Connecticut, happens to be the highest mountain in that state. Happily, the town is webbed with hiking trails—including one of the more dramatic, open ridgeline sections of the Appalachian Trail. Given that you can drive almost to the top of Mount Everett and that you can park at several other trailheads that access high-elevation trails—and paths to several waterfalls (the cascades of Race Brook and Bear Rock as well as Bash Bish)—you would assume this place was one of the better-known, more popular spots to hike. Not so. Mount Washington seems to be a well-kept hikers' secret (see *Hiking* and *Green Space*). Mount Washington is no longer the state's smallest town (as it was in previous editions of this book); the population is now a whopping 135 and triples in summer. The center of the village is marked by the small **Union Church** (ecumenical, open summers only) and tiny town hall. Note the old cemetery on West Street and Blueberry Hill Farm under *Selective Shopping*.

TO SEE

MUSEUMS
Chesterwood (298-3579). Go 3 miles west of Stockbridge on MA 102, turn left onto MA 183; follow signs. Open May through October, daily 10–5. $6.50 adults, $3.50 aged 13–18, $1.50 6–12; family rate $16. This 160-acre estate served as summer home for 33 years to Daniel Chester French (1850–1931), whose Minuteman statue in Concord established his eminence as a sculptor at age 25. By 1895, when he discovered Stockbridge, he was internationally respected and able to maintain this elaborate summer home and studio, which commands, as he put it, the "best dry view" he'd ever seen. Maintained by the National Trust, the property includes the mansion, a Barn Gallery with special exhibits, and the studio, now exhibit space for plaster casts of many of the sculptor's works, including the statue that now sits in Washington's Lincoln Memorial. Visitors are welcome to stroll the grounds, which include a wooded path—the Hemlock Glade—overlooking Monument Mountain. Frequent events are staged throughout the summer, and there is also a November sale (at the gift store) and a Christmas tour.
The **Norman Rockwell Museum** (298-4100), MA 183 (0.6 mile) south of the junction of MA 183 and MA 102, three miles west of Stockbridge. Open daily 10–5 in summer; November through April, weekdays 11–4, weekends 10–5. Closed Thanksgiving, Christmas, New Year's Day. Rockwell's studio is open May through October. Admission: $8 adults, $2 aged 6–18. Norman Rockwell (1894–1978) lived his last 50 years in Stockbridge and is represented here by some 200 works, including *The Four Freedoms* and many original paintings for the *Saturday Evening Post* covers. Works also include illustrations he made for *Collier's Maga-*

zine on '60s civil rights incidents. The handsome new museum is on a 36-acre estate with views (and picnic facilities) overlooking the Housatonic River.

HISTORIC HOMES

Naumkeag (298-3239), Prospect Hill Road, Stockbridge. Open Memorial Day to Columbus Day, Tuesday through Sunday and Monday holidays, 10–5. $6.50 adults for house and garden, $5 for garden only; $2.50 aged 6–12; members free. The Trustees of Reservations maintain this gabled and shingled 26-room "cottage." It was designed by McKim, Mead, and White in 1885 for one of the leading lawyers of the day, Joseph Hodges Choate, who endeared himself to his wealthy colleagues by reversing an income-tax law that Congress had passed in 1894. The gardens are as exceptional as the house.

Mission House (298-3239), Main Street, Stockbridge. Open Memorial Day weekend to Columbus Day, Tuesday through Sunday and Monday holidays 10–5. Adults $5, children $2.50. John Sergeant, idealistic young missionary to the Stockbridge tribe, built this house for his bride in 1739. He built it not on MA 102 where it now stands (known as the "Plain" at the time, this site held Native American wigwams), but up on the hill where the town's few white families lived, among them the Williamses. Sergeant's wife was Abigail Williams, a lady of pretensions, and the house is elaborately built for its time and place. It was salvaged and moved to this site in 1929. It's maintained by the Trustees of Reservations.

Colonel John Ashley House (229-8600), in Ashley Falls, well marked from US 7, south of Sheffield Village. Open Memorial Day weekend through mid-October, Wednesday through Sunday and Monday holidays 1–5. $5 adults, $2.50 children. The oldest house in Berkshire County (1735), this house was the site of the 1773 drafting of the Sheffield Resolves denouncing the British Parliament. The home is beautifully paneled, restored, and furnished. You learn about Mum Bet, purportedly the first slave to sue for, and win, her freedom under due process of law. The house and nearby Bartholomew's Cobble (see *Green Space*) are maintained by the Trustees of Reservations.

Merwin House (298-4703), 14 Main Street, Stockbridge. Open June through mid-October, Tuesday, Thursday, Saturday, and Sunday, with tours on the hour noon–4. $4 adults, $3.50 seniors, $2 children. An 1825 home preserved to look the way it did as a late-19th-century summer home. It's maintained by the Society for the Protection of New England Antiquities.

ARTS CENTERS

The Berkshire Theater Festival (298-5536), East Main Street (MA 102), Stockbridge. Celebrating its 68th season in 1996, the festival is staged in a building designed by Stanford White in 1887 as the Stockbridge Casino, restored and moved to its present site in the 1920s by Mabel Choate (mistress of Naumkeag). The plays are all by American playwrights, and the performers are aspiring actors; a young Katharine Hepburn, Ethel Barrymore, James Cagney, and Dustin Hoffman all performed here. The season runs late June through August; children's theater is staged Thursday and Saturday at noon under a tent.

The Berkshire Choral Festival (229-8526), 245 Undermountain Road (Berkshire School), Sheffield. A summer series of five Saturday concerts featuring as many as 200 voices and the Springfield Symphony.

Aston Magna Festival (528-3595), St. James Church, Main Street, Great Barrington; 17th-, 18th-, and early-19th-century music, very professionally played on period instruments.

The Mahaiwe Theater (528-0100), 14 Castle Street, Great Barrington. This wonderfully ornate theater was built in 1905 to present original plays, something it still does along with stubbornly preserving its single movie screen.

TO DO

BICYCLING
There's a fine little book, *Short Bike Rides in the Berkshires*, by Lewis C. Cuyler (Berkshire House, $9.95), that describes 30 routes. *The Bicyclist's Guide to the South Berkshires* (Freewheel Publishers, Lenox, $14.95) is also an excellent book. Bicycles can be rented from **Gaffer's Outdoors** (229-0063), US 7, Sheffield; and from **Berkshire Bike & Blade** (528-5555), 284 Main Street, Great Barrington.

BIRDING
Thousand Acre Swamp, off Norfolk Road, south of Southfield, left on Hotchkiss. A birdwatcher's delight.

BOATING
The placid Housatonic is ideal for lazy rides down the river. Trips are detailed in the *AMC River Guide—Central/Southern New England.* Canoe rentals and shuttle service are available from **Gaffer's Outdoors** (229-0063), 216 Main Street (US 7), in Sheffield; and from **Clarke Outdoors** (203-672-6365), which also offers kayak lessons, not far south of the border on US 7 in West Cornwall, Connecticut.

CAR RACING
Lime Rock Park (203-435-0896), Lakeville, Connecticut. Open April through October Saturday and holidays. Sports-car superstars who race here include Paul Newman.

FISHING
For a detailed listing of every pond and river stocked with bass, pickerel, perch, hornpout, and trout, check the annual (free) "Berkshires Official Guide."

GOLF

Egremont Country Club (528-4222), MA 23, South Egremont, offers 18 holes, moderate greens fees. **Greenock Country Club** (243-3323), West Park Street, Lee, offers nine holes, moderate greens fees. **Wyantenuck Country Club** (528-3229), Sheffield Road, Great Barrington, offers 18 holes, pricey greens fees.

MINIATURE GOLF

A Berkshire trip isn't complete without a visit to the indoor Rainbow's End Miniature Golf (18 holes) at the **Cove Lanes** in Great Barrington (US 7).

HIKING

More than 100,000 acres of Berkshire County (75 percent) is wooded, and 86 miles of the Appalachian Trail traverse the county. The number and variety of walking and hiking trails, many dating back to the 19th century, are amazing. They are described in several books, notably *Hikes & Walks in the Berkshire Hills* by Lauren R. Stevens ($9.95), *A Guide to Natural Places in the Berkshire Hills* by Rene Laubach ($9.95), and *Wildflowers of the Berkshire & Taconic Hills* by Joseph G. Strauch Jr. ($12.95), all published by Berkshire House, based in South Lee. *The Appalachian Mountain Club Guide to Massachusetts and Rhode Island* ($16.95) is also extremely helpful (get the 1995 edition), published by AMC Books. **Berkshire Hiking Holidays** (499-9648), based in Lenox, offers 3–6-day trips that combine lodging, hiking, and canoeing, as well as summer cultural events for individuals and groups.

(See also *Green Space—Walks.*)

SWIMMING

State parks and forests offer some of the most pleasant as well as most accessible swimming in this area (see *Green Space—Parks and State Forests*). For a fee you can also swim at **Prospect Lake Park** (528-4158), a private campground in North Egremont; at the **Egremont Country Club** (528-4222), South Egremont; at **Kinne's Grove** on Lake Garfield in Monterey; and at **Card Lake** in West Stockbridge.

TENNIS

Tennis Village School, West Stockbridge, two hard-surface courts. **Sheffield Racquet Club** (229-7968), four clay courts, clubhouse. **Greenock Country Club** (243-3323), Lee, two courts. **Egremont Country Club** (528-4222), South Egremont, four courts.

CROSS-COUNTRY SKIING

Bucksteep Manor (623-5535; 1-800-645-2825), Washington Mountain Road, Washington. With an 1800-foot elevation and 25 km of trails on 400 acres, this area is usually snow covered in winter. Trails are groomed and tracked, and there are rentals and guided tours in October Mountain State Forest; also lodging and dining on the premises.

Butternut (528-0610), Great Barrington. Adjacent to the alpine area are 4 miles of trails connecting with Beartown State Forest.

(Also see *Green Space.*)

DOWNHILL SKIING

Butternut (528-2000), Great Barrington; west on MA 23. Still owned by the same family that founded it almost 40 years ago, Butternut is known for its grooming and for the beauty of its design—both on and off the slopes.
Vertical drop: 1000 feet.
Terrain: 22 trails.
Lifts: One quad, one triple, four double chairs.
Snowmaking: 98 percent of area.
Rates: $38 adults, $28 juniors, weekends; $30 and $20 midweek.

Catamount (528-1262; 1-800-342-1840), South Egremont, MA 23. Catamount straddles the New York/Massachusetts line, overlooking the rolling farm country of the Hudson Valley. It's been in business more than 40 years as a family area. The newly enlarged base lodge is pleasant.
Vertical drop: 1000 feet.
Terrain: 23 slopes and trails.
Lifts: Four chair lifts, three T bars.
Snowmaking: 85 percent of area.
Rates: $37 adults, $25 juniors, weekends; $25 and $15 midweek; night skiing Wednesday and Thursday $15, $19 Saturday.

Otis Ridge (269-4444), MA 23 in Otis. A long-established family ski area that limits lift ticket sales to 800 per day and operates a Ski Camp (aged 8–16) near the top of its trails.
Vertical drop: 400 feet.
Terrain: 10 slopes and trails.
Lifts: One double chair, five tows.
Snowmaking: 80 percent of area.
Facilities: Lodging and food at the slopeside Grouse House (269-4446).

GREEN SPACE

PARKS AND STATE FORESTS

The Massachusetts Department of Environmental Management (DEM) publishes a handy map/guide of its Berkshire holdings and maintains a visitor-friendly regional office on US 7 south of Pittsfield: 442-8928.

Beartown State Forest (528-0904), Blue Hill Road, Monterey; 10,555 acres. The high tablelands stretching northwest from Monterey are known as "Beartown," the upper end dropping down to the Housatonic River in South Lee. Accessible from both MA 102 in South Lee and MA 17 in Monterey, the area includes 35-acre **Benedict Pond,** an artificially formed pond good for swimming (there are sanitary but no changing facilities), picnicking, and boating (no motors). There are also a dozen campsites plus lean-tos along the **Appalachian Trail.** You can drive or hike to the summit of **Mount Wilcox;** a 1½-mile trail circles the pond there.

Mount Washington State Forest (582-0330), East Street, Mount Washington. This 4500-acre tract fills the southwest corner of Massachusetts. It's best known for **Bash Bish Falls,** a dramatic 60-foot falls that rushes down a 1000-foot-deep gorge, finally plunging some 80 feet around two sides of a mammoth boulder and dropping into a perfect pool that's labeled "No Swimming." Needless to say this sign is frequently ignored (rangers are on duty weekends only) and, sad to say, divers occasionally die here. Don't swim, but do explore this special place. Access is via MA 23, MA 41, and Mt. Washington Road in South Egremont; take the wooded, winding Falls Road to "the upper parking lot"—from which a rugged ¼-mile trail meanders steeply down through pines to the falls. Continue down the road to "the lower parking lot" in New York's **Taconic State Park** if you prefer to walk a level path to the bottom of the falls. From this lot you can also access the steep but short trail to the upper rim of the falls—which continues (via the South Taconic Trail) to Alander Mountain. The forest includes 15 primitive, walk-in camping sites with pit toilets, spring water, and fireplaces on the way to Alander Mountain. In June mountain laurel blooms throughout the forest. (Also see Mount Everett State Reservation in this section and Mount Washington under *Villages.*)

Mount Everett State Reservation (528-0330), also in the town of Mount Washington, features a road to the top of Mount Everett, the 2602-foot-high mountain (second highest in Massachusetts) that commands an overview of Berkshire County to the north. Dogwood blooms in spring, mountain laurel in June, and there is blueberrying in August. **Guilder Pond,** accessible by car, is filled with pink water lilies during late July and much of August. (Also see Race Brook Falls, Bash Bish Falls, and [under *Villages*] Mount Washington.)

October Mountain State Forest (243-1178), a total of 15,710 acres accessible from US 20 in both Lenox and Lee. Camping is the big draw here, but there are just 50 sites. **Schermerhorn Gorge** is a popular hike and many miles of trails also used for winter skiing and snowmobiling. Much of this area was once impounded by Harry Payne Whitney as a game preserve (it included buffalo, moose, and Angora goats as well as smaller animals). Halfway Pond is a good fishing spot.

Otis State Forest (528-0904), off MA 23 on Nash Road in West Otis. Boating (no motors) is permitted in **Upper Spectacle Pond,** and there are extensive cross-country ski trails, part of which traverse the original road that Henry Knox labored over with cannons in the winter of 1775–76.

Tolland State Forest (269-7268) off MA 8 in Otis offers 90 campsites (85 of them for tents); also picnic space for 100, and swimming, fishing, and boating in **Otis Reservoir.**

Sandisfield/Cookson State Forests (258-4774). The state forest holdings are scattered around Sandisfield; the most popular section is just over the New Marlboro line (MA 57) on **York Lake,** a 40-acre dammed area near the headquarters of Sandy Brook. Here you can swim, boat (no motors), and picnic (there are tables, grills, and fireplaces). There are also 10 wilderness campsites.

PICNICKING

Bowker Woods, MA 183 between Stockbridge and Chesterwood; drive in at the sign. There's a pine grove by a small pond, good for picnics. (Also see Monument Mountain under *Walks.*)

WALKS

Monument Mountain on US 7 north of Great Barrington. This peak is one of the most distinctive in the state: a long ridge of pinkish quartzite, scarcely 15 feet wide in some places, 1700 feet high. The climb is lovely any day, whether by the Hickey or the Monument Trail. The hillside is covered with red pine and, in June, with flowering mountain laurel. A Bryant poem tells of a Native American maiden, disappointed in love, who hurled herself from "Squaw Peak." Nathaniel Hawthorne, Herman Melville, and O.W. Holmes all picnicked here in 1850.

Bartholomew's Cobble (229-8600), marked from MA 7A in Ashley Falls south of Sheffield. This 200-acre tract takes its name from the high limestone knolls or cobbles of marble and quartzite that border the glass-smooth Housatonic River. We recommend the pine-carpeted Ledges Trail, a (theoretically) 45-minute loop with many seductive side trails down to the river or up into the rocky heights. A booklet guide is available from the naturalist when the property is open (mid-April to mid-October, Wednesday through Sunday and holidays, 9-5; $2 adults, $1 children). There are exhibits in the Bailey Trailside Museum.

Tyringham Cobble, ½ mile from Tyringham Center on Jerusalem Road. The Appalachian Trail crosses a portion of this 206-acre property: steep upland pasture and woodland, including a part of Hop Brook, with views of the valley and village below. Note that the Trustees of Reservations also maintain 446-acre **McLennan Reservation** on Fenn Road, 2 miles south of Tyringham center: steep, wooded slopes with one of the county's most spectacular views.

Laurel Hill, Stockbridge. A path leads from the elementary school on Main Street to a stone seat designed by Daniel Chester French. Marked trails continue across the Housatonic to Ice Glen (a ravine) and to Laura's Tower (a steel tower); another trail leads along the crest of the spur of Beartown Mountain.

Berkshire Botanical Garden (298-3926), Stockbridge, junction of MA 102 and MA 183. Open year-round. This botanical garden is on 15 acres that include a pond. There are shrubs, trees, perennial borders, greenhouses, herbs, periodic lectures and workshops. Admission charged mid-May to mid-October: $2 adults, $1 seniors, $.50 children.

WATERFALLS
Bash Bish Falls. The area's most famous and dramatic waterfall—a 60-foot fall plunging through a sheer gorge (see also Mount Washington State Forest under *Parks and State Forests*).

Race Brook Falls in Sheffield: A series of five cascades and a picnic area. From the turnout on MA 41 north of the Stage Coach Inn, follow red blazes for 1½ miles.

Umpachene Falls. At the New Marlboro Church in the village center turn south; follow signs to Mill River. Just before the metal bridge there is a dirt road forking right; from here follow signs.

Becket Falls. Two-tenths of a mile up Brooker Hill from the Becket Arts Center (MA 8 and Pittsfield Road) there is a shallow turnout in which to park. It's a steep scramble down to view the 25-foot-high cascade.

Campbell Falls State Park, accessible from MA 57 in New Marlboro, then a forest road to this site: The Whiting River pours over a split ledge and cascades 80 feet down a precipitous declivity. There are picnic tables, toilets, and foot trails.

Sages Ravine. A strikingly cut chasm with a series of falls, best accessed from Salisbury Road in Mount Washington.

LODGING

Note: Lodging tax varies from town to town. At this writing, in Great Barrington and Lee it is 9.7 percent; in Sheffield and Egremont it's 5.7 percent. Also note that prices tend to soar during Tanglewood season (July and August), and many inns require a minimum 2- or 3-night stay on weekends.

INNS
The Red Lion Inn (298-5545) Main Street, Stockbridge 01250. Probably the most famous inn in Massachusetts, a rambling white clapboard beauty built in 1897. Staying here is like stepping into a Norman Rockwell painting, and there isn't a musty or dusty corner in the entire inn. Even the cheapest, shared-bath rooms are carefully furnished with real and reproduction antiques and bright prints, and there are some splendid rooms with canopy beds. The inn's long porch, festooned with flowers and amply furnished with rockers in warm weather, is the true center of Stockbridge in summer, as is the hearth in its lobby in winter. There is a large, formal dining room, a cozy pub, and, in summer, a garden café by the pool. There are now actually a choice of 111 guest rooms (90 with private bath, two handicapped accessible) if you count rooms and suites in the annex, the newest of which is the old Stockbridge firehouse that Norman Rockwell painted. $70–250 per room; children are free but there's a $20 charge per cot.

The Old Inn on The Green (229-3131), New Marlboro 01230. Back in the early '70s Bradford Wagstaff and Leslie Miller (husband and wife) restored this fine 1760, double-porched inn in a beautiful village center; more recently they converted a turn-of-the-century, Norman-style barn at Gedney Farm down the road into 15 fantasy guest rooms and suites, many with fireplaces and tiled whirlpools. From $90 with shared bath in the old inn to $245 for the master suite at Gedney Farm, continental breakfast included. (Also see *Dining Out.*)

Windflower (528-2720; 1-800-992-1993), 684 South Egremont Road (MA 23), Great Barrington 01230. We keep returning to this gracious, turn-of-the-century country mansion that's become such a hospitable country inn. The common rooms are just the right combination of elegance and comfort. Most of the 13 guest rooms have canopy or four-poster beds and/or fireplaces, the plumbing is fine (check out the deep clawfoot tub in room #5), and the food is famous (see *Dining Out*); but what really makes this place is the welcoming family who run it: veteran innkeepers Gerry and Barbara Liebert and their chef-daughter Claudia with her green-thumbed and handy husband, John Ryan. Facilities include a landscaped pool; golf and tennis are across the road at the Egremont Country Club. $170–220 per room double occupancy is less than it sounds because it includes an exceptional four-course dinner (otherwise $27.50 prix fixe) and a full breakfast.

The Williamsville Inn (274-6118), MA 41, West Stockbridge 01266. Open year-round for rooms, in winter just Thursday through Sunday for dining. The 1797 house is known for its fine dining and its flower and sculpture gardens; facilities also include a pool and tennis court. All 16 guest rooms have private bath, and many have fireplaces or wood stove. $105–185 per couple. (Also see *Dining Out.*)

The Egremont Inn (528-2111), Box 418, South Egremont 01258. This three-story, double-porched landmark is in the middle of a classic crossroads village. The inn dates, in part, from 1780 and (as is frequently the case) is under new ownership. We wish Steve and Karen Waller well and applaud the bright upholstery in the lobby and other common rooms, but at this writing the 21 rooms (all with private bath) vary in comfort. Facilities include a dining room, pool, and two tennis courts, and in winter Catamount ski area is just down the road. $85–170 per room.

The Weathervane Inn (528-9580), MA 23, South Egremont 01258. A gracious, 200-year-old inn on 10 acres. Rooms all have private bath, antiques. There is a bar by the living room hearth, and the attractive dining room is open to the public. There's also a TV room and a pool. $95–135 B&B, $175 MAP, $525 MAP for a 3-night weekend in July and August.

Federal House (243-1824), MA 102, South Lee 01260. A columned 1824 mansion built by the founder of the Hurlbut Paper Company, now widely respected as a restaurant with six handsomely furnished guest rooms with private baths. $95–155 depending on the season (ask about multiple-day, off-season packages); guests receive 20 percent off dinner (see *Dining Out.*)

Stagecoach Hill Inn (229-8585), 854 South Undermountain Road, Sheffield 01257. A genuine old stage stop in 1829 has been a lodging and dining landmark off and on ever since. The new innkeeper, Sandra MacDougall, has spiffed up the old tavern (a great little pub with a hearth and reasonably priced menu) and the formal dining room over which her son, chef David Essenfeld, presides. Upstairs are seven rooms furnished with a pleasing mix of family heirlooms, antiques, and period reproductions; the three third-floor rooms share a bath; four rooms are in the cottage out back. The trail to the cascades along the Race Brook Trail and up to the Appalachian Trail is just next door. $50–125 depending on the room and season.

The Morgan House Inn (243-0181), 33 Main Street, Lee 01238. This building has always been a downtown landmark: a stagecoach stop since 1853 and now the place the bus stops. Since acquiring it in 1993, Lenora and Stuart Bowen have established a good reputation for the dining room and have been gradually renovating the rooms. Guests can sit and rock on the second-floor porch. $72–145 per room in summer includes full breakfast.

Thornewood Inn & Spencer's Restaurant (528-3828), 453 Stockbridge Road (junction of US 7 and MA 183), Great Barrington 01230. This pleasant place includes a popular restaurant and 12 guest rooms, all with private bath; inquire about the two-room suite, good for families, in the carriage house. Facilities include a pool. $65–165.

BED & BREAKFASTS

In Great Barrington 01230

Elling's Bed & Breakfast (528-4103), PO Box 6, 250 Maple Avenue (MA 23 West). Ray and Jo Elling have been in the bed & breakfast business longer than most people, and their experience has bred an easy, friendly atmosphere. The handsome, white clapboard house dates back to 1746, and its guest wing, containing six rooms, has its own low-beamed living room with fireplace and TV. The rooms are nicely furnished with antiques; one has a private bath, and the others are no more than two to a bath. The house sits high on a knoll above the road, commanding a view of fields backed by hills. There's a deep, sandy swimming hole in the river on the property and plenty of inviting space to roam. Breakfast is buffet style: fresh-baked muffins and homemade jams. $65–85.

LittleJohn Manor (528-2882), PO Box 148, MA 23 at the Newsboy Monument. Built as the gardener's cottage for a former estate, this delightful house has four guest rooms sharing two baths. The hosts, Paul DuFour and Herby Littlejohn, formerly managed a largish inn in Maine. They pride themselves on their full English breakfasts (complete with genuine "bangers") and teas (homemade scones and all). They also bottle and sell their wine vinegar. Their other pride is the garden, carefully planted to bloom continuously from spring through fall. Savaged by the tornado that whipped through town on Memorial Day of 1995, both the house and garden have undergone major repairs since. $60–90 with

breakfast. Paul is a justice of the peace, and weddings can be arranged.
The Turning Point Inn (528-4777), RD 2 Box 140. Open year-round. Built as the Pixley Tavern in 1800, this striking double-doored inn, nicely renovated, offers six guest rooms (four with private bath) in the main house and a two-bedroom cottage with kitchenette. There's a cheery parlor, also a great country kitchen in which guests are permitted to make their coffee and tea. Irving Yost and his daughter Jamie serve ample, whole-grain breakfasts. Lake Buel is just down the road, and Butternut Basin ski area is a few minutes' drive. $80–100 includes full, healthy (plenty of grains) breakfasts. $200 per night for the cottage.

Seekonk Pines (528-4192; 1-800-292-4192), 142 Seekonk Cross Road (at MA 23). An expansive old home with spreading gardens and a large common room with a fireplace and piano; a well-stocked guest pantry is off the dining room, with its table set for eight. Guest rooms feature antiques and antique quilts. Hostess Linda Best paints the watercolors displayed throughout the house, and her husband, Christian, makes dollhouses like the one in the living room. The grounds harbor a swimming pool and a number of pet llamas. $70–105.

Wainright Inn (528-2062), 518 South Main Street (US 7), south of town. Said to date from 1766, this large, Victorian-looking house was expanded to its present shape by Franklin Pope, an electrical genius recognized for a number of inventions (a couple in partnership with Thomas Edison), but who died while tinkering with a transformer in his basement here. This is an informal place, good for children. It also offers a full handicapped-accessible, ground-floor room and accepts dogs. There are eight rooms, all but two with private bath and some with working fireplaces. $50–100 per room.

In Egremont 01230

☞ **Baldwin Hill Farm** (528-4092), 121 Baldwin Hill Road N/S. This is a very special place: a Victorian farmhouse that's been in the Burdsall family for over three generations. Dick's grandfather bought the 450-acre hilltop farm as a summer place in 1912, adding touches like the mammoth fieldstone fireplace in one of the two living rooms. While Dick was growing up here (attending classes in the one-room schoolhouse), this was a serious dairy farm, and though there are no more cows, the surrounding fields are still hayed. Quite possibly the most beautifully sited B&B in Berkshire County, the house commands a sweeping view of mountains. All four guest rooms have good views, but our favorite is the bay window room with chairs positioned for enjoying the view of Mount Everett to the south; this twin-bedded room has a closeted sink but shares a bath with the adjoining room. Inviting common spaces include a comfortably furnished screened-in porch and seats in the landscaped garden; there's also a pool. $70–94 per couple.

Bread & Roses (528-1099), corner of MA 71 and Baldwin Hill Road, North Egremont (mailing address: Star MA 65, Box 50, Great Barrington

01230). A sophisticated but informal home with two parlors, a wrap-around porch, and five guest rooms, all with private baths. Elliot Lowell is a local attorney who works out of the house, and Julie Lowell is an accomplished breakfast chef. French is spoken. $95 per couple.

In Lee 01238

☞ **Historic Merrell Tavern Inn** (243-1794; 1-800-243-1794), 1565 Pleasant Street (MA 102), South Lee 01260. This is a standout: a double-porched inn built in 1794 with a third-floor ballroom added in 1837, a stagecoach stop for much of the 19th century. Difficult as it is to believe, it stood vacant for 75 years before Chuck and Faith Reynolds purchased it in 1981 and spent years restoring the fine detailing, adding appropriate colors, wallpaper, and a mural or two. Nine of the guest rooms have working fireplaces (all have private bath), and all have been carefully decorated with an eye to comfort as well as style. Guests breakfast in the canary-colored tap room with its original circular bar in the corner. Grounds slope in the back to the Housatonic River. $75–155 per couple includes breakfast and tea; children are $15 extra; 3-night minimum in summer, but weekday specials begin at $55 off-season.

Applegate Bed and Breakfast (243-4451; 1-800-691-9012), 279 West Park Street. This place is a winner: a 1920s mansion with a pillared portico that's spacious and comfortable. Host Rick Cannata is a pilot, and Nancy, a semi-retired flight attendant who obviously has a knack for both decorating and people. Common rooms are filled with photos of past guests. A grand piano is tucked into a corner of the living room, which has built-in bookcases and window seats, a fireplace, and space for reading or playing backgammon. Guest rooms vary in size from huge (Room 1, with its king-sized four-poster, fireplace, and steam shower with two shower heads) to quite snug, but we like Room 6, with its large bed tucked under the eaves. Nancy keeps local menus and a book for guest comments on restaurants. Breakfast here is by candlelight. Amenities include a pool, a guest fridge, and plenty of lawn. Rick has turned the Carriage House into a two-bedroom apartment with a complete kitchen and a whirlpool tub. $85–225 depending on the room, day, and season. Inquire about winter and spring packages.

☞ **Chambery Inn** (243-2221; 1-800-537-4321), 199 Main Street. This unlikely lodging place, a parochial school built in 1885, was rescued from the wrecker's ball and moved to its present site by Joe Toole (whose grandfather was in the first class to attend the school). As you might suspect, the rooms are huge, with 13-foot-high tin ceilings, 8-foot-tall windows—and blackboards (chalk is supplied). A continental breakfast is delivered to your room. $85–195 depending on the season and day.

Haus Andreas, RR 1, Box 605-B, Stockbridge Road. A majestic mansion with an 18th-century core and turn-of-the-century lines (it was land-scaped and modernized by George Westinghouse Jr.). It is now home for Sally and Ben Schenck. Rooms and suites are all furnished in antiques and have private bath; several have working fireplaces, and a one-bedroom cottage by the pool has kitchen facilities and a hearth in the living room. $60–150 for rooms, children over 10 welcome. $160–250 for suites.

In Sheffield 01257

☞ **Staveleigh House** (229-2129), 59 South Main Street (US 7). Dorothy Marosy and Marion Whitman, longtime friends, have created a truly homey Berkshire retreat. We don't mean homey as in cluttered and shabby, because every wing chair and sofa is brightly, tastefully upholstered, and every room is furnished with flair. There are five guest rooms, one with private bath and two downstairs, off by themselves overlooking the garden. My favorite is a symphony in blues and whites with a wicker chaise longue and rocker. The house was built as a parsonage in 1818, and it's set back from US 7 with inviting gardens out back. Breakfast is an event here: puffed pancakes, individually baked and topped with apple slivers, for instance. $70–95 per room including breakfast.

☞ **Ivanhoe Country House** (229-2143), 254 South Undermountain Road (MA 41). This is an exceptional find: gracious, friendly, comfortable. Guests are welcome to play games or the piano, watch TV, or dip into the library of the paneled Chestnut Room where a fire burns in winter and French doors create an airy feel in summer. There are nine rooms, some with kitchenettes, all with access to fridges. One 2-bedroom unit with a glassed-in porch can sleep a family. Continental breakfast appears outside each bedroom in the morning (rooms all have eating space). In summer use the pool and the hiking trails up to the five cascades along the Race Brook Trail, leading to a spectacular stretch of the Appalachian Trail across Mount Race; in winter you can poke around the inn's own 25 acres on skis. $55–150 (two-bedroom unit with bath) on weekends in summer. Well-behaved, leashed (at all times) dogs are welcome for an extra $10 (Carole and Dick Maghery raise golden retrievers).

Orchard Shade (229-8463), 84 Maple Avenue. This is a find that is easy to miss, on a side street in the middle of the village. What you notice first is the expansive screened-in porch on which paying guests have been rocking since 1888. The older part of the house dates from 1841. The eight rooms are attractively homey, and several connect to form family suites; seven share three baths. Longtime hosts Debbie and Henry Thorton are welcoming; the extensive garden includes a pool. Family-style dinner is served Saturday. From $55 single to $150 for a two-bedroom suite with private bath.

☞ **Race Brook Lodge** (229-2916), 684 Undermountain Road (MA 41). "If you have a lemon, squeeze it" is the way architect David Rothstein describes the way he has transformed a 1790s barn into one of Berkshire County's more distinctive and inviting places to stay. "This is a chintz-free zone," Rothstein quips about the lack of antiques and frills in his 20 guest rooms (14 in the barn and 6 more divided between two cottages). The open beams and angles of the old barn remain, but walls are white and stenciled; rooms are furnished with bright, southwest Native American rugs and spreads. As you would expect in a barn, the common room is large and multileveled, with some good artwork. It serves as the setting for a summer series of Sunday jazz concerts (Rothstein was the last manager of the legendary Berkshire Music Barn). The lodge caters to hikers and walkers, encouraging guests to climb the Race Brook Trail that measures 1½ miles in distance and rises almost 2000 feet in elevation—past a series of five cascades—to Mount Race (see Mount Washington under *Villages*). Children are welcome, and the $65–125 rates don't rise during Tanglewood season; no minimum stay required, either.

In Stockbridge 01262

Cherry Hill Farm Bed & Breakfast (298-3535; 298-5452), PO Box 1245. As we traveled up the long drive to this imposing, Georgian-style 1890s mansion, we worried that a butler would shoo us away. Not so. Nick Swan and his father, Jack, couldn't have been more welcoming, explaining that the house had been in their family since the 1930s and that families—even young children—are welcome. Guests breakfast around the formal dining table in the paneled dining room and sleep in large, high-ceilinged rooms (five have working fireplaces but most share baths). Views are across fields to Monument Mountain. The extensive grounds include a tennis court, pond, and walking/cross-country trails. $60–150 all year.

The Inn at Stockbridge (298-3337), US 7, Box 2033. This white-pillared mansion was built in 1906, set on 12 acres with ample woods and meadow to tramp around in. Flowers, comfortable blue chintz chairs, and books fill the living room, where a fire is lit on rainy days. There's an attractive pool in the garden. Breakfast is served either in the formal dining room or on the back porch. There are eight guest rooms, each different, all with private bath. $80–135.

Berkshire Thistle Bed & Breakfast (298-3188), PO Box 1227, US 7. Gene Elling is a second-generation B&B host (his parents operate Elling's B&B), and this modern house is guest friendly. Set on 5 sloping acres, well back from US 7, it offers open, airy common space and a large deck. There are four clean, crisp guest rooms (five in a pinch); breakfast is "expanded continental" midweek but on weekends is very full, all made from scratch. Children over 8 years. $65–125.

Elsewhere

The Golden Goose (243-3008), Box 336, Main Road, Tyringham 01264-0336. This inviting old house is in the middle of a peaceful valley village. Lilija and Jospeh Rizzo invite amateur musicians to try their hand at the baby grand piano and push open the beveled French doors to enjoy the view from the large deck. Guest rooms are furnished with antiques; breakfast, which usually includes homemade applesauce and hot biscuits, is served family style at the oak table. There are private

Main Street Stockbridge at Christmastime *by Norman Rockwell*

baths and a small efficiency apartment with its own entrance; guests also have access to a fridge and BBQ. They are encouraged to walk through nearby Tyringham Cobble (see *Green Space*), which connects with the Appalachian Trail. The inn is set in its own 6 acres. $70–120.

New Boston Inn (258-4477), junction of MA 8 and US 7, Sandisfield 01255. The former ladies' parlor in this 1737 stagecoach stop is now the breakfast room, the pub is just for guests, and the ballroom upstairs is now "The Gathering Room," a great space with a billiards table, TV, piano, plenty of room to read and play games, and matching fireplaces at either end of the room. The six upstairs guest rooms have low ceilings, wide floorboards, and private baths. $95 includes a full breakfast.

WHERE TO EAT

DINING OUT
In Egremont

The Old Mill (528-1421), MA 23, South Egremont. Dining Tuesday through Sunday. No reservations for groups of fewer than five, so come early or expect a wait in the pleasant bar where a lighter tavern menu is offered. The vintage-1797 gristmill by Hubbard Brook makes a simple, elegant setting for 85 guests. Your meal might begin with duck liver mousse pâté ($5) and you might dine on sautéed scallops with Shiitake mushrooms, ginger, and sake ($17). A grilled veal chop with red wine shallot butter is $22. Save room for desserts like *profiteroles au chocolat.*

Windflower Inn (528-2720), 684 South Egremont Road (MA 23), Egremont. Open by reservation for dinner. This chef-owned and -oper-

ated inn features fresh ingredients and everything made from scratch. In summer an unusual variety of greens, other vegetables, fruits, and herbs are grown in the inn garden, and in winter chef Claudia Liebert and her mother, Barbara (a semi-retired chef and innkeeper), shop carefully and selectively in local markets. The dining room is candle- and firelit, with well-spaced tables and muted colors. Inn guests order their dinners before arriving, and outside guests can order when they reserve. A four-course prix fixe ($27.50) dinner includes a choice of three entrées. The specialty of the house is roast duckling with plum sauce. You might begin with a hearty corn chowder with red potatoes and bell peppers and finish with a brandied chocolate apricot torte. The wine list is well chosen and remarkably reasonable in price.

Elm Court Inn (528-0325), MA 71, North Egremont. Dinner served except Tuesday and Wednesday. The large, low-ceilinged dining room gleams with polished wood. Chef-owner Urs Bieri earns high praise for his classic German/Swiss dishes like filet goulash forestiere with rosti potato ($17.25), veal à la Suisse and Wiener schnitzel. Rack of lamb Provençale ($24) and breast of duck on a potato pancake ($19.50) are also staples.

John Andrews (528-3469), MA 23, South Egremont. Open for dinner nightly and for Sunday brunch. We love the warm, earth-toned walls and soft lighting, not to mention the menu that includes so many of our favorite foods that the choice is difficult: grilled leg of lamb, grilled eggplant with red-onion relish and red wine herb jus, for instance ($15); or red snapper with a parsley crust, pine nuts, balsamic syrup, and olive oil ($18.50). Tortellini with artichokes, spinach, and Mascarpone is $12.50. Leave room for dessert.

Swiss Hutte Inn & Restaurant (528-6200), MA 23 at Catamount ski area in South Egremont. Open in the winter and summer seasons for lunch and dinner. A Swiss chef-owner; outdoor patio as well as inside seating. Specialties include Wiener schnitzel and Swiss rosti; save room for dessert. Entrées average $15.

In Great Barrington

Boiler Room Cafe (528-4280), 405 Stockbridge Road (US 7). Serving dinner Wednesday through Saturday and holiday Sundays. Michelle Miller has relocated from her original site at the Buggy Whip Factory and expanded into three artfully decorated dining rooms. On an April evening you might begin with a flan of fresh morels with asparagus and spring greens ($7) and feast on braised veal pot roast with Mexican spices, soft tortillas, and spicy black beans ($18); or try Mediterranean shellfish stew with monkfish and cod ($19).

Castle Street Cafe (528-5244), 10 Castle Street. Closed Tuesday. A café and wine bar featuring local farm products, fresh fish, pasta, grilled meats, and homemade desserts. You might begin with steamed mussels ($5) and dine on a Castle burger with straw potatoes ($9), eggplant roulade (stuffed with three cheeses, $12), or grilled salmon in a red wine sauce with lentils ($17). Dessert options usually include the "world's best chocolate mousse cake."

Painted Lady Restaurant (528-1662), 785 South Main Street (US 7). Open daily for dinner 5–10, Sunday 4–9. We have never met anyone with a bad word for this combination of Italian and Continental cuisine, served in Victorian splendor. You might dine on veal caldostana (served on a bed of spinach and topped with prosciutto, artichokes, plum tomatoes, and mozzarella; $16.40) or simply on eggplant Parmesan with angelhair marinara ($12.50).

La Tomate (528-3003), 12 Railroad Street. Closed Monday. Open for lunch Thursday through Saturday, dinner Tuesday through Sunday. This storefront restaurant would be recognized as exceptional even in Provence—the source of the particular dishes and flavors in which chef-owner Jean Claude Vierne specializes. Dinner pastas like linguine a l'épice (spicy pasta, chicken breast, eggplant, and pepper) are $10, while the scaloppine Cirois (sautéed veal scaloppine, lemon sauce, and Provençal sauce) is $19. A bouillabaisse of lobster, shellfish, saffron, and herbs is $22. You can lunch on "le Burger" or on a salmon, bacon, lettuce, and tomato sandwich ($6.50). The wine list is extensive.

Elsewhere

La Bruschetta Ristorante (232-7141), West Stockbridge. Most people rave about this place, but we have heard complaints too; best to judge for yourself. You might begin with fresh pumpkin and sage ravioli tossed with lemon sage butter and reggiano Parmesan ($5.25), and dine on fresh spinach gnocchi served with prosciutto field mushroom cream sauce ($11.95) or osso buco Milanese (the veal is kosher; $15.75).

Federal House (243-1824), MA 102, South Lee. Open for dinner and Sunday brunch. Rated highly, the small dining rooms in this 1824 pillared mansion are the place to dine on *escalopine* of veal gnocchi *italienne* ($15.50) or *escalope* of salmon with caviar ($16.50); Châteaubriand Bouquetiere for two is $38.

Williamsville Inn (274-6580), MA 41, West Stockbridge. Dining by candlelight is from a "Country French" menu.

Lenox House Restaurant (637-1341), US 7/US 20, Lenox. Open for dinner nightly in summer; from September through May, closed Monday through Wednesday. Candlelight and elegantly set tables provide the atmosphere. Specialties include veal Picatta, bouillabaisse, and roast duckling. Open for lunch ($4–10) and dinner ($14–20).

The Red Lion Inn (298-5545), Main Street, Stockbridge. Breakfast, lunch, and dinner served daily. The Lion's Den is open except midweek in winter, good for a reasonably priced tavern menu. The formal and quite wonderful old main dining room requires tie and jackets for dinner. The menu holds few surprises, but that's okay. You can lunch on salmon cakes or a grilled chicken salad (both $9.50) and dine on chicken Boursin ($18.50), roast prime rib of Angus beef ($25), or sirloin of venison with wild mushrooms in red wine sauce (that's the surprise: $23.50). For dessert we recommend the Red Lion Indian pudding ($3.50). The wine list is extensive, ranging from $16.50 for a California chardonnay to $150 for a 1987 French Burgundy.

Truc Orient Express (232-4204), Harris Street, West Stockbridge. Open for lunch and dinner, weekends until 10. A Vietnamese restaurant that's been here since '79, offering a pleasant, woven-straw and white-tablecloth decor and food that can be as spicy as you specify. Specialties include hotpot ($24). Entrées begin at $11.50 for sweet-and-sour chicken and average $15.

The Old Inn on the Green and Gedney Farm (229-3131), New Marlboro. Open for lunch in the Gallery Cafe at Gedney Farm, July through October, Thursday through Sunday 11–2:30; for dinner on the garden terrace and in the four small, candlelit (there's no other light) dining rooms of the 18th-century inn itself every night July through October (Thursday through Sunday, November through June). On Saturday nights dinner is prix fixe, reservations required.

Stagecoach Hill Inn (229-8585), 854 South Undermountain Road (MA 41), Sheffield. Closed Wednesday; call to check if dinner is being served. The formal dining room in this classic brick stage stop has new owners and a new lease on life. The menu in the adjacent, pubby tavern represents one of the few bargains in the Berkshires: baked steak and mushroom pie on grilled tomatoes, and grilled chicken and portobello pot pie with roasted garlic and a mashed potato crust, both $9.

The Hillside (528-3123), MA 57, New Marlboro. Closed Monday year-round, Tuesday too in winter, otherwise open for dinner. Ask Berkshire residents what their favorite restaurants are, and this low-key but elegant restaurant is always mentioned. Specialties are Continental classics like onion soup, melon and prosciutto, and veal dishes. $13.95–19.95.

The Cottage Cafe (229-3411), The Buggy Whip Factory, Main Street, Southfield. Open for lunch Friday through Monday and dinner Thursday through Monday, 5:30–9:30. Occupying the space pioneered by the Boiler Room Cafe. You can lunch on a baked cottage puff (fresh spinach, ricotta, and lump crabmeat wrapped in phyllo leaves) or a three-onion tart (sautéed leeks, scallions, and yellow onions baked in a creamy herbed custard). Dinner might be a spicy lamb curry ($14.95) or roasted eggplant with tomato, garlic, and fresh herbs ($12.95).

The Morgan House (243-0181), Main Street, Lee. The center of town since stagecoach days, this place is a sure bet for either lunch or dinner, especially since chef-owner Lenora Bowen has taken over the kitchen. Specialties include chicken in a popover and roast duckling with rum sauce and spiced pecans. Entrees $12–15.

EATING OUT

In Great Barrington

20 Railroad Street (528-9345). Open daily for lunch and dinner, also for Sunday brunch. Railroad Street was still dingy in 1977 when this friendly pub opened. Since then the side street has filled with boutiques and restaurants, but this one still stands out. The menu is huge, ranging through soups, chilis, nachos, salads, pocket sandwiches, burgers, and reubens, and featuring daily specials like chicken Marbella or veal Mariera. The ornate, 28-foot-long bar was moved from the Commodore Hotel in Manhattan to Great Barrington in 1919 and served as the centerpiece of a speakeasy until 1933—when it became one of the first legal bars in town.

Bronze Dog Cafe (528-5678), Great Barrington Railroad Station (turn off Main Street at the information center). Spacious and artfully decorated, this is the kind of place where you tend to linger. The menu changes constantly, but the night we stopped by you could dine on grilled marinated lamb kebob with saffron rice, vegetables, and grilled fruit; or on rosemary lemon-roasted chicken with garlic mashed potatoes and vegetables (both $12.95).

Jodi's Country Cookery (528-6064), 327 Stockbridge Road. Open daily for breakfast, lunch, and dinner. Jodi and Steven Amaruso have created a bright, attractive space that's popular with locals and visitors alike, dedicated to good food at affordable prices without being dull. The baked sole is stuffed with real, moist crabmeat ($14.95), and the chicken Florentine is layered with fresh spinach, prosciutto, and mozzarella (both $14.95). Try the lox for breakfast and a grilled sandwich for lunch. Sesame noodles with oriental vegetables is $10.95.

Hickory Bill's Barb-B-Que (528-1444), US 7, next to the Boiler Room Cafe. Open Tuesday through Saturday for lunch and dinner. Bill Ross is behind the counter serving "authentic Texas-style" pork, beef back rib, chicken, and even kielbasa that's been barbecued for 12 hours over hickory wood; it's served with a choice of collards, beans, slaw, or salad. Picnic tables out back overlook the Housatonic. For dessert, try the sweet potato pie.

Four Brothers (528-9684), US 7. This restaurant is part of an upstate New York chain, but it doesn't seem that way. The decor is classic Greek, complete with plants and fake grape arbor. Generally regarded as having the best pizzas, Greek salads, and lasagne around; there's also fried fish and eggplant casserole ($4.50). Dinners range from a small pizza ($3.50) to $6.50 for honey-dipped fried chicken.

Martin's (528-5455), 49 Railroad Street. Open daily for breakfast and lunch. Breakfast is an all-day affair, the omelets are a feast, and the burgers are outstanding, too. Beer and herbal teas are served, and crayons are at every table; inspired customers of all ages can design their own place mats.

In Lee

Cactus Cafe (243-4300), 54 Main Street. Open for breakfast on weekends, otherwise lunch and dinner daily. A zany storefront, middle-of-town place that uses no lard and offers a mean chili con queso and smoked mushroom and eggplant quesadilla. Beers include carta blanca, and there's sangria or wine by the glass.

Joe's Diner (243-9756), 63 Center Street, South Lee. Open 24 hours a day. Choose from a counter or a booth and watch the town saunter in and out. The food is good too.

Sullivan Station (243-2082), the Lee railroad station, Railroad Street (off Main Street behind the Chambery Inn). Open daily for lunch, dinner, and anything in between.

In West Stockbridge

Shaker Mill Tavern (232-8565), West Stockbridge. Open for lunch and dinner. This large, attractive dining place is furnished in "eclectic" (stained glass, etc.). The huge menu offers everything from pizzas and burgers to pesto pignoli and baked stuffed scrod. A variety of beer is served.

In South Egremont

Mom's Country Cafe (528-2414), MA 23 in the village. A great little way-stop, with flowery paper and friendly service, that's open for both lunch and dinner. A good choice of salads and sandwiches, pastas, veal and chicken dishes, and seafood.

The Store (528-2289), Main Street (next to the firehouse). Open for lunch. Craig and Donna Faedi have created a delightful deli/café specializing in local produce and products.

The Gaslight Cafe, Main Street. We miss the old Gaslight Cafe with its marble soda fountain, but the new version is still a good bet for breakfast (try the Shays Rebellion omelet) or lunch, and there are tables out back.

Elsewhere

Olde Otis Inn Pizza Shoppe (269-0220), junction of MA 8 and MA 23, Otis. Closed Wednesday. Open Monday and Tuesday 11–3, Thursday and Sunday 11–8, Friday and Saturday 11–9. It's just nice to know that this place is here, miles from anywhere, to get a bite to eat, let alone good homemade soups, fresh breads, and standout pizza.

Naji's (298-5465), 40 Main Street, Stockbridge. Good for lunch. Anyone who knew the old Alice's Restaurant of Arlo Guthrie's song will do a double take at the present trompe l'oeil pillars and busts in this familiar space. The deli case is full of Middle Eastern delicacies like stuffed grape leaves and falafel. The tables are a bit small, the plates are paper, and the utensils, plastic, but this is still an oasis of sorts.

Jack's Grill & Restaurant (274-1000), Main Street, Housatonic. Open for lunch only for large groups by reservation, for dinner except Monday and Tuesday. Owned by the Fitzpatricks of Red Lion Inn fame, this former company store (for the workers in this classic 19th-century mill village) is decorated with nostalgia items like tube radios and a model train, filled with sounds of the '40s and '50s. The menu ranges from hamburgers and linguine with tomato sauce to grilled salmon, lamb, and sirloin.

SNACKS

Berkshire Ice Cream (232-4111), West Stockbridge. We love the story and the taste of this creamy ice cream. The roots are in Ipswich, where Norbert V. White founded White Farms Golden Guernsey Dairy in 1953, and the update is in West Stockbridge where Norby's son Matthew founded Berkshire Ice Cream, convincing a number of local residents to buy a share in the cows of his start-up herd. The ice cream comes from the milk of the dairy's own prize-winning Guernsey herd; and whatever the secret, the 65 flavors of ice cream, frozen yogurt, and sherbet taste pretty good.

Mystery Cafe (229-0075), US 7, Sheffield, occupying the lucky space formerly known as Mary's Place. The café offers a half-dozen mismatched tables, cappuccino, chocolate cheesecake and other temptations like "Death by chocomint"; it also has a full line of paperback mystery books. You can lunch on the "soup of the day."

SELECTIVE SHOPPING

ANTIQUES SHOPS

South Berkshire is one of the antiques centers of New England. Sheffield alone harbors more than two dozen stores, and South Egremont has almost the same number. A pamphlet listing Berkshire County antiques dealers is available from every store and from the sources listed under *Guidance.*

ARTS AND CRAFTS

Great Barrington Pottery (274-6259), MA 41, Housatonic. The handsome, nicely glazed pieces are fired in a Japanese wood-burning kiln.

Visitors are invited to the daily performance of "the ancient tea ceremony" between 1 and 4 in the Kyoto-style teahouse; silk flowers are also sold.

Joyous Spring Pottery (528-4115), Art School Road, Monterey. Open daily 10–5 in summer; otherwise call ahead. Striking unglazed vases and other decorative pieces, fired continuously day and night for 10 days, an ancient Japanese technique called "yaki-shime."

Pond House Studio (243-2271), 47 Center Street, Lee. Bowls handmade from sections of trees found locally. These are one-of-a-kind art forms, very special.

Fellerman & Raabe Glassworks (229-8533), South Main Street (US 7), Sheffield. Open daily Tuesday through Friday 8–6, Saturday through Monday 11–6. Don't miss this place. The showroom is a riot of brilliant colors and fascinating shapes: bowls, perfume bottles, dishes, jewelry. Visitors are welcome to watch Stephen Fellerman and other artists blow and shape these pieces of art.

Butler Sculpture Park (229-8924), 481 Shunpike Road, Sheffield. Open May through October 10–5 daily; by appointment in winter. Robert Butler fashions large, brightly colored abstract sculptures in his studio, which features a gallery with views over the Sheffield Valley. The building sits atop a hillside that's been landscaped with wooded paths into a truly remarkable sculpture garden.

Undermountain Weavers (274-6565), MA 41, Housatonic. A studio workshop in a barn is the source of classic men's sports jackets, women's suits and skirts, ties and scarves, ponchos and blankets; most designed and fabricated here from Shetland wools and rare Chinese cashmere.

October Mountain Stained Glass (528-6681), 343 Main Street. A variety of quality stained glass: lampshades, bottles, jewelry, custom work.

Housatonic Galleries, MA 183, Housatonic. The old mill village of Housatonic harbors a number of interesting studios and galleries, which traditionally hold open house on the first Friday and Saturday of each month.

West Stockbridge has become a cluster point for galleries and studios. These include **Hoffman Pottery** (232-4646), 103 MA 4, featuring brightly patterned functional pieces; **New England Stained Glass Studio** (232-7181), 5 Center Street, featuring Tiffany reproductions; **The Contemporary Sculptors Guild** (232-7187), 32 Main Street, showcasing a 3-acre sculpture garden on the Williams River; and **Clay Forms Studio** (232-4339), Austerlitz Road, the source of Leslie Klein's ceramic visions.

BOOKSTORES

Apple Tree Books (243-2012), 87 Main Street, Lee. A small general bookstore specializing in Native American books; it also carries jewelry. The owner's rabbit, two birds, and dog are always present, making this a cozy place to browse.

The Bookloft (528-1521), Barrington Plaza, Great Barrington. A large, attractive, general bookstore with a wide variety of titles, both new and used; a good children's section.

CHRISTINA TREE

At Monterey Chevre Farm

FARMS

Monterey Chevre (528-2138), off New Marlboro Road, 2 miles off MA 23 in Monterey. Getting there is half the fun since the back roads leading to the farm are beautiful, and what a find. Wayne Dunlop and Susan Sellew have chosen to supply local restaurants and customers rather than go big time—an option that is very real given the quality of their goat cheese, in five varieties (plain, with chives and garlic, no salt, with thyme and olive oil, and a peppered log). The cheese is available in various sizes from the fridge at the dairy at prices well below what you pay in local stores. Children will love seeing the baby goats, but adult supervision is a must.

Blueberry Hill Farm (528-1479), East Street, Mount Washington. If you don't happen to have your own blueberry patch, this is the next best thing: pick-your-own wild blueberries (in-season of course) in one of the Berkshires' most beautiful settings (see Mount Washington under *Villages*).

Windy Hill Farm (298-3217), 686 Stockbridge Road, Great Barrington. Open April through Christmas daily 9–5. Pick-your-own apples (over 25 varieties), cider press, container-grown nursery stock.

SHOPPING COMPLEXES

The Buggy Whip Factory (229-3676), Southfield. A long, picturesque, sagging wooden tannery, said to date from 1792, now houses one of the largest gatherings of antiques dealers in the county as well as an artisans' gallery and a variety of other stores, including the Neuma Factory Store (featuring beautiful men's and women's hand-crafted cotton sweaters).

Jenifer House Commons, US 7, north of Great Barrington. The former Jenifer House now offers an assortment of antiques and boutiques, also a brew pub.

Railroad Street, Great Barrington. The boutiques change frequently here but are always worth checking out.

West Stockbridge. A village full of riverside shops.

SPECIAL SHOPS

Berkshire Cupboard (528-1880), 297 Main Street, Great Barrington. The prime source for Berkshire products, books, prints, maps, cards, T-shirts, and history.

The Rookery (528-3323), MA 23, South Egremont. It's difficult to miss the display of concrete garden and lawn ornaments. This is a longtime family business and local landmark.

Country Curtains (298-5565) at the Red Lion Inn, Stockbridge. A phenomenon rather than just a store, nationally known through its catalog. Country Curtains is a source of a wide variety of matching curtains and beddings, beautifully displayed in the rear of the Red Lion Inn.

Kenver, Ltd. (538-2330), MA 23, South Egremont. Housed in an 18th-century tavern, a long-established source of ski- and sportswear.

SPECIAL EVENTS

May: **Chesterwood Antique Auto Show,** Stockbridge. **Memorial Day Parade,** Great Barrington.

July: **Fireworks** and **Independence Day music** at Tanglewood.

August: **Berkshire Crafts Fair,** at the high school, Great Barrington. **Annual Antiques Show,** midmonth at Berkshire Botanical Garden. **Monument Mountain Author Climb,** commemorating the day in 1850 that Melville, Hawthorne, and Holmes met and picnicked on Monument Mountain.

September: **Barrington Fair** at the Great Barrington Fairgrounds.

October: **Berkshire Botanical Garden Harvest Festival,** Stockbridge. **Halloween Walk Through Ice Glen** (a Stockbridge tradition), usually followed by a bonfire.

December: **Naumkeag** is decorated for Christmas. *A Christmas Carol* is read in Stockbridge Library.

CENTRAL BERKSHIRE

To many visitors Lenox and the Berkshires are virtually synonymous. Home of the Boston Symphony Orchestra's world-famous summer music festival at Tanglewood, Lenox has come to epitomize all the intense cultural life of the Berkshires: music, dance, art, theater, and resident literati, past and present.

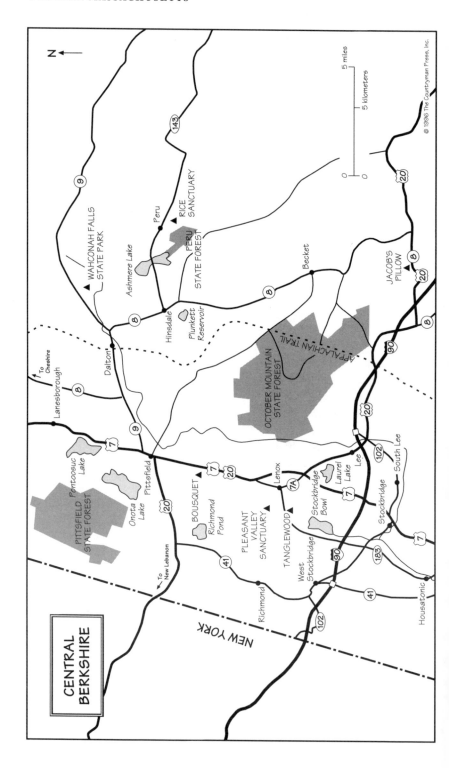

Writers such as Henry Wadsworth Longfellow, Nathaniel Hawthorne, Herman Melville, and Oliver Wendell Holmes Sr. were among the first Berkshire summer residents. Their lyric descriptions of its inspirational scenery attracted wealthy rusticators—who built great summer mansions (often coyly called "cottages") and terraced cornfields into formal gardens.

The stock market crash of 1928, the Depression, and the federal income tax thinned the ranks of the Berkshires' wealthy elite. The mansions remained, however, and were frequently taken over by private schools, religious orders, or cultural institutions.

In 1937 the Boston Symphony Orchestra (BSO) made Tanglewood its summer home. Dancers, musicians, actors, and writers began flocking to the Lenox area, attracted by the presence of the Berkshire Playhouse, Jacob's Pillow Dance Festival, and the BSO—all still in creative summer residence at former private estates.

High-culture happenings attract a steady flow of summer visitors to central Berkshire. Happily, this busy arts scene is staged in tranquil countryside that is far more than a backdrop. Since the 1840s, both picnicking and hiking (along bench-spotted paths and up gentle mountains) have been considered the thing to do in the Berkshires. With more than 100,000 acres of state forest and a sizable number of other public preserves, the area remains one of the most inviting to explore on foot.

Many old mansions, some well-nigh baronial, are now inns and bed & breakfasts. Regardless of decor or degree of luxury, their rates vary wildly through the year. On weekends during "Tanglewood season" (July and August) you can pay Manhattan prices for a modest room and queue up for an equally pricey dinner. With the exception of fall foliage season, however, during midweek—even in August—you pay less and don't wait in line.

Off-season, prices drop substantially, and culture doesn't disappear. The BSO might be gone but galleries and museums remain, as do many musicians and artists. In winter there are also hundreds of miles of cross-country ski trails and several ski areas to enjoy.

AREA CODE
413

GUIDANCE
The Berkshires Visitors Bureau (443-9186; outside Massachusetts 1-800-237-5747), Berkshire Common, Pittsfield 01201. Open Monday through Friday 9–5. This is the source of "The Berkshires Vacation Guide," a thick biannual listing of attractions, lodgings, and dining. The bureau also keeps track of vacancies during crunch periods and can refer callers to inns and motels with space. The Pittsfield Information Booth, across Main Street at the park, is open June through mid-October, Monday through Thursday 9–5, Friday and Saturday 9–8, Sunday 10–noon; Labor Day to Columbus Day, weekends only.

Lenox Chamber of Commerce (637-3646), in the old Lenox Academy building, 75 Main Street. Open year-round. Summer: Monday through Thursday 10–4, Friday and Saturday 10–6, Sunday 10–2. Winter: Monday 10–noon, 1–3; Tuesday through Saturday 9:30–4:30. A very helpful walk-in center with an extensive pamphlet rack. Free lodging referrals, which during Tanglewood season include many private homes.

GETTING THERE

By air: Pittsfield is 37 miles from Albany Airport, 70 miles from Bradley Field in Windsor Locks, Connecticut.

By train: AMTRAK's Lakeshore Limited from Boston to Chicago stops in Pittsfield (1-800-872-7245).

By bus: From Boston **Peter Pan** (1-800-343-9999) and **Greyhound** (1-800-231-2222) serve Lenox, Lee, and Pittsfield. From New York City, **Providence Bonanza** (617-720-4110) serves Great Barrington, Lee, Lenox, and Pittsfield.

Abbot's Taxi (243-1645) in Lee serves Boston, New York, Albany, and Connecticut airports, as well as making local runs.

GETTING AROUND

The Berkshire Regional Transit Authority (499-2782) links Great Barrington, Lee, Lenox, and Stockbridge with Pittsfield; hours are geared to commuters rather than to visitors. Fare is $.60 per town.

Local taxis include Abbot's (see above) and **Alexis Taxi & Powell Limousine Service** (442-3531; outside Berkshire County 1-800-345-3531) in Pittsfield.

MEDICAL EMERGENCY

Berkshire Medical Center (447-2000), 725 North Street, Pittsfield: 24-hour emergency care.

Lenox Ambulance (637-2345), 14 Walker Street, Lenox: 24-hour emergency service.

VILLAGE

Lenox evolved in stages. Its first boost came from its rise from farm to shire town or county seat in 1787, a status that gave it graceful Federal buildings like the courthouse (the present library with its luxurious reading rooms, gallery, and outdoor reading park), the Academy (now housing the chamber of commerce), and the Church on the Hill. In the 1860s, when county government shifted to Pittsfield, a new breed of summer visitor brought visible change. Intellectual and literary families from Boston had been spending their summers in town for a decade, but now the very rich began buying up large holdings. By the turn of the century more than 75 elaborate summer "cottages" were scattered along every ridge in town. Lenox's glory years as the inland Newport were brief, ended by the Great Depression and the federal income tax. The resort might have vanished entirely had it not been for the BSO and its

Hancock Shaker Village

then-novel Berkshire Music Festival. Concert halls were not yet air-conditioned, and symphony music typically ceased during the summer. The orchestra selected Lenox as its summer home because Tanglewood (a forested estate named by Hawthorne, who wrote *Tanglewood Tales* there) was given to it by a patron.

Many other local estates are occupied by nonprofit institutions—ranging from the Kripalu Center for Yoga and Health at what was Shadowbrook (Andrew Carnegie's grand home overlooking Stockbridge Bowl), to Shakespeare & Company, a theater group performing at The Mount (former residence of Pulitzer Prize–winning novelist Edith Wharton, whose best-known work, *Ethan Frome,* is set in the Berkshires). The Mount, built in 1902, is also open in summer for tours.

Lenox remains essentially a country village but has become an increasingly sophisticated one in recent years.

TO SEE

MUSEUMS AND HISTORIC HOMES

Berkshire Museum (443-7171), Main Street (US 7, just south of the park), Pittsfield. Open Tuesday through Saturday 10–5, Sunday 1–5 (Monday in July and August). An example of what a regional museum should be, this complex was founded in 1903 by Dalton philanthropist Zenas Crane. The 18 galleries display both permanent and changing exhibits and there are frequent films, performances, lectures, and concerts in the Little Cinema, a 300-seat theater. The permanent collection includes Hudson River School landscapes and early American portraits by Church, Inness, and Copley, plus mobiles by Alexander Calder. There are also 15th- to 18th-century European works and ancient artifacts, including a 2000-year-old mummy. Children love the natural his-

THE BERKSHIRE MUSEUM

The Touch the Sea exhibit at Pittsfield's Berkshire Museum

tory collection of shells, gemstones, and fossils and the new aquarium featuring fish from throughout the world, as well as the reptiles, spiders, local animals, and birds. A special Berkshire section includes a birchbark canoe.

Hancock Shaker Village (443-0188), 5 miles west of Pittsfield on US 20, junction with MA 41. From Boston take the West Stockbridge exit on the Mass. Pike (take MA 41 North to US 20 West). Open daily April through November 9:30–5. Adults $10, children $5. In 1961 the village's 20 buildings were about to be sold to a neighboring racetrack when a group of Pittsfield residents rallied and bought the entire community—including 1000 acres—from its last Shaker sisters. The buildings have been restored, including the much-copied and -photographed round, stone barn. A scattering of tidy buildings grouped around the 1830 brick dining hall and surrounded by its own orchards and meadows, the village looks like some primitive painter's vision of the heavenly kingdom. Founded in 1790, this "City of Peace" prospered in the mid-19th century (some 250 Brethren were divided among six "families" in the 1830s), and it survived 170 years. The guides, craftsmen, and furnishings all tell about the dancing monks and nuns who turned farming, craftsmanship, and invention into visible prayers. Note the frequent special events staged throughout the year. During July, August, and part of September traditional Shaker dinners are served in the brick building; the cost is $38. (For reservations call 443-0188.) A snack bar and picnic areas are on the grounds. The gift shop sells yarn, herbs, and baked goods made on the premises. Inquire about the Shaker Trail leading to the adjacent Pittsfield State Forest, traveling past the sites of old Shaker dwellings and religious ceremonies and by the Shaker-built "Great Wall of the Berkshires." You might also want to continue a few miles west on US 20 to the **Mount Lebanon Shaker Village** (518-784-9500) in New Lebanon, New York. Far less developed as a museum than its Hancock neighbor, this village has been preserved primarily as the Darrow School; while approaching the dozen "Church Family" buildings along the quiet dirt road, it's easy to imagine away a century.

Arrowhead (442-1793), 789 Holmes Road (off US 7/US 20,) Pittsfield. Open Memorial Day through October, Monday through Saturday 10–4:30, Sunday 11–3:30. It was in this 18th-century house, purchased in 1850 when he was 31, that Herman Melville wrote *Moby Dick*. The grandly conceived story of the great white whale and the mad sea captain who obsessively pursues it was put on paper in a study overlooked by the looming, probably inspiring, mass of Mount Greylock. The house is sparsely furnished, but it conveys a sense of Melville during the 13 years he lived here, writing *Moby Dick* and a number of other works that brought him no fame or money in his lifetime. The house is headquarters for the Berkshire County Historical Society, and a film on Berkshire history is shown. There is a nature trail.

Crane Museum (684-2600), off MA 8, near Pioneer Mill on Housatonic Street, Dalton. Open June through mid-October, Monday through Friday 2–5. Free and worth a stop. Housed in the rag room of the Old Stone Mill (1846) by the Housatonic, the displays tell the story of paper making and include a fascinating variety of paper money. Crane Paper is the sole supplier of "money paper" to the United States Mint; the company has been in the family for five generations.

ART CENTERS

In no other part of the country are so many quality music, dance, and theater productions found so near each other. Almost any day of the summer you can choose from a rich menu of live performances, many at prices far below what they would command in New York or Boston.

Tanglewood Music Festival (637-1600), Tanglewood, entrance on West Street (MA 183, west of Lenox village). The Boston Symphony Orchestra's summer concert series, June through August, has been held since the 1930s in a fan-shaped, open-sided hall understatedly referred to as "The Shed." It actually seats more than 5000 people and has splendid acoustics. A new addition to Tanglewood is 1200-seat Seiji Ozawa Hall, named for the BSO's longtime music director. The hall is striking architecturally and has won several design awards. More than 14,000 people regularly converge on Tanglewood on weekends, but a concert is never sold out—there is always room on the grounds of the 500 acres. Many Sunday concertgoers actually prefer the lawn and come several hours before concert time, dressed in high resort style (or any old way at all), and often with elaborate picnic hampers that have been known to include white linen tablecloths and candelabras. The lawn at Tanglewood is one of New England's great people-watching places. In addition to the symphonic concerts (Friday and Saturday evenings and Sunday afternoons) there are weekly chamber music concerts and open rehearsals, the annual Festival of Contemporary Music, and almost daily concerts by young musicians of the Tanglewood Music Center. The Boston Pops performs each summer as well. Prices for BSO shed concerts are $12–70; Ozawa Hall, $12–30. A detailed schedule and order form is available by contacting the Tanglewood Ticket Office (before May 31), Symphony Hall, Boston 02115 (617-266-1492; after May contact Tanglewood in Lenox 01240, 637-5165).

Berkshire Performing Arts Theater at the National Music Center (637-4718, tickets and schedule; 637-1800, information), 70 Kemble Street, Lenox. Housed in a former boys' school, the center focuses on American music of all sorts. Plans call for a museum of American music, library and archive, recording studios, and residence and retirement facilities for professional musicians. The center presents a season-long program of pop, folk, blues, and jazz performances by well-known artists in its 1200-seat, air-conditioned hall.

Jacob's Pillow Dance Festival (243-0745), George Carter Road, Becket (off US 20, eight miles east of Lee). America's oldest dance festival, Jacob's Pillow presents a 10-week summer program of classic and experimental dance. Located on a onetime hilltop farm, the Pillow was founded in the 1930s by the famed dancer Ted Shawn as both a school for dancers and a performance center. As well as scheduled productions, informal impromptu performances are going on all the time. There is a pleasant alfresco restaurant, the Pillow Cafe. Tickets are $10–35.

Armstrong Chamber Concerts (637-3646; 203-868-0522), Town Hall Theater, Lenox. Unique programs by noted artists using combinations of instruments in a wide spectrum of musical styles. April through November.

Berkshire Opera Company (243-1343), Cranwell Opera House, US 20, Lenox. Full productions of traditional and modern operas sung in English. July and August.

TO DO

FOR FAMILIES

Berkshire Scenic Railway (637-2210), Housatonic Street and Willow Creek Road, Lenox. A railroading museum in the restored turn-of-the-century Lenox train station that includes exhibits and model railroads.

Admission to the museum is free. Also offered are short narrated train rides around the museum grounds. $1.50 adults, $1 children and seniors.
Alpine Slide at Jiminy Peak. See "North Berkshire."

BICYCLING

An authoritative (good maps and descriptions) book by a local cyclist is *Bike Rides in the Berkshires,* by Lewis C. Cuyler (Berkshire House Publishers, $8.95). Rentals are available from **Plaine's Ski and Cycle Center** (499-0294), 55 West Housatonic Street, Pittsfield. (Also see "North Berkshire" and "South County.")

BOATING

Boat rentals are available at **Pontoosuc Lake** in Pittsfield (Quirk's Marine, 447-7512); also at **Greenwater Pond** in Becket, **Laurel Lake** in Lee, **Hoosac Lake** in Cheshire, and **Richmond Pond** in Richmond. The placid Housatonic is ideal for lazy rides down the river. Trips are detailed in the *AMC River Guide—Central/Southern New England.*

Canoes can be rented at **Quirk's Marine** (447-7512), Pittsfield; and **Main Street Sports & Leisure** (637-4407), Lenox. **Berkshire Hiking Holidays** (637-4442), PO Box 2231, Lenox, offers canoeing/lodging/hiking packages.

FISHING

For a detailed listing of every pond and river stocked with bass, pickerel, perch, hornpout, and trout, check the Berkshire Visitors Bureau "Summer Guide." **Points North Hunting and Fishing Outfitters** in Adams (see "North Berkshire") offer sport-fishing trips.

Pilobus Dance Theater at the Jacob's Pillow Dance Festival

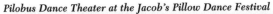

HIKING

See the trails described in *Green Space* (also see "North Berkshire" and "South County").

HORSEBACK RIDING

Aspinwall-Bayville Stables (637-0245), US 7, Lenox; supervised trail rides. **R & C Stables** (637-0613) at Eastover Resort, East Street, Lenox; supervised trail rides. **Twin Ponds Farm** (518-733-6793), off MA 22, Stephentown, New York; trail rides, $20 an hour, $50 for 3 hours (kids' pony rides $3).

GOLF

The local courses are the 18-hole **Country Club of Pittsfield** (447-8500); the outstanding 18-hole **Cranwell Golf Course** (637-0441) in Lenox; and the 18-hole **Wahconah Country Club** (684-1333) in Dalton.

SWIMMING

Under *Green Space* in this section check Wahconah Falls, and Pittsfield; under *Green Space* in "South County" check Beartown, Sandisfield, Tolland. For a fee ($5 adults, $1 children) you can also swim at: **Prospect Lake Park** (528-4158), a private campground in North Egremont (there are picnic tables in the pines and a float); the **Egremont Country Club** (528-4222) at Ashmere Lake and Plunkett Reservoir in Hinsdale; **Onota** and **Pontoosuc Lakes** in Pittsfield; **Card Lake** in West Stockbridge; and the **YMCA Outdoor Center** (three pools) on Pontoosuc Lake.

TENNIS

Berkshire West Athletic Club (499-4600), Dan Fox Drive, Pittsfield; four outdoor and five indoor courts. **Jiminy Peak Resort** (738-5500), Hancock; six asphalt courts. Fee. **Cranwell Resort** (637-0441), US 20, Lenox; two Har-Tru courts. **Ponterril/YMCA** (447-7405; 499-0640), US 7, Pontoosuc Lake, Pittsfield; six clay courts, fee for nonmembers.

CROSS-COUNTRY SKIING

Canterbury Farm Bed & Breakfast (623-8765), Fred Snow Road, Becket, offers 11 miles of tracked trails at an average elevation of 1700 feet; rental equipment.
(Also see *Green Space.*)

DOWNHILL SKIING

Bousquet (442-8316), Pittsfield. The Berkshires' oldest ski area, founded in 1932, and the one that pioneered both the ski train and night skiing. Noted for friendly slopes ideal for beginning and intermediate skiers; 750-foot vertical drop and 21 trails. Open daily in winter, also nightly except Sunday. Marked from US 7/US 20 south of town. Tickets $10–15.

Jiminy Peak (738-5500), Corey Road, Hancock (between US 7 and MA 43). Central Berkshires' big mountain and the focal point of a large, four-season resort. The vertical drop is 1140 feet, and about 40 percent of the terrain is rated expert. Twenty-eight trails, seven chair lifts, one

bar, 95 percent snowmaking. Night skiing. Open daily in-season until
10:30. Tickets $37 weekends, $30 weekdays.

GREEN SPACE

Pleasant Valley Wildlife Sanctuary (637-0320), 472 West Mountain Road,
Lenox. This 730-acre Massachusetts Audubon Sanctuary includes part
of Lenox Mountain and Yokun Brook. It has beaver ponds and meadows, a hemlock gorge, a hummingbird garden, a summer trailside museum, and 7 miles of trails, used in winter for cross-country skiing. $3
adults, $2 children and seniors.
Canoe Meadows Wildlife Sanctuary, Holmes Road off US 7, south of
Pittsfield. This Massachusetts Audubon Sanctuary offers a mix of wetlands and croplands with 5 miles of trails. No rest rooms. $2 adults, $1
children and seniors.
Dorothy Frances Rice Wildlife Refuge in Peru: South Road off MA 143
from the town center. Three hundred acres, walking trails, self-guiding
trails, owned by the New England Forestry Foundation.
STATE PARKS AND FORESTS
John F. Kennedy State Park in Lenox on US 7. The grounds of the
former Aspinwall Hotel offer hiking trails, good for cross-country skiing
in winter.
Pittsfield State Forest (442-8992) totals 9695 acres. From the corner of
US 20 and US 7 in Pittsfield, drive west on West Street, north on Chur-
chill Street, and west on Cascade to the entrance. $2 day-use fee. A 5-
mile circular paved road travels beside Lulu Brook to Berry Pond,
where there is camping (13 sites) and boating (no motors); 18 more
sites are located at Parker Brook, with a picnic area across the way and
another at the Lulu Brook swimming area. A ski lodge, located near the
ski jump, can be rented by groups in summer; it's used as a warming hut
in winter. Trails lead to the Taconic Skyline Trail, a spectacular ridge
route leading north into Vermont. Tranquillity Trail, a paved, ¾-mile
loop through spruce woods, has been designed for wheelchair access.
There are taped descriptions of flora and fauna. In June the forest harbors 40 acres of azaleas. Balance Rock—a 165-ton boulder poised on
another rock—is accessible via Balance Rock Road from US 7 in Lanes-
boro. The camping fee is $4 or $5, depending on the site.
Wahconah Falls State Park (442-8992), off MA 9 in Dalton, 3 miles east
of the town center. A 2-minute walk brings you from the parking area
down to picnic tables, scattered among the smooth rocks above the falls;
swimming is permitted in the small pool at their base.
Peru State Forest (442-8992), off MA 143 in Peru; south on Curtin Road,
1 mile from Peru Center. Garnet Hill (2178 feet) yields a good view of
the surrounding country, and there is fishing in Garnet Lake.

LODGING

During July and August the general Berkshire policy is a minimum 2- or 3-night stay on weekends. Note that the Lenox Chamber of Commerce refers guests to private homes during this period.

RESORTS

Eastover (637-0625), 430 East Street, Lenox 01240. This 1000-acre estate has been offering "old-fashioned fun" since 1947; 165 rooms, some in a turn-of-the-century gilded "cottage," most in motel-style annexes. Facilities include a small ski slope with a chair lift, an ice rink, driving range, seven tennis courts, horseback riding, indoor and outdoor pools. Other amenities include a huge dance hall, a Civil War museum, and a herd of buffalo! Weeks and weekends are tightly scheduled, with the unusual twist that some programs are geared exclusively to singles, others to families, still others to couples. Liquor is not served at Eastover. Weekends are $80–101 per person per night including all meals.

The Ponds at Foxhollow (637-1469), US 7, Lenox 01240. A new clubhouse is the centerpiece for this 48-unit, 225-acre condominium resort that offers swimming (indoor and outdoor pool), tennis, hot tub and sauna, exercise and game rooms. The one- and two-bedroom units are large and have air-conditioning and fireplaces. One-week rentals only in July and August, $1100–1400. Weekend packages and daily rates at other times.

Blantyre (637-3556; off-season 298-3806), Blantyre Road, Lenox 01240. Built in 1902 to replicate an ancestral home in Scotland, this magnificent, Tudor-style mansion was lovingly restored to its original glory in 1980 by Jack and Jane Fitzpatrick, owners of the Red Lion Inn in Stockbridge. There is a baronial entry hall, a truly graceful music room with crystal chandeliers, sofas covered in petit point, a piano, and a harp. Guests dine in the paneled dining room, either around the long formal table or in the adjoining, smaller octagonal room. Dinner is open to the public by reservation. Guest rooms are impeccably furnished with antiques, and most have fireplaces. There are 85 well-kept acres with four tennis courts, a swimming pool (with hot tub and sauna), and competition croquet courts (grounds and buildings are not open to the public for viewing). Open mid-May through October. Room rates are $225–400; suites, $285–585; cottages, $160–475.

Wheatleigh (637-0610), West Hawthorne Road, Lenox 01240. This yellow brick palazzo was built in 1893 and set in 22 acres that now include a swimming pool and tennis courts. Tanglewood is around the corner. There are 17 large and elegantly decorated rooms, all with private bath, about half with fireplaces. The restaurant is expensive but award-winning. This is a special and impressive place, but we find the atmosphere stiff and a bit pretentious (probably sour grapes because we can't afford it). $155–525 in-season, $155–375 off-season.

Cranwell Resort & Golf Club (637-1364; 1-800-CRANWEL), US 20, Lenox 01240. A 380-acre, 64-room resort with a hilltop view. The imposing main building was built as a grand private home in 1893 and long used as a Jesuit boys preparatory school. Rooms in the main house are luxurious and furnished with period antiques; those in various outbuildings are pleasant but more simply furnished. There are two dining rooms, a lounge, meeting rooms (one the old chapel), and a heated outdoor pool. The big attraction, however, is the 18-hole, PGA championship golf course, the area's most challenging. $229–389 in-season with continental breakfast.

Seven Hills (637-0060; 1-800-869-6518), 40 Plunkett Street, Lenox 01240. This 1911 Tudor Revival mansion is set in 27 terraced and landscaped acres. The 52 rooms vary from bright, motel-style doubles out in the garden annex to classic old bedrooms with flowery wallpaper and working fireplaces in the main house. New management has refurbished the place from top to bottom, brightening rooms and enlarging many common spaces. The restaurant has a good local reputation and is open for dinner. Facilities include a pool and tennis courts; a path leads down to Laurel Lake. Open year-round. Rates, with continental breakfast, are $179–299 in the manor house, $125–179 in the annex.

INNS

Apple Tree Inn (637-1477), 334 West Street, Lenox 01240. This century-old house sits high on a hill overlooking the Stockbridge Bowl, just across from the main entrance to Tanglewood. The view is one of the loveliest in the Berkshires, enhanced by flowering apple trees and lush rose gardens. (Owner Greg Smith cultivates no fewer than 300 varieties of roses.) Each of the 13 rooms in the main house has been imaginatively, lovingly restored and furnished, four with working fireplaces. The 20 rooms in the modern lodge are motel-style but pleasant and handy to the pool, which commands an extraordinary view. The other great view is from the circular, glass-walled dining room, open to the public and popular with concertgoers. Light meals are also available in the oak-beamed tavern after Tanglewood concerts. $150–300 in Tanglewood season, $75–240 the rest of the year.

The Village Inn (637-0020; 1-800-253-0917), 16 Church Street, Lenox 01240. On a quiet back street in Lenox village, this cozy old inn—built in 1770—offers 32 rooms (all with private bath and telephones), a comfortable screened porch, and a Victorian-style parlor. There is usually someone sitting on the stool in front of the check-in desk, which doubles as a bar. The inn is open to the public for breakfast, tea, and dinner. $70–195 summer and fall, $50–150 the rest of the year.

Gateways Inn and Restaurant (637-2532), 71 Walker Street, Lenox 01240. Built by Harley Procter of Procter & Gamble in 1912 to resemble (the story goes) a cake of Ivory soap, which it does—one with black shutters. Although best known as a restaurant, this elegant small inn offers nine rooms, one a suite with two fireplaces that was Arthur Fiedler's favorite place to stay when he conducted at Tanglewood. All rooms have private baths. The restaurant has long been considered one of the area's best. Room rates are $170–205.

BED & BREAKFASTS

In Lenox 01240

Candlelight Inn (637-1555), 53 Walker Street. In the heart of Lenox village and better known as a restaurant than an inn, the Candlelight has eight attractive guest rooms upstairs, all with air-conditioning and private baths. There are four dining rooms plus a pub on the premises. Open year-round. $90–155 in-season, $65–120 off-season.

☞ **The Gables Inn** (637-3416), 81 Walker Street. This gracious old village home housed Edith Wharton while she was constructing The Mount. Central to everything in the village, it has 18 bedrooms with private baths. Half of them also have fireplaces. Rates, with continental breakfast, are $90–195 in summer and fall, $75–160 the rest of the year.

Cliffwood Inn (637-3330), 25 Cliffwood Street. Built in 1904 as the summer home of the American ambassador to France, the inn is airy and elegant with seven guest rooms, six with working fireplaces. (One has a fireplace in the bathroom.) In summer, breakfast is served on the veranda overlooking the garden and pool; in winter, by the fireplace in the gracious oval dining room. $110–200 in-season, $72–126 the rest of the year.

Garden Gables (637-0193), 141 Main Street (US 7). Owners Mario and Lynn Mekinda live in as well as run Garden Gables, and the result is a notably cheery and homey feeling. The triple-gabled, white clapboard house—built in 1780—is set well back from the road and within walking distance of the village shops and restaurants. Rooms are bright and comfortable, and all have private baths (three also have whirlpools). Eight rooms have fireplaces, and others have private porches. The ample grounds convey a sense of being out in the country, and the outdoor, guests-only pool is one of the biggest in Berkshire County. $90–200 in-season, $65–145 off-season.

☞ **Walker House** (637-1271; 1-800-235-3098), 64 Walker Street. This expanded Federal-era (1804) house has a Victorian feel inside, nicely decorated with interesting art and inviting common rooms. A flower-garnished and wicker-furnished veranda overlooks the expansive back garden. Five of the eight guest rooms, each named for a composer, have fireplaces, and all have charm. Innkeepers Peggy and Richard Houdek know the area thoroughly and happily share their knowledge with guests. Breakfast, tea, and bicycles are included in the rates. $70–180 in-season, $60–120 the rest of the year.

Birchwood Inn (637-2600; 1-800-524-1646), 7 Hubbard Street. This grand hilltop mansion dates back to 1762. There are 10 rooms in the main house (eight with private bath), and two suites in the carriage house. The library parlor is a gracious, welcoming room that takes up one side of the house. There is a nice view of Lenox from the porch, and

Kennedy Park is nearby. Rates, which include afternoon wine and cheese as well as full breakfast, are $89–199 in-season, $60–135 off-season.

Cornell Inn (637-0562), 209 Main Street (MA 7A). This B&B is really a complex of buildings: The 10 rooms in the 1880's main building have private baths, and there are four more rooms in the carriage house and an additional 10 in recently renovated, two-centuries-old McDonald House next door, all with fireplaces, whirlpools, four-posters, entertainment centers, and decks. Continental breakfast weekdays, full breakfast buffet on Sunday. Restaurant and pub. $59–199 in-season.

Brook Farm (637-3013), 15 Hawthorne Street. A handsome yellow Victorian house on a quiet byway south of the village, Brook Farm is furnished to fit its period (1889). There are 12 guest rooms, all with private baths, four with fireplaces. Breakfast is served buffet-style in the elegant green dining room overlooking the garden, and afternoon tea is served. There is a pool and a comfortable lounging parlor with fireplace. The previous owners were poetry enthusiasts who accumulated a large library of poetry books and tapes and encouraged poetry reading on the premises. Present owners Joe and Anne Miller keep up this tradition but are not quite as passionate about verse as were their predecessors. $75–170 in-season, $65–110 off-season.

The Kemble Inn (637-4113; 1-800-353-4113), 2 Kemble Street. The newest (1994) luxury bed & breakfast inn in Lenox, the Kemble Inn is a Georgian Revival mansion built in 1881 by US Secretary of State Frederick Freylinghuysen and named for tart-tongued actress Fanny Kemble—a frequent Lenox visitor in the last century. Owner Richard Reardon is a contractor and has completely renovated and modernized the house. All 12 guest rooms have baths and air-conditioning and one room, which has a black marble fireplace, is handicapped accessible. The building is elegant, but the decor—plastic plants and awful paintings of Quebec landscapes with price tags attached—doesn't match it. $100–295, depending on season and time of week.

Whistler's Inn (637-0975), 5 Greenwood Street (corner of MA 7A). A mostly Tudor-style mansion with large, opulent common rooms including a ballroom, library, music room, and dining room. The formal garden is Italianate. There are 11 guest rooms, all with private bath. A full breakfast is served. Innkeeper Richard Mears is a novelist, wife Joan, an artist. No surprise then that the library is well stocked, the walls hung with interesting art, and the atmosphere distinctly cultural. The inn is across from the Church on the Hill and an easy walk from both village shops and Kennedy Park. $90–200 in summer, $70–160 off-season.

Rookwood (637-9750), 11 Stockbridge Road. A turreted, 19-room Victorian inn within walking distance of Tanglewood. All rooms have private baths, and seven have fireplaces. Rates, which include afternoon tea as well as breakfast, are $140–225 in high season, $75–130 low season.

The Hilltop Inn (637-1746), 174 Main Street. A handsome old house at the crest of Main Street. It was recently restored by Vito Perulli, owner of Gateways Inn, so thoroughly that the place seems more like a Victorian reproduction than the real thing. The six guest rooms are furnished in period style, and all have bathrooms, fireplaces, air-conditioning, and cable TV. The Norman Rockwell suite also has a canopy bed and a splendiferous bathroom. There is a wraparound porch and a combination sitting and breakfast room looking out on the garden. $125–195 in-season, $96–160 off-season.

Underledge (637-0236), 106 Cliffwood Street. This formal, turn-of-the-century home has eight rooms, five with working fireplaces, all with large windows. Located on a mansion-lined street, it borders Kennedy Park with its extensive trails for walking and skiing. This was the Lanoues' home before they opened it to guests, and there is a friendly, family feel to the place. $115–175 in-season, $60–125 the rest of the year.

Amadeus House (637-4770), 15 Cliffwood Street. A large, comfortable, 19th-century house with seven guest rooms and a small rentable apartment. Two rooms share a bath, the rest have their own. All rooms are named for composers. Amadeus was, of course, Mozart's middle name, and his room is unusually nice with a sitting area, wood stove, and porch. House amenities include a large collection of classical CDs. Owners Marty Gottron and John Felton are a friendly, interesting couple—both with a journalism background—who like to spend time with their guests. $55–175 in the summer/fall season, $55–155 the rest of the year.

Elsewhere in Central Berkshire

White Horse Inn (442-2512), 378 South Street, Pittsfield 01201. Open May through November. A large, turn-of-the century house with eight guest rooms, all with private bath, several with fireplaces. On a busy street but set well back from it. In summer, continental breakfast is served on the deck. $75–135.

The Dalton House (684-3854), 955 Main Street, Dalton 01226. This handsome old home was built by a former Hessian soldier in 1810. There is a large, informal sitting area with old beams, wood-lined walls, and a "Loafing Loft." Breakfast buffet is served in the Garden Room. The gardens are extensive, and there is a pool. The 11 rooms have private baths and some have fireplaces. In summer and fall, $68–115; winter and spring, $58–85.

Canterbury Farm Bed & Breakfast (623-8765), Becket 01223. This early-19th-century home stands on its own 200 acres surrounded by gardens, fields, and woods crisscrossed with ski trails. The four guest rooms, one with a fireplace, share two baths. There are two sitting rooms with color TV, a piano, and games in the library. $65–85 per couple includes a full breakfast, $15 for an extra person in the room. Ten percent less for more than 4 days' lodging.

OTHER LODGING

Canyon Ranch in the Berkshires (637-4100; 1-800-742-9000), Bellefontaine, 91 Kemble Street, Lenox 01240. Sister to the famous spa in

Arizona, this spectacularly deluxe, 150-acre fitness resort is blessed with a superb setting. The focal point is a grand 1890s manor house that is a replica of the Petit Trianon of Louis XVI. Guests sleep in the more modest 120-room inn, a clapboard building in traditional New England style. Just about every health and fitness program imaginable is offered, and instruction and equipment are state of the art. Meals are dietary but also gourmet and delicious. Canyon Ranch has been called "a cross between boot camp and heaven," but guests (who have included many celebrities) almost invariably depart glowing and enthusiastic. All this doesn't come cheap: 3-night packages are $1150–1270 including meals (but not taxes or service), based on double occupancy of a standard room. For a day-use fee of $220–280, nonguests can have two physical services (such as massage or shiatsu), eat lunch, and use all sports facilities.

Hilton Inn Berkshire (499-2000), Berkshire Common at West Street, Pittsfield. This is the Berkshires' only high-rise and very much a part of the county seat. There are 175 rooms, an indoor pool, café, and a highly regarded restaurant. $99–189 summer and fall, $79–129 winter and spring.

Kripalu Center for Yoga and Health (637-3280), MA 183, Stockbridge 01262 (just beyond Tanglewood on the Lenox-Stockbridge line). This nationally known Yoga-based holistic health center offers a structured daily regimen and a variety of weekend, week-long, and longer programs. Kripalu is housed in Shadowbrook, a former Jesuit novitiate on the grounds of Andrew Carnegie's 300-acre estate, which overlooks the Stockbridge Bowl and is within walking distance of Tanglewood. The center's founder, Yogi Amrit Desai, is no longer in residence, but the staff are committed members of a Yoga community and unusually friendly and helpful. The center can accommodate up to 300 guests, who come from around the country to study Yoga and meditation and learn stress-reduction techniques. Many people, however, come simply for the holistic food, massage and other body work, and peace, quiet, and beauty. Facilities include whirlpools, saunas, hiking and cross-country trails, beach, boats, and tennis; also a children's program during summer months. Rates, which include vegetarian meals and use of all facilities, run from $80 a day in a dormitory to $190 for a private room with bath. Special program packages and introductory rates are usually available.

WHERE TO EAT

DINING OUT

Gateways Inn (637-2532), 71 Walker Street, Lenox. Open for dinner. A well-known restaurant in a 1912 mansion. The specialty is Italian cuisine with a variety of pasta dishes. Entrées in the $12–20 range.

Wheatleigh (637-0610), West Hawthorne Road, Lenox. Open for lunch and brunch in-season; closed Monday. This Florentine palazzo, within walking distance of Tanglewood, features "creative cuisine": pheasant with cognac sauce or rack of lamb, for instance. The renowned Wheat-leigh Dining Room has a prix fixe menu of $68. The Grill Room is à la carte with entrées in the $15–25 range.

Village Inn (637-0020), 16 Church Street, Lenox. The dining room has a pronounced country inn feel. The specialty is regional American cuisine with an emphasis on New England dishes. Entrées are $12–25. Afternoon tea is served and, on Sunday, both brunch and an elaborate, English-style high tea.

Apple Tree (637-1477), 224 West Street, Lenox. The round corner dining room, twinkling with myriad small white lights, seems suspended above the Stockbridge Bowl, which it overlooks. Continental cuisine and homemade desserts. Entrées are $10–25.

Cafe Lucia (637-2460), 90 Church Street, Lenox. Open daily for dinner, July through September, closed Sunday the rest of the year. A remodeled art gallery is the setting for appreciating classic Italian dishes such as osso buco or chicken Scarparello. Moderate to expensive.

The Candlelight Inn (637-1555), 35 Walker Street, Lenox. A charming, candlelit dining room and outdoor dining in summer. American and continental dishes such as cold poached salmon with chive ramoulade ($18.95) or cold marinated spinach linguine with shrimp and garlic vinaigrette ($14.95).

Church Street Cafe (637-2745), 69 Church Street, Lenox. A lively, popular restaurant with an eclectic and always interesting menu. There is a pleasant dining patio and several connecting dining rooms, the walls of which are hung with paintings by local artists. Entrées under $25.

Roseborough Grill and Country Restaurant (637-2700), 83 Church Street, Lenox. Open daily from 8 AM in summer; closed Tuesday and Wednesday off-season. A rustic dining room specializing in charcoal-grilled fish, chicken, beef, and ribs. All baking done on the premises. Dinner entrées are $13–20.

Blantyre (637-3556), 16 Blantyre Road, Lenox. Open May through November, Blantyre is a baronial mansion that epitomizes the Berkshires' Gilded Age glory; dining in its grand restaurant is a memorable (and expensive) experience. The cuisine is French (of course), prepared with care, and served with flair. The wine list is vast and varied. The prix fixe menu is $65 per person. Dinner is by reservation only. In summer lunch is also served, on the terrace overlooking the formal garden.

Seven Hills (637-0060), 40 Plunkett Street, Lenox. Open daily 5–9:30 PM year-round. The dining room of this grand, 1911 Tudor mansion serves classical Continental cuisine in appropriately elegant surroundings. If traditional sauces and dishes are too rich for you, however, there is also an alternative, "heart healthy" menu. Most entrées are in the $25–30 range. Dinner only. (Reservations recommended.)

Lenox House (637-1341), 55 Pittsfield-Lenox Road, Lenox. Open daily for lunch, dinner, and snacks. Antiques and shining copper give this restaurant a New England feeling also reflected in the menu. Specialties include dishes such as New England seafood pie. Most entrées are $10–24.

Truffles and Such (447-9592), Allendale Shopping Center (MA 8 and MA 9), Pittsfield. New American cuisine in a sleek, contemporary setting. The menu includes dishes like Caribbean crabcake with green peppercorns, and chicken livers with green apples. Most entrées are $10–24.

Dakota (499-7900), US 7, Lenox/Pittsfield line. There is a large fieldstone fireplace in the dining room, which is supposed to resemble an Adirondack lodge. Specialties include seafood, hand-cut steaks, and mesquite-grilled fish. Open for dinner daily and Sunday brunch. Most entrées are $12–20.

EATING OUT

Village Snack Shop (637-2564), 35 Housatonic Street, Lenox. Great breakfasts, soups, sandwiches, and luncheon specials. Inexpensive. Popular local hangout and gossip exchange (if they don't know about it at the Village Snack Shop, it didn't happen).

Lenox Pizza House (637-2590), 7 Franklin Street, Lenox. Serving up Greek-style pan pizzas, grinders, Greek salads, and so on, for more than 20 years. A liquor license, and they deliver.

Elizabeth's Cafe Pizzeria (448-8244), 1264 East Street (across from the GE plant), Pittsfield. A small, inexpensive, but interesting eatery. Soups are great; real Italian polenta is a specialty. There are marvelous salads.

The Highland (442-2457), 100 Fenn Street, Pittsfield. An oasis for the frugal diner since 1936. The most expensive item on the menu is sirloin steak at $9.95. The cheapest dish, a staple since the Great Depression, is the $2.95 spaghetti. No credit cards. No reservations. No pretensions.

SELECTIVE SHOPPING

Body and Soul (637-3014), 63 Church Street, Lenox. Natural body-care products and gifts.

Naomi's Herbs (637-0616), 11 Housatonic Street, Lenox. Dried herbs and flowers. Potpourri fragrances, herbs, and oils.

Stones Throw Antiques (637-2733), 57 Church Street, Lenox. Prints, glass, china, and other 19th-century decorative objects.

The Cottage (447-9643), 31 South Street, Pittsfield. A stylish shop with tableware, baskets, gourmet foods, soaps, clothing, jewelry, and more.

The Bookstore (637-3390), 9 Housatonic Street, Lenox. An inviting bookstore with a large and varied selection. Stocks books of regional interest and by authors with local connections—such as Edith Wharton.

Either/Or Bookstore (637-8055), Brushwood Farm, MA 7 and MA 20, Lenox. "A roadside rest for the mind." Side-by-side children's and adults' stores.

The Book Maze (537-1701), Lenox House Country Shops, MA 7 and MA 20, Lenox. Lots of books, gifts, CDs, cassettes, and bargains.

Yankee Candle (499-3626), Pittsfield-Lenox Road, Lenox. Candles (including dip-your-own), gifts, and bath accessories.

The lawn of the Tanglewood Music Festival

SPECIAL EVENTS

June: Opening of **Tanglewood concert series.**
July: **Independence Day parade and celebrations,** Pittsfield.

NORTH BERKSHIRE

In the very northwest corner of Massachusetts, northern Berkshire County is a ruggedly beautiful landscape of steep-sided wooded hills and isolated valleys veined with fast-rushing rivers. Although geographically out of the way, North Berkshire's natural beauty attracts a stream of visitors year-round.

Dividing and dominating the area is the massive presence of 3491-foot-high Mount Greylock, the state's tallest mountain. Greylock is not an isolated peak but a range containing the three highest mountains in Massachusetts and rising steeply above the countryside on four sides. Geologically, Mount Greylock is part of New York's Taconic Range, Berkshire's western wall. To the east, the highest peaks of the Hoosac Range hedge northern Berkshire from the Hilltowns.

Greylock is topped by Massachusetts's official war monument, from which you can supposedly see 100 miles. It is the only New England mountain with a place to stay on top (built in the 1930s by the Civilian Conservation Corps, Bascom Lodge is maintained by the Appalachian Mountain Club). The surrounding 10,000-acre state reservation offers excellent hiking and some of the finest views in New England.

Given what it has to offer, the reservation is underused. Even in foliage season, when the mountain and the countryside colors are spectacular, relatively few visitors take the trouble to drive to the summit (it's accessible from both the region's major highways, MA 2 and US 7), let alone hike up.

Everyone stops in Williamstown, the area's "village beautiful." Sited at the junction of MA 2 and US 7 and home of prestigious Williams College, Williamstown is the quintessentially gracious old college town. It is also internationally known for its two superb art museums, the Sterling and Francine Clark Art Institute and the Williams College Museum of Art. In summer, moreover, the Williamstown Theater Festival draws its audience from all over.

Neighboring North Adams is, by contrast, a blue-collar mill town that has lost most of its industries—shoes, textiles, rugs, boxes, bricks, biscuits, and electronic parts. Its future, however, looks more promising. Many of the former factory buildings are being put to interesting new uses (one is now a Shiitake mushroom farm), and plans are well advanced to convert the largest mill complex, the sprawling former Sprague Electric Works, into MASS MOCA, a museum of contemporary art and a multidisciplinary cultural center that will include galleries, artists' studios, restaurants, and lodging.

The first view of North Adams for most motorists is from the Western Summit, one of the high points on the Mohawk Trail (MA 2), just before they take the precipitous plunge down the back of the Hoosac Range along the zigs and zags of the famous (in winter, infamous) Hairpin Turn. Because the range is so steep, early locomotives were unable to climb it, which meant a railroad couldn't run directly from Boston to the west. Massachusetts's industries were handicapped, and Boston's future as a major port was in doubt until a 4.7-mile-long railroad tunnel was finally blasted through the Hoosac Range in 1875. It took 25 years, involved new engineering techniques (including pioneering use of the explosive nitroglycerin), and cost the lives of nearly 200 workers and $20 million (an enormous sum for the time) to complete. The story of the Hoosac Tunnel and the boom years its construction brought to North Adams is well told at the Western Gateway Heritage State Park in downtown North Adams.

Whereas North Adams manufactured a variety of products, its smaller sister town of Adams was primarily known for its textile mills. The old mills, many of them imposing examples of late-19th-century industrial architecture, still stand, and some now house discount outlets.

In McKinley Square at the center of North Adams stands a bronze

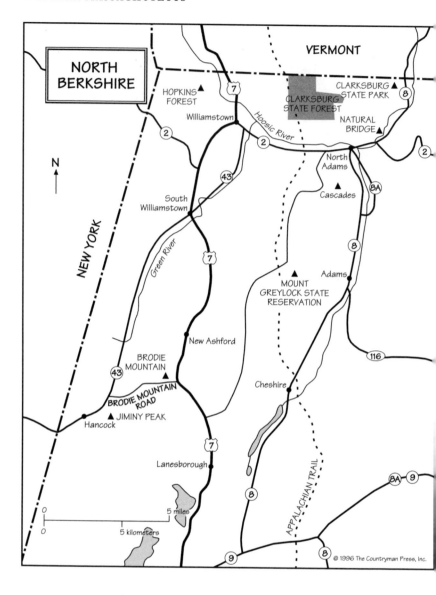

statue of President William McKinley, arms outstretched pleadingly as they were when he asked Congress to pass a tariff protecting American textile manufacturers from foreign competition. The protective tariff was responsible for Adams's period of greatest prosperity and directly benefited a local industrialist and longtime friend of McKinley, William Plunkett, owner of the Berkshire Cotton Manufacturing Company. A grateful and grieving Plunkett erected the statue after McKinley's assassination in 1901.

Mount Greylock towers over Adams, visible everywhere. The high plateau above the town, known as Greylock Glen, has been proposed for a series of developments over the years. A four-season facility, featuring golf and cross-country skiing, is presently planned. The entire mountain is webbed with hiking trails.

AREA CODE
413

GUIDANCE
Berkshire Visitors Bureau (443-9186; 1-800-237-5747), plaza level, Berkshire Common, West Street (next to the Hilton Hotel), Pittsfield. Berkshire County's official tourist information center offering information about lodging, dining, and cultural attractions. Maps, brochures, and guidebooks are available. A seasonal **tourist information booth** in Park Square, Pittsfield, is staffed and stocked with maps and brochures.

Northern Berkshire Chamber of Commerce (663-3735), in the Holiday Inn at 40 Main Street, North Adams. Open Monday through Friday 9–5. A seasonal information booth is maintained at the gatehouse to the Windsor Mill on Union Street.

Western Gateway Heritage State Park (663-6312), 9 Furnace Street Bypass (Building No. 4), North Adams. Tourist materials are available at the park information desk.

Williamstown Tourist Board Booth (458-4922; 458-9077), intersection of MA 2 and US 7, Williamstown. A well-stocked and usually staffed information booth in the heart of town.

MEDICAL EMERGENCY
North Adams Regional Hospital (663-6701), Hospital Avenue, North Adams. **Northern Berkshire Family Medicine** (743-7084; 664-7785), 1 Commercial Street, Adams. **Williamstown Medical Associates** (458-8182), 197 Adams Road, Williamstown.

Village Ambulance Service (call 911), Williamstown.

GETTING THERE
By bus: **Bonanza** (458-9371; 1-800-556-3815) serves North Adams and Williamstown from Boston and New York.

GETTING AROUND
Williamstown, North Adams, Adams, Cheshire, and Lanesborough are all served by buses of **BRTA,** the **Berkshire Regional Transit Authority** (499-2782; 1-800-292-6636).

VILLAGES

Williamstown. From its earliest years Williamstown has been an orderly, elegantly planned, and education-minded community. It was founded in 1753 as West Hoosac, and at their first meeting the seven original proprietors passed what would now be called zoning laws. Meadows and uplands were divided, and settlers were required to clear a minimum of 5 acres of land and build a house at least 15 by 18 feet, a substantial dwelling by frontier standards. An exact replica of one of these "regulation" houses, built as a town bicentennial project using mid-18th-century tools and methods, stands in Field Park, a remnant of the original town Green. Two years after the settlement was founded, Colonel Ephraim Williams Jr.—who had commanded the local fort and first surveyed the area—wrote a will endowing "a free school forever," provided that the township fell within Massachusetts (New York claimed it) and was renamed Williamstown. Shortly after making his will, Williams was killed in upstate New York fighting the French, but the conditions of his will weren't met for many years.

Because the border between Massachusetts and New York was long disputed, the school, now Williams College, couldn't be founded until 1791. It quickly, however, became central to town life. In 1815, when finances were shaky and the trustees considered moving the school to a less isolated location, local people pledged enough money to keep it in town. Williams College has long been one of the country's most respected liberal arts schools, and its well-endowed campus is very beautiful. Because of its small student body (about 2000) compared to the number of applicants for admission each year, it is also one of the hardest of all American colleges to get into.

The town has been a tourist destination since the mid-19th century. As early as the 1830s, local mineral springs began attracting visitors, and by the Civil War, Williamstown was an established resort with some large hotels and palatial summer homes. The old resort hotels are long gone, but there are some comfortable modern ones, plus motels and a spate of bed & breakfasts, many of the latter in fine old houses. Bucolic South Williamstown still has a number of gentlemen's farms, some quite grand.

The Sterling and Francine Clark Art Institute alone is worth a trip to Williamstown, and its world-class collection is complemented by that of the first-rate Williams College Museum of Art. The summer theater festival is one of the best of its kind in the country. All in all, Williamstown, a jewel of a village set within a circle of mountains, deserves more than a quick stop.

TO SEE

Williams College (597-3131) enrolls some 2000 students, almost equally divided between men and women and drawn from throughout the US and more than 40 countries. Tours of the 450-acre campus are available at the admissions office (next to the Adams Memorial Theater). Few other colleges are as entwined with their communities. Be sure to pick up the "Guide to the Campus," with a map that covers half of town. Buildings of interest to the general public (in addition to the art museum) include the following entries.

Edgar Degas's bronze Little Dancer of Fourteen Years, *found at Williamstown's Sterling and Francine Clark Art Institute*

Chapin Library of rare books in Stetson Hall sits behind Thompson Memorial Chapel, across Main Street from the Museum of Art. It's worth visiting to see the college's priceless collection of documents from the American Revolution. Original copies of the Declaration of Independence, of the Articles of Confederation, of two early versions of the Bill of Rights, and of a draft of the Constitution are exhibited (closed Saturday and Sunday).

Hopkins Observatory (597-2188), dedicated in 1838, is one of the first observatories in the country. Free shows are offered here in the Milham Planetarium most Fridays; since space is limited, make reservations.

Adams Memorial Theatre, Main Street. Since 1954 this theater has been the principal venue of the renowned Williamstown Theatre Festival, which presents some 240 performances of different productions each July and August (see *Entertainment*).

MUSEUMS

Sterling and Francine Clark Art Institute (458-9545), 225 South Street, Williamstown. Open Tuesday through Sunday 10–5. Free. This collection rivals that of many city museums. There are medieval works like a 15th-century panel painting by Piero della Francesca and works by such masters as Fragonard, Turner, and Goya. The museum is best known for its French impressionist paintings (Monet, Degas, Pissaro, and no fewer than 30 Renoirs) and for its American period pieces (Winslow Homer, John Singer Sargent, and Frederic Remington). The white marble building and its modern red granite addition contrast nicely with the meadow next door and the clapboard farmhouse across the street. In summer there is an outdoor café. The parklike lawns have picnic tables. A path (used for cross-country skiing in winter) leads over a brook and up Stone Hill. The museum sponsors a series of films and lectures.

Williams College Museum of Art (597-2429). Open Tuesday through Saturday 10–5, Sunday 1–5, free; housed in a striking building that combines a vintage 1846, two-story octagon with a major three-story addition (full of unconventional spaces) designed by Charles Moore. The museum has an outstanding permanent collection of American 19th- and 20th-century works by Eakins, Hassam, Feininger, Rivers, and Hopper, and represents the world's largest collection of works by Maurice Prendergast. Exhibits constantly change.

Williamstown House of Local History, Elizabeth S. Botsford Memorial Library (458-5369), Main Street. Monday through Friday 10–5:30; Wednesday 10–8; Saturday 10–1. Built in 1815 as a residence for the college treasurer, this homey library building retains many original features, including a curved staircase and graceful fireplace mantels. The House of Local History wing contains an extensive collection that includes spinning wheels, Civil War uniforms, old ice skates, photos, and much more.

FOR FAMILIES

Western Heritage Gateway State Park (663-6312), Furnace Street (MA 8), downtown North Adams. Open daily 10–5. Free. Housed in a former railroad freight yard, the park tells the epic story of the construction of the 4.7-mile-long Hoosac Tunnel, one of 19th-century America's greatest engineering feats. The tunnel took 25 years to build, from 1850 to 1875, claimed nearly 200 lives, and cost $20 million. In a replica of a section of tunnel, an audiovisual presentation takes visitors back in time with the sounds of dripping water, pickaxes striking stone, nitroglycerin explosions, and a political debate about the merits of the massive project. There are also changing arts and crafts exhibits. Other buildings in the park complex contain restaurants and shops.

Natural Bridge State Park (663-6392 summer; 663-6392 winter), MA 8, North Adams (½ mile north of the Heritage State Park). The centerpiece of this 49-acre park is an unusual natural formation, a white marble bridge spanning a steep gorge. The only one of its kind in North America, the bridge was created eons ago by melting glaciers. Picnic tables and nature trails. In summer, a park interpreter is on hand to explain the geological forces that created the bridge.

Alpine Slide at Jiminy Peak (738-5500), Corey Road (between US 7 and MA 43), Hancock. Memorial Day to Labor Day daily, weekends in May and September, 10:30 AM to 10 PM.

(Also see Mount Greylock State Reservation under *Green Space.*)

TO DO

BICYCLING

Biking is popular on the back roads around Williamstown, especially on MA 43 along the Green River. Rental 10-speeds are available in Williamstown from **The Spoke** (458-3456) on Main Street and from **The Mountain Goat** (458-8445) on Water Street, which also rents mountain bikes. **Jiminy Peak** (738-5500) rents 10-speeds in summer.

CANOEING

The Hoosic River is good for canoeing. Canoe and kayak rentals as well as sales and guidance can be found at **Berkshire Outfitters** (743-5900), MA 8 in Adams.

FISHING

The Green River can be rewarding for anglers, as can town-owned Bridges Pond and, in Hemlock, Broad and Roaring Brooks. **Points North Outfitters** (743-4030), MA 8, North Adams, sells fly-fishing gear, runs fly-fishing schools, and offers guided trips on the Deerfield River.

GOLF

The Taconic Golf Club (458-3997), Meachem Street, open daily mid-April to mid-November; and the **Waubeeka Golf Links** (458-8355), South Williamstown, open daily April to mid-November.

HIKING

The Hopkins Memorial Forest (597-2346), Northwest Hill Road, Willamstown, is a 2000-acre preserve owned by Williams College with a network of hiking (and, in winter, cross-country skiing) and nature trails. Some connect with the Taconic Crest Trail, on which you can hike to New York and Vermont. Also here are the Hopkins Farm Museum and a botanical garden.

(Also see Mount Greylock Reservation under *Green Space*.)

HORSEBACK RIDING

Bonnie Lea Farm (458-3149), US 7, Williamstown. Lessons $15 an hour, trail rides $35 for 2 hours.

SWIMMING

Sands Spring Pool and Spa (458-5205), Sands Spring Road (off US 7, north of Williamstown at the Cozy Corner motel), is an attractive pool, fed by the town's mineral springs. Billed as the oldest spa in the United States, it was formally established in 1813. This old-fashioned complex—run by the same family since 1950—includes a snack bar, changing rooms, sauna, whirlpool, and video machines. The pool is sparkling clean, 74 degrees, and genuinely exhilarating. Open May through September, weekdays 11–7:30; weekends and holidays 10-8. The fee is $7.50 adults, $6.50 children.

The Margaret Lindley Park (MA 2 and US 7), Williamstown, is a well-kept town pool with changing rooms and picnic tables; daily charge for

nonresidents. Open summer and school vacation, daily 11–7.
(See also Clarksburg State Park under *Green Space*.)

TENNIS

There is a free town court off Main Street, across from the Maple Terrace
Motel, Williamstown. **Williams College** (597-3131) maintains 12 clay
and 12 hard-top tennis courts (fee and reservations). For a fee you can
also use the indoor courts at **Brodie Mountain Tennis and Racquetball Club** (458-4677) in New Ashford and at **Jiminy Peak** (738-5500)
in Hancock, both on US 7.

CROSS-COUNTRY SKIING

Brodie Mountain (443-4752) maintains roughly 16 miles of trails with a
good deal of variety. Wide, tracked trails are lit at night (used by the
Williams College Ski Team), and less formal trails run through pastures
and up into the wooded Mount Greylock State Reservation. Rentals
are available here and in Williamstown at the **Mountain Goat** (458-
8445) and at **Goff's** (458-3605). Cross-country skiers are also welcomed
on the Taconic Golf Course, in Hopkins Forest, and on the Stone Hill
trails. (Also see *Green Space*.)

DOWNHILL SKIING

Brodie Mountain (443-4752), US 7, New Ashford (10 minutes south of
Williamstown). Named for an 18th-century Irishman, Brodie is also
known as Kelly's Irish Alps (it's owned by the Kelly family), famed for its
Leprechaun Lounge and its green snow on St. Patrick's Day. It's also a
respectable ski hill with lodging and a year-round campground.
Vertical drop: 1250 feet.
Terrain: 28 miles of slopes and trails.
Lifts: Four chairs, two tows.
Snowmaking: 95 percent of area.
Facilities: Night skiing; nursery (infants accepted).
Rates: $30–35 adults.

Jiminy Peak (738-5500), Corey Road, Hancock 01237, sits high in the Jeri-
cho Valley, a narrow corridor that runs east-west between MA 43 and
US 7 in Hancock. It is a self-contained winter resort with rental condos
and a 105-suite inn (see *Lodging*).
Vertical drop: 1200 feet.
Skiing Terrain: 28 slopes and trails.
Lifts: Seven chairs, one J-bar.
Snowmaking: 95 percent of area.
Facilities: Night skiing; nursery (2 years and up).
Rates: $26–37 adults.

ICE SKATING

The Williams College Lansing Chapman Rink (597-2433) is open to the
public for a small fee. Outdoor skating at Bridges Pond and Frog Pond.

GREEN SPACE

Mount Greylock State Reservation (499-4262; 499-4263), Rockwell Road (between US 7 and MA 8), Lanesborough. There are two main approaches to the summit, from Lanesborough and from North Adams. From US 7 in Lanesborough follow the Mount Greylock Reservation signs to the Park Visitors Center and continue up Rockwell Road another 9 miles. We recommend this route because the information center offers guidance on this 10,000-acre reservation with its 45 miles of trails, 35 rustic campsites, and a picnic area with a dramatic overlook (at nearby Stony Ledge). From North Adams, one road to the top is marked from MA 8 at the Western Gateway Heritage State Park, and the other is the Notch Road from MA 2.

The Appalachian Trail crosses the summit of Mount Greylock, which at 3491 feet is the roof of Massachusetts. The reservation's chief points of interest include the following:

The Summit Veterans Memorial Tower is a 92-foot-high granite tower built in 1933 as a memorial to all Bay State men killed in the nation's wars. On a clear day five states can be seen from the top of the tower. **Bascom Lodge** is a handsome fieldstone lodge built on the summit in the 1930s by the Civilian Conservation Corps and now run by the Appalachian Mountain Club. It is one of the nicest stops along the Appalachian Trail, welcoming motorists, day hikers, and trail walkers alike. A shop sells trail snacks, maps, and guides, and there is a snack bar with a gourmet view. Accommodation includes both private and dorm-style rooms. (See *Lodging.*) **The Cascades:** A waterfall formed by Notch Brook as it tumbles into a pool below, this is a popular 1-hour hike from MA 2. Park on Marion Avenue and pick up the path at the end of the street. Cross the footbridge and follow the trail.

PICNICKING

Stone Hill. A 55-acre town park, accessible from Stone Hill Road off South Street, Williamstown, offers wooded trails and a stone seat with a view.

Mount Hope Park. Sixteen acres on MA 43, Williamstown. Mount Hope Park has picnic tables by the confluence of the Hopper and Green Rivers.

STATE PARK AND FOREST

Clarksburg State Park and Clarksburg State Forest (664-8345 summer; 442-8928 winter), Middle Road, Clarksburg. Together, the park and forest cover 3250 wooded acres that are particularly beautiful in foliage season. The park's **Mauserts Pond** has a day-use area with swimming, picnic facilities, and a pavilion. There is a scenic nature trail around the pond and 50 campsites nearby. (Nominal fee.)

(In "West Franklin County/Mohawk Trail," also see Savoy Mountain State Forest, with its beautiful Tannery Falls, swimming in North Pond, and camping at South Pond, all not far from Adams.)

LODGING

INNS

The Williams Inn (458-9371), Main Street (junction of MA 2 and US 7), Williamstown 01267. A modern, Colonial Revival–style hostelry in the heart of town with 100 guest rooms, all with full bath, TV, and air-conditioning. Amenities include an indoor swimming pool and sauna. The dining room is open for breakfast, lunch, and dinner, and lighter fare is served in the tavern lounge. Doubles are $100–150.

The Orchards (458-9611), 222 Adams Road (off MA 2), Williamstown 01267. Located in a commercial strip on the edge of town, The Orchards is a sand-colored complex that includes both a 49-room hotel and a large and popular restaurant (see *Dining Out*). The contemporary exterior doesn't even suggest the interior, which is that of an English country house and filled with antiques, including a collection of 65 vintage silver teapots. Rooms overlook interior courtyards and feature four-poster beds, goosefeather and down pillows, and tasteful touches like TVs concealed in armoires. $125–220.

The Country Inn (738-5500; outside Massachusetts 1-800-882-8859), Jiminy Peak, Corey Road, Hancock 01237. There are 105 one-bedroom efficiency suites in this complex, part of a four-season resort. Downhill skiing in winter, miniature golf, tennis, and an alpine slide in summer. Year-round amenities include a restaurant and lounge. $95–195.

LODGE

Bascom Lodge (443-0011), Mount Greylock Reservation, Lanesborough 01237. Located just below the highest point in Massachusetts—the summit of Greylock—Bascom Lodge is a handsome fieldstone building erected in the 1930s to house the US army officers who ran the local Civilian Conservation Corps forestry program. It accommodates up to 36 guests in both private rooms and dorms. Sheets, blankets, and towels are provided. The entire lodge can be rented, and it's a great place for weddings. A full breakfast ($5) and dinner ($10) are served. $70–80.

BED & BREAKFASTS

In Williamstown 01267

Riverbend Farm (458-3121; 1-800-418-2057), 643 Simonds Road (US 7). Many B&Bs try to cultivate a colonial ambience but Riverbend Farm doesn't have to try: It's an authentic 1770 former tavern listed on the National Register of Historic Places. The present cozy parlor was originally the tavern taproom, where the Battle of Bennington was planned and where Colonel Ephraim Williams signed his will endowing Williams College. Owners David and Judy Loomis have lovingly restored the place, preserving the wood paneling, wide floorboards, and massive central chimney—which serves five working fireplaces. A full and elegant breakfast is served at a long table by the hearth in the old "keep-ing room" or kitchen. Five guest rooms share two bathrooms. $80–100.

Williamstown Bed and Breakfast (458-9202), 30 Cold Spring Road. A spacious 1880s house nicely but unfussily furnished in period style. Three good-sized guest rooms with private baths. The full breakfast always includes a hot entrée and home-baked bread and muffins. $70–80.

The House on Main Street (458-3031), 1120 Main Street. Built in the early 1700s, this house was moved to its present site in the 1830s, en-larged and Victorianized in the 1870s, and remodeled and modernized by the Riley family in 1986. There are six large, sunny, and cheerfully decorated guest rooms, three with private baths and the others sharing one and a half bathrooms. A full breakfast is served in the country-style kitchen. Guests have the use of a parlor and a large screened porch. $75–90.

Goldberry's (458-3935), 39 Cold Spring Road. An elegant Federal house, built in the 1830s as a girls school or "female seminary." The three bedrooms all have private baths. The full breakfast includes fresh fruit, and tea or cider is served in the afternoon. A deck looks out on the gar-den. $75.

In South Williamstown 01267

Field Farm Guest House (458-3135), 554 Sloan Road (off MA 43, near the intersection with US 7). The only B&B run by the Trustees of Res-ervations, this is a gem. Built in 1948 as the country home of a wealthy Williams College alumnus, the beautifully appointed, California-style ranch house is surrounded by 300 acres of gardens and meadows that include a fish pond and a sweeping view of Mount Greylock and the Taconic Range. The five guest rooms all have private baths, views, and balconies or decks. $90 with enhanced continental breakfast.

In North Adams 01247

Blackinton Manor (663-5795), 1391 Massachusetts Avenue, Blackinton Village. An elegant, Federal-style mansion with Italianate embellish-ments built in 1849 by Sanford Blackinton, a wealthy textile manufac-turer whose mill was nearby. Musician owners Dan and Betsey Epstein—Dan a classical pianist, Betsey an opera singer and cantor—bought the nearly derelict manor in 1992 and have completely restored it. There are five guest rooms furnished with antiques. Private baths. The Epsteins frequently give concerts for guests. Rooms are $70–120 with full breakfast.

Twin Sisters Inn (663-6933), 1111 South Street/Curran Highway (MA 8). A former turn-of-the-century carriage house remodeled into a country retreat in the 1930s. Surrounded by 10 acres of lawns and garden. Four pleasant guest rooms share two full baths. Continental break-fast. $50–60, double occupancy.

WHERE TO EAT

DINING OUT
In Williamstown

Robin's Restaurant (458-4489), 117 Latham (foot of Spring Street). Open for lunch and dinner. An elegant eating place anytime, but with a large pine tree–shaded deck that makes it particularly pleasant in warm weather. The cuisine blends Mediterranean and innovative American with dishes such as a mixed grill of duck leg confit and sausages, and grilled salmon steak with red and green pestos. Most entrées are in the $15–25 range.

Savories (458-2175), 123 Water Street. Open Tuesday through Sunday, dinner 4–10. A cozy, tavern atmosphere. Steak, grilled salmon, and pasta dishes are particular specialties. Most entrées are $10–25.

Hobson's Choice (458-9101), 159 Water Street. Open for lunch and dinner. A friendly, unpretentious (the outside could use a coat of paint), roadhouse-style restaurant with old-fashioned wooden booths. Very popular with the college crowd, and there is often a line to get in. Seafood is always on the menu, and there are all-you-can-eat specials. Soups are homemade. Entrées are usually $10–20.

The Orchards (458-9611), US 2, Williamstown. Open for lunch and dinner; Sunday brunch. An elegant formal dining room serving basically Continental cuisine. Tables are set with Irish linen and decorated with fresh flowers. The dining room walls are covered with plush velvet. Dinner entrées are in the $20–30 range.

Cobble Cafe (458-5930), 27 Spring Street. A pleasant, intimate restaurant right downtown. The menu is innovative and contemporary with great salads and interesting pasta dishes. Open for breakfast (usually around 6:30 AM), lunch, and dinner. Dinner entrées in the $12–20 range.

In North Adams

Due Baci Ristorante (664-6581), 40 Main Street (the Holiday Inn). A serious but unstuffy restaurant run by a local dentist (and chef) and his son. The menu is basically northern Italian with veal in white wine sauces a specialty. Open for breakfast, lunch, and dinner. Lunch features an all-you-can-eat buffet for $5.25. Most dinner entrées are $10–15.

EATING OUT
In Williamstown

Cozy Corner Restaurant (458-3854), 850 Simonds Road (US 7). Breakfast, lunch, and dinner. An unpretentious roadhouse with low prices and a loyal following. Fish-and-chips and pizza are specialties.

Purple Pub (458-3306), Bank Street (just off Spring Street). Open for lunch and dinner. A friendly little place that really feels like a pub. Good sandwiches and burgers, daily specials. Fast and friendly service. There is a small outdoor dining area.

Misty Moonlight Diner (458-3305), 408 Main Street (MA 2). A family restaurant with a 1950s atmosphere. Open 7 AM–10 PM, and serves breakfast all day.

Chopsticks (458-5750), 412 Main Street (MA 2). Open for lunch and dinner. A solid and popular Chinese restaurant with a large menu featuring dishes from different regions of China. The lounge specializes in "exotic tropical drinks" (not easy to find in North Berkshire) and also carries imported Chinese beers.

In North Adams

Freight Yard Pub (663-6547), Western Gateway Heritage State Park. Open for lunch and dinner. A friendly, informal place with something of a sports-bar atmosphere. Burgers, seafood, and Italian dishes are always on the menu. Locally made kielbasa a specialty. There is an outdoor dining patio.

Jack's Hot Dogs (664-9006), 12 Eagle Street (off Main Street). Lunch, dinner, and noshing in between. A local institution that's been in the same family for more than seven decades. If you like hot dogs with all the trimmings (including sauerkraut), Jack's is the place.

ENTERTAINMENT

Williamstown Theater Festival (597-3399), PO Box 517, Williamstown. For more than 40 years this festival has offered some of the best theater in the Northeast from the last week of June through August. Both new and classic plays are presented, featuring top actors and actresses. Most performances are on the main stage of the 521-seat Adams Memorial Theater, but other venues are also used.

The Williamstown Community Theatre and the College's **Williams Theater** perform during winter months.

The Sterling and Francine Clark Art Institute (see *To See*) presents a variety of films, lectures, and plays throughout the year.

Images Cinema (458-5812), 40 Spring Street, Williamstown. A classic college-town movie house showing foreign films and interesting domestic ones.

SELECTIVE SHOPPING

Delftree Farm (664-4907), 2340 Main Street, North Adams. Housed in an old brick factory building, Delftree Farm grows some 8000 pounds of prized Shiitake mushrooms a week. Here, at the source, the mushrooms sell for $8–10 a pound, depending on quality—far less than the price in a big-city gourmet shop.

Pottery Plus (458-2143), 25 Spring Street, Williamstown. Handmade jewelry, crafted wooden items, pottery, glass, and such.

ANTIQUES SHOPS

Collector's Warehouse (458-9686), 105 North Street (US 7), Williamstown. Open Wednesday through Saturday 12:30–5. Miscellaneous antiques and collectibles, including glassware, jewelry, frames, dolls, linen, and furniture.

The Library Antiques (458-3436), 70 Spring Street, Williamstown. Closed Wednesday. A series of rooms filled with antiques of all sorts. Browsers welcome.

Saddleback Antique (458-5852), US 7, Williamstown. A dealers' group shop in an old schoolhouse. All sorts of antiques, including furniture, pottery, and posters.

Amber Springs Antiques (442-1237), Main Street (US 7), Lanesborough. Open daily March through December; weekends and by appointment January and February. American furnishings and tools, pottery, advertising, country store items, and trivia.

BOOKSTORES

Water Street Books (458-8071), 26 Water Street, Williamstown. Well-stocked general bookstore. Particularly good selection of books on the Berkshires and by area authors.

Green River Books (458-0058), 96 Water Street, Williamstown. An attractive secondhand bookstore that also carries a lot of like-new publishers' remainders. Books on a wide range of subjects, but a particularly strong emphasis on art, children's, first editions, and rare and antiquarian books. Poetry readings are held regularly and there is a reading deck out back, overlooking the river.

FACTORY OUTLETS

Old Stone Mill (743-1015), 5 Hoosac Street, Adams. Savings of up to 75 percent on a wide variety of wallpapers, many with matching fabrics, comforters.

Novtex (664-4207), 510 State Road (MA 2), North Adams. Laces, ribbons, crafts supplies, and notions at big savings.

Interior Alternatives Outlet (743-1986), 5 Hoosac Street, Adams. Waverly fabrics, wallpaper, bedding, Oriental and area rugs.

Berkshire Sportswear (664-4931), 121 Union Street, Windsor Mill. Factory firsts and seconds women's sportswear, specialty knits.

SPECIAL EVENTS

June: **La Festa,** a multiethnic festival in North Adams featuring entertainment, crafts, and food (last three weekends).

Late July through early August: **Susan B. Anthony Days** commemorate the suffragette, who was born in Adams. Main Street is closed off and filled with booths, games, and food stalls.

Mid- to late August: **Adams Agricultural Fair.**

First weekend in October: **Northern Berkshire Fall Foliage Festival** in North Adams. Includes races, games, suppers, and sales, and culminates with a big parade that traditionally coincides with peak foliage colors.

Columbus Day weekend: **Mount Greylock Ramble**—a traditional mass climb of "their" mountain by Adams residents.

General Index

Lodging Index

Books from The Countryman Press

Explorer's Guides

The alternative to mass-market guides with their homogenized listings. Explorer
Guides focus on independently owned inns, motels, and restaurants, and on fami
and cultural activities reflecting the character and unique qualities of the area.

A selection of our books about Massachusetts and the Northeast

We offer a variety of fiction, nonfiction, and outdoor recreation guides. Our book
are available through bookstores, or they may be ordered directly from th
publisher. To order, or for a complete catalog, please contact:

The Countryman Press
PO Box 175AP
Woodstock, VT 05091
1-800-245-4151